HOW DO YOU FACE LIFE AND ITS CHALLENGES?

— A Life-Saving guide to help you with Living Life —

Stella Louise

Maple Leaf Publishing Inc.
Alberta Canada

Copyright © 2020 Stella Louise

All rights reserved. No part of this book may be reproduced or transmitted in any form or by any means, electronic or mechanical, including photocopying, recording, or by any information storage and retrieval system, without written permission of the publisher.

ISBN: 978-1-77419-030-2 (Paperback)
ISBN: 978-1-77419-031-9 (Ebook)
Print Information available on the last page.
Rev. Date: February 7, 2020

MAPLE LEAF PUBLISHING INC.
3rd Floor 4915 54 St Red Deer,
Alberta T4N 2G7 Canada

General Inquiries & Customer Service
Phone: 1-(403)-356-0255
Toll Free: 1-(888)-498-9380
Email: info@mapleleafpublishinginc.com

My heart says of you, "Seek his face!"
Your face, LORD, I will seek.
Psalm 27:8

Each of you should use whatever gift you have received to serve others, as faithful stewards of God's grace in its various forms.
1 Peter 4:10

To my husband, Wendell, daughter, Numa, and son, Adrian, and my sisters in Christ, Dawn Blair, Michal Farkess, and my sister-in-law, Fannie Shelton
Thank you for being an encouragement in helping me to share thoughts of God.

Contents

INTRODUCTION — 1

GOD'S LOVE — 3
JANUARY 1
Exodus 1:22–2:10

ADORATION — 4
JANUARY 2
Psalm 103:1–18

ADORATION — 6
JANUARY 3
Colossians 3:12–17

AGING 7
JANUARY 4 — 7
    Doctrine of God
Deuteronomy 34:1–12

AGING — 9
JANUARY 5
Psalm 92:12–15

AGING — 10
JANUARY 6
God's Care
Isaiah 46:4–13

AGING 12
JANUARY 7 — 12
    Living Like Christ/Spiritual Growth
1 Timothy 4:6–11

ANGER — 13
JANUARY 8
Ephesians 4:25–32

BIBLE 14
Nehemiah 8:1–8

BIBLE 15
JANUARY 10
Nehemiah 8:2–6; Acts 8:4–8

BIBLE 16
JANUARY 11
Psalm 119:89–96

BIBLE 18
JANUARY 12
Psalm 119:161–168

BIBLE 19
JANUARY 13
1 John 1:1–4

BIBLE 20
JANUARY 14
Bible Study/Obedience
Philippians 1:27–30

BIBLE 21
JANUARY 15
Doctrine of God
Psalm 119:17–19, 130–134

BIBLE 23
JANUARY 16
Holy Spirit/Spiritual Transformation
1 Samuel 3:1–10

BIBLE 24
JANUARY 17
Psalm 119:97–104

BIBLE 25
JANUARY 18
    Holy Spirit
Hebrews 1:1–12

JANUARY 19 27
LOVE FOR GOD
Deuteronomy 6:1–12

CHRIST 28
JANUARY 20
    Christ's Birth
Nahum 1:7–15

CHRIST 30
JANUARY 21
    Christ's Birth
John 8:12–20

CHRIST 31
JANUARY 22
    Christ, Messiah/Savior/Evangelism/Salvation
Matthew 28:16–20

CHRIST 32
JANUARY 23
    Christ/Messiah/Savior
Mark 14:32–39

CHRIST'S DEITY 33
JANUARY 24
    Fear
Luke 2:8–20

CHRIST'S DEITY 35
JANUARY 25
Luke 2:8–20

CHRIST'S DEITY 36
JANUARY 26
    Christ/Savior/Messiah
John 1:1–14

CHRIST'S DEITY 38
JANUARY 27
    Christ Jesus/Savior
John 10:1–9

CHRIST'S DEITY 39
JANUARY 28
    Savior/Messiah
John 15:12–17

CHRIST'S DEITY 40
JANUARY 29
    Christ/Savior
1 Corinthians 1:18–31

CHRIST'S DEITY 42
JANUARY 30
    Savior/Messiah
Philippians 2:1–11

CHRIST'S DEITY 43
JANUARY 31
    Jesus
    The Messiah/Savior
James 2:8–26

CHRIST'S DEITY 45
FEBRUARY 1
    False Teaching
John 8:31–38

CHRIST 46
FEBRUARY 2
    Living Like Christ
Matthew 10:35–42

FEBRUARY 3 47
LIVING LIKE CHRIST
1 Peter 2:9–12

CHRIST'S BIRTH 48
FEBRUARY 4
    Prayer/Temptation
Luke 2:25–38

CHRIST 50
FEBRUARY 5
    Prayer
Luke 10:38–11:4

CHRIST/SAVIOR/MESSIAH 51
FEBRUARY 6
    Pray/Temptation
Luke 22:39–46

FEBRUARY 7 52
SALVATION
John 4:31–34

CHRIST'S CRUCIFIXION 53
FEBRUARY 8
    Love of God
Psalm 22:1–10

FEBRUARY 9 55
CHRIST/SAVIOR
John 17:1–5

FEBRUARY 10 56
CHRIST/CRUCIFIXION
    Resurrection/Messiah/Savior
John 20:24–31

FEBRUARY 11 57
SALVATION
Hebrews 9:19–28

CHRIST'S DEATH 58
FEBRUARY 12
    Salvation
Psalm 103:1–18

FEBRUARY 13 61
CHRIST'S BIRTH
Isaiah 9:1–7

FEBRUARY 14 63
CHRIST'S BIRTH
Luke 2:8–14

FEBRUARY 15 64
SALVATION
Luke 24:13–32

CHRIST'S DEATH 65
FEBRUARY 16
    Christ/Savior/Messiah
John 18:10–14, 36–37

CHRIST'S DEATH 67
FEBRUARY 17
    Salvation
Romans 3:21–26

CHRIST'S DEATH 68
FEBRUARY 18
    Evangelism
1 Peter 3:8–16

CHRIST'S RETURN   69
FEBRUARY 19
Matthew 25:1–13

CHRIST'S RETURN   70
FEBRUARY 20
Luke 2:21–35

FEBRUARY 21   72
CHRIST'S RETURN
1 Thessalonians 4:13–18

FEBRUARY 22   73
CHRIST'S RETURN
   Love of God
Revelation 22:12–21

FEBRUARY 23   74
CHRIST'S RETURN
   Suffering
2 Thessalonians 1:3–12

FEBRUARY 24   76
CHRIST'S RESURRECTION
   Trusting God
Luke 24:13–35

FEBRUARY 25   77
CHRIST'S RETURN
   Trust in God
2 Peter 3:8–15

CHURCH UNITY   78
FEBRUARY 26
Romans 15:1–7

FEBRUARY 27   80
LIVING WITH OTHER BELIEVERS IN CHRIST
1 Corinthians 14:6–12, 26

FEBRUARY 28 — 81
CHURCH UNITY
Serving Others
2 Corinthians 1:3–7

FEBRUARY 29 — 82
GOD'S CARE/WORRY
Matthew 6:25–34

CHURCH WORSHIP — 83
MARCH 1
Acts 2:42–47

CONTENTMENT — 84
MARCH 2
Consumerism
Ecclesiastes 1:1–11

MARCH 3 — 86
CONTENTMENT
Philippians 4:10–19

MARCH 4 — 87
CONTENTMENT
Age/God's Care
2 Corinthians 12:6–10

MARCH 5 — 88
CONTENTMENT
Christian Living
Matthew 20:1–16

DEATH — 90
MARCH 6
Resurrection of Believers
John 11:17–27

MARCH 7   91
DEATH
    Heaven
1 Thessalonians 4:13–18

DISCIPLESHIP   92
MARCH 8
    Discipleship
Luke 9:57–62

MARCH 9   93
DISCIPLESHIP
Luke 9:57–62

MARCH 10   *94*
GOD CARES/PARENTING
Proverbs 22:1–16

ENCOURAGEMENT   96
MARCH 11
Exodus 17:8–16

MARCH 12   97
ENCOURAGEMENT
Ephesians 4:25–32

MARCH 13   98
ENCOURAGEMENT
1 Thessalonians 4:1–12

MARCH 14   100
BIBLE/EVANGELISM
3 John 1:1–8

MARCH 15   101
ENCOURAGEMENT
    Living for Christ
1 Thessalonians 4:1–12

MARCH 16 102
ENCOURAGEMENT
    Love for Others
Ephesians 4:2–6

MARCH 17 103
ENCOURAGEMENT
    Stories of Faith
Hebrews 11:32–12:3

EVANGELISM 104
MARCH 18
Psalm 42

MARCH 19 106
EVANGELISM
Matthew 5:1–16

MARCH 20 108
EVANGELISM
Mark 5:1–20

MARCH 21 109
EVANGELISM
John 6:34–51

MARCH 22 111
EVANGELISM
John 6:34–51

MARCH 23 112
EVANGELISM
Acts 1:1–8

MARCH 24 113
EVANGELISM
2 Corinthians 2:14–17

MARCH 25 114
EVANGELISM
    Christ the Savior
John 1:1–8

MARCH 26 115
EVANGELISM
    God's Care
Mark 1:16–22

MARCH 27 116
HUMAN NATURE
Philippians 3:17–21

MARCH 28 117
EVANGELISM
    Living for Christ
Matthew 10:26–32

MARCH 29 118
EVANGELISM
    Living Like Christ
2 Corinthians 2:12–17

MARCH 30 119
EVANGELISM
    Love for Others
Mark 14:3–9

MARCH 31 120
EVANGELISM
    Relationship
Luke 8:40–48

APRIL 1 121
EVANGELISM
    Salvation
Luke 5:27–32

APRIL 2 122
EVANGELISM
    Salvation
2 Corinthians 4:1–6

APRIL 3 123
EVANGELISM
    Salvation
2 Corinthians 4:1–6

FAITH 124
APRIL 4
    Christ, Savior
Romans 4: 18–25

APRIL 5 125
FAITH
    Doctrine of God
    Salvation
1 John 5:1–13

APRIL 6 126
TRUST
Hebrews 11:8–16

APRIL 7 127
FALSE PROPHETS
Matthew 7:12–23

APRIL 8 129
FEAR
Mark 4:35–5:1

APRIL 9 130
FEAR
    God's Care
Psalm 27:1–8

APRIL 10 131
FEAR
      Trust in God
Numbers 13:25–14:9

APRIL 11 133
FEAR
      Trust in God
Numbers 13:25–14:9

APRIL 12 135
FEAR
      Worry
Psalm 34:1–10

FELLOWSHIP WITH GOD 137
APRIL 13
Hebrews 2:1–4

FORGIVENESS 138
APRIL 14
      Sin
2 Samuel 22:26–37

APRIL 15 139
FORGIVENESS
Psalm 86:5–15

FORGIVENESS 141
APRIL 16
Ephesians 4:25–32

FRIENDSHIP 142
APRIL 17
      Compassion
Job 11:7–20

GIVING 144
APRIL 18
    Serving Others
Acts 20:22–35

GOD 145
APRIL 19
Genesis 12:1–4; 17:1–2

APRIL 20 147
GOD
Psalm 100

APRIL 21 148
DOCTRINE OF GOD
2 Chronicles 20:1–13

APRIL 22 149
DOCTRINE OF GOD
    Bible/Prayer
Judges 2:7–19

APRIL 23 151
DOCTRINE OF GOD
    Doing the Right Thing
2 Chronicles 16:7–14

APRIL 24 152
DOCTRINE OF GOD
    Protection
Joshua 20:1–9

APRIL 25 153
DOCTRINE OF GOD
    Grace
Matthew 5:43–48

APRIL 26   **154**
DOCTRINE OF GOD
      Strength/Suffering
Isaiah 40:27–31

APRIL 27   **156**
GOD
Suffering/Trust
Habakkuk 3:16–19

APRIL 28   **157**
GOD
Waiting on God
Numbers 14:39–45 157

APRIL 29   **158**
WAITING ON GOD
Psalm 25:1–15

APRIL 30   **160**
GOD
      Worship
Psalm 68:7–10, 19–20

MAY 1   **161**
GOD'S CARE
Psalm 37:21–31

MAY 2   **163**
GOD'S CARE
      Relationship
Acts 20:17–20, 35–38

MAY 3   **164**
GOD'S CARE
Psalm 116:5–9

MAY 4 165
GOD'S CARE
Psalm 121

MAY 5 167
GOD'S CARE
Psalm 139:1–18

MAY 6 169
GOD'S CARE
You Matter
Ecclesiastes 1:1–11

MAY 7 171
GOD'S CARE
Isaiah 50:4–10

MAY 8 173
GOD'S CARES
Christ the Savior
Psalm 34:15–22

MAY 9 174
GOD'S CARE
Grief
Psalm 34:15–22

MAY 10 175
GOD'S CARE
Life Struggles
Lamentations 5:8–22

MAY 11 177
GOD'S CARE
    Miracles/Trust in God
Mark 8:1–13   *177*

MAY 12   **179**
GOD'S CARE
    Salvation
John 10:1–11

MAY 13   **180**
GOD'S CARE
    Suffering
Psalm 55:4–23

MAY 14   **183**
GOD'S CARE
    Trusting God
1 Chronicles 29:14–19

MAY 15   **184**
GOD'S CARE
    Suffering/Trust in God
Proverbs 18:4–12

MAY 16   **185**
GOODNESS OF GOD
Genesis 3:1–8

MAY 17   **186**
GOD'S GRACE
    Love and Mercy
Ephesians 2:4–7

GOD'S LOVE   **187**
MAY 18
Genesis 16:1–13

MAY 19 189
GOD'S LOVE
Numbers 33:1–15, 36–37

MAY 20 190
GOD'S LOVE
Psalm 36:5–12

MAY 21 192
GOD'S LOVE
Lamentations 3:21–26

MAY 22 193
GOD'S LOVE
    Serving Others
Haggai 2:15–23

MAY 23 194
GOD'S LOVE
Matthew 6:25–34

MAY 24 195
LOVE OF GOD
Acts 9:1–19

MAY 25 197
GOD'S LOVE
Romans 5:6–11

MAY 26 198
GOD' LOVE
Romans 8:12–17

MAY 27   199
GOD'S LOVE
Romans 8:31–38

MAY 28   200
GOD'S LOVE
1 John 4:7–19

HOPELESSNESS   201
MAY 29
Psalm 146:1–10

MAY 30   203
GOD'S PRESENCE
Hebrews 13:1–6

MAY 31   204
SUFFERING
     God's Love
Psalm 110

JUNE 1   206
SUFFERING
Job 23:1–12

JUNE 2   207
GRATITUDE
Psalm 119:9–16

GRATITUDE   209
JUNE 3
Colossians 3:12–17

GRIEF   **210**
JUNE 4
John 16:28–33

JUNE 5   **211**
GRIEF
    Heaven
John 11:1–4, 38–44

HEAVEN   **212**
JUNE 6
Colossians 3:1–11

JUNE 7   **213**
HEAVEN
Hebrews 11:8–16

JUNE 8   **214**
FALL/SIN
Revelation 22:1–5

JUNE 9   **215**
HEAVEN
    Salvation
John 14:1–6

HOLY SPIRIT   **216**
JUNE 10
Exodus 4:1–12

JUNE 11   **218**
HOLY SPIRIT
2 Kings 2:1–12

JUNE 12   **219**
HOLY SPIRIT
Acts 2:1–12

JUNE 13 221
HOLY SPIRIT
    Life Struggles
John 14:16–27

HUMILITY 222
JUNE 14
Philippians 2:1–11

JUNE 15 223
INJUSTICE
    Love for Others
Mark 10:13–16

JUNE 16 224
JOY
    Fulfilled Joy
John 16:17–24

JUDGING OTHERS 225
JUNE 17
John 3:9–21

JUNE 18 227
JUDGING
    God's Love
John 7:53–8:11

LEGACY 228
JUNE 19
2 Chronicles 21:4–20

JUNE 20 230
LEGACY
    Living for Christ
Proverbs 22:1–12

JUNE 21 231
LEGACY
      Stories of Faith
Psalm 145:1–13

LIFE STRUGGLES 234
JUNE 22
      Trust in God
Isaiah 40:21–31

JUNE 23 236
TRUST IN GOD
2 Timothy 3:10–15

LIVING FOR CHRIST 237
JUNE 24
Matthew 5:13–16

JUNE 25 238
LIVING FOR CHRIST
1 Peter 3:9–12

JUNE 26 239
OBEDIENCE
2 Kings 12:1–15

JUNE 27 240
SERVING OTHERS
Ephesians 6:5–9

JUNE 28 241
LIVING FOR CHRIST
      Serving Others
Colossians 2:20–3:4

LIVING LIKE CHRIST   **242**
JUNE 29
Psalm 141:1–4

JUNE 30   **243**
LIVING LIKE CHRIST
2 Peter 1:12–21

JULY 1   **244**
PERSONAL BEHAVIOR/THE TONGUE
Psalm 141

JULY 2   **246**
LIVING LIKE CHRIST
Ephesians 5:1–16

JULY 3   **247**
LIVING LIKE CHRIST
Philippians 4:4–9

JULY 4   **248**
LIVING LIKE CHRIST
Philippians 4:4–9

JULY 5   **249**
LIVING LIKE CHRIST
Colossians 3:12–17

JULY 6   **250**
LIVING LIKE CHRIST
James 1:22–27

JULY 7   **251**
LIVING LIKE CHRIST
    Spiritual Transformation
James 3:1–12

JULY 8   252
LIVING LIKE CHRIST
    Spiritual Transformation
James 3:1–12

LONELINESS   254
JULY 9
2 Timothy 4:9–18

LORD'S SUPPER   255
JULY 10
Mark 8:11–21

LOVE FOR GOD   256
JULY 11
Psalm 86:1–13

JULY 12   258
LOVE FOR GOD
Isaiah 49:13–21

JULY 13   259
LOVE FOR GOD
1 Peter 1:1–9

LOVE FOR OTHERS   261
JULY 14
Deuteronomy 10:12–22

JULY 15   262
LOVE
Luke 7:36–50

JULY 16   263
LOVE FOR OTHERS
Romans 13:8–11

JULY 17 264
LOVE OF GOD
    Christian Living/Love for Others
1 Corinthians 13

JULY 18 266
LOVE FOR OTHERS
2 Corinthians 1:3–7

JULY 19 267
LOVE FOR OTHERS
Philippians 2:1–11

JULY 20 268
LOVING OTHERS
    Living Like Christ
1 John 2:3–11

JULY 21 269
LOVE FOR OTHERS
1 John 3:16–17

JULY 22 270
LOVE FOR OTHERS
    Confrontation
Proverbs 27:5–10

JULY 23 271
LOVE AND SERVING OTHERS
James 1:22–27

JULY 24 272
RACISM
2 Corinthians 5:16–21

MARRIAGE — 273
JULY 25 — 273

Prayer

1 Peter 3:7–12 — 273

MATERIALISM — 275
JULY 26 — 275

Idolatry

Matthew 6:24–34 — 275

JULY 27 — 276
PRIORITIES — 276
Luke 12:22–34 — 276

MOTIVES — 277
JULY 28 — 277

Serving Others

Matthew 6:1–6 — 277

OBEDIENCE — 278
JULY 29 — 278
Deuteronomy 5:28–33 — 278

JULY 30 — 279
OBEDIENCE — 279
Deuteronomy 6:1–12 — 279

JULY 31 — 280
Deuteronomy 30:11–20 — 280

AUGUST 1 — 282
OBEDIENCE — 282

Sin

Jeremiah 7:1–11 — 282

AUGUST 2 — 283
SPIRITUAL TRANSFORMATION
John 8:39–47

AUGUST 3 — 284
OBEDIENCE
Trust in God
Jeremiah 1:4–9

AUGUST 4 — 285
OBEDIENCE
Jonah 4

PARENTING — 286
AUGUST 5
Stories of Faith
Psalm 78:1–8

AUGUST 6 — 288
THE LOVE OF GOD
Luke 15:11–24

PATIENCE — 290
AUGUST 7
Galatians 5:13–26

PERSONAL BEHAVIOR — 291
AUGUST 8
Living Like Christ
Psalm 34:11–18

PERSECUTION — 292
AUGUST 9
Acts 6:8–15; 7:59–60

AUGUST 10 293
EVANGELISM/GOD'S CARE
Jeremiah 1:1–10

PRAYER 295
AUGUST 11
Psalm 46

AUGUST 12 296
PRAYING
Psalm 71:1–12

AUGUST 13 298
PRAY
Psalm 91

AUGUST 14 300
PRAYER
Psalm 122:6–9

AUGUST 15 301
PRAYER
1 Kings 18:41–45

AUGUST 16 302
PRAYER
2 Chronicles 6:12–21

AUGUST 17 304
PRAYER
2 Chronicles 13:10–18

AUGUST 18 305
PRAYER
Matthew 6:5–10

AUGUST 19 *PRAYER* Matthew 16:1–4	**306**
AUGUST 20 *PRAYER* **Doctrine of God** Ephesians 3:14–21	**307**
AUGUST 21 *PRAYER* 1 Thessalonians 5:12–28	**308**
AUGUST 22 *PRAYER* **Fellowship with God** Matthew 14:13–23	**309**
AUGUST 23 *PRAYER* **God's Care** Matthew 6:25–34	**310**
AUGUST 24 *PRAYER* Matthew 26:39–42; 27:45–46	**311**
AUGUST 25 *HOLY SPIRIT INTERCESSION* Romans 8:22–34	**312**
AUGUST 26 *PRAYER* **Rest/Serving Others** Luke 9:1–2, 10–17	**314**

AUGUST 27   **315**
PRAYER
    Spiritual Discipline
Matthew 14:22–36

AUGUST 28   **317**
PRAYER
    Suffering
2 Kings 19:9–20

AUGUST 29   **318**
    Prayer
Isaiah 37:9–22, 33

AUGUST 30   **320**
PRAYER
Luke 18:1–8

AUGUST 31   **321**
PRAYER
    Suffering
John 17:6–19

SEPTEMBER 1   **322**
PRAYER
1 Thessalonians 5:16–28

SEPTEMBER 2   **323**
PRAYER
Hebrews 4:14–16

PURPOSE   **324**
SEPTEMBER 3
    Spiritual Gifts/Serving Others
1 Peter 4:7–11

RELATIONSHIPS 325
SEPTEMBER 4
    Enemies/Listening
1 Samuel 25:14–33

SEPTEMBER 5 327
RELATIONSHIPS
    Evangelism
Luke 19:1–9

SEPTEMBER 6 328
RELATIONSHIPS
    Forgiving Others
Luke 6:27–36

SEPTEMBER 7 329
RELATIONSHIPS
    Leadership/Love
Philemon 8–18

SEPTEMBER 8 330
RELATIONSHIPS
    Spiritual Transformation
Proverbs 27:5–17

SEPTEMBER 9 332
RELATIONSHIPS
    Spiritual Transformation
Proverbs 27:5–17

REPENTANCE 334
SEPTEMBER 10
    Christ/Messiah
Isaiah 40:1–11

SEPTEMBER 11 — 336
REPENTANCE
Salvation
Mark 10:17–27

SEPTEMBER 12 — 338
SIN
Psalm 51:7–17

SEPTEMBER 13 — 339
REPENTANCE
Sin
1 Samuel 25:1–12

SEPTEMBER 14 — 341
REPENTANCE
Forgiveness of Sin
Joel 2:12–17

RESPECT — 343
SEPTEMBER 15
Ezra 5:6–17

REST — 344
SEPTEMBER 16
Exodus 18:14–24

SEPTEMBER 17 — 345
REST
Mark 6:7–13, 30–32

SEPTEMBER 18 — 347
REST
God's Care
Matthew 11:25–30

SEPTEMBER 19   348
RESTING
    Waiting/Witnessing
John 4:4–14

SALVATION   349
SEPTEMBER 20
Isaiah 12

SEPTEMBER 21   350
SALVATION
Psalm 146

SEPTEMBER 22   352
SALVATION
Mark 2:13–17

SEPTEMBER 23   353
SALVATION
Luke 1:67–79

SEPTEMBER 24   355
SALVATION
Luke 4:14–21

SEPTEMBER 25   356
SALVATION
    Christ, Savior and Messiah
Romans 3:21–26

SEPTEMBER 26   357
SALVATION
John 1:1–14

SEPTEMBER 27   358
SALVATION
John 6:53–69

SEPTEMBER 28 — 360
SALVATION
John 8:31–37

SEPTEMBER 29 — 361
SALVATION
Hebrews 10:19–25

SEPTEMBER 30 — 362
SALVATION
1 Peter 1:3–9

OCTOBER 1 — 363
SALVATION
1 Peter 1:17–23

OCTOBER 2 — 364
SALVATION
1 Peter 2:4–10

OCTOBER 3 — 365
SALVATION
    Spiritual Growth
Philippians 3:1–8

SATAN — 366
OCTOBER 4
    Temptation
Genesis 3:1–7

OCTOBER 5 — 368
TEMPTATION
Genesis 3:1–7

OCTOBER 6 — 369
TEMPTATION
Mark 14:32–42

SERVING OTHERS 370
OCTOBER 7
  Serving
Exodus 31:1–11

OCTOBER 8 371
SERVING
1 Kings 12:1–15

OCTOBER 9 373
SERVING OTHERS
Galatians 6:2–10

OCTOBER 10 374
SERVING OTHERS
  Love
Philippians 1:27–2:4

OCTOBER 11 375
SERVING OTHERS
  Stewardship and Giving
Matthew 25:31–40

SIN 376
OCTOBER 12
  Forgiveness
Romans 7:14–25

OCTOBER 13 377
SPIRITUAL GROWTH
Roman 7:15–25

OCTOBER 14 379
SIN
  Temptation
Genesis 4:1–8

OCTOBER 15 — 380
SIN
Temptation
1 Corinthians 10:1–13

OCTOBER 16 — 381
SIN
Temptation
1 Corinthians 10:1–13

SPIRITUAL GIFTS — 383
OCTOBER 17
1 Corinthians 12:4–14

SPIRITUAL GROWTH — 384
OCTOBER 18
Proverbs 2:1–5

OCTOBER 19 — 385
SPIRITUAL GROWTH
Luke 19:1–10

OCTOBER 20 — 386
SPIRITUAL GROWTH
Living with Other Believers
Ephesians 4:1–16

SPIRITUAL TRANSFORMATION — 387
OCTOBER 21
Romans 12:1–8

OCTOBER 22 — 388
SPIRITUAL TRANSFORMATION
1 Corinthians 9:24–27

OCTOBER 23   389
SPIRITUAL TRANSFORMATION
2 Corinthians 5:12–21

OCTOBER 24   391
SPIRITUAL TRANSFORMATION
Galatians 5:16–25

OCTOBER 25   392
SPIRITUAL TRANSFORMATION
Revelation 2:12–17

OCTOBER 26   393
SPIRITUAL TRANSFORMATION
   God's Care
2 Peter 1:1–10

OCTOBER 27   394
SPIRITUAL TRANSFORMATION
   God's Love
1 Corinthians 6:9–11; 13:4–7

OCTOBER 28   395
SPIRITUAL TRANSFORMATION
   Holy Spirit
Ezekiel 18:25–32

OCTOBER 29   396
SPIRITUAL TRANSFORMATION
   Loving Others
Ephesians 2:1–10

OCTOBER 30   398
SPIRITUAL TRANSFORMATION
   Living Like Christ
Psalm 138:7–8; Ephesians 2:6–10

SUFFERING 399
OCTOBER 31
Psalm 40:1–5

NOVEMBER 1 400
GOD
Exodus 13:17–22

NOVEMBER 2 401
SUFFERING
Isaiah 61:1–4

NOVEMBER 3 403
SUFFERING
　　God's Care
Psalm 35:17–28

NOVEMBER 4 405
SUFFERING
　　God's Care
Psalm 55:4–23

NOVEMBER 5 407
SUFFERING
　　God's Care
John 14:15–21

NOVEMBER 6 409
HEAVEN
Philippians 1:12–26

NOVEMBER 7 410
SUFFERING
　　Salvation
Psalm 119:71–75

NOVEMBER 8 411
SUFFERING
    Trust in God
James 1:2–12

TEMPTATION 412
NOVEMBER 9
Isaiah 53:1–6

NOVEMBER 10 414
CHRIST/SAVIOR
Hebrews 2:10–18

THANKFULNESS 415
NOVEMBER 11
Job 40:1–14

NOVEMBER 12 417
THANKFULNESS
    Creation
Psalm 136:1–9

NOVEMBER 13 418
THANKFULNESS
    Worship
Psalm 139:14–18

THE TONGUE 419
NOVEMBER 14
James 3:1–12

THE TONGUE 421
NOVEMBER 15
James 3:1–12

TRIALS   **422**
NOVEMBER 16
Psalm 13:1–6

NOVEMBER 17   **423**
GOD'S WILL
1 Peter 1:1–9

NOVEMBER 18   **424**
GOD'S SOVEREIGNTY
Psalm 121

NOVEMBER 19   **426**
GOD'S LOVE
Job 7:11–21

NOVEMBER 20   **427**
SURRENDER
John 16:25–33

SURRENDER   **428**
NOVEMBER 21
Psalm 94:3–23

NOVEMBER 22   **431**
GOD'S GRACE
Lamentations 3:1–3, 25–33

NOVEMBER 23   **432**
TRUST
Psalm 107:23–32

NOVEMBER 24   **434**
TRIALS
Psalm 32:1–6; Matthew 11:28–30

NOVEMBER 25   **435**
TRIALS
Matthew 5:38–48

NOVEMBER 26   **436**
GOD'S PRESENCE
John 16:25–33

NOVEMBER 27   **437**
GOD'S SOVEREIGNTY
James 1:1–8

TRUST IN GOD   **438**
NOVEMBER 28
Exodus 16:11–31

NOVEMBER 29   **440**
TRUST IN GOD
Judges 7:1–8

NOVEMBER 30   **441**
TRUST IN GOD
Psalm 18:1–6

DECEMBER 1   **442**
TRUST IN GOD
Psalm 20

DECEMBER 2   **444**
TRUST IN GOD
Psalm 77:1–15

DECEMBER 3   **446**
TRUST IN GOD
Proverbs 3:1–18

DECEMBER 4 448
TRUST IN GOD
    God's Care/Suffering
Proverbs 18:4–12

DECEMBER 5 450
TRUST IN GOD
Isaiah 55:6–13

DECEMBER 6 452
TRUST IN GOD
Isaiah 55:6–13

DECEMBER 7 454
TRUST IN GOD
Matthew 8:23–28

DECEMBER 8 455
TRUST IN GOD
    Honesty
Luke 16:1–10

DECEMBER 9 456
TRUST IN GOD
Hebrews 10:32–11:6

DECEMBER 10 458
TRUST IN GOD
Revelation 3:7–13

DECEMBER 11 459
TRUST IN GOD
    Fear
Numbers 14:1–9

DECEMBER 12 460
TRUST IN GOD
    Suffering
2 Kings 6:8–17

DECEMBER 13 462
TRUST IN GOD
    Suffering
2 Kings 6:8–17

DECEMBER 14 463
SUFFERING
Philippians 4:8–13

DECEMBER 15 464
SUFFERING/TRUST
Hebrews 12:1–11

DECEMBER 16 465
SUFFERING
James 1:2–4

DECEMBER 17 466
TEMPTATION
Genesis 39:1–12

DECEMBER 18 468
WAITING ON GOD
1 Chronicles 17:1–20

UNITY 470
DECEMBER 19
Ephesians 4:1–6

WISDOM
DECEMBER 20 470
1 Kings 4:29–34

DECEMBER 21 471
DISCERNMENT
Proverbs 19:15–25

DECEMBER 22 473
MENTOR
Ecclesiastes 12:6–14

DECEMBER 23 474
COUNSEL
1 Corinthians 1:18–25

DECEMBER 24 475
WISDOM
    Faith/Grace
James 1:1–8

DECEMBER 25 476
WISDOM
James 3:13–17

WITNESSING 477
DECEMBER 26
    Testimony
2 Corinthians 3:1–11

DECEMBER 27 478
WISDOM
Acts 8:26–35

DECEMBER 28 **480**
THE CALL
1 Samuel 3:1–10

WORSHIP **481**
DECEMBER 29
    The Doctrine of God
Psalm 100

DECEMBER 30 **482**
WORSHIP
Ezra 3:7–13

DECEMBER 31 **483**
WORSHIP
    Encouragement
Acts 4:32–37; 9:26–27

INTRODUCTION

Like millions of people, each one of us faces challenges every day in our life.

However, it is not the challenge itself, but how we choose to face the challenge and how we choose to give the problem to God.

How does God think and what does God say about the challenges you are facing? Does He see the challenge or problem the same as you do? Each difficulty we face, God sees it as an opportunity to show Himself as Jehovah, the relational God, who wants to have a relationship with each believer. He wants to reveal Himself as Elohim, the Strong Creator God and as Adonai, who is Master over All. All that He has created and that nothing is impossible for Him. Each challenge has a set of circumstances that makes it possible for God to do something.

After having faced many challenges in life, I have concluded that only God had the answer and the advice I needed to solve my dilemma at that moment. Learning to seek God first, I have learned that regrets, heartaches, and not to mention, headaches were avoidable.
Learning what God's Word has to say about life has changed my perspective profoundly.

As you read this devotional, the table of contents will help you find where to go according to the situation you are facing. Even though that day's reading may be on a different topic, you can read it as well as finding the day that is dealing with the subject matter you are facing. The scripture index will help you find what scriptures were used and where to find it in the book. As you read this book each day, it will encourage you to saturate your mind and heart with the unfailing Word of God. It will have a profound impact on how you think.

Spending time with God, the Strong Creator, who is Master over All, you will soon learn He wants to have a relationship with you to tell how much He loves you.

God's Love
January 1
Exodus 1:22–2:10

The story of a baby boy who was born, but a king wanted him to die.
This was a sad time for his mother and father, and it made them cry.
A precious little baby boy, what had he done?
Why would a king want to kill someone's precious, loved son?
What could they do?
Nonetheless, God had a plan for his life, and it all came true.
God gave him two mothers whose love for him was dear.
By the things they taught him, it would become quite clear.
One taught him how to live in the palace of the Egyptian king.
The other mother showed and taught him how to
worship his God, Jehovah, the King of Kings.
To Him, he will learn to worship, praise, pray, and sing.
This little boy will learn many amazing things.
This baby boy: Moses is his name.
The story of his life brought glory, worship, and praise to God,
and because of his life history, many were never the same.

When your life is in the hands of God, He will take you,
an ordinary person, and do extraordinary things.

Exodus 1:22–2:10

22 Then Pharaoh gave this order to all his people: "Every Hebrew boy that is born you must throw into the Nile, but let every girl live."
The Birth of Moses
2 Now a man of the tribe of Levi married a Levite woman, 2 and she became pregnant and gave birth to a son. When she saw that he was a fine child, she hid him for three months. 3 But when she could hide him no longer, she got a papyrus basket[a] for him and coated it with tar and pitch. Then she placed the child in

it and put it among the reeds along the bank of the Nile. 4 His sister stood at a distance to see what would happen to him.

5 Then Pharaoh's daughter went down to the Nile to bathe, and her attendants were walking along the riverbank. She saw the basket among the reeds and sent her female slave to get it. 6 She opened it and saw the baby. He was crying, and she felt sorry for him. "This is one of the Hebrew babies," she said. 7 Then his sister asked Pharaoh's daughter, "Shall I go and get one of the Hebrew women to nurse the baby for you?"

8 "Yes, go," she answered. So the girl went and got the baby's mother. 9 Pharaoh's daughter said to her, "Take this baby and nurse him for me, and I will pay you." So the woman took the baby and nursed him. 10 When the child grew older, she took him to Pharaoh's daughter and he became her son. She named him Moses,[b] saying, "I drew him out of the water."

Adoration
January 2
Psalm 103:1–18

I took the time to think about the goodness of God and all He will do.
What I have learned is how much God loves
me, and I have learned that it is true.
I need not forget His benefits of comfort, advantage, and ease.
I always want to know how my God to please.
He heals my body and forgives my sins.
He has come into my heart because I have welcomed Him in.
He has redeemed me with love and compassion, rescuing my soul.
God is my Father; I am more precious to Him than silver and gold.
As the heavens are high above the earth,
So intense and potent for me is God's love
because, to Him, I am of great worth.
As far as the East is from the West have my sins been removed from me.
It is pleasing to know from sin's control I have been set free.
From everlasting to everlasting, my God will always love me.

This is what I am looking forward to having in eternity.
How do you know God loves you?

Psalm 103:1–18

1
Praise the Lord, my soul;
all my inmost being, praise his holy name.
2
Praise the Lord, my soul,
and forget not all his benefits—
3
who forgives all your sins
and heals all your diseases,
4
who redeems your life from the pit
and crowns you with love and compassion,
5
who satisfies your desires with good things
so that your youth is renewed like the eagle's.
6
The Lord works righteousness
and justice for all the oppressed.
7
He made known his ways to Moses,
his deeds to the people of Israel:
8
The Lord is compassionate and gracious,
slow to anger, abounding in love.
9
He will not always accuse,
nor will he harbor his anger forever;
10
he does not treat us as our sins deserve
or repay us according to our iniquities.

11
For as high as the heavens are above the earth,
so great is his love for those who fear him;
12
as far as the east is from the west,
so far has he removed our transgressions from us.
13
As a father has compassion on his children,
so the Lord has compassion on those who fear him;
14
for he knows how we are formed,
he remembers that we are dust.
15
The life of mortals is like grass,
they flourish like a flower of the field;
16
the wind blows over it and it is gone,
and its place remembers it no more.
17
But from everlasting to everlasting
the Lord's love is with those who fear him,
and his righteousness with their children's children—
18
with those who keep his covenant
and remember to obey his precepts.

Adoration
January 3
Colossians 3:12–17

God, I want to give thanks to You through Jesus Christ.
I thank You very much for the peace that rules my heart
and keeps me filled with joy to be true and right.
I want the message of Christ to be in me.

It gives me songs of adoration to sing about eternity.
This is how I will live today;
In whatever I will do or whatever I will say,
I will do so in the name of Jesus to bring praise
and thanksgiving to my God as I pray.
This has put a song in my heart to sing.
Because, Jesus, You are my Lord, Savior, and eternal King.
Music of Christ will keep joy in your heart.

Colossians 3:12–17

12 Therefore, as God's chosen people, holy and dearly loved, clothe yourselves with compassion, kindness, humility, gentleness and patience. 13 Bear with each other and forgive one another if any of you has a grievance against someone. Forgive as the Lord forgave you. 14 And over all these virtues put on love, which binds them all together in perfect unity. 15 Let the peace of Christ rule in your hearts, since as members of one body you were called to peace. And be thankful. 16 Let the message of Christ dwell among you richly as you teach and admonish one another with all wisdom through psalms, hymns, and songs from the Spirit, singing to God with gratitude in your hearts. 17 And whatever you do, whether in word or deed, do it all in the name of the Lord Jesus, giving thanks to God the Father through him

Aging
January 4
Doctrine of God
Deuteronomy 34:1–12

Age is something we all understand.
The purpose of this number is out of our command.
It is God who has total control when He has a call on your life.

It is His decision at what age He will call
you, so just obey and do not fight.
When this season of life begins for you,
There will be some challenges, and there will be some fun too.
Age may be a number that you will understand.
But it is God who has age at His full command.
Are you ready to be used by God, no matter what happens?

Deuteronomy 34: 1–12

The Death of Moses

34 Then Moses climbed Mount Nebo from the plains of Moab to the top of Pisgah, across from Jericho. There the Lord showed him the whole land—from Gilead to Dan, 2 all of Naphtali, the territory of Ephraim and Manasseh, all the land of Judah as far as the Mediterranean Sea, 3 the Negev and the whole region from the Valley of Jericho, the City of Palms, as far as Zoar. 4 Then the Lord said to him, "This is the land I promised on oath to Abraham, Isaac and Jacob when I said, 'I will give it to your descendants.' I have let you see it with your eyes, but you will not cross over into it."
5 And Moses the servant of the Lord died there in Moab, as the Lord had said. 6 He buried him in Moab, in the valley opposite Beth Peor, but to this day no one knows where his grave is. 7 Moses was a hundred and twenty years old when he died, yet his eyes were not weak nor his strength gone. 8 The Israelites grieved for Moses in the plains of Moab thirty days, until the time of weeping and mourning was over.
9 Now Joshua son of Nun was filled with the spirit of wisdom because Moses had laid his hands on him. So the Israelites listened to him and did what the Lord had commanded Moses.
10 Since then, no prophet has risen in Israel like Moses, whom the Lord knew face to face, 11 who did all those signs and wonders the Lord sent him to do in Egypt—to Pharaoh and to all his officials and to his whole land. 12 For no one has ever shown the mighty power or performed the awesome deeds that Moses did in the sight of all Israel

Aging
January 5
Psalm 92:12–15

Aging is something we all will have to face.
Aging is best experienced when it is done with God's grace.
It can be full of tranquillity, without thinking about the things
that went wrong to make you feel uncomfortable and guilty.
Aging can also be full of courage, kindness, and mirth.
This is to encourage you to see aging as experiencing
life with a new mind-set to be birthed.
Growing old with God is what life is all about.
Thinking about who God is brings so much joy
it will make you jump and shout.
It is life that is full of indescribable treasures.
Treasures that cannot be measured.
Growing old with God does not convey uselessness.
It is a life that defines faithfulness.

Aging can be described as a bottle of fine wine:
the older it gets, the better it is.

Psalm 92:12–15

12
The righteous will flourish like a palm tree,
they will grow like a cedar of Lebanon;
13
planted in the house of the Lord,
they will flourish in the courts of our God.
14
They will still bear fruit in old age,
they will stay fresh and green,
15
proclaiming, "The Lord is upright;
he is my Rock, and there is no wickedness in him."

Aging
January 6
God's Care
Isaiah 46:4–13

One day, I looked into the mirror, and what did I see?
Someone who was aging looking back at me.
Hair was turning gray.
Even with the use of dye, the gray will always stay.
Sagging skin? A nip and tuck should do the trick.
However, other challenges in life it cannot fix.
Reminding me that growing old is happening each and every day.
With growing old, there are many struggles to face.
How do you face the challenge of growing old?
How do you deal with the changes that you cannot put on hold?
How do you deal with the changes in life that should be years of gold?
The fear of growing old? God wants to be there for you.
He will teach you how to number your days in
the aging process as you go through.
God will be there to carry, sustain, and rescue you; know that this is true.
As you fulfill your purpose in life, you have
the wisdom to know what to do.
As you grow older each day, let the heart of you grow new.

Do you remember the time when you wanted to be older?

Isaiah 46:4–13

4
Even to your old age and gray hairs
I am he, I am he who will sustain you.
I have made you and I will carry you;
I will sustain you and I will rescue you.
5
"With whom will you compare me or count me equal?
To whom will you liken me that we may be compared?

6
Some pour out gold from their bags
and weigh out silver on the scales;
they hire a goldsmith to make it into a god,
and they bow down and worship it.
7
They lift it to their shoulders and carry it;
they set it up in its place, and there it stands.
From that spot it cannot move.
Even though someone cries out to it, it cannot answer;
it cannot save them from their troubles.
8
"Remember this, keep it in mind,
take it to heart, you rebels.
9
Remember the former things, those of long ago;
I am God, and there is no other;
I am God, and there is none like me.
10
I make known the end from the beginning,
from ancient times, what is still to come.
I say, 'My purpose will stand,
and I will do all that I please.'
11
From the east I summon a bird of prey;
from a far-off land, a man to fulfill my purpose.
What I have said, that I will bring about;
what I have planned, that I will do.
12
Listen to me, you stubborn-hearted,
you who are now far from my righteousness.
13
I am bringing my righteousness near,
it is not far away;
and my salvation will not be delayed.
I will grant salvation to Zion,
my splendor to Israel.

Aging
January 7
Living Like Christ/Spiritual Growth
1 Timothy 4:6–11

As we are aging, our bodies are decaying.
The body is aging and slowly decomposing and fading away.
Some of us exercise to slow the process of
wishing youthfulness will always stay.
While exercise is good for the body, what about the soul?
What do you do for the soul as you grow old?
Labor and strive to put your hope in the living Christ.
His death to save all people from sin was a sacrifice.
The body is growing older with each new day.
Because of sin, it will stay this way.
However, as a believer in Christ, this does not need to be.
You will receive a new body for eternity.
Just wait and see.

Is it getting harder to look into the mirror? Then think about eternity.

1 Timothy 4:6–11

6 If you point these things out to the brothers and sisters, you will be a good minister of Christ Jesus, nourished on the truths of the faith and of the good teaching that you have followed. 7 Have nothing to do with godless myths and old wives' tales; rather, train yourself to be godly. 8 For physical training is of some value, but godliness has value for all things, holding promise for both the present life and the life to come. 9 This is a trustworthy saying that deserves full acceptance. 10 That is why we labor and strive, because we have put our hope in the living God, who is the Savior of all people, and especially of those who believe. 11 Command and teach these things.

Anger
January 8
Ephesians 4:25–32

There is a rage rising inside me.
How can I control this anger so no one will see?
A smile came along my way.
I know Jesus had to have sent it because He knew I needed it today.
It took away the anger and the rage too.
Lord Jesus, I wish to thank You.
It kept me from speaking words that would have been unkind.
Those words someone would have kept in the mind.
That beautiful smile really did make my day.
I wish to be compassionate, kind, and forgiving, and watch what I say.
Thank You, Jesus, for forgiving me; I thank You very
much for the gift of a smile that has set me free.

It is amazing how a smile can have a bearing on anger.

Ephesians 4:25–32

25 Therefore each of you must put off falsehood and speak truthfully to your neighbor, for we are all members of one body. 26 "In your anger do not sin": Do not let the sun go down while you are still angry, 27 and do not give the devil a foothold. 28 Anyone who has been stealing must steal no longer, but must work, doing something useful with their own hands, that they may have something to share with those in need. 29 Do not let any unwholesome talk come out of your mouths, but only what is helpful for building others up according to their needs, that it may benefit those who listen. 30 And do not grieve the Holy Spirit of God, with whom you were sealed for the day of redemption. 31 Get rid of all bitterness, rage and anger, brawling and slander, along with every form of malice. 32 Be kind and compassionate to one another, forgiving each other, just as in Christ God forgave you. Bible

Bible
January 9
Nehemiah 8:1–8

The Bible, the Word of God, is an amazing book.
It is easy to see that after taking the first look.
Though many were associated with writing it, there is only one author.
It has been preserved through the ages.
There are sixty-six books that fill its pages.
Listen attentively when you read.
You will get the desire to praise God indeed.
Lift your voice in praise while your hands are raised.
Amen, amen, so be it; God should be worshipped. He should be praised.
Bow down, and worship Him with your face to the ground.
Worshipping God can be very profound.

When you look in the Bible, are you reading it to learn
and know God, or to say you have read it?

Nehemiah 8:1–8

8
1 all the people came together as one in the square before the Water Gate. They told Ezra the teacher of the Law to bring out the Book of the Law of Moses, which the Lord had commanded for Israel.
2 So on the first day of the seventh month Ezra the priest brought the Law before the assembly, which was made up of men and women and all who were able to understand. 3 He read it aloud from daybreak till noon as he faced the square before the Water Gate in the presence of the men, women and others who could understand. And all the people listened attentively to the Book of the Law.
4 Ezra the teacher of the Law stood on a high wooden platform built for the occasion. Beside him on his right stood Mattithiah, Shema, Anaiah, Uriah, Hilkiah and Maaseiah; and on his left were Pedaiah, Mishael, Malkijah, Hashum, Hashbaddanah, Zechariah and Meshullam.
5 Ezra opened the book. All the people could see him because he

was standing above them; and as he opened it, the people all stood up. 6 Ezra praised the Lord, the great God; and all the people lifted their hands and responded, "Amen! Amen!" Then they bowed down and worshiped the Lord with their faces to the ground. 7 The Levites—Jeshua, Bani, Sherebiah, Jamin, Akkub, Shabbethai, Hodiah, Maaseiah, Kelita, Azariah, Jozabad, Hanan and Pelaiah— instructed the people in the Law while the people were standing there. 8 They read from the Book of the Law of God, making it clear and giving the meaning so that the people understood what was being read.

Bible
January 10
Nehemiah 8:2–6; Acts 8:4–8

Pay attention. Pay very close attention to what the Lord has to say.
Listen attentively every day.
However, the mind can go on an adventure in wondering.
It can easily be distracted while in the excitement of pondering.
Lord, please help me to listen and not just hear.
Please make your message to me very clear.
Help me not only to watch but to see.
This is something that I need to learn how to be.
Help my focus to be on the present and not in an absent state of mind.
Lord, I need to be listening to You all the time.
Lord, speak to me today.
My intention is to pay close attention to everything You have to say.

How well we hear is how well we listen.

Nehemiah 8:2–6

2 So on the first day of the seventh month Ezra the priest brought the Law before the assembly, which was made up of men and women and all who were able to understand. 3 He read it aloud from daybreak till noon as he faced the square before the Water Gate in

the presence of the men, women and others who could understand. And all the people listened attentively to the Book of the Law.
4 Ezra the teacher of the Law stood on a high wooden platform built for the occasion. Beside him on his right stood Mattithiah, Shema, Anaiah, Uriah, Hilkiah and Maaseiah; and on his left were Pedaiah, Mishael, Malkijah, Hashum, Hashbaddanah, Zechariah and Meshullam.
5 Ezra opened the book. All the people could see him because he was standing above them; and as he opened it, the people all stood up. 6 Ezra praised the Lord, the great God; and all the people lifted their hands and responded, "Amen! Amen!" Then they bowed down and worshiped the Lord with their faces to the ground.

Acts 8:4–8

Philip in Samaria
4 Those who had been scattered preached the word wherever they went. 5 Philip went down to a city in Samaria and proclaimed the Messiah there. 6 When the crowds heard Philip and saw the signs he performed, they all paid close attention to what he said. 7 For with shrieks, impure spirits came out of many, and many who were paralyzed or lame were healed. 8 So there was great joy in that city.

Bible
January 11
Psalm 119:89–96

The Bible has much to say about how we should live each day.
When your heart is heavy, weighed down by
circumstances of everyday affairs,
Causing you to be filled with despair,
It may cause you to wonder, Does God really care?
God will not abandon or desert you.
Reading the Bible will tell you what God wants you to do.
His Word is timeless; let it be your guide.
Then you will know that God is always at your side.

The Bible is a compass and a map, telling you how to get through your day.

Psalm 119:89–96

ל Lamedh

89
Your word, Lord, is eternal;
it stands firm in the heavens.

90
Your faithfulness continues through all generations;
you established the earth, and it endures.

91
Your laws endure to this day,
for all things serve you.

92
If your law had not been my delight,
I would have perished in my affliction.

93
I will never forget your precepts,
for by them you have preserved my life.

94
Save me, for I am yours;
I have sought out your precepts.

95
The wicked are waiting to destroy me,
but I will ponder your statutes.

96
To all perfection I see a limit,
but your commands are boundless.

Bible
January 12
Psalm 119:161–168

The Bible is the written Word of God, filled with much treasure.
It is something of great value that cannot be measured.
It is of great value and will guide you through life.
Life that was given to those who would believe in His Son, Jesus Christ.
Dig into the scriptures, and you will find precious stones
of rubies, of promises that can be yours and mine.
They are ours to keep all the time.
Precious stones of rubies of hope.
When you dig into the scriptures, it will teach you how to cope.
Precious stones of silver, gold, and jasper will fill
your heart with the wisdom of peace.
This is something that will continue to be in your heart and never cease.
Sapphire, a precious stone, is to be desired and inspire you to love.
These treasures are all given to us from God above.
No matter how often you are in God's Word, you
will always find something to be treasured.

Psalm 119:161–168

w Sin and Shin
161
Rulers persecute me without cause,
but my heart trembles at your word.
162
I rejoice in your promise
like one who finds great spoil.
163
I hate and detest falsehood
but I love your law.
164

Seven times a day I praise you
for your righteous laws.
165
Great peace have those who love your law,
and nothing can make them stumble.
166
I wait for your salvation, Lord,
and I follow your commands.
167
I obey your statutes,
for I love them greatly.
168
I obey your precepts and your statutes,
for all my ways are known to you.

Bible
January 13
1 John 1:1–4

Word of Life, how I need You.
With all that is happening in my life, how will I make it through?
Word of Life, how I need you.
Words are important, but I do not know exactly what words to say.
Word of Life, I will pray to You today.
This is what I would like to say:
Keep me in Your hands throughout the day.
I will trust you because You are powerful and You speak the truth.
All that I need I will always find in no one else but You.

Jesus is the Word of Life that speaks words that matter.

1 John 1:1–4

The Incarnation of the Word of Life

1 That which was from the beginning, which we have heard, which we have seen with our eyes, which we have looked at and our hands have touched—this we proclaim concerning the Word of life. 2 The life appeared; we have seen it and testify to it, and we proclaim to you the eternal life, which was with the Father and has appeared to us. 3 We proclaim to you what we have seen and heard, so that you also may have fellowship with us. And our fellowship is with the Father and with his Son, Jesus Christ. 4 We write this to make our joy complete.

Bible
January 14
Bible Study/Obedience
Philippians 1:27–30

Study your Bible so you will learn to live for Christ
as you mature spiritually and grow.
Be exhorted to have the conduct from applying the Word of truth.
This is what Christ has asked from his gospel
of good news for all believers to do.
Be requested to be consistent and persist in applying the Word of life.
This is why Christ was sacrificed.
The character of believers is to become one in God's holy Son;
In Christ to remain steadfastness with peace and
gladness; there will be times this will not be fun.
To have harmony with humility that will last for an eternity;
Suffering from being a living sacrifice,
This is having the willingness to suffer for the holiness of Christ;
Live to be obedient and not have a life that is full of shame.
Live for God's Word, which is for our good,
and it will bring glory to His name.
Studying God's Word and applying it is a life of living in obedience.

Philippians 1:27–30

Life Worthy of the Gospel

27 Whatever happens, conduct yourselves in a manner worthy of the gospel of Christ. Then, whether I come and see you or only hear about you in my absence, I will know that you stand firm in the one Spirit, striving together as one for the faith of the gospel 28 without being frightened in any way by those who oppose you. This is a sign to them that they will be destroyed, but that you will be saved—and that by God. 29 For it has been granted to you on behalf of Christ not only to believe in him, but also to suffer for him, 30 since you are going through the same struggle you saw I had, and now hear that I still have

Bible
January 15
Doctrine of God
Psalm 119:17–19, 130–134

Learning and memorizing God's Word, how difficult is it to do?
If you hide it in your heart, will it continue to speak to you?
As you treasure God's Word, store it up in
your heart and refreshes it each day.
As you meditate on it, you will know how to
pray and what you need to say.
As your body grows old, do not allow your heart to grow cold.
Keeping God's Word stored in your heart, is storing treasure of gold.
Your mind may experience memory loss; however, it will
not separate you from His love and care for you.
God's Word will continue to live and strive in you,
because it is the Living Word and it is the Truth.

"I have hidden your word in my heart."
Psalm 119:11

Psalm 119:17–19

17
Be good to your servant while I live,
that I may obey your word.
18
Open my eyes that I may see
wonderful things in your law.
19
I am a stranger on earth;
do not hide your commands from me.

Psalm 119:130–134

130
The unfolding of your words gives light;
it gives understanding to the simple.
131
I open my mouth and pant,
longing for your commands.
132
Turn to me and have mercy on me,
as you always do to those who love your name.
133
Direct my footsteps according to your word;
let no sin rule over me.
134
Redeem me from human oppression,
that I may obey your precepts.

Bible
January 16
Holy Spirit/Spiritual Transformation
1 Samuel 3:1–10

When God speaks to you, do you hear?
Are you in the Bible to permit God near?
When God speaks, is the Holy Spirit guiding you?
Are you listening so you know what you need to do?
When He speaks, do you hear His voice?
Does it help you to know you can make a choice?
A choice to obey.
A choice not to delay.
When God speaks, it is how well you listen to hear.
Learning His Word to apply it to your life will permit Him to be near.

When God speaks, are you listening?

1 Samuel 3:1–10

The Lord Calls Samuel
3 The boy Samuel ministered before the Lord under Eli. In those days the word of the Lord was rare; there were not many visions. 2 One night Eli, whose eyes were becoming so weak that he could barely see, was lying down in his usual place. 3 The lamp of God had not yet gone out, and Samuel was lying down in the house of the Lord, where the ark of God was. 4 Then the Lord called Samuel. Samuel answered, "Here I am." 5 And he ran to Eli and said, "Here I am; you called me."
But Eli said, "I did not call; go back and lie down." So he went and lay down.
6 Again the Lord called, "Samuel!" And Samuel got up and went to Eli and said, "Here I am; you called me."
"My son," Eli said, "I did not call; go back and lie down."

7 Now Samuel did not yet know the Lord: The word
of the Lord had not yet been revealed to him.
8 A third time the Lord called, "Samuel!" And Samuel got
up and went to Eli and said, "Here I am; you called me."
Then Eli realized that the Lord was calling the boy. 9 So Eli told
Samuel, "Go and lie down, and if he calls you, say, 'Speak, Lord, for
your servant is listening.'" So Samuel went and lay down in his place.
10 The Lord came and stood there, calling as at
the other times, "Samuel! Samuel!"
Then Samuel said, "Speak, for your servant is listening."

Bible
January 17
Psalm 119:97–104

God's Word, how sweet it is;
tantamount to my taste.
It teaches me how to live life at God's pace.
When I do not, it's a life lived in haste that will
accomplish nothing—a life filled with waste.
God's Word will bring about a life filled with spiritual transformation.
Empowered by the Holy Spirit, life changing in restoration.
God's Word, how sweet and gratifying it is to me.
It is a powerful presence in my life for eternity.
How does God's Word, the Bible influence your life?

Psalm 119:97–104

מ Mem
97
Oh, how I love your law!
I meditate on it all day long.

98
Your commands are always with me
and make me wiser than my enemies.
99
I have more insight than all my teachers,
for I meditate on your statutes.
100
I have more understanding than the elders,
for I obey your precepts.
101
I have kept my feet from every evil path
so that I might obey your word.
102
I have not departed from your laws,
for you yourself have taught me.
103
How sweet are your words to my taste,
sweeter than honey to my mouth!
104
I gain understanding from your precepts;
therefore I hate every wrong path.

Bible
January 18
Holy Spirit
Hebrews 1:1–12

Speak to me Lord; I want to hear.
Speak, speak; please, Lord, draw Your servant near.
I want to understand every word of Your command. Speak,
Lord, speak to me as You take me by my hand.
Speak, Lord, speak; through Your Holy Spirit, please talk to me.
I want to learn more about Jesus and live with Him in eternity.
I will listen to all You have to say.
Speak, Lord, please speak, for I am listening to You each day.

Speak, Lord, please speak. I know You are listening whenever I pray.
Speak, Lord; I want to know what You have to say.

What is God saying to you today from the Bible?

Hebrews 1:1–12

God's Final Word: His Son
1 In the past God spoke to our ancestors through the prophets at many times and in various ways, 2 but in these last days he has spoken to us by his Son, whom he appointed heir of all things, and through whom also he made the universe. 3 The Son is the radiance of God's glory and the exact representation of his being, sustaining all things by his powerful word. After he had provided purification for sins, he sat down at the right hand of the Majesty in heaven. 4 So he became as much superior to the angels as the name he has inherited is superior to theirs.
The Son Superior to Angels
5 For to which of the angels did God ever say,
"You are my Son;
today I have become your Father"?
Or again,
"I will be his Father,
and he will be my Son"?
6 And again, when God brings his firstborn into the world, he says,
"Let all God's angels worship him."
7 In speaking of the angels he says,
"He makes his angels spirits,
and his servants flames of fire."
8 But about the Son he says,
"Your throne, O God, will last for ever and ever;
a scepter of justice will be the scepter of your kingdom.
9
You have loved righteousness and hated wickedness;
therefore God, your God, has set you above your companions
by anointing you with the oil of joy."
10 He also says,

"In the beginning, Lord, you laid the foundations of the earth,
and the heavens are the work of your hands.
11
They will perish, but you remain;
they will all wear out like a garment.
12
You will roll them up like a robe;
like a garment they will be changed.
But you remain the same,
and your years will never end."

January 19
Love for God
Deuteronomy 6:1–12

Hide God's Word in your heart and understand
what it means to live by God's commands.
Treasure His Word, how to live each day,
Then you will know how to obey.
Discuss it, think about it when you lie down and when you get up.
Let it fill your mind like an empty cup.
Use His Word to make all your decisions for today.
Praying His Word into your life will help you know the way.
How God's Word is treasured!
That is how a person's love for God can be measured.
God's Word can be measured in a person's life by how that person lives.

Deuteronomy 6:1–12

Love the Lord Your God

6 These are the commands, decrees and laws the Lord your God directed me to teach you to observe in the land that you are crossing the Jordan to possess, 2 so that you, your children and their children after them may fear the Lord your God as long as you live by keeping all his

decrees and commands that I give you, and so that you may enjoy long life. 3 Hear, Israel, and be careful to obey so that it may go well with you and that you may increase greatly in a land flowing with milk and honey, just as the Lord, the God of your ancestors, promised you.
4 Hear, O Israel: The Lord our God, the Lord is one. 5 Love the Lord your God with all your heart and with all your soul and with all your strength. 6 These commandments that I give you today are to be on your hearts. 7 Impress them on your children. Talk about them when you sit at home and when you walk along the road, when you lie down and when you get up. 8 Tie them as symbols on your hands and bind them on your foreheads. 9 Write them on the door frames of your houses and on your gates.
10 When the Lord your God brings you into the land he swore to your fathers, to Abraham, Isaac and Jacob, to give you—a land with large, flourishing cities you did not build, 11 houses filled with all kinds of good things you did not provide, wells you did not dig, and vineyards and olive groves you did not plant—then when you eat and are satisfied, 12 be careful that you do not forget the Lord, who brought you out of Egypt, out of the land of slavery.

Christ
January 20
Christ's Birth
Nahum 1:7–15

What is happening in the news today?
How will this new information enable and encourage me to pray?
Will this news bring me hope?
Will it help me know how in life to cope?
Will it bring me joy and peace?
Will this peace and joy be mine to keep?
Peace and joy, only God can give.
It is excellent news because it will help me know how I am to live.
News to know God is a refuge in times of unrest.
I do not need to be concerned because God will do what is best.

God will bring me peace.
It will never cease.

Good news is knowing the love of God.

Nahum 1:7–15

7
The Lord is good,
a refuge in times of trouble.
He cares for those who trust in him,
8
but with an overwhelming flood
he will make an end of Nineveh;
he will pursue his foes into the realm of darkness.
9
Whatever they plot against the Lord
he will bring to an end;
trouble will not come a second time.
10
They will be entangled among thorns
and drunk from their wine;
they will be consumed like dry stubble.
11
From you, Nineveh, has one come forth
who plots evil against the Lord
and devises wicked plans.
12 This is what the Lord says:
"Although they have allies and are numerous,
they will be destroyed and pass away.
Although I have afflicted you, Judah,
I will afflict you no more.
13
Now I will break their yoke from your neck
and tear your shackles away."

14
The Lord has given a command concerning you, Nineveh:
"You will have no descendants to bear your name.
I will destroy the images and idols
that are in the temple of your gods.
I will prepare your grave,
for you are vile."
15
Look, there on the mountains,
the feet of one who brings good news,
who proclaims peace!
Celebrate your festivals, Judah,
and fulfill your vows.
No more will the wicked invade you;
they will be completely destroyed.

Christ
January 21
Christ's Birth
John 8:12–20

In a world of darkness is where I have been.
It was a world of sin.
A life filled with hurt, pain, confusion, humiliation, and shame.
To many, like me, life was just a game.
The Christmas story of Jesus's birth
changed my life by letting me know what I am worth.
This Light I followed.
It changed my tomorrow.
Christmas has a new meaning for me.
Christmas is about why Christ came to this world to set me free.
It freed me to live with Him who truly loves me for eternity.

There is no better gift than the one God has given
to us: the gift of His Son, Jesus Christ.

John 8:12–20

Dispute Over Jesus's Testimony

12 When Jesus spoke again to the people, he said, "I am the light of the world. Whoever follows me will never walk in darkness, but will have the light of life."

13 The Pharisees challenged him, "Here you are, appearing as your own witness; your testimony is not valid."

14 Jesus answered, "Even if I testify on my own behalf, my testimony is valid, for I know where I came from and where I am going. But you have no idea where I come from or where I am going. 15 You judge by human standards; I pass judgment on no one. 16 But if I do judge, my decisions are true, because I am not alone. I stand with the Father, who sent me. 17 In your own Law it is written that the testimony of two witnesses is true. 18 I am one who testifies for myself; my other witness is the Father, who sent me."

19 Then they asked him, "Where is your father?"

"You do not know me or my Father," Jesus replied. "If you knew me, you would know my Father also." 20 He spoke these words while teaching in the temple courts near the place where the offerings were put. Yet no one seized him, because his hour had not yet come.

Christ
January 22
Christ, Messiah/Savior/Evangelism/Salvation
Matthew 28:16–20

As believers, we have been given the command to go throughout the lands;
With the goal to reach every man;
With sharing the gospel of Jesus Christ, witnessing to
what will make life pleasant, enjoyable, and right.
We are to make disciples of all ethnicities to save all humanity.
Be sensitive to everyone you meet today as they each go on their way.
You may not know what is precisely in their hearts or on their minds.
Sharing Jesus with them will not be wasting their time.

The extraordinary mission of testifying to the
death and resurrection of Jesus Christ
should be fulfilled in every Christian's life.

Do not let sharing the gospel of Jesus Christ be a challenge
in hindering others to know to about Him.

Matthew 28:16–20

The Great Commission
16 Then the eleven disciples went to Galilee, to the mountain
where Jesus had told them to go. 17 When they saw him, they
worshiped him; but some doubted. 18 Then Jesus came to them and
said, "All authority in heaven and on earth has been given to me.
19 Therefore go and make disciples of all nations, baptizing them
in the name of the Father and of the Son and of the Holy Spirit,
20 and teaching them to obey everything I have commanded you.
And surely I am with you always, to the very end of the age."

Christ
January 23
Christ/Messiah/Savior
Mark 14:32–39

Jesus fell, and with intense prayer, He poured out His heart that day.
His spirit, soul, body, and mind were in anguish as he prayed.
Those first crushing hours bathed in the suffering
of distress and agony beyond belief.
He was preparing Himself before His Father to undertake
the sin of the world, and there was only grief.
The extreme suffering arose out of physical, mental,
and emotional anguish with no relief.
The agony and suffering pressed down on Him as an olive press.
It caused His sweat to be like drops of blood from distress.
He endured the pain as it crushed Him for my sin.

It was pain that continued until His life came to an end.
It was punishment He bore for how I have lived my life.
It was during the time of prayer of my Lord and Savior, Jesus Christ.
I do not understand all that Jesus has done for me.
Father God, please help me to appreciate the
depth of this love for eternity.

Gethsemane is Hebrew for oil press; this is what sin did to Jesus as He prayed at Gethsemane—my sin was pressing life from Him.

Mark 14:32–39

Gethsemane

32 They went to a place called Gethsemane, and Jesus said to his disciples, "Sit here while I pray." 33 He took Peter, James and John along with him, and he began to be deeply distressed and troubled. 34 "My soul is overwhelmed with sorrow to the point of death," he said to them. "Stay here and keep watch." 35 Going a little farther, he fell to the ground and prayed that if possible the hour might pass from him. 36 "Abba, Father," he said, "everything is possible for you. Take this cup from me. Yet not what I will, but what you will." 37 Then he returned to his disciples and found them sleeping. "Simon," he said to Peter, "are you asleep? Couldn't you keep watch for one hour? 38 Watch and pray so that you will not fall into temptation. The spirit is willing, but the flesh is weak." 39 Once more he went away and prayed the same thing.

Christ's Deity
January 24
Fear
Luke 2:8–20

God came to us as a child and for us not to be in fear.
Immanuel, God is with us. Our God is near.

God sent us His Son. Because of Him, we are dear.
Ordinary people are who we are.
How can we speak to Almighty God, who
we may think and feel is very far?
Almighty God, how may we come to You and be near?
How may we speak to You and enter into Your presence
while not feeling terror or being in fear?
It is through this child, Jesus Christ, that we can come.
He is God's holy beloved Son.
We may enter God's presence, and this is the only way.
It is through Jesus Christ, and it is through Him we will pray.
We are to pray to God in Jesus's name every day.

It is through Jesus that we may come before God.

Luke 2:8–20

8 And there were shepherds living out in the fields nearby, keeping watch over their flocks at night. 9 An angel of the Lord appeared to them, and the glory of the Lord shone around them, and they were terrified. 10 But the angel said to them, "Do not be afraid. I bring you good news that will cause great joy for all the people. 11 Today in the town of David a Savior has been born to you; he is the Messiah, the Lord. 12 This will be a sign to you: You will find a baby wrapped in cloths and lying in a manger."
13 Suddenly a great company of the heavenly host
appeared with the angel, praising God and saying,
14
"Glory to God in the highest heaven,
and on earth peace to those on whom his favor rests."
15 When the angels had left them and gone into heaven, the shepherds said to one another, "Let's go to Bethlehem and see this thing that has happened, which the Lord has told us about."
16 So they hurried off and found Mary and Joseph, and the baby, who was lying in the manger. 17 When they had seen him, they spread the word concerning what had been told them about this child, 18 and all who heard it were amazed at what the shepherds said to them. 19 But

Mary treasured up all these things and pondered them in her heart. 20 The shepherds returned, glorifying and praising God for all the things they had heard and seen, which were just as they had been told.

Christ's Deity
January 25
Luke 2:8–20

As the shepherds watched their flocks at night,
A great company of angels appeared with news of delight.
The shepherds were in fear.
They were experiencing God's presence as being near.
Skepticism was not in their thinking, bringing a challenge to their belief.
The angel's message was one of peace of God's favor that gave relief.
Their faith took them on the journey to
Bethlehem to be a witness, they told.
They saw Mary, Joseph, and the baby Jesus lying in
a manger. They watched history unfold.
They went and spread the word of what they saw and what they heard.
They were worshipping God with every word.
All who heard were amazed, giving God such praise.
It was something, for Mary, that could not be measured.
It was something that was to be treasured.
The shepherd returned, with much worship
and praise for what God had done.
They saw their Messiah, Savior, Redeemer—God's begotten Son.

Behold the birth of the Savior of the world, Jesus Christ!

Luke 2:8–20

8 And there were shepherds living out in the fields nearby, keeping watch over their flocks at night. 9 An angel of the Lord appeared to them, and the glory of the Lord shone around them, and they were terrified. 10 But the angel said to them, "Do not be afraid. I bring you good news that will

cause great joy for all the people. 11 Today in the town of David a Savior has been born to you; he is the Messiah, the Lord. 12 This will be a sign to you: You will find a baby wrapped in cloths and lying in a manger."
13 Suddenly a great company of the heavenly host appeared with the angel, praising God and saying,
14
"Glory to God in the highest heaven,
and on earth peace to those on whom his favor rests."
15 When the angels had left them and gone into heaven, the shepherds said to one another, "Let's go to Bethlehem and see this thing that has happened, which the Lord has told us about."
16 So they hurried off and found Mary and Joseph, and the baby, who was lying in the manger. 17 When they had seen him, they spread the word concerning what had been told them about this child, 18 and all who heard it were amazed at what the shepherds said to them. 19 But Mary treasured up all these things and pondered them in her heart.
20 The shepherds returned, glorifying and praising God for all the things they had heard and seen, which were just as they had been told.

Christ's Deity
January 26
Christ/Savior/Messiah
John 1:1–14

The Word is alive today.
What does He have to say?
Who and What is the Word, and what does it have to do with me?
The Word is the Light that came to bring
life, to live with God for eternity.
The Word is Jesus Christ, who came to this world to sacrifice His life.
As the Living Word, He spoke words of truth.
His Word told us what we need to do;
How to live a life not controlled by sin;
For this kind of life always kept Satan and his darkness in.

Choose this day to make Jesus the Messiah, your Savior,
and Lord, and He will be more than a Friend. Jesus
Christ alone died on the cross has conquered sin.
Jesus is the actual, pure and real light, which is filled with grace and truth.
Now that you know who the Word is and what He came to do,
What do you want Him to do for you?

How is the Living Word living in you?

John 1:1–14

The Word Became Flesh
1 In the beginning was the Word, and the Word was with God, and the Word was God. 2 He was with God in the beginning. 3 Through him all things were made; without him nothing was made that has been made. 4 In him was life, and that life was the light of all mankind. 5 The light shines in the darkness, and the darkness has not overcome it.
6 There was a man sent from God whose name was John.
7 He came as a witness to testify concerning that light, so that through him all might believe. 8 He himself was not the light; he came only as a witness to the light.
9 The true light that gives light to everyone was coming into the world. 10 He was in the world, and though the world was made through him, the world did not recognize him. 11 He came to that which was his own, but his own did not receive him. 12 Yet to all who did receive him, to those who believed in his name, he gave the right to become children of God— 13 children born not of natural descent, nor of human decision or a husband's will, but born of God.
14 The Word became flesh and made his dwelling among us. We have seen his glory, the glory of the one and only Son, who came from the Father, full of grace and truth.

Christ's Deity
January 27
Christ Jesus/Savior
John 10:1–9

Why do I need a Savior? What good will it do?
What will a Savior offer me that I can depend on as truth?
Will He be a mediator for me for the wrongs I have done?
The Bible tells me this would be God's Holy and Righteous Son.
He is the Good Shepherd who will protect the sheep.
He will watch over them even while they sleep.
Jesus wants to be the mediator between God and me for my sins.
All I need to do is to ask with a sincere heart, and He will come in.
My sin is forgiven, and my life is made a new.
It is what Jesus as my Shepherd has come to do.
I am a lost sheep who needs a Shepherd to protect and show me the way.
I need a Shepherd to watch over me each and every day.
I want to thank You, Jesus, for dying for me.
Thank You very much for my salvation for eternity.

A compass will tell you the direction you are traveling, and GPS will show you how to get there; however, Jesus, the Good Shepherd, will not only tell you the direction you are going, and how to get to heaven, He will also protect you along the way and get you there for sure.

John 10:1–9

The Good Shepherd and His Sheep
10 "Very truly I tell you Pharisees, anyone who does not enter the sheep pen by the gate, but climbs in by some other way, is a thief and a robber. 2 The one who enters by the gate is the shepherd of the sheep. 3 The gatekeeper opens the gate for him, and the sheep listen to his voice. He calls his own sheep by name and leads them out. 4 When he has brought out all his own, he goes on ahead of them, and his sheep follow him because they know his voice. 5 But they will never

follow a stranger; in fact, they will run away from him because they do not recognize a stranger's voice." 6 Jesus used this figure of speech, but the Pharisees did not understand what he was telling them.
7 Therefore Jesus said again, "Very truly I tell you, I am the gate for the sheep. 8 All who have come before me are thieves and robbers, but the sheep have not listened to them. 9 I am the gate; whoever enters through me will be saved. They will come in and go out, and find pasture.

Christ's Deity
January 28
Savior/Messiah
John 15:12–17

How do you see Jesus Christ?
In how He lived His life?
Do you think He was approachable and welcomed all who
came to Him, no matter who they may have been?
While you are thinking about this, think about
yourself and how you have sinned.
Do you think any undesirable person would have an
opportunity to live with Him for eternity?
If you were in the crowd watching, listening, and heard Him speak,
Would you be moved with compassion for those among
you who are physically and spiritually weak?
What would you think of His power to witness Him
subduing demons at the sound of His voice?
They obey His command because He is God's
Son and they did not have a choice.
What would you think if you witnessed Him
calming violent storms over the sea?
Resurrecting the dead and thinking, That could be me.
How do you see Jesus Christ?
Do you focus only on His power and not how He lived His life?
Do you see Him as a superhero and there is no relationship to be had?

If you do, that would be very sad.
He deserves our obedience, and yet He can be called our friend.
How you relate to Jesus is how you see your sin.

How do you relate to Jesus?

John 15:12–17

12 My command is this: Love each other as I have loved you. 13 Greater love has no one than this: to lay down one's life for one's friends. 14 You are my friends if you do what I command. 15 I no longer call you servants, because a servant does not know his master's business. Instead, I have called you friends, for everything that I learned from my Father I have made known to you. 16 You did not choose me, but I chose you and appointed you so that you might go and bear fruit—fruit that will last—and so that whatever you ask in my name the Father will give you. 17 This is my command: Love each other.

Christ's Deity
January 29
Christ/Savior
1 Corinthians 1:18–31

Oh, the cross, the message that it gave.
All who believe it will be forgiven and saved.
It's a message you must understand before you can believe.
You must know the One who died and appreciates
the gift of eternal life to receive.
The power and compelling meaning of the cross
and its complete forgiveness of our sin.
Jesus Christ, the Messiah, became our Savior
and will never have to die for us again.
He took upon himself the cost of our iniquities and transgression.
Live each day for Him, with a heart and attitude
of gratitude and with no confusion.

Let Jesus Christ becomes your Lord and Savior because He loves you. Loving you for eternity is all He wishes to do.

Know the power of the cross.

1 Corinthians 1:18–31

Christ Crucified Is God's Power and Wisdom
18 For the message of the cross is foolishness to those who are perishing, but to us who are being saved it is the power of God. 19 For it is written:
"I will destroy the wisdom of the wise;
the intelligence of the intelligent I will frustrate."
20 Where is the wise person? Where is the teacher of the law? Where is the philosopher of this age? Has not God made foolish the wisdom of the world? 21 For since in the wisdom of God the world through its wisdom did not know him, God was pleased through the foolishness of what was preached to save those who believe. 22 Jews demand signs and Greeks look for wisdom, 23 but we preach Christ crucified: a stumbling block to Jews and foolishness to Gentiles, 24 but to those whom God has called, both Jews and Greeks, Christ the power of God and the wisdom of God. 25 For the foolishness of God is wiser than human wisdom, and the weakness of God is stronger than human strength. 26 Brothers and sisters, think of what you were when you were called. Not many of you were wise by human standards; not many were influential; not many were of noble birth. 27 But God chose the foolish things of the world to shame the wise; God chose the weak things of the world to shame the strong. 28 God chose the lowly things of this world and the despised things—and the things that are not—to nullify the things that are, 29 so that no one may boast before him. 30 It is because of him that you are in Christ Jesus, who has become for us wisdom from God—that is, our righteousness, holiness and redemption. 31 Therefore, as it is written: "Let the one who boasts boast in the Lord."

Christ's Deity
January 30
Savior/Messiah
Philippians 2:1–11

When Jesus came into this world, fame He did not seek.
He came being humble and meek.
Those who followed Him were encouraged with love.
Love that brought comfort from God above.
He was compassionate, and He gave it with joy and much pleasure.
We as believers are to have the same mind-set
as Christ, and it should be treasured.
Selfish ambition should not be a part of a believer's life.
Do not be conceited, because that will not be living for Christ.
Jesus humbly offered Himself as a sacrifice for all our sins.
What are you doing to allow Him into your heart, to welcome Him in?

He humbled himself by becoming obedient
to death—even death on a cross!
Philippians 2:8

Philippians 2:1–11

Imitating Christ's Humility
2 Therefore if you have any encouragement from being united with Christ, if any comfort from his love, if any common sharing in the Spirit, if any tenderness and compassion, 2 then make my joy complete by being like-minded, having the same love, being one in spirit and of one mind. 3 Do nothing out of selfish ambition or vain conceit. Rather, in humility value others above yourselves, 4 not looking to your own interests but each of you to the interests of the others.
5 In your relationships with one another, have
the same mindset as Christ Jesus:
6
Who, being in very nature God,

did not consider equality with God something
to be used to his own advantage;
7
rather, he made himself nothing
by taking the very nature of a servant,
being made in human likeness.
8
And being found in appearance as a man,
he humbled himself
by becoming obedient to death—
even death on a cross!
9
Therefore God exalted him to the highest place
and gave him the name that is above every name,
10
that at the name of Jesus every knee should bow,
in heaven and on earth and under the earth,
11
and every tongue acknowledge that Jesus Christ is Lord,
to the glory of God the Father.

Christ's Deity
January 31
Jesus
The Messiah/Savior
James 2:8–26

God is real, and the demons surely know.
They stand in fear before God and His Son,
Jesus Christ, because the Bible says so.
So, how real is your faith, if works you will not do?
Your words and your hands should be as one and not do as two.
Let your words speak of your faith.
While your hands do the work, your faith proclaims.

Then the two have become one because they are one and the same.
Faith without works does not bring praise to Jesus's holy name.
The kingdom of darkness once held you in prison because of sin.
Jesus, the Son of God, rescued and accepted you as an eternal friend.

How does your faith work?

James 2:8–26

8 If you really keep the royal law found in Scripture, "Love your neighbor as yourself," you are doing right. 9 But if you show favoritism, you sin and are convicted by the law as lawbreakers. 10 For whoever keeps the whole law and yet stumbles at just one point is guilty of breaking all of it. 11 For he who said, "You shall not commit adultery," also said, "You shall not murder." If you do not commit adultery but do commit murder, you have become a lawbreaker. 12 Speak and act as those who are going to be judged by the law that gives freedom, 13 because judgment without mercy will be shown to anyone who has not been merciful. Mercy triumphs over judgment.

Faith and Deeds
14 What good is it, my brothers and sisters, if someone claims to have faith but has no deeds? Can such faith save them? 15 Suppose a brother or a sister is without clothes and daily food. 16 If one of you says to them, "Go in peace; keep warm and well fed," but does nothing about their physical needs, what good is it? 17 In the same way, faith by itself, if it is not accompanied by action, is dead.
18 But someone will say, "You have faith; I have deeds." Show me your faith without deeds, and I will show you my faith by my deeds. 19 You believe that there is one God. Good! Even the demons believe that—and shudder.
20 You foolish person, do you want evidence that faith without deeds is useless? 21 Was not our father Abraham considered righteous for what he did when he offered his son Isaac on the altar? 22 You see that his faith and his actions were working together, and his faith was made complete by what he did. 23 And the scripture was fulfilled

that says, "Abraham believed God, and it was credited to him as righteousness," and he was called God's friend. 24 You see that a person is considered righteous by what they do and not by faith alone. 25 In the same way, was not even Rahab the prostitute considered righteous for what she did when she gave lodging to the spies and sent them off in a different direction? 26 As the body without the spirit is dead, so faith without deeds is dead.

Christ's Deity
February 1
False Teaching
John 8:31–38

What is truth, and what is it to me?
Having truth, will it keep me free?
Free from lies in the deception of sin.
Will it permit me to know an enemy from a true and loyal friend?
Will this truth teach me how to live a life knowing
good from bad, right from wrong?
Will this truth keep me morally strong?
There is only one Truth, and this Truth will set you free.
This Truth will teach you to be free for eternity.
Free from lies and what sin can and will do to you.
This Truth is Jesus Christ, and His word is true.
Believe and accept Jesus, and He will show you the way
to have a fully satisfying life each and every day.

Everyone wants the truth, but does everyone know what truth is?

John 8:31–38

Dispute Over Whose Children Jesus's Opponents Are
31 To the Jews who had believed him, Jesus said, "If you hold to my teaching, you are really my disciples. 32 Then you will know the truth, and the truth will set you free."

33 They answered him, "We are Abraham's descendants and have never been slaves of anyone. How can you say that we shall be set free?" 34 Jesus replied, "Very truly I tell you, everyone who sins is a slave to sin. 35 Now a slave has no permanent place in the family, but a son belongs to it forever. 36 So if the Son sets you free, you will be free indeed. 37 I know that you are Abraham's descendants. Yet you are looking for a way to kill me, because you have no room for my word. 38 I am telling you what I have seen in the Father's presence, and you are doing what you have heard from your father."

Christ
February 2
Living Like Christ
Matthew 10:35–42

When you live for Christ, it will be a life of love, devotion, and sacrifice.
It will be a life esteeming the needs and the
welfare of others; with adoration
in showing your appreciation of what Christ has done for you.
Jesus lived what He taught.
From that, you will learn to give.
Living for Christ is the joy of learning what life is all about.
Willingness to share it with others, with love
and care, will make you want to shout.
You will lose nothing when you are living a life of sacrifice.
It is a matter of living life for Jesus Christ.

Have you experienced what it means to live for Christ?

Matthew 10:35–42

35 For I have come to turn
"'a man against his father,
a daughter against her mother,
a daughter-in-law against her mother-in-law—

36
a man's enemies will be the members of his own household.'
37 "Anyone who loves their father or mother more than me is not worthy of me; anyone who loves their son or daughter more than me is not worthy of me. 38 Whoever does not take up their cross and follow me is not worthy of me. 39 Whoever finds their life will lose it, and whoever loses their life for my sake will find it.
40 "Anyone who welcomes you welcomes me, and anyone who welcomes me welcomes the one who sent me. 41 Whoever welcomes a prophet as a prophet will receive a prophet's reward, and whoever welcomes a righteous person as a righteous person will receive a righteous person's reward. 42 And if anyone gives even a cup of cold water to one of these little ones who is my disciple, truly I tell you, that person will certainly not lose their reward."

February 3
Living Like Christ
1 Peter 2:9–12

How can your lifestyle honor God today?
Listening to practical advice will help you to live in a godly way.
Refrain from that which is sinfully wrong,
as that is against your very soul.
Instead, live a life where your behavior will reflect
on living a life that is spiritually whole.
When others see your attitude and behavior, it
should be the one that God would approve.
Honorable living is not focused on selfish thoughts, words, and deeds.
It is living focused on pleasing God and meeting others' needs.
It is living in a way that others will notice and that
will draw them to God's way of life.
It is living a life filled with experiencing God's
love, and it will be a life of sacrifice.

As a believer in Christ, you are one of God's chosen people.

1 Peter 2:9–12

9 But you are a chosen people, a royal priesthood, a holy nation, God's special possession, that you may declare the praises of him who called you out of darkness into his wonderful light. 10 Once you were not a people, but now you are the people of God; once you had not received mercy, but now you have received mercy.

Living Godly Lives in a Pagan Society

11 Dear friends, I urge you, as foreigners and exiles, to abstain from sinful desires, which wage war against your soul. 12 Live such good lives among the pagans that, though they accuse you of doing wrong, they may see your good deeds and glorify God on the day he visits us.

Christ's Birth
February 4
Prayer/Temptation
Luke 2:25–38

Do not become discouraged or impatient when you
are waiting for answers to your prayer.
God's schedule is not the same as yours, and
your time is not the same as His time.
Waiting with expectancy and patience, please bear this in mind.
God's timing is never late or behind.
Nonetheless, His timing is always on time.
His timing is always perfect, which is worth the wait.
When He sent Jesus as the Messiah, it affected many who had faith.
Continue to pray, and let it never come to an end.
Many had prayed and waited for the Messiah
to come and to take away their sin.
Jesus is the answer to all our prayers for hope.

Luke 2:25–38

25 Now there was a man in Jerusalem called Simeon, who was righteous and devout. He was waiting for the consolation of Israel, and the Holy Spirit was on him. 26 It had been revealed to him by the Holy Spirit that he would not die before he had seen the Lord's Messiah. 27 Moved by the Spirit, he went into the temple courts. When the parents brought in the child Jesus to do for him what the custom of the Law required, 28 Simeon took him in his arms and praised God, saying:

29
"Sovereign Lord, as you have promised,
you may now dismiss your servant in peace.
30
For my eyes have seen your salvation,
31
which you have prepared in the sight of all nations:
32
a light for revelation to the Gentiles,
and the glory of your people Israel."

33 The child's father and mother marveled at what was said about him. 34 Then Simeon blessed them and said to Mary, his mother: "This child is destined to cause the falling and rising of many in Israel, and to be a sign that will be spoken against, 35 so that the thoughts of many hearts will be revealed. And a sword will pierce your own soul too." 36 There was also a prophet, Anna, the daughter of Penuel, of the tribe of Asher. She was very old; she had lived with her husband seven years after her marriage, 37 and then was a widow until she was eighty-four. She never left the temple but worshiped night and day, fasting and praying. 38 Coming up to them at that very moment, she gave thanks to God and spoke about the child to all who were looking forward to the redemption of Jerusalem.

Christ
February 5
Prayer
Luke 10:38–11:4

Come and sit at Jesus's feet and listen to what He has to say.
It will be food for thought for your life today.
Come and sit at Jesus's feet and listen to what He has to say.
When you go before God you will know how to pray.
Come and sit at Jesus's feet and watch the world go by.
Do not feel bad if no one stops and tell you hi.
Come and sit at Jesus's feet.
You must listen and not fall asleep.
He will teach everything you need to know.
Learn them for they will encourage you to spiritually grow.
He is the Bread of life.
He gave His life for you for your sin as a sacrifice.

Physical food our body needs each day, but our soul
needs spiritual food each day for eternity.

Luke 10:38–11:4

At the Home of Martha and Mary
38 As Jesus and his disciples were on their way, he came to a village where a woman named Martha opened her home to him. 39 She had a sister called Mary, who sat at the Lord's feet listening to what he said. 40 But Martha was distracted by all the preparations that had to be made. She came to him and asked, "Lord, don't you care that my sister has left me to do the work by myself? Tell her to help me!"
41 "Martha, Martha," the Lord answered, "you are worried and upset about many things, 42 but few things are needed—or indeed only one. Mary has chosen what is better, and it will not be taken away from her."

Jesus's Teaching on Prayer
11 One day Jesus was praying in a certain place. When he finished, one of his disciples said to him, "Lord, teach us to pray, just as John taught his disciples."
2 He said to them, "When you pray, say:
"'Father,
hallowed be your name,
your kingdom come.
3
Give us each day our daily bread.
4
Forgive us our sins,
for we also forgive everyone who sins against us.
And lead us not into temptation.'
"

Christ/Savior/Messiah
February 6
Pray/Temptation
Luke 22:39–46

Temptation always wants to control you,
Getting you to do the things you do not want to do.
You must pray temptation away.
You must do this every day.
It wants you to not do God's will.
Jesus taught that to temptation we should not yield.
Remember, in our own strength alone,
temptation we cannot fight and win.
Temptation's goal is to get us to yield to sin.
Remember, you must pray, pray every day.
Do not allow temptation to have its way.

Sin battle has been fought and won by Jesus Christ.

Luke 22:39–46

Jesus Prays on the Mount of Olives
39 Jesus went out as usual to the Mount of Olives, and his disciples followed him. 40 On reaching the place, he said to them, "Pray that you will not fall into temptation." 41 He withdrew about a stone's throw beyond them, knelt down and prayed, 42 "Father, if you are willing, take this cup from me; yet not my will, but yours be done." 43 An angel from heaven appeared to him and strengthened him. 44 And being in anguish, he prayed more earnestly, and his sweat was like drops of blood falling to the ground.
45 When he rose from prayer and went back to the disciples, he found them asleep, exhausted from sorrow. 46 "Why are you sleeping?" he asked them. "Get up and pray so that you will not fall into temptation."

February 7
Salvation
John 4:31–34

What would quench my thirst for life?
What would satisfy my appetite and feel just right?
Is it a hunger for life? What must it be?
Who can quench this thirst and hunger that are deep inside of me?
Jesus Christ is the Living Bread, the only One
who can satisfy this hunger deep within.
He is all that my soul needs to no longer have the desire to sin.
Satisfying my hunger to no end.
He is the Living Water who will quench my thirst.
To Him I will always go first.
Whenever I am thirsty for the truth, He will
always tell me what I need to do.
He is the Living Word who will tell me what is right and what
is wrong, how I am weak but in Him I can be strong.
He can satisfy all my hunger and my thirst to no end.

Jesus is my Lord, Savior, Redeemer, and my faithful, loyal Friend.
Jesus is the Living Bread and Water, the Living
Word who help me not to think the same.
I will think differently, always remembering to pray in His holy name.
It is my soul that has a deep hunger and thirst that need to be satisfied.
I will never be hungry or thirsty again, because
Jesus will always be at my side.

If you have a hunger and thirst for life, Jesus
is the only One who can satisfy.

John 4:31–34

31 Meanwhile his disciples urged him, "Rabbi, eat something."
32 But he said to them, "I have food to eat that you know nothing about."
33 Then his disciples said to each other, "Could
someone have brought him food?"
34 "My food," said Jesus, "is to do the will of him
who sent me and to finish his work.

Christ's Crucifixion
February 8
Love of God
Psalm 22:1–10

While on the cross, Christ endured the pain of isolation.
This is the realization of the agony of His suffering as a propitiation.
He cried out to His Father when God looked away,
When He saw all of my sins on Him that day.
God, His Father, had forsaken Him while He
suffered under the burden of my sins.
He was alone, isolated; there was no one, not one single friend.
He endured the abandonment until the work of the
cross was finished and His life came to an end.

As a sinner, my sins nailed Jesus to His cross; He stayed there because He wanted to become my Savior, Lord, and faithful Friend.

Jesus is always with believers; He will never leave them alone.

Psalm 22:1–10

Psalm 22
For the director of music. To the tune of "The Doe of the Morning." A psalm of David.
1
My God, my God, why have you forsaken me?
Why are you so far from saving me,
so far from my cries of anguish?
2
My God, I cry out by day, but you do not answer,
by night, but I find no rest.
3
Yet you are enthroned as the Holy One;
you are the one Israel praises.
4
In you our ancestors put their trust;
they trusted and you delivered them.
5
To you they cried out and were saved;
in you they trusted and were not put to shame.
6
But I am a worm and not a man,
scorned by everyone, despised by the people.
7
All who see me mock me;
they hurl insults, shaking their heads.
8
"He trusts in the Lord," they say,
"let the Lord rescue him.

Let him deliver him,
since he delights in him."
9
Yet you brought me out of the womb;
you made me trust in you, even at my mother's breast.
10
From birth I was cast on you;
from my mother's womb you have been my God.

February 9
Christ/Savior
John 17:1–5

Jesus finished the work God gave Him to do.
It glorified the Father, and the Father glorified Him too.
This was all done to save man from sin.
It was to clean the sinner's heart, and it allows God's love to come in.
This has made Jesus become the sinner's Friend.
The crucifixion, the work of the cross, was the sacrifice of the Lamb,
Inasmuch as He loved me just as I am.
Thank You, Father God, for sending Your Son, Jesus, to die for me.
Thank You, Jesus, for what You did on the cross at Calvary.

Jesus died so that you and I might live.

John 17:1–5

Jesus Prays to Be Glorified
17 After Jesus said this, he looked toward heaven and prayed: "Father, the hour has come. Glorify your Son, that your Son may glorify you. 2 For you granted him authority over all people that he might give eternal life to all those you have given him. 3 Now this is eternal life: that they know you, the only true God, and Jesus Christ, whom you have sent. 4 I have brought you glory on earth by finishing

the work you gave me to do. 5 And now, Father, glorify me in your presence with the glory I had with you before the world began."

February 10
Christ/Crucifixion
Resurrection/Messiah/Savior
John 20:24–31

Jesus is the Messiah, God's holy Son.
When He was crucified on the cross, how many souls were won?
Why would Jesus die for me?
Why would He die when He was free?
He committed no sin. He had no shame.
He had done nothing to shame His holy name.
He was crucified as the Messiah for the sin of man.
Few truly understood then, and many do not understand now.
He was resurrected as the Savior to all who would believe.
They would be given salvation to live in heaven with Him eternally.
The scars remained in His side, hands, and feet.
As Lord, the scars no longer hurt but were there to lead His lost sheep.
Do you know Jesus as the Christ?
Do you understand why He would sacrifice His life?
Do you doubt, like Thomas, because you truly want to believe?
Or do you doubt because Satan's lies have you deceived?

Did Jesus die for you?

John 20:24–31

Jesus Appears to Thomas
24 Now Thomas (also known as Didymus), one of the Twelve, was not with the disciples when Jesus came. 25 So the other disciples told him, "We have seen the Lord!"

But he said to them, "Unless I see the nail marks in
his hands and put my finger where the nails were, and
put my hand into his side, I will not believe."
26 A week later his disciples were in the house again, and Thomas
was with them. Though the doors were locked, Jesus came and
stood among them and said, "Peace be with you!" 27 Then he
said to Thomas, "Put your finger here; see my hands. Reach out
your hand and put it into my side. Stop doubting and believe."
28 Thomas said to him, "My Lord and my God!"
29 Then Jesus told him, "Because you have seen me, you have believed;
blessed are those who have not seen and yet have believed."

The Purpose of John's Gospel
30 Jesus performed many other signs in the presence of his
disciples, which are not recorded in this book. 31 But these are
written that you may believe that Jesus is the Messiah, the Son
of God, and that by believing you may have life in his name.

February 11
Salvation
Hebrews 9:19–28

We are waiting for Christ to appear a second time.
It will not be for Him to die for the sacrifice of
our sin—please keep this in mind.
We are waiting to receive the salvation for our sin.
What a joy it is to possess a gift that is so precious from a loving friend.
With the peace He has made with God for our sin,
We are thankful to have a relationship with
God that is made right with peace.
Peace and joy that will never cease.
We can enter into God's presence with thanksgiving, worship, and praise.
With humble hearts, voices of admiration, and hands raised,
We will sing, sing, sing.
To Christ, our Savior, who is our sacrifice and our King.

Lord Jesus, thank You for my salvation.

Hebrews 9:19–28

19 When Moses had proclaimed every command of the law to all the people, he took the blood of calves, together with water, scarlet wool and branches of hyssop, and sprinkled the scroll and all the people. 20 He said, "This is the blood of the covenant, which God has commanded you to keep." 21 In the same way, he sprinkled with the blood both the tabernacle and everything used in its ceremonies. 22 In fact, the law requires that nearly everything be cleansed with blood, and without the shedding of blood there is no forgiveness. 23 It was necessary, then, for the copies of the heavenly things to be purified with these sacrifices, but the heavenly things themselves with better sacrifices than these. 24 For Christ did not enter a sanctuary made with human hands that was only a copy of the true one; he entered heaven itself, now to appear for us in God's presence. 25 Nor did he enter heaven to offer himself again and again, the way the high priest enters the Most Holy Place every year with blood that is not his own. 26 Otherwise Christ would have had to suffer many times since the creation of the world. But he has appeared once for all at the culmination of the ages to do away with sin by the sacrifice of himself. 27 Just as people are destined to die once, and after that to face judgment, 28 so Christ was sacrificed once to take away the sins of many; and he will appear a second time, not to bear sin, but to bring salvation to those who are waiting for him.

Christ's Death
February 12
Salvation
Psalm 103:1–18

Lord God, I want to praise You,
For Your steadfast love and mercies too.
So many blessings; I have no idea the amount
because they are too numerous to count.

You have given me forgiveness, healing, deliverance,
provision, renewal, and protection too.
Lord, I am so blessed that I do not know what to do
but give You praise for my salvation today.
You are loving me in so many different ways.

Salvation is a gift that continues to give.

Psalm 103:1–18

A psalm of David.
1
Praise the Lord, my soul;
all my inmost being, praise his holy name.
2
Praise the Lord, my soul,
and forget not all his benefits—
3
who forgives all your sins
and heals all your diseases,
4
who redeems your life from the pit
and crowns you with love and compassion,
5
who satisfies your desires with good things
so that your youth is renewed like the eagle's.
6
The Lord works righteousness
and justice for all the oppressed.
7
He made known his ways to Moses,
his deeds to the people of Israel:
8
The Lord is compassionate and gracious,
slow to anger, abounding in love.

9
He will not always accuse,
nor will he harbor his anger forever;
10
he does not treat us as our sins deserve
or repay us according to our iniquities.
11
For as high as the heavens are above the earth,
so great is his love for those who fear him;
12
as far as the east is from the west,
so far has he removed our transgressions from us.
13
As a father has compassion on his children,
so the Lord has compassion on those who fear him;
14
for he knows how we are formed,
he remembers that we are dust.
15
The life of mortals is like grass,
they flourish like a flower of the field;
16
the wind blows over it and it is gone,
and its place remembers it no more.
17
But from everlasting to everlasting
the Lord's love is with those who fear him,
and his righteousness with their children's children—
18
with those who keep his covenant
and remember to obey his precepts.

February 13
Christ's Birth
Isaiah 9:1–7

What hope is there when you cannot see the light?
When the darkness is intense, and nothing is going right?
What ray of hope is there when you cannot find your way?
Do not give up. Instead, have faith, and pray.
Have faith in God and the Light that have
penetrated the darkness, making a way.
The brilliance of the Light in the darkness will shine through.
That Light is Jesus Christ, and He came to the
world so that He could die to save you.
Darkness will not win.
It will not overcome, because Jesus has conquered sin.
Receive the Light. It is here for you.
Jesus is the Light of the World, and this is true.

Only Jesus can bring light into your world of darkness.

Isaiah 9:1–7

9 Nevertheless, there will be no more gloom for those who were in distress. In the past he humbled the land of Zebulun and the land of Naphtali, but in the future he will honor Galilee of the nations, by the Way of the Sea, beyond the Jordan—

2

The people walking in darkness
have seen a great light;
on those living in the land of deep darkness
a light has dawned.

3

You have enlarged the nation
and increased their joy;
they rejoice before you

as people rejoice at the harvest,
as warriors rejoice
when dividing the plunder.

4

For as in the day of Midian's defeat,
you have shattered
the yoke that burdens them,
the bar across their shoulders,
the rod of their oppressor.

5

Every warrior's boot used in battle
and every garment rolled in blood
will be destined for burning,
will be fuel for the fire.

6

For to us a child is born,
to us a son is given,
and the government will be on his shoulders.
And he will be called
Wonderful Counselor, Mighty God,
Everlasting Father, Prince of Peace.

7

Of the greatness of his government and peace
there will be no end.
He will reign on David's throne
and over his kingdom,
establishing and upholding it
with justice and righteousness
from that time on and forever.
The zeal of the Lord Almighty
will accomplish this.

February 14
Christ's Birth
Luke 2:8–14

God gave His one and only Son to renew the life in you.
This life is filled with joy, mercy, peace, grace, and love too.
To know the love God has for you and the joy that it brings!
It will take away all the burdens that are on your heart
and replace them with songs of gladness to sing.
Oh, the joy of having a Savior and knowing the love He has for you!
It will truly make a difference in your life, no
matter what you may be going through.

What joy it is to know Jesus has come to give you joy.

Luke 2:8–14

8 And there were shepherds living out in the fields nearby, keeping watch over their flocks at night. 9 An angel of the Lord appeared to them, and the glory of the Lord shone around them, and they were terrified. 10 But the angel said to them, "Do not be afraid. I bring you good news that will cause great joy for all the people. 11 Today in the town of David a Savior has been born to you; he is the Messiah, the Lord. 12 This will be a sign to you: You will find a baby wrapped in cloths and lying in a manger."
13 Suddenly a great company of the heavenly host
appeared with the angel, praising God and saying,
14
"Glory to God in the highest heaven,
and on earth peace to those on whom his favor rests."

February 15
Salvation
Luke 24:13–32

How many times has Jesus come my way?
Because I did not recognize Him, I did not know what to say.
I knew He spoke with love and truth.
His words I held on to because they brought me comfort too.
I did not see the wounds in His hands or His feet.
Jesus, please forgive me.
Jesus came again, and when He spoke in that
moment, His words touched my soul.
My heart was awake, and I felt alive, refreshed, and not worn out and old.
I was filled with joy, and I was thankful to say,
"Jesus, thank You for dying for me at Calvary Hill that dark, gloomy day.

Have you seen Jesus today?

Luke 24:13–32

On the Road to Emmaus
13 Now that same day two of them were going to a village called Emmaus, about seven miles from Jerusalem. 14 They were talking with each other about everything that had happened. 15 As they talked and discussed these things with each other, Jesus himself came up and walked along with them; 16 but they were kept from recognizing him. 17 He asked them, "What are you discussing together as you walk along?"
They stood still, their faces downcast. 18 One of them, named Cleopas, asked him, "Are you the only one visiting Jerusalem who does not know the things that have happened there in these days?"
19 "What things?" he asked.
"About Jesus of Nazareth," they replied. "He was a prophet, powerful in word and deed before God and all the people. 20 The chief priests and our rulers handed him over to be sentenced to death, and they crucified him; 21 but we had hoped that he was the one who was

going to redeem Israel. And what is more, it is the third day since all this took place. 22 In addition, some of our women amazed us. They went to the tomb early this morning 23 but didn't find his body. They came and told us that they had seen a vision of angels, who said he was alive. 24 Then some of our companions went to the tomb and found it just as the women had said, but they did not see Jesus."

25 He said to them, "How foolish you are, and how slow to believe all that the prophets have spoken! 26 Did not the Messiah have to suffer these things and then enter his glory?" 27 And beginning with Moses and all the Prophets, he explained to them what was said in all the Scriptures concerning himself. 28 As they approached the village to which they were going, Jesus continued on as if he were going farther. 29 But they urged him strongly, "Stay with us, for it is nearly evening; the day is almost over." So he went in to stay with them.

30 When he was at the table with them, he took bread, gave thanks, broke it and began to give it to them. 31 Then their eyes were opened and they recognized him, and he disappeared from their sight. 32 They asked each other, "Were not our hearts burning within us while he talked with us on the road and opened the Scriptures to us?"

Christ's Death
February 16
Christ/Savior/Messiah
John 18:10–14, 36–37

When circumstances cause you to react too quickly,
without thinking, What is the right thing to do?
If history were to repeat itself, would you do something
different, or would do the same as before?
Or do you not even have a clue?
We must be focused to do God's will.
No matter how you may feel,
Restraint must be used.

Some may refuse.
Never be out of control when doing the work of Jesus Christ.
Remember, in being a strong conqueror,
restraint will become a way of life.
You must think with your heart and know in your head what you will do.
Your actions can have consequences, and there is no one to blame but you.
Do you see restraint as a weakness that needs the strength to be
in control, or it is a strength that will control a weakness?

John 18:10–14

10 Then Simon Peter, who had a sword, drew it and
struck the high priest's servant, cutting off his right
ear. (The servant's name was Malchus.)
11 Jesus commanded Peter, "Put your sword away! Shall
I not drink the cup the Father has given me?"
12 Then the detachment of soldiers with its commander and the
Jewish officials arrested Jesus. They bound him 13 and brought
him first to Annas, who was the father-in-law of Caiaphas, the high
priest that year. 14 Caiaphas was the one who had advised the Jewish
leaders that it would be good if one man died for the people.

John 18:36-37

36 Jesus said, "My kingdom is not of this world. If it were,
my servants would fight to prevent my arrest by the Jewish
leaders. But now my kingdom is from another place."
37 "You are a king, then!" said Pilate.
Jesus answered, "You say that I am a king. In fact, the
reason I was born and came into the world is to testify to
the truth. Everyone on the side of truth listens to me."

Christ's Death
February 17
Salvation
Romans 3:21–26

Christ was a sacrifice of atonement for me.
Shedding His blood for sin so I could be made free.
By faith, I have received this gift of salvation for eternity.
I have been made right with God by the justification of grace.
Being right with God is a gift that He has given to the whole human race.

If you do not have Jesus, how can you make things right with God?

Romans 3:21–26

Righteousness Through Faith
21 But now apart from the law the righteousness of God has been made known, to which the Law and the Prophets testify. 22 This righteousness is given through faith in Jesus Christ to all who believe. There is no difference between Jew and Gentile, 23 for all have sinned and fall short of the glory of God, 24 and all are justified freely by his grace through the redemption that came by Christ Jesus. 25 God presented Christ as a sacrifice of atonement, through the shedding of his blood—to be received by faith. He did this to demonstrate his righteousness, because in his forbearance he had left the sins committed beforehand unpunished— 26 he did it to demonstrate his righteousness at the present time, so as to be just and the one who justifies those who have faith in Jesus.

Christ's Death
February 18
Evangelism
1 Peter 3:8–16

Be encouraged to share your faith.
Give the reason why you want to love and not hate.
Give the reason why you want to honor Christ, because
of the transformation that places in you.
The transformation would be so obvious that it will
make others envy you, and they will want it too.
Let the sharing of your faith influence you to treat
others with compassion and humility.
Not returning evil for evil or insult for insult,
but pursuing peace as an actuality.
Keep your tongue from speaking evil, and then deceiving
with your speech is something you will not do.
When you share your faith, it is the way that God wants to use you.

How do you express Christ's importance to you?

1 Peter 3:8–16

Suffering for Doing Good
8 Finally, all of you, be like-minded, be sympathetic, love one another, be compassionate and humble. 9 Do not repay evil with evil or insult with insult. On the contrary, repay evil with blessing, because to this you were called so that you may inherit a blessing. 10 For,
"Whoever would love life
and see good days
must keep their tongue from evil
and their lips from deceitful speech.
11
They must turn from evil and do good;
they must seek peace and pursue it.

12
For the eyes of the Lord are on the righteous
and his ears are attentive to their prayer,
but the face of the Lord is against those who do evil."
13 Who is going to harm you if you are eager to do good? 14 But even if you should suffer for what is right, you are blessed. "Do not fear their threats; do not be frightened." 15 But in your hearts revere Christ as Lord. Always be prepared to give an answer to everyone who asks you to give the reason for the hope that you have. But do this with gentleness and respect, 16 keeping a clear conscience, so that those who speak maliciously against your good behavior in Christ may be ashamed of their slander.

Christ's Return
February 19
Matthew 25:1–13

Preparing for Christ's return is something we must do every day.
Live each day for Christ's return as you work and play.
We need to be attentive while we wait.
His return is something we should always anticipate.
There is still much work that needs to be done
before the coming of God's holy Son.
Now is the time to make sure your heart is right.
Do not wait until the last minute, because He could come day or night.
When Christ returns, He will not wait for you
if you have not done what He has told you to do.

Are you prepared for Christ's return?

Matthew 25:1–13

The Parable of the Ten Virgins
25 "At that time the kingdom of heaven will be like ten virgins who took their lamps and went out to meet the bridegroom. 2 Five of

them were foolish and five were wise. 3 The foolish ones took their lamps but did not take any oil with them. 4 The wise ones, however, took oil in jars along with their lamps. 5 The bridegroom was a long time in coming, and they all became drowsy and fell asleep.

6 "At midnight the cry rang out: 'Here's the bridegroom! Come out to meet him!'

7 "Then all the virgins woke up and trimmed their lamps. 8 The foolish ones said to the wise, 'Give us some of your oil; our lamps are going out.'

9 "'No,' they replied, 'there may not be enough for both us and you. Instead, go to those who sell oil and buy some for yourselves.'

10 "But while they were on their way to buy the oil, the bridegroom arrived. The virgins who were ready went in with him to the wedding banquet. And the door was shut.

11 "Later the others also came. 'Lord, Lord,' they said, 'open the door for us!'

12 "But he replied, 'Truly I tell you, I don't know you.'

13 "Therefore keep watch, because you do not know the day or the hour.

Christ's Return
February 20
Luke 2:21–35

Jesus Christ may come any day.
Prepare your heart and do not delay.
Always remember, Jesus can come any day.
God is faithful in keeping His promises; His word He will never break.
Know this for sure and do not hesitate.
Simeon's faith was strong, and he did believe.
He saw his Messiah, and he was not deceived.
Praise God today for the coming of Christ.
Praise Him; praise Him for His love and His sacrifice.
Jesus will return, and it will be soon.
No one knows the time or the date; whether it will be
in the morning, the evening, or the afternoon.

Jesus could return today.
Do what you need to do for the Messiah's return and do not delay.

Are you prepared for the Messiah's return?

Luke 2:21–35

21 On the eighth day, when it was time to circumcise the child, he was named Jesus, the name the angel had given him before he was conceived.
Jesus Presented in the Temple
22 When the time came for the purification rites required by the Law of Moses, Joseph and Mary took him to Jerusalem to present him to the Lord 23 (as it is written in the Law of the Lord, "Every firstborn male is to be consecrated to the Lord"), 24 and to offer a sacrifice in keeping with what is said in the Law of the Lord: "a pair of doves or two young pigeons."
25 Now there was a man in Jerusalem called Simeon, who was righteous and devout. He was waiting for the consolation of Israel, and the Holy Spirit was on him. 26 It had been revealed to him by the Holy Spirit that he would not die before he had seen the Lord's Messiah. 27 Moved by the Spirit, he went into the temple courts. When the parents brought in the child Jesus to do for him what the custom of the Law required, 28 Simeon took him in his arms and praised God, saying:
29
"Sovereign Lord, as you have promised,
you may now dismiss your servant in peace.
30
For my eyes have seen your salvation,
31
which you have prepared in the sight of all nations:
32
a light for revelation to the Gentiles,
and the glory of your people Israel."
33 The child's father and mother marveled at what was said about him.
34 Then Simeon blessed them and said to Mary, his mother: "This child is destined to cause the falling and rising of many in Israel, and to

be a sign that will be spoken against, 35 so that the thoughts of many hearts will be revealed. And a sword will pierce your own soul too."

February 21
Christ's Return
1 Thessalonians 4:13–18

How can I be relieved of this world's suffering, sorrow, pain, and fear?
What do I need to know, what do I need to hear?
Is this all there is to life? Is this the way things should be?
What will become of me? Is there a life for an eternity?
If I die today, where will I go?
Can someone tell me? I want to know.
I want to know the truth. I want to know what I need to do.
There is life after death for everyone who is alive and who has lived.
Giving your life to Christ for the salvation that He gives.
You can live with Him in heaven for eternity.
This is life, this is how living should be.
Ask for forgiveness for the sins you have done.
Accepting Jesus Christ as your Savior and Lord as God's holy Son;
Live for Him, and sin's control of your life will be gone.
Thank You, Jesus, for my new life.
Thank You very much for Your sacrifice.
Jesus, if You return today,
I know that, to heaven, I am on my way.

If Jesus returns today, will you be ready?

1 Thessalonians 4:13–18

Believers Who Have Died
13 Brothers and sisters, we do not want you to be uninformed about those who sleep in death, so that you do not grieve like the rest of mankind, who have no hope. 14 For we believe that Jesus died and rose again, and so we believe that God will bring with Jesus those

who have fallen asleep in him. 15 According to the Lord's word, we tell you that we who are still alive, who are left until the coming of the Lord, will certainly not precede those who have fallen asleep. 16 For the Lord himself will come down from heaven, with a loud command, with the voice of the archangel and with the trumpet call of God, and the dead in Christ will rise first. 17 After that, we who are still alive and are left will be caught up together with them in the clouds to meet the Lord in the air. And so we will be with the Lord forever. 18 Therefore encourage one another with these words.

February 22
Christ's Return
Love of God
Revelation 22:12–21

Come, Lord Jesus. I wait for You.
Come, Lord Jesus. I know You are coming, for this is true.
Come, Lord Jesus. I am waiting for You.
Come, Lord Jesus. The wait has been long.
As I wait for You, Jesus, my faith is becoming strong.
I will be in Your presence one day soon.
Come, Lord Jesus. Will it be this afternoon?
Come, Lord Jesus. I want to be away from death, sickness, pain, and fear.
Come, Lord Jesus. It is You who I wish to be near.
Come, Lord Jesus. This world is dark and difficult to live in.
Come, Lord Jesus. This world is dark and difficult because of sin.
Come, Lord Jesus. Will it be in the morning, the evening, or afternoon?
Come, Lord Jesus. Please let it be soon.

"Come, Lord Jesus." Revelation 22:20

Revelation 22:12–21

Epilogue: Invitation and Warning
12 "Look, I am coming soon! My reward is with me, and I will give to each person according to what they have done. 13 I am the Alpha and the Omega, the First and the Last, the Beginning and the End.
14 "Blessed are those who wash their robes, that they may have the right to the tree of life and may go through the gates into the city. 15 Outside are the dogs, those who practice magic arts, the sexually immoral, the murderers, the idolaters and everyone who loves and practices falsehood.
16 "I, Jesus, have sent my angel to give you this testimony for the churches. I am the Root and the Offspring of David, and the bright Morning Star."
17 The Spirit and the bride say, "Come!" And let the one who hears say, "Come!" Let the one who is thirsty come; and let the one who wishes take the free gift of the water of life.
18 I warn everyone who hears the words of the prophecy of this scroll: If anyone adds anything to them, God will add to that person the plagues described in this scroll. 19 And if anyone takes words away from this scroll of prophecy, God will take away from that person any share in the tree of life and in the Holy City, which are described in this scroll.
20 He who testifies to these things says, "Yes, I am coming soon."
Amen. Come, Lord Jesus.
21 The grace of the Lord Jesus be with God's people. Amen.

February 23
Christ's Return
Suffering
2 Thessalonians 1:3–12

Christ will return one day,
To right the wrongs that sin has on display.
He will come with His mighty angels to war against evil and its deeds.
Righteousness has won. This is true indeed.
This will bring relief to those who had faith and belief.

Life in a sinful world is so full of grief.
Jesus as the believer's Savior and Lord will come
one day to make this wrong right.
Then the world will be filled with love, joy, peace, and God's glorious light.
Stand firm in your faith.
Jesus will return, and He will not hesitate.
Evil and sin will no longer be;
They will be destroyed for eternity.

Sin has had its day.

2 Thessalonians 1:3–12

Thanksgiving and Prayer
3 We ought always to thank God for you, brothers and sisters, and rightly so, because your faith is growing more and more, and the love all of you have for one another is increasing. 4 Therefore, among God's churches we boast about your perseverance and faith in all the persecutions and trials you are enduring. 5 All this is evidence that God's judgment is right, and as a result you will be counted worthy of the kingdom of God, for which you are suffering. 6 God is just: He will pay back trouble to those who trouble you 7 and give relief to you who are troubled, and to us as well. This will happen when the Lord Jesus is revealed from heaven in blazing fire with his powerful angels. 8 He will punish those who do not know God and do not obey the gospel of our Lord Jesus. 9 They will be punished with everlasting destruction and shut out from the presence of the Lord and from the glory of his might 10 on the day he comes to be glorified in his holy people and to be marveled at among all those who have believed. This includes you, because you believed our testimony to you. 11 With this in mind, we constantly pray for you, that our God may make you worthy of his calling, and that by his power he may bring to fruition your every desire for goodness and your every deed prompted by faith. 12 We pray this so that the name of our Lord Jesus may be glorified in you, and you in him, according to the grace of our God and the Lord Jesus Christ.

February 24
Christ's Resurrection
Trusting God
Luke 24:13–35

Jesus has risen, and this is a fact.
When you meet Him, how will you react?
He has risen, and what are you expected to do?
You need to be ready to meet Him as He makes Himself known to you.
As you do, it will be clear that all the Bible has said about Him is true.
Expect Him to come alongside you and show
you how you are to live today.
The risen Jesus is alive; to Him you are to always
give praise and worship as you pray.

Are you expecting to experience Jesus today?

Luke 24:13–35

On the Road to Emmaus
13 Now that same day two of them were going to a village called Emmaus, about seven miles from Jerusalem. 14 They were talking with each other about everything that had happened. 15 As they talked and discussed these things with each other, Jesus himself came up and walked along with them; 16 but they were kept from recognizing him. 17 He asked them, "What are you discussing together as you walk along?"
They stood still, their faces downcast. 18 One of them, named Cleopas, asked him, "Are you the only one visiting Jerusalem who does not know the things that have happened there in these days?"
19 "What things?" he asked.
"About Jesus of Nazareth," they replied. "He was a prophet, powerful in word and deed before God and all the people. 20 The chief priests and our rulers handed him over to be sentenced to death, and they crucified him; 21 but we had hoped that he was the one who was going to redeem Israel. And what is more, it is the third day since all this took place. 22 In addition, some of our women amazed us. They

went to the tomb early this morning 23 but didn't find his body. They came and told us that they had seen a vision of angels, who said he was alive. 24 Then some of our companions went to the tomb and found it just as the women had said, but they did not see Jesus."

25 He said to them, "How foolish you are, and how slow to believe all that the prophets have spoken! 26 Did not the Messiah have to suffer these things and then enter his glory?" 27 And beginning with Moses and all the Prophets, he explained to them what was said in all the Scriptures concerning himself. 28 As they approached the village to which they were going, Jesus continued on as if he were going farther. 29 But they urged him strongly, "Stay with us, for it is nearly evening; the day is almost over." So he went in to stay with them.

30 When he was at the table with them, he took bread, gave thanks, broke it and began to give it to them. 31 Then their eyes were opened and they recognized him, and he disappeared from their sight. 32 They asked each other, "Were not our hearts burning within us while he talked with us on the road and opened the Scriptures to us?"

33 They got up and returned at once to Jerusalem. There they found the Eleven and those with them, assembled together 34 and saying, "It is true! The Lord has risen and has appeared to Simon." 35 Then the two told what had happened on the way, and how Jesus was recognized by them when he broke the bread.

February 25
Christ's Return
Trust in God
2 Peter 3:8–15

Please do not delay; Jesus Christ is on His way.
For some, the wait may feel long.
Please wait; there are many who do not yet belong.
Christ is waiting patiently for them to hear the
message of salvation and believe,
No longer living a life of being deceived.

He waits for them, just as He has waited for you.
He understands that waiting is not easy to do.
However, as you wait, witness to the lost and do not hesitate.
Witness, witness, telling others of what Christ has done for you.
Witness until He returns; that is what you need to do.

Are you ready for the return of Christ?

2 Peter 3:8–15

8 But do not forget this one thing, dear friends: With the Lord a day is like a thousand years, and a thousand years are like a day. 9 The Lord is not slow in keeping his promise, as some understand slowness. Instead he is patient with you, not wanting anyone to perish, but everyone to come to repentance.
10 But the day of the Lord will come like a thief. The heavens will disappear with a roar; the elements will be destroyed by fire, and the earth and everything done in it will be laid bare.
11 Since everything will be destroyed in this way, what kind of people ought you to be? You ought to live holy and godly lives 12 as you look forward to the day of God and speed its coming. That day will bring about the destruction of the heavens by fire, and the elements will melt in the heat. 13 But in keeping with his promise we are looking forward to a new heaven and a new earth, where righteousness dwells.
14 So then, dear friends, since you are looking forward to this, make every effort to be found spotless, blameless and at peace with him.
15 Bear in mind that our Lord's patience means salvation, just as our dear brother Paul also wrote you with the wisdom that God gave him.

Church Unity
February 26
Romans 15:1–7

Church unity is essential in relationships of acceptance, but it is far more than toleration.

Unity in the church is not to focus on individuality but on unification.
Christ wants us to have an attitude of bringing glory
to God by having one mind and one voice.
When we come together to glorify God, it is done by choice.
That choice will empower believers to endure
persecution as a price for their faith.
The bond of church unity is so powerful in God's love that
persecution and oppression are not seen as a mistake.
Together, we must strive.
God is always on our side.
Satan wants to bring division.
However, this is not God's vision.
Coming together is what each believer in Christ must do.
That oneness is how God's love will be shown through.
Let that oneness always be in you.

God's love always comes forward in unity.

Romans 15:1–7

15 We who are strong ought to bear with the failings of the weak and not to please ourselves. 2 Each of us should please our neighbors for their good, to build them up. 3 For even Christ did not please himself but, as it is written: "The insults of those who insult you have fallen on me." 4 For everything that was written in the past was written to teach us, so that through the endurance taught in the Scriptures and the encouragement they provide we might have hope. 5 May the God who gives endurance and encouragement give you the same attitude of mind toward each other that Christ Jesus had, 6 so that with one mind and one voice you may glorify the God and Father of our Lord Jesus Christ. 7 Accept one another, then, just as Christ accepted you, in order to bring praise to God.

February 27
Living with Other Believers in Christ
1 Corinthians 14:6–12, 26

The true believer of Christ will help the church to grow and stay healthy.
When believers are working together, using their gifts and
talents, the church will flourish and be wealthy.
This will make the church a safe place to be until
we go to be with Christ for eternity.
The church will grow like a healthy plant with a sweet fragrance of love.
A sweet fragrance that is sent from God above.
God did not ask the church to be perfect but to be
diligent in serving and in living for Jesus Christ.
This will allow the world to see the beauty of His sacrifice.

When the church works for unity, all experience the love of Christ.

1 Corinthians 14:6–12

6 Now, brothers and sisters, if I come to you and speak in tongues, what good will I be to you, unless I bring you some revelation or knowledge or prophecy or word of instruction? 7 Even in the case of lifeless things that make sounds, such as the pipe or harp, how will anyone know what tune is being played unless there is a distinction in the notes? 8 Again, if the trumpet does not sound a clear call, who will get ready for battle? 9 So it is with you. Unless you speak intelligible words with your tongue, how will anyone know what you are saying? You will just be speaking into the air. 10 Undoubtedly there are all sorts of languages in the world, yet none of them is without meaning. 11 If then I do not grasp the meaning of what someone is saying, I am a foreigner to the speaker, and the speaker is a foreigner to me. 12 So it is with you. Since you are eager for gifts of the Spirit, try to excel in those that build up the church.

1 Corinthians 14:26

Good Order in Worship
26 What then shall we say, brothers and sisters? When you come together, each of you has a hymn, or a word of instruction, a revelation, a tongue or an interpretation. Everything must be done so that the church may be built up.

**February 28
Church Unity
Serving Others
2 Corinthians 1:3–7**

Showing others comfort may not be what you think.
It is not the comfort of an easy chair,
Or the ambience that will fill the air.
It is not the tranquillity of a cozy room that
would inspire one to be delighted.
However, it is when God has shown you comfort
while you are hurting during troubled times.
During these times, you need someone to
help you take worry off your mind.
You need to be refreshed with encouragement
that helps to see you through.
You need someone who knows how to be there for you.
Having been comforted during times of need,
You will be able to identify and understand how
to meet someone else's need indeed.

Now you have an idea what to do with challenging
times when that the season is over.

2 Corinthians 1:3–7

Praise to the God of All Comfort

3 Praise be to the God and Father of our Lord Jesus Christ, the Father of compassion and the God of all comfort, 4 who comforts us in all our troubles, so that we can comfort those in any trouble with the comfort we ourselves receive from God. 5 For just as we share abundantly in the sufferings of Christ, so also our comfort abounds through Christ. 6 If we are distressed, it is for your comfort and salvation; if we are comforted, it is for your comfort, which produces in you patient endurance of the same sufferings we suffer. 7 And our hope for you is firm, because we know that just as you share in our sufferings, so also you share in our comfort.

February 29
God's Care/ Worry
Matthew 6:25–34

Worry is knocking at my door, causing me
to be anxious and fearful too.
Lord, this uneasiness is heavy.
What should I do?
His knocking is getting persistent, Lord, I am in need of You.
I will not answer his call; no matter what he says, I know it is not true.
I do not need to worry, because I have put my faith in You.
Lord, I know You care about creation, and I know You
care about me, so I do not need to worry; my
mind of worry can be set free.

Worrying may not change the situation; however, it will
raise your blood pressure and give you wrinkles.

Matthew 6:25–34

Do Not Worry

25 "Therefore I tell you, do not worry about your life, what you will eat or drink; or about your body, what you will wear. Is not life more than food, and the body more than clothes? 26 Look at the birds of the air; they do not sow or reap or store away in barns, and yet your heavenly Father feeds them. Are you not much more valuable than they? 27 Can any one of you by worrying add a single hour to your life? 28 "And why do you worry about clothes? See how the flowers of the field grow. They do not labor or spin. 29 Yet I tell you that not even Solomon in all his splendor was dressed like one of these. 30 If that is how God clothes the grass of the field, which is here today and tomorrow is thrown into the fire, will he not much more clothe you—you of little faith? 31 So do not worry, saying, 'What shall we eat?' or 'What shall we drink?' or 'What shall we wear?' 32 For the pagans run after all these things, and your heavenly Father knows that you need them. 33 But seek first his kingdom and his righteousness, and all these things will be given to you as well. 34 Therefore do not worry about tomorrow, for tomorrow will worry about itself. Each day has enough trouble of its own.

Church Worship
March 1
Acts 2:42–47

What does a church need to grow?
To be vibrant where spiritual awareness will flow?
It is essential to follow the instruction of God's Word that will show
the fellowship of believers as they spiritually grow.
Learning to pray in seeking to know God's guidance every day.
Learning how to worship, to study and to fellowship
together in the unity it will bring.
It is the joy of being strengthened together in
bringing worship to our Lord and King.

We are learning now how to fellowship and worship for eternity.

Acts 2:42–47

The Fellowship of the Believers
42 They devoted themselves to the apostles' teaching and to fellowship, to the breaking of bread and to prayer. 43 Everyone was filled with awe at the many wonders and signs performed by the apostles. 44 All the believers were together and had everything in common. 45 They sold property and possessions to give to anyone who had need. 46 Every day they continued to meet together in the temple courts. They broke bread in their homes and ate together with glad and sincere hearts, 47 praising God and enjoying the favor of all the people. And the Lord added to their number daily those who were being saved.

Contentment
March 2
Consumerism
Ecclesiastes 1:1–11

Contentment, contentment; how the heart longs to be.
Contentment, contentment; that is what I want for me.
How will I know when enough is enough, and there is no need for more?
I have learned when I am filled with the desire to
have Jesus. Life will be satisfying for sure.
The world cannot give you contentment.
It is filled with resentment.
Resenting that you do not have more and what you do not need.
The world's way is to advertise to you that
you should be unsatisfied indeed.
Contentment, contentment; how my heart longs to be.
Having Jesus in my heart is what contentment is to me.

Having Jesus in your life is how life is supposed to be lived.

Ecclesiastes 1:1–11

Everything Is Meaningless
1 The words of the Teacher, son of David, king in Jerusalem:
2
"Meaningless! Meaningless!"
says the Teacher.
"Utterly meaningless!
Everything is meaningless."
3
What do people gain from all their labors
at which they toil under the sun?
4
Generations come and generations go,
but the earth remains forever.
5
The sun rises and the sun sets,
and hurries back to where it rises.
6
The wind blows to the south
and turns to the north;
round and round it goes,
ever returning on its course.
7
All streams flow into the sea,
yet the sea is never full.
To the place the streams come from,
there they return again.
8
All things are wearisome,
more than one can say.
The eye never has enough of seeing,
nor the ear its fill of hearing.
9
What has been will be again,

what has been done will be done again;
there is nothing new under the sun.
10
Is there anything of which one can say,
"Look! This is something new"?
It was here already, long ago;
it was here before our time.
11
No one remembers the former generations,
and even those yet to come
will not be remembered
by those who follow them.

March 3
Contentment
Philippians 4:10–19

I need to learn the lesson of contentment,
So my heart will not be filled with resentment.
Contentment will put my heart at rest.
It will allow me to enjoy God's very best.
There will be no need to complain or grumble.
I will have the right attitude of being humble.
Circumstances God does not need to change to help me to grow.
Change needs to be made in me so contentment will show;
Then the lesson of contentment has been learned.
This is what my heart has long yearned.

Contentment will solve the problem that advertisement creates.

Philippians 4:10–19

Thanks for Their Gifts

10 I rejoiced greatly in the Lord that at last you renewed your concern for me. Indeed, you were concerned, but you had no

opportunity to show it. 11 I am not saying this because I am in need, for I have learned to be content whatever the circumstances. 12 I know what it is to be in need, and I know what it is to have plenty. I have learned the secret of being content in any and every situation, whether well fed or hungry, whether living in plenty or in want. 13 I can do all this through him who gives me strength. 14 Yet it was good of you to share in my troubles. 15 Moreover, as you Philippians know, in the early days of your acquaintance with the gospel, when I set out from Macedonia, not one church shared with me in the matter of giving and receiving, except you only; 16 for even when I was in Thessalonica, you sent me aid more than once when I was in need. 17 Not that I desire your gifts; what I desire is that more be credited to your account. 18 I have received full payment and have more than enough. I am amply supplied, now that I have received from Epaphroditus the gifts you sent. They are a fragrant offering, an acceptable sacrifice, pleasing to God. 19 And my God will meet all your needs according to the riches of his glory in Christ Jesus.

March 4
Contentment
Age/God's Care
2 Corinthians 12:6–10

How do you live life accepting the way things are and
not the way you want and expect them to be?
How do you do this joyfully?
When age tells you it will limit your body as to what it can do.
This restraint can cause all kinds of physical limitations on you.
Whether the limitations are physical, emotional,
or intellectual all can be tested.
To help you to be responsible and accountable, it will enable you to go
through your day trusting with faith in God to do for you what is best.
Rather than complaining, feeling sorry for yourself
because of what you are going through.
Trusting in God's care, knowing He will provide and take care of you.

Focus on your weaknesses with joy and delight.
Because your strength will come from God, as He
uses what is wrong. He will use it right.

Whatever your difficulties of hardship or persecution
in life may be, God will use it for good, for:
"Therefore I will boast all the more gladly about my weaknesses,
so that Christ's power may rest on me."
2 Corinthians 12:9

2 Corinthians 12:6–10

6 Even if I should choose to boast, I would not be a fool, because I would be speaking the truth. But I refrain, so no one will think more of me than is warranted by what I do or say, 7 or because of these surpassingly great revelations. Therefore, in order to keep me from becoming conceited, I was given a thorn in my flesh, a messenger of Satan, to torment me. 8 Three times I pleaded with the Lord to take it away from me. 9 But he said to me, "My grace is sufficient for you, for my power is made perfect in weakness." Therefore I will boast all the more gladly about my weaknesses, so that Christ's power may rest on me. 10 That is why, for Christ's sake, I delight in weaknesses, in insults, in hardships, in persecutions, in difficulties. For when I am weak, then I am strong.

March 5
Contentment
Christian Living
Matthew 20:1–16

The life that God has given to me is not to be used in comparing
what He is doing in others with what He is doing in me.
Comparing what others have should not be.
The obsession with comparing is not God's way.
When this is being done, it is not okay.
This is being proud with jealousy. The truth is that

God does not want this behavior to be in me or in you.
Be content with focusing on the life God has
given to you, with thanksgiving too.
The obsession with comparison says God has
favorites, which definitely is not true.
God does not compare. So, do not let behavior of comparison be in you.

Contentment has a way of bringing peace to the heart.

Matthew 20:1–16

The Parable of the Workers in the Vineyard
20 "For the kingdom of heaven is like a landowner who went out early in the morning to hire workers for his vineyard. 2 He agreed to pay them a denarius for the day and sent them into his vineyard.
3 "About nine in the morning he went out and saw others standing in the marketplace doing nothing. 4 He told them, 'You also go and work in my vineyard, and I will pay you whatever is right.' 5 So they went.
"He went out again about noon and about three in the afternoon and did the same thing. 6 About five in the afternoon he went out and found still others standing around. He asked them, 'Why have you been standing here all day long doing nothing?'
7 "'Because no one has hired us,' they answered.
"He said to them, 'You also go and work in my vineyard.'
8 "When evening came, the owner of the vineyard said to his foreman, 'Call the workers and pay them their wages, beginning with the last ones hired and going on to the first.'
9 "The workers who were hired about five in the afternoon came and each received a denarius. 10 So when those came who were hired first, they expected to receive more. But each one of them also received a denarius. 11 When they received it, they began to grumble against the landowner. 12 'These who were hired last worked only one hour,' they said, 'and you have made them equal to us who have borne the burden of the work and the heat of the day.'
13 "But he answered one of them, 'I am not being unfair to you, friend. Didn't you agree to work for a denarius? 14 Take your

pay and go. I want to give the one who was hired last the same as I gave you. 15 Don't I have the right to do what I want with my own money? Or are you envious because I am generous?' 16 "So the last will be first, and the first will be last."

Death
March 6
Resurrection of Believers
John 11:17–27

When a loved one dies, the pain is so real.
There appears to be no comfort for how you feel.
However, when the departed are believers, the
farewell is temporary, to say the least.
They will be there with the Lord. They will no
longer be in a state of being deceased.
Rest assured, they will be in the Lord's mighty hands.
This is faith on which you can stand.
Even when you cry out from your pain because they are no longer here,
Jesus hears your cries because He has a listening ear.
He knows you need comforting, so He will be
near, and there will be nothing to fear.
This is a transition, changing in life that will take place.
It will not be easy, but it is something we will have to face.
However, when you focus on life, eternity will now come to mind.
You and your loved one will one day be living
together again in eternity for all time.

Jesus does not want you to be in pain forever;
He wants you to have joy for eternity.

John 11:17–27

Jesus Comforts the Sisters of Lazarus
17 On his arrival, Jesus found that Lazarus had already been in the tomb for four days. 18 Now Bethany was less than two miles from Jerusalem, 19 and many Jews had come to Martha and Mary to comfort them in the loss of their brother. 20 When Martha heard that Jesus was coming, she went out to meet him, but Mary stayed at home.
21 "Lord," Martha said to Jesus, "if you had been here, my brother would not have died. 22 But I know that even now God will give you whatever you ask."
23 Jesus said to her, "Your brother will rise again."
24 Martha answered, "I know he will rise again in the resurrection at the last day."
25 Jesus said to her, "I am the resurrection and the life. The one who believes in me will live, even though they die; 26 and whoever lives by believing in me will never die. Do you believe this?"
27 "Yes, Lord," she replied, "I believe that you are the Messiah, the Son of God, who is to come into the world."

March 7
Death
Heaven
1 Thessalonians 4:13–18

How ready are you when death occurs in your life?
Will you be ready? It could happen tonight.
Death is real, and many do not know when it will take place.
When death will be staring them in the face.
If you have accepted Jesus Christ, then you have been saved through grace.
Hope in Jesus Christ will take fear's place.
Death, I know one day you will be here.
Hope and faith in Jesus have taken away all my fears.

The differences between heaven and hell is that their accommodations are not temporary. They are permanent.

1 Thessalonians 4:13–18

Believers Who Have Died

13 Brothers and sisters, we do not want you to be uninformed about those who sleep in death, so that you do not grieve like the rest of mankind, who have no hope. 14 For we believe that Jesus died and rose again, and so we believe that God will bring with Jesus those who have fallen asleep in him. 15 According to the Lord's word, we tell you that we who are still alive, who are left until the coming of the Lord, will certainly not precede those who have fallen asleep. 16 For the Lord himself will come down from heaven, with a loud command, with the voice of the archangel and with the trumpet call of God, and the dead in Christ will rise first. 17 After that, we who are still alive and are left will be caught up together with them in the clouds to meet the Lord in the air. And so we will be with the Lord forever. 18 Therefore encourage one another with these words.

Discipleship
March 8
Discipleship
Luke 9:57–62

What does it mean to be a follower of Jesus Christ?
What do you have to gain, and what will you have to sacrifice?
Where will you have to go?
Will life be fast or slow?
When you make this decision, will you truly know?
As a follower of Jesus Christ, your life will no longer be your own to negotiate and navigate as to what you want to do.
As a follower of Jesus, He will have full authority over you.
This decision will take some thought, depending
on where in life you will be.

Living for Jesus, you will want to be free.
Free from the slavery of sin that has had a hold on humanity.
Challenges you are sure to face.
However, each one will be met with God's saving grace.

The world will tell you life is a gamble and play your
cards right; however, how do you play for eternity?

Luke 9:57–62

The Cost of Following Jesus
57 As they were walking along the road, a man said
to him, "I will follow you wherever you go."
58 Jesus replied, "Foxes have dens and birds have nests,
but the Son of Man has no place to lay his head."
59 He said to another man, "Follow me."
But he replied, "Lord, first let me go and bury my father."
60 Jesus said to him, "Let the dead bury their own dead,
but you go and proclaim the kingdom of God."
61 Still another said, "I will follow you, Lord; but first
let me go back and say goodbye to my family."
62 Jesus replied, "No one who puts a hand to the plow and
looks back is fit for service in the kingdom of God."

March 9
Discipleship
Luke 9:57–62

As a follower of Jesus, there are some friendships
that you may need to change.
As a follower of Jesus, nothing will stay the same.
Friendship with Jesus will ask much from you.
You will not always do the things that you used to do.
There will be some people who will not understand why
you would allow Him to bring change into your life.

Why would it be filled with the need to sacrifice?
As a follower of Jesus, much will be asked and required of you.
Just remember, it will be a life filled with joy of being useful too.

There will be people who will not understand why you would
want to be a follower of Jesus, but that will be okay.

Luke 9:57–62

The Cost of Following Jesus
57 As they were walking along the road, a man said
to him, "I will follow you wherever you go."
58 Jesus replied, "Foxes have dens and birds have nests,
but the Son of Man has no place to lay his head."
59 He said to another man, "Follow me."
But he replied, "Lord, first let me go and bury my father."
60 Jesus said to him, "Let the dead bury their own dead,
but you go and proclaim the kingdom of God."
61 Still another said, "I will follow you, Lord; but first
let me go back and say goodbye to my family."
62 Jesus replied, "No one who puts a hand to the plow and
looks back is fit for service in the kingdom of God."

March 10
God Cares/Parenting
Proverbs 22:1–16

The future is in the hands of children; bring them up so they will know
they are to learn about Jesus as they grow—
Grow in knowledge to understand they are to
live and learn to obey God's command.
What He says is good and right, so they will have God's insight.
Tomorrow's leaders they will be.
They need to know how to live for God and not plant corruptible seeds.

Teach children, so they will grow.
As they become older, they will know which way they are to go.

It will be children who will become tomorrow's leaders.
Who will teach them, and what will they learn?

Proverbs 22:1–16

A good name is more desirable than great riches;
to be esteemed is better than silver or gold.
2
Rich and poor have this in common:
The Lord is the Maker of them all.
3
The prudent see danger and take refuge,
but the simple keep going and pay the penalty.
4
Humility is the fear of the Lord;
its wages are riches and honor and life.
5
In the paths of the wicked are snares and pitfalls,
but those who would preserve their life stay far from them.
6
Start children off on the way they should go,
and even when they are old they will not turn from it.
7
The rich rule over the poor,
and the borrower is slave to the lender.
8
Whoever sows injustice reaps calamity,
and the rod they wield in fury will be broken.
9
The generous will themselves be blessed,
for they share their food with the poor.

10
Drive out the mocker, and out goes strife;
quarrels and insults are ended.
11
One who loves a pure heart and who speaks with grace
will have the king for a friend.
12
The eyes of the Lord keep watch over knowledge,
but he frustrates the words of the unfaithful.
13
The sluggard says, "There's a lion outside!
I'll be killed in the public square!"
14
The mouth of an adulterous woman is a deep pit;
a man who is under the Lord's wrath falls into it.
15
Folly is bound up in the heart of a child,
but the rod of discipline will drive it far away.
16
One who oppresses the poor to increase his wealth
and one who gives gifts to the rich—both come to poverty.

Encouragement
March 11
Exodus 17:8–16

May I take this opportunity to encourage
you today as you go on your way?
With the challenges you will face, you will need God's amazing grace.
In our shared journey of faith, hope is what I want to offer you.
I know you have hope to offer me too.
We need each other to stay strong.
Especially when things are going wrong.
We will be committed to take each other before God's holy throne.
In prayer is where we will be, praying for each other continually.

May I take this opportunity to be an encouragement to you today as you go on your way? Oh, yes, I pray that you will have a great day.

Be an encouragement to someone's today, even with just a smile.

Exodus 17:8–16

The Amalekites Defeated

8 The Amalekites came and attacked the Israelites at Rephidim. 9 Moses said to Joshua, "Choose some of our men and go out to fight the Amalekites. Tomorrow I will stand on top of the hill with the staff of God in my hands." 10 So Joshua fought the Amalekites as Moses had ordered, and Moses, Aaron and Hur went to the top of the hill. 11 As long as Moses held up his hands, the Israelites were winning, but whenever he lowered his hands, the Amalekites were winning. 12 When Moses' hands grew tired, they took a stone and put it under him and he sat on it. Aaron and Hur held his hands up—one on one side, one on the other—so that his hands remained steady till sunset. 13 So Joshua overcame the Amalekite army with the sword. 14 Then the Lord said to Moses, "Write this on a scroll as something to be remembered and make sure that Joshua hears it, because I will completely blot out the name of Amalek from under heaven." 15 Moses built an altar and called it The Lord is my Banner. 16 He said, "Because hands were lifted up against the throne of the Lord, the Lord will be at war against the Amalekites from generation to generation."

March 12
Encouragement
Ephesians 4:25–32

Let today be a new beginning.
A life filled with joy and not one that is focused on sinning.
Let today be a new beginning.
A life filled with God's joy and peace.

This is the kind of life you will never want to crease.
Let it not be only in your attitude.
Let it be in who you are with gratitude.
Lying, stealing, using abusive language, being
bitter and angry all will have to cease.
These attitudes and behaviors will not bring peace.
Only in the power of the Holy Spirit can change take place.
It is the power that is from God and through His amazing grace.

Encouraging words to the spirit will bring
healing to overcome any adversities.

Ephesians 4:25–32

25 Therefore each of you must put off falsehood and speak truthfully to your neighbor, for we are all members of one body. 26 "In your anger do not sin": Do not let the sun go down while you are still angry, 27 and do not give the devil a foothold. 28 Anyone who has been stealing must steal no longer, but must work, doing something useful with their own hands, that they may have something to share with those in need. 29 Do not let any unwholesome talk come out of your mouths, but only what is helpful for building others up according to their needs, that it may benefit those who listen. 30 And do not grieve the Holy Spirit of God, with whom you were sealed for the day of redemption. 31 Get rid of all bitterness, rage and anger, brawling and slander, along with every form of malice. 32 Be kind and compassionate to one another, forgiving each other, just as in Christ God forgave you.

March 13
Encouragement
1 Thessalonians 4:1–12

Encourage your fellow believers to follow Jesus as their Lord.
Show compassion while being in one accord.
With passion urgently inspire each other to live a life that is pure.

When this is done daily, it will happen for sure.
As the church intercedes for those who believe;
The body will remain healthy and strong,
Enabling the desire to live godly and right, not evilly and wrong.
We are connected to each other through our Lord, Jesus Christ.
Use every opportunity to encourage other
believers in living spiritually and right.

Believers are linked together, connected to form a
strong chain of encouragement and support.

1 Thessalonians 4:1–12

Living to Please God

4 As for other matters, brothers and sisters, we instructed you how to live in order to please God, as in fact you are living. Now we ask you and urge you in the Lord Jesus to do this more and more. 2 For you know what instructions we gave you by the authority of the Lord Jesus.
3 It is God's will that you should be sanctified: that you should avoid sexual immorality; 4 that each of you should learn to control your own body in a way that is holy and honorable, 5 not in passionate lust like the pagans, who do not know God; 6 and that in this matter no one should wrong or take advantage of a brother or sister. The Lord will punish all those who commit such sins, as we told you and warned you before. 7 For God did not call us to be impure, but to live a holy life. 8 Therefore, anyone who rejects this instruction does not reject a human being but God, the very God who gives you his Holy Spirit.
9 Now about your love for one another we do not need to write to you, for you yourselves have been taught by God to love each other. 10 And in fact, you do love all of God's family throughout Macedonia. Yet we urge you, brothers and sisters, to do so more and more, 11 and to make it your ambition to lead a quiet life: You should mind your own business and work with your hands, just as we told you, 12 so that your daily life may win the respect of outsiders and so that you will not be dependent on anybody.

March 14
Bible/Evangelism
3 John 1:1–8

I thank you so much for the help and encouragement I received today.
It motivated and inspired me as I went on my way.
Your words of inspiration were what I needed in order to hear.
It was the guiding light that lets me know that Jesus is near.
Now I know that I can do the same.
I will be an encouragement to others in helping
them to praise Jesus's name.
Each believer has so much to offer, and there is so much to do.
As you work for God's kingdom, be encouraged to inspire others too.

How do you encourage others in their journey of faith in Jesus Christ?

3 John 1–8

1 The elder,
To my dear friend Gaius, whom I love in the truth.
2 Dear friend, I pray that you may enjoy good health and that all may go well with you, even as your soul is getting along well. 3 It gave me great joy when some believers came and testified about your faithfulness to the truth, telling how you continue to walk in it. 4 I have no greater joy than to hear that my children are walking in the truth. 5 Dear friend, you are faithful in what you are doing for the brothers and sisters, even though they are strangers to you. 6 They have told the church about your love. Please send them on their way in a manner that honors God. 7 It was for the sake of the Name that they went out, receiving no help from the pagans. 8 We ought therefore to show hospitality to such people so that we may work together for the truth.

March 15
Encouragement
Living for Christ
1 Thessalonians 4:1–12

Be motivated today,
With encouragement by the words I say.
Give your best to know and please our God every day.
Let this provide an incentive to you.
To be persistent in your faith in everything that you say and do.
Be inspired to keep living for God on your journey of faith.
In confidence and with hope, no matter the many mistakes.
Be motivated to keep up the good work today.
In everything you do and in everything you say.

Words of encouragement are always nice to hear while serving the Lord.

1 Thessalonians 4:1–12

Living to Please God

4 As for other matters, brothers and sisters, we instructed you how to live in order to please God, as in fact you are living. Now we ask you and urge you in the Lord Jesus to do this more and more. 2 For you know what instructions we gave you by the authority of the Lord Jesus.
3 It is God's will that you should be sanctified: that you should avoid sexual immorality; 4 that each of you should learn to control your own body in a way that is holy and honorable, 5 not in passionate lust like the pagans, who do not know God; 6 and that in this matter no one should wrong or take advantage of a brother or sister. The Lord will punish all those who commit such sins, as we told you and warned you before. 7 For God did not call us to be impure, but to live a holy life. 8 Therefore, anyone who rejects this instruction does not reject a human being but God, the very God who gives you his Holy Spirit.
9 Now about your love for one another we do not need to write to you, for you yourselves have been taught by God to love each other. 10 And in fact, you do love all of God's family throughout

Macedonia. Yet we urge you, brothers and sisters, to do so more and more, 11 and to make it your ambition to lead a quiet life: You should mind your own business and work with your hands, just as we told you, 12 so that your daily life may win the respect of outsiders and so that you will not be dependent on anybody.

March 16
Encouragement
Love for Others
Ephesians 4:2–6

I have struggles of which I do not want you to be aware.
I feel you could not understand or care.
I will do everything and anything to prevent them from being known.
This is the part of me I do not want to get shown.
Honesty is very difficult for me.
My fear of being hurt is what keeps me from being free.
Your encouragement helped me to know
that vulnerability is the healthiest way to go.
Being stimulated by you is helping me to understand and see.
You understand my struggles because you
have experienced the same as me.
This is giving me hope.
Your love, support, and patience encourage me to know how I am to cope.

How am I to understand your pain if you do not tell me?

Ephesians 4:2–6

2 Be completely humble and gentle; be patient, bearing with one another in love. 3 Make every effort to keep the unity of the Spirit through the bond of peace. 4 There is one body and one Spirit, just as you were called to one hope when you were called; 5 one Lord, one faith, one baptism; 6 one God and Father of all, who is over all and through all and in all.

March 17
Encouragement
Stories of Faith
Hebrews 11:32–12:3

Be encouraged; heaven is watching and cheering you on.
As you travel on your journey of faith, be committed
to Jesus Christ, God's holy Son.
Those who have gone before you persevered in
their great trials of endurance against sin.
They are the great cloud of witnesses in heaven who will welcome you in.
Listen, listen to their cheers.
They are telling you there is nothing to fear.
That Jesus Christ is always near.
To give you the strength to run this race.
The race of faith through God's amazing grace.

As a believer in Jesus Christ, all of heaven is
cheering you on in your faith journey.

Hebrews 11:32–12:3

32 And what more shall I say? I do not have time to tell about Gideon, Barak, Samson and Jephthah, about David and Samuel and the prophets, 33 who through faith conquered kingdoms, administered justice, and gained what was promised; who shut the mouths of lions, 34 quenched the fury of the flames, and escaped the edge of the sword; whose weakness was turned to strength; and who became powerful in battle and routed foreign armies. 35 Women received back their dead, raised to life again. There were others who were tortured, refusing to be released so that they might gain an even better resurrection. 36 Some faced jeers and flogging, and even chains and imprisonment. 37 They were put to death by stoning; they were sawed in two; they were killed by the sword. They went about in sheepskins and goatskins, destitute, persecuted and mistreated— 38 the world was not worthy of them. They wandered in deserts and mountains, living in caves and in holes in the ground.

39 These were all commended for their faith, yet none of them received what had been promised, 40 since God had planned something better for us so that only together with us would they be made perfect.
12 Therefore, since we are surrounded by such a great cloud of witnesses, let us throw off everything that hinders and the sin that so easily entangles. And let us run with perseverance the race marked out for us, 2 fixing our eyes on Jesus, the pioneer and perfecter of faith. For the joy set before him he endured the cross, scorning its shame, and sat down at the right hand of the throne of God. 3 Consider him who endured such opposition from sinners, so that you will not grow weary and lose heart.

Evangelism
March 18
Psalm 42

My soul will not be at rest, for I thirst for my God when I am oppressed.
My soul cries out for you, Lord God; I want and need Your rest.
Without You, Lord God, I cannot do my best.
How my soul cries out for You.
The longing is so deep, no one and nothing can fulfill it. What do I do?
You, O God, are the meaning of life.
No one can fill Your place to make life good and right.
My heart cries out. I am desperate for Your presence to be with me.
My soul finds peace because I know I will be with You for eternity.

Your soul knows it needs God; do you?

Psalm 42

For the director of music. A maskil of the Sons of Korah.
1
As the deer pants for streams of water,
so my soul pants for you, my God.
2
My soul thirsts for God, for the living God.

When can I go and meet with God?
3
My tears have been my food
day and night,
while people say to me all day long,
"Where is your God?"
4
These things I remember
as I pour out my soul:
how I used to go to the house of God
under the protection of the Mighty One
with shouts of joy and praise
among the festive throng.
5
Why, my soul, are you downcast?
Why so disturbed within me?
Put your hope in God,
for I will yet praise him,
my Savior and my God.
6
My soul is downcast within me;
therefore I will remember you
from the land of the Jordan,
the heights of Hermon—from Mount Mizar.
7
Deep calls to deep
in the roar of your waterfalls;
all your waves and breakers
have swept over me.
8
By day the Lord directs his love,
at night his song is with me—
a prayer to the God of my life.
9
I say to God my Rock,

> "Why have you forgotten me?
> Why must I go about mourning,
> oppressed by the enemy?"
>
> 10
> My bones suffer mortal agony
> as my foes taunt me,
> saying to me all day long,
> "Where is your God?"
>
> 11
> Why, my soul, are you downcast?
> Why so disturbed within me?
> Put your hope in God,
> for I will yet praise him,
> my Savior and my God.

March 19
Evangelism
Matthew 5:1–16

It is so amazing to see how God is working through me.
He says I am the light that He is using to draw to
Him so that others can experience and see
His love, patience, kindness, and humility.
There are just so many ways to share God so others will experience Him.
Remember as light of the world, your light needs to be bright and not dim.
Hearts will be mended, and lives will be changed.
When your light shines, someone's world of darkness will not be the same.
Shine, shine, shine. Let your light shine in the world that is around you.
God will do amazing things for others as He works through
me and as He works through you. Know that this is true.

When you enter a room, let your light shine for Jesus.

Matthew 5:1–16

Introduction to the Sermon on the Mount

5 Now when Jesus saw the crowds, he went up on a mountainside and sat down. His disciples came to him, 2 and he began to teach them.

The Beatitudes

He said:

3
"Blessed are the poor in spirit,
for theirs is the kingdom of heaven.

4
Blessed are those who mourn,
for they will be comforted.

5
Blessed are the meek,
for they will inherit the earth.

6
Blessed are those who hunger and thirst for righteousness,
for they will be filled.

7
Blessed are the merciful,
for they will be shown mercy.

8
Blessed are the pure in heart,
for they will see God.

9
Blessed are the peacemakers,
for they will be called children of God.

10
Blessed are those who are persecuted because of righteousness,
for theirs is the kingdom of heaven.

11 "Blessed are you when people insult you, persecute you and falsely say all kinds of evil against you because of me. 12 Rejoice and be glad, because great is your reward in heaven, for in the same way they persecuted the prophets who were before you.

Salt and Light

13 "You are the salt of the earth. But if the salt loses its saltiness, how can it be made salty again? It is no longer good for anything, except to be thrown out and trampled underfoot.
14 "You are the light of the world. A town built on a hill cannot be hidden. 15 Neither do people light a lamp and put it under a bowl. Instead they put it on its stand, and it gives light to everyone in the house. 16 In the same way, let your light shine before others, that they may see your good deeds and glorify your Father in heaven.

March 20
Evangelism
Mark 5:1–20

As a believer, you must tell how much Jesus has done for you.
Your story is important, as it is filled with the truth.
By telling your story, others will come to know,
There is someone who knows my experience,
and now I know where I need to go.
Tell your story, so others will hear
that the love of Jesus Christ for them is so very dear.
Tell it! Tell it! Don't be ashamed.
Because it will bring glory, honor, worship, and praise to His holy name.

Let the redeemed of the LORD tell their story.
Psalm 107:2

Mark 5:1–20 New

Jesus Restores a Demon-Possessed Man
5 They went across the lake to the region of the Gerasenes. 2 When Jesus got out of the boat, a man with an impure spirit came from the tombs to meet him. 3 This man lived in the tombs, and no one could bind him anymore, not even with a chain. 4 For he had often been chained hand and foot, but he tore the chains apart and broke the irons on his feet.

No one was strong enough to subdue him. 5 Night and day among the tombs and in the hills he would cry out and cut himself with stones. 6 When he saw Jesus from a distance, he ran and fell on his knees in front of him. 7 He shouted at the top of his voice, "What do you want with me, Jesus, Son of the Most High God? In God's name don't torture me!" 8 For Jesus had said to him, "Come out of this man, you impure spirit!"
9 Then Jesus asked him, "What is your name?"
"My name is Legion," he replied, "for we are many." 10 And he begged Jesus again and again not to send them out of the area.
11 A large herd of pigs was feeding on the nearby hillside. 12 The demons begged Jesus, "Send us among the pigs; allow us to go into them." 13 He gave them permission, and the impure spirits came out and went into the pigs. The herd, about two thousand in number, rushed down the steep bank into the lake and were drowned.
14 Those tending the pigs ran off and reported this in the town and countryside, and the people went out to see what had happened.
15 When they came to Jesus, they saw the man who had been possessed by the legion of demons, sitting there, dressed and in his right mind; and they were afraid. 16 Those who had seen it told the people what had happened to the demon-possessed man—and told about the pigs as well. 17 Then the people began to plead with Jesus to leave their region.
18 As Jesus was getting into the boat, the man who had been demon-possessed begged to go with him. 19 Jesus did not let him, but said, "Go home to your own people and tell them how much the Lord has done for you, and how he has had mercy on you." 20 So the man went away and began to tell in the Decapolis how much Jesus had done for him. And all the people were amazed.

March 21
Evangelism
John 6:34–51

Have you heard the good news?
Let me make sure I tell it to you right.
It is about the Living Bread, which is the Bread of Life.

It is none other than Jesus Christ.
When you have tried the Bread of Life, you will never be hungry again.
This is good news that you would want to share with all of your friends.
This is the good news of the gospel of Jesus to take away all of your sins.
Have you heard the good news?
You can have a new life and be born again.
You can have a life that will not be controlled by sin.

Sharing Jesus Christ will give someone new life.

John 6:34–51

34 "Sir," they said, "always give us this bread." 35 Then Jesus declared, "I am the bread of life. Whoever comes to me will never go hungry, and whoever believes in me will never be thirsty. 36 But as I told you, you have seen me and still you do not believe. 37 All those the Father gives me will come to me, and whoever comes to me I will never drive away. 38 For I have come down from heaven not to do my will but to do the will of him who sent me. 39 And this is the will of him who sent me, that I shall lose none of all those he has given me, but raise them up at the last day. 40 For my Father's will is that everyone who looks to the Son and believes in him shall have eternal life, and I will raise them up at the last day."
41 At this the Jews there began to grumble about him because he said, "I am the bread that came down from heaven." 42 They said, "Is this not Jesus, the son of Joseph, whose father and mother we know? How can he now say, 'I came down from heaven'?" 43 "Stop grumbling among yourselves," Jesus answered. 44 "No one can come to me unless the Father who sent me draws them, and I will raise them up at the last day. 45 It is written in the Prophets: 'They will all be taught by God.' Everyone who has heard the Father and learned from him comes to me. 46 No one has seen the Father except the one who is from God; only he has seen the Father. 47 Very truly I tell you, the one who believes has eternal life. 48 I am the bread of life. 49 Your ancestors ate the manna in the wilderness, yet they died. 50 But here is the bread that comes down from heaven,

which anyone may eat and not die. 51 I am the living bread that came down from heaven. Whoever eats this bread will live forever. This bread is my flesh, which I will give for the life of the world."

March 22
Evangelism
John 6:34–51

May I share my bread with you today?
It is the best bread, I have to say.
It is like no other, once you have tasted and see.
This bread is for the dying that was given on Calvary.
This bread is the Living Bread, the Bread of Life.
This Bread is Jesus Christ.
What a joy it is to share with you.
This Living Bread, and it is good news.
This Bread will last for eternity, and this is true.
As you take this Bread of Life, share it with others too.
Tell them what Jesus has done for you.

When people are hungry for life, share Jesus with them.

John 6:34–51

34 "Sir," they said, "always give us this bread." 35 Then Jesus declared, "I am the bread of life. Whoever comes to me will never go hungry, and whoever believes in me will never be thirsty. 36 But as I told you, you have seen me and still you do not believe. 37 All those the Father gives me will come to me, and whoever comes to me I will never drive away. 38 For I have come down from heaven not to do my will but to do the will of him who sent me. 39 And this is the will of him who sent me, that I shall lose none of all those he has given me, but raise them up at the last day. 40 For my Father's will is that everyone who looks to the Son and believes in him shall have eternal life, and I will raise them up at the last day."

41 At this the Jews there began to grumble about him because he said, "I am the bread that came down from heaven." 42 They said, "Is this not Jesus, the son of Joseph, whose father and mother we know? How can he now say, 'I came down from heaven'?" 43 "Stop grumbling among yourselves," Jesus answered. 44 "No one can come to me unless the Father who sent me draws them, and I will raise them up at the last day. 45 It is written in the Prophets: 'They will all be taught by God.' Everyone who has heard the Father and learned from him comes to me. 46 No one has seen the Father except the one who is from God; only he has seen the Father. 47 Very truly I tell you, the one who believes has eternal life. 48 I am the bread of life. 49 Your ancestors ate the manna in the wilderness, yet they died. 50 But here is the bread that comes down from heaven, which anyone may eat and not die. 51 I am the living bread that came down from heaven. Whoever eats this bread will live forever. This bread is my flesh, which I will give for the life of the world."

March 23
Evangelism
Acts 1:1–8

Let's talk today about who Jesus is and what He had to say.
He was a man who had a mission to change lives each and every day.
He is the Son of God, who sacrificed His life for the sin of man.
This is love that few will understand.
This is salvation, which is a free gift to all who would believe.
A gift to live with God and Christ eternally.
There is nothing you can do to earn salvation, which is a gift given in love.
This gift came from God above.

Trust Jesus as your Savior and Lord, and live each day for Him.

Acts 1:1–8 New

Jesus Taken Up Into Heaven

1 In my former book, Theophilus, I wrote about all that Jesus began to do and to teach 2 until the day he was taken up to heaven, after giving instructions through the Holy Spirit to the apostles he had chosen. 3 After his suffering, he presented himself to them and gave many convincing proofs that he was alive. He appeared to them over a period of forty days and spoke about the kingdom of God. 4 On one occasion, while he was eating with them, he gave them this command: "Do not leave Jerusalem, but wait for the gift my Father promised, which you have heard me speak about. 5 For John baptized with water, but in a few days you will be baptized with the Holy Spirit."
6 Then they gathered around him and asked him, "Lord, are you at this time going to restore the kingdom to Israel?"
7 He said to them: "It is not for you to know the times or dates the Father has set by his own authority. 8 But you will receive power when the Holy Spirit comes on you; and you will be my witnesses in Jerusalem, and in all Judea and Samaria, and to the ends of the earth."

March 24
Evangelism
2 Corinthians 2:14–17

An aroma of Christ I want to be.
A fragrance Christ can enjoy for all eternity.
Spending time with my Lord is changing me.
People will pay attention to the aroma that I wear of my King.
To some, it is a fragrance of life; to others, it is
a fragrance of death that it will bring.
However, the fragrance of Christ will make the heart want to sing.

Are you wearing the fragrance of life or the fragrance of death?

2 Corinthians 2:14–17

14 But thanks be to God, who always leads us as captives in Christ's triumphal procession and uses us to spread the aroma of the knowledge of him everywhere. 15 For we are to God the pleasing aroma of Christ among those who are being saved and those who are perishing. 16 To the one we are an aroma that brings death; to the other, an aroma that brings life. And who is equal to such a task? 17 Unlike so many, we do not peddle the word of God for profit. On the contrary, in Christ we speak before God with sincerity, as those sent from God.

March 25
Evangelism
Christ the Savior
John 1:1–8

You have the light. Let it shine through.
The world needs to see Jesus living in, and through, you.
You are the light, a witness that the world needs to see.
How to live for Jesus now and have life with Him for eternity.
Letting your light shine as you stand firm for
what is true, good, holy, and right.
Bring light into the world of darkness so people
will know how to have spiritual insight.
Be a witness in sharing your testimony of all
Christ has done and is doing for you.
The world needs to see Jesus's light shining through.

Your smile may be what someone needs to see as the light of Jesus.

John 1:1–8

The Word Became Flesh
1 In the beginning was the Word, and the Word was with God, and the Word was God. 2 He was with God in the beginning. 3 Through

him all things were made; without him nothing was made that has been made. 4 In him was life, and that life was the light of all mankind. 5 The light shines in the darkness, and the darkness has not overcome it.
6 There was a man sent from God whose name was John.
7 He came as a witness to testify concerning that light, so that through him all might believe. 8 He himself was not the light; he came only as a witness to the light.

March 26
Evangelism
God's Care
Mark 1:16–22

Your life has a purpose; that is why you are here.
Value yourself, because to Jesus Christ you are very dear.
Living your life for Him, there is something He wants you to do.
Being a witness as someone whose life He has
transformed and is living proof of the truth.
The truth of faith and belief of why Jesus has died for you.
As a believer in Jesus, a call has been made on your life.
To carry the message of Christ
to all who would believe.
His message of love and salvation they would freely receive.
No matter what people may have once thought of you,
When Jesus enters your life, you will become a living proof:
That God's Word is the Living Truth.

As a believer, God has a plan for your life.

Mark 1:16–22

Jesus Calls His First Disciples
16 As Jesus walked beside the Sea of Galilee, he saw Simon and his brother Andrew casting a net into the lake, for they were fishermen.

17 "Come, follow me," Jesus said, "and I will send you out to fish for people." 18 At once they left their nets and followed him. 19 When he had gone a little farther, he saw James son of Zebedee and his brother John in a boat, preparing their nets. 20 Without delay he called them, and they left their father Zebedee in the boat with the hired men and followed him.
Jesus Drives Out an Impure Spirit
21 They went to Capernaum, and when the Sabbath came, Jesus went into the synagogue and began to teach. 22 The people were amazed at his teaching, because he taught them as one who had authority, not as the teachers of the law.

March 27
Human Nature
Philippians 3:17–21

As a follower of Christ, I want to be an example for others to follow.
I will not let my faith be shallow and hollow.
I want to be real in my faith so others will see Jesus Christ living in me.
I want my faith to be real; I want my faith to be true.
I want my faith to be where others will say,
"I want that kind of faith too. I want to live for
Jesus. I want to be just like you."
I want to be an example for others to follow.
So, there will be believers to live for Jesus for today and for tomorrow.

Who are you being an example to follow living for Christ,
and whose example are you following to live for Christ?

Philippians 3:17–21

17 Join together in following my example, brothers and sisters, and just as you have us as a model, keep your eyes on those who live as we do. 18 For, as I have often told you before and now tell you again even with tears, many live as enemies of the cross of Christ. 19 Their destiny is

destruction, their god is their stomach, and their glory is in their shame. Their mind is set on earthly things. 20 But our citizenship is in heaven. And we eagerly await a Savior from there, the Lord Jesus Christ, 21 who, by the power that enables him to bring everything under his control, will transform our lowly bodies so that they will be like his glorious body.

March 28
Evangelism
Living for Christ
Matthew 10:26–32

Jesus had compassion for those lost in sin.
He wanted to become their Savior, Lord, Redeemer, and eternal Friend.
He saw that they were helpless as sheep.
They needed a Shepherd whose love would be deep
and who would be there in a heartbeat.
Receiving Jesus as your Savior and Lord, you cannot keep it to yourself.
You need to share it to help someone else.
Share the love of Christ as you live for Him.
It will let others know that life will be bright
and purposeful, not dreary and dim.

Share Christ with someone today.

Matthew 10:26–32

26 "So do not be afraid of them, for there is nothing concealed that will not be disclosed, or hidden that will not be made known. 27 What I tell you in the dark, speak in the daylight; what is whispered in your ear, proclaim from the roofs. 28 Do not be afraid of those who kill the body but cannot kill the soul. Rather, be afraid of the One who can destroy both soul and body in hell. 29 Are not two sparrows sold for a penny? Yet not one of them will fall to the ground outside your Father's care. 30 And even the very hairs of your head are all numbered. 31 So don't be afraid; you are worth more than many sparrows.

32 "Whoever acknowledges me before others, I will also acknowledge before my Father in heaven.

March 29
Evangelism
Living Like Christ
2 Corinthians 2:12–17

As a sweet sacrifice of praise, I will smell like Christ.
Having His fragrance, I will have the smell of life.
It will draw others to me.
Because I am wearing the smell of eternity.
The fragrance of eternity is a smell that is
exquisite, beautiful, delicate, and rare.
Because of what went into it: God's pure love
for us with considerable care.
Spread the fragrance of Christ and you will see,
People will want to wear it for eternity.

The fragrance of Christ is living a godly life.

2 Corinthians 2:12–17

Ministers of the New Covenant
12 Now when I went to Troas to preach the gospel of Christ and found that the Lord had opened a door for me, 13 I still had no peace of mind, because I did not find my brother Titus there. So I said goodbye to them and went on to Macedonia. 14 But thanks be to God, who always leads us as captives in Christ's triumphal procession and uses us to spread the aroma of the knowledge of him everywhere. 15 For we are to God the pleasing aroma of Christ among those who are being saved and those who are perishing. 16 To the one we are an aroma that brings death; to the other, an aroma that brings life. And who is equal to such a task? 17 Unlike so many,

we do not peddle the word of God for profit. On the contrary, in Christ we speak before God with sincerity, as those sent from God.

March 30
Evangelism
Love for Others
Mark 14:3–9

Don't worry, my friend, I will be here for you today.
I will do what I can as God shows me the way.
The love of Christ I will give to you today in what I do and in what I say.
Know I am limited in what I can do.
However, Jesus is not limited in what He will do for you.
I am grateful for this opportunity to give you my best.
I know my Lord and Savior, Jesus, will do the rest.

Give your best in doing what you can for Jesus today.

Mark 14:3–9

3 While he was in Bethany, reclining at the table in the home of Simon the Leper, a woman came with an alabaster jar of very expensive perfume, made of pure nard. She broke the jar and poured the perfume on his head. 4 Some of those present were saying indignantly to one another, "Why this waste of perfume? 5 It could have been sold for more than a year's wages and the money given to the poor." And they rebuked her harshly. 6 "Leave her alone," said Jesus. "Why are you bothering her? She has done a beautiful thing to me. 7 The poor you will always have with you, and you can help them any time you want. But you will not always have me. 8 She did what she could. She poured perfume on my body beforehand to prepare for my burial. 9 Truly I tell you, wherever the gospel is preached throughout the world, what she has done will also be told, in memory of her."

March 31
Evangelism
Relationship
Luke 8:40–48

Guarding my personal space and privacy is something I possess.
It is something I desire to keep, I must confess.
As I grow in my relationship with Christ, He wants
to touch the hurting world through me.
He wants to reach the hurting with His love, to be with Him for eternity.
He wants to touch them with His encouragement,
mercy, comfort, and grace.
When He brings them into my life, this will be done at His pace.
I need to be a window that Jesus can use so others can see,
The face of Jesus wanting to touch their lives to love them for eternity.

How are you allowing Jesus to use you to touch the hurting?

Luke 8:40–48

Jesus Raises a Dead Girl and Heals a Sick Woman
40 Now when Jesus returned, a crowd welcomed him, for they were all expecting him. 41 Then a man named Jairus, a synagogue leader, came and fell at Jesus' feet, pleading with him to come to his house 42 because his only daughter, a girl of about twelve, was dying. As Jesus was on his way, the crowds almost crushed him. 43 And a woman was there who had been subject to bleeding for twelve years, but no one could heal her. 44 She came up behind him and touched the edge of his cloak, and immediately her bleeding stopped.
45 "Who touched me?" Jesus asked.
When they all denied it, Peter said, "Master, the people are crowding and pressing against you."
46 But Jesus said, "Someone touched me; I know that power has gone out from me."

47 Then the woman, seeing that she could not go unnoticed, came trembling and fell at his feet. In the presence of all the people, she told why she had touched him and how she had been instantly healed. 48 Then he said to her, "Daughter, your faith has healed you. Go in peace."

April 1
Evangelism
Salvation
Luke 5:27–32

Welcome, welcome, welcome; all are welcome.
With open arms I welcome you
to receive the love of Jesus, because His love is real and true.
I welcome you, because it is only what Jesus would do.
I want to share His love with you.
Through the eyes of love.
In Jesus's love, all are welcome from God above.

You are welcome to receive the love of God through His Son, Jesus Christ.

Luke 5:27–32

Jesus Calls Levi and Eats With Sinners
27 After this, Jesus went out and saw a tax collector by the name of Levi sitting at his tax booth. "Follow me," Jesus said to him, 28 and Levi got up, left everything and followed him. 29 Then Levi held a great banquet for Jesus at his house, and a large crowd of tax collectors and others were eating with them. 30 But the Pharisees and the teachers of the law who belonged to their sect complained to his disciples, "Why do you eat and drink with tax collectors and sinners?" 31 Jesus answered them, "It is not the healthy who need a doctor, but the sick. 32 I have not come to call the righteous, but sinners to repentance."

April 2
Evangelism
Salvation
2 Corinthians 4:1–6

Let the truth be made known.
Jesus Christ sits on His throne.
He has conquered death and sin.
The Prince of this world has been defeated.
He did not win.
Jesus has destroyed death; through the gospel,
He has brought life and light.
The immortality of life will be a joy and a delight.
Though some who are skeptics haven't heard or believed.
The joy of knowing salvation they have not received.
However, there are some who have believed but are
living in their own strength and being deceived.
With the truth, allow Jesus to illuminate your mind.
You will experience freedom to live in victory all the time.

Do you understand why you need salvation?

2 Corinthians 4:1–6

Present Weakness and Resurrection Life
4 Therefore, since through God's mercy we have this ministry, we do not lose heart. 2 Rather, we have renounced secret and shameful ways; we do not use deception, nor do we distort the word of God. On the contrary, by setting forth the truth plainly we commend ourselves to everyone's conscience in the sight of God. 3 And even if our gospel is veiled, it is veiled to those who are perishing. 4 The god of this age has blinded the minds of unbelievers, so that they cannot see the light of the gospel that displays the glory of Christ, who is the image of God.
5 For what we preach is not ourselves, but Jesus Christ as Lord, and ourselves as your servants for Jesus' sake. 6 For God, who said, "Let light

shine out of darkness," made his light shine in our hearts to give us the light of the knowledge of God's glory displayed in the face of Christ.

April 3
Evangelism
Salvation
2 Corinthians 4:1–6

You have an opportunity to share the gospel with someone today.
Words of life are what you should say.
Know these are powerful words that will convict.
Some will receive Christ, while others will have a fit.
Life without Christ is a life of sin.
It is a life of being in annoyance, suffering, with mental
and emotional pain and torment from within.
Hearing the gospel and understanding what it will do,
You will see it is a life filled with God's love for you.

Share the gospel with someone today.

2 Corinthians 4:1–6

Present Weakness and Resurrection Life
4 Therefore, since through God's mercy we have this ministry, we do not lose heart. 2 Rather, we have renounced secret and shameful ways; we do not use deception, nor do we distort the word of God. On the contrary, by setting forth the truth plainly we commend ourselves to everyone's conscience in the sight of God. 3 And even if our gospel is veiled, it is veiled to those who are perishing. 4 The god of this age has blinded the minds of unbelievers, so that they cannot see the light of the gospel that displays the glory of Christ, who is the image of God. 5 For what we preach is not ourselves, but Jesus Christ as Lord, and ourselves as your servants for Jesus' sake. 6 For God, who said, "Let light shine out of darkness," made his light shine in our hearts to give us the light of the knowledge of God's glory displayed in the face of Christ.

Faith
April 4
Christ, Savior
Romans 4: 18–25

What is faith that I should hope for and believe?
Will this trust give me the confidence that I will
have what I have hoped to receive?
Do you have confidence that your faith is strong?
Will it be there for you no matter what may go wrong?
What do you put your faith in?
When life tells you that you will have to start again,
What do you put your faith in?
That will put a smile on your face, a great, broad grin.
Putting your faith in Jesus Christ is the most righteous thing to be done.
It is putting faith in no one else but God's holy and righteous Son.
He will never leave you, no matter what you will go through.
He will always be here for you.
What is faith that you should hope in and trust to receive?
Having Jesus as your Savior and Lord because
you trust in Him and believe.

Having faith takes a strong belief.

Romans 4:18–25

18 Against all hope, Abraham in hope believed and so became the father of many nations, just as it had been said to him, "So shall your offspring be." 19 Without weakening in his faith, he faced the fact that his body was as good as dead—since he was about a hundred years old—and that Sarah's womb was also dead. 20 Yet he did not waver through unbelief regarding the promise of God, but was strengthened in his faith and gave glory to God, 21 being fully persuaded that God had power to do what he had promised. 22 This is why "it was credited to him as righteousness." 23 The words "it was credited to him" were written not for him alone, 24 but also for us,

to whom God will credit righteousness—for us who believe in him who raised Jesus our Lord from the dead. 25 He was delivered over to death for our sins and was raised to life for our justification.

April 5
Faith
Doctrine of God
Salvation
1 John 5:1–13

The things of this world I do not want it to have control over me.
How do I resist it and become mentally and spiritually free?
I have learned you must have faith in the Son of God, Jesus Christ.
He died for the world's sin, as a sacrifice.
You must keep God's commandments and of this world not be a part.
This takes much faith; it will be hard.
To live in this world, it will take a life.
A life in Jesus Christ is to live right.
You will experience life's ups and downs,
While it takes away your smile and gives you a frown.
Some battles you will conquer with victory, while
some battles you will experience defeat.
But with a life in Jesus, this pattern of losing does not have to repeat.
To overcome the world is something you can do.
Just live a life of obedience with faith, doing what Jesus tells you to.

Victory or defeat is how you understand how to live life.

1 John 5:1–13

Faith in the Incarnate Son of God
5 Everyone who believes that Jesus is the Christ is born of God, and everyone who loves the father loves his child as well. 2 This is how we know that we love the children of God: by loving God and carrying out his commands. 3 In fact, this is love for God: to

keep his commands. And his commands are not burdensome, 4 for everyone born of God overcomes the world. This is the victory that has overcome the world, even our faith. 5 Who is it that overcomes the world? Only the one who believes that Jesus is the Son of God.
6 This is the one who came by water and blood—Jesus Christ. He did not come by water only, but by water and blood. And it is the Spirit who testifies, because the Spirit is the truth. 7 For there are three that testify:
8 the Spirit, the water and the blood; and the three are in agreement.
9 We accept human testimony, but God's testimony is greater because it is the testimony of God, which he has given about his Son. 10 Whoever believes in the Son of God accepts this testimony. Whoever does not believe God has made him out to be a liar, because they have not believed the testimony God has given about his Son. 11 And this is the testimony: God has given us eternal life, and this life is in his Son. 12 Whoever has the Son has life; whoever does not have the Son of God does not have life.

Concluding Affirmations

13 I write these things to you who believe in the name of the Son of God so that you may know that you have eternal life.

April 6
Trust
Hebrews 11:8–16

In the journey of life, I am a stranger and a foreigner on this earth.
Traveling to many places, this journey is of spiritual worth,
Because it has given me a spiritual rebirth.
It has taught me to live by faith.
Faith to believe that God is faithful to fulfill His
promises; in them He will not hesitate.
With my faith, pressing forward, God will be my guide.
He will never leave me. He will always stay at my side.
A stranger and a foreigner on this earth I may be.
But I am a citizen of heaven; it is my home for eternity.

Where is your eternal home?

Hebrews 11:8–16

8 By faith Abraham, when called to go to a place he would later receive as his inheritance, obeyed and went, even though he did not know where he was going. 9 By faith he made his home in the promised land like a stranger in a foreign country; he lived in tents, as did Isaac and Jacob, who were heirs with him of the same promise. 10 For he was looking forward to the city with foundations, whose architect and builder is God. 11 And by faith even Sarah, who was past childbearing age, was enabled to bear children because she considered him faithful who had made the promise. 12 And so from this one man, and he as good as dead, came descendants as numerous as the stars in the sky and as countless as the sand on the seashore. 13 All these people were still living by faith when they died. They did not receive the things promised; they only saw them and welcomed them from a distance, admitting that they were foreigners and strangers on earth. 14 People who say such things show that they are looking for a country of their own. 15 If they had been thinking of the country they had left, they would have had opportunity to return. 16 Instead, they were longing for a better country—a heavenly one. Therefore God is not ashamed to be called their God, for he has prepared a city for them.

April 7
False Prophets
Matthew 7:12–23

I need to discern so I will learn to know the truth from a lie.
Though I am a little lamb, precious as I am, I need
to know the wolves from the sheep.
Many come to deceive; I do believe, so I would not know their true intent.
Masquerading in many disguises.
These false prophets come to deceive with plenty of surprises.
I will know them by their fruit.
Their work of sin would be the proof.
I must also be aware of those who come in the Lord's name.

Doing the work of the Lord as if they are playing a game.
My Lord will tell them to leave, because He will not know them indeed.
I may be one of Jesus's little lambs.
I love people and I love the truth, because this is who I am.

How do you know the truth from a lie?

Matthew 7:12–23

12 So in everything, do to others what you would have them do to you, for this sums up the Law and the Prophets.
The Narrow and Wide Gates
13 "Enter through the narrow gate. For wide is the gate and broad is the road that leads to destruction, and many enter through it. 14 But small is the gate and narrow the road that leads to life, and only a few find it.
True and False Prophets
15 "Watch out for false prophets. They come to you in sheep's clothing, but inwardly they are ferocious wolves. 16 By their fruit you will recognize them. Do people pick grapes from thornbushes, or figs from thistles? 17 Likewise, every good tree bears good fruit, but a bad tree bears bad fruit. 18 A good tree cannot bear bad fruit, and a bad tree cannot bear good fruit. 19 Every tree that does not bear good fruit is cut down and thrown into the fire. 20 Thus, by their fruit you will recognize them.
True and False Disciples
21 "Not everyone who says to me, 'Lord, Lord,' will enter the kingdom of heaven, but only the one who does the will of my Father who is in heaven. 22 Many will say to me on that day, 'Lord, Lord, did we not prophesy in your name and in your name drive out demons and in your name perform many miracles?' 23 Then I will tell them plainly, 'I never knew you. Away from me, you evildoers!'

April 8
Fear
Mark 4:35–5:1

Today may seem calm, but a storm is on the way.
Now is a great time to get down on your knees and pray.
Maybe now you are encountering a storm of
tragedy or something of a great loss.
It has brought you fear at a great cost.
Face your fears with a determination to allow Jesus to see you through.
He will calm your fears and strengthen your faith too.
There is no need to be afraid, so let Jesus take care of you.

Make Jesus your anchor during life's storms.

Mark 4:35–5:1

Jesus Calms the Storm
35 That day when evening came, he said to his disciples, "Let us go over to the other side." 36 Leaving the crowd behind, they took him along, just as he was, in the boat. There were also other boats with him. 37 A furious squall came up, and the waves broke over the boat, so that it was nearly swamped. 38 Jesus was in the stern, sleeping on a cushion. The disciples woke him and said to him, "Teacher, don't you care if we drown?"
39 He got up, rebuked the wind and said to the waves, "Quiet! Be still!" Then the wind died down and it was completely calm.
40 He said to his disciples, "Why are you so afraid? Do you still have no faith?"
41 They were terrified and asked each other, "Who is this? Even the wind and the waves obey him!"
Jesus Restores a Demon-Possessed Man
5 They went across the lake to the region of the Gerasenes.

April 9
Fear
God's Care
Psalm 27:1–8

The way is dark, and I am controlled by fear.
I call out to Jesus. Jesus, Jesus, are you near?
I feel so afraid, and there is darkness all around.
I am too terrified to make a sound.
I call out to Jesus. Jesus, Jesus, are you near?
This darkness has caused me so much fear.
Jesus, You are my Savior, and Your light will shine through.
Jesus, Jesus I need You.
You understand my fears that have brought me so many tears.
Thank You very much for listening when I pray.
Thank You for being with me every day.

When you are afraid, do you call on Jesus?

Psalm 27:1–8

1
The Lord is my light and my salvation—
whom shall I fear?
The Lord is the stronghold of my life—
of whom shall I be afraid?
2
When the wicked advance against me
to devour me,
it is my enemies and my foes
who will stumble and fall.
3
Though an army besiege me,
my heart will not fear;
though war break out against me,
even then I will be confident.

> **4**
> One thing I ask from the Lord,
> this only do I seek:
> that I may dwell in the house of the Lord
> all the days of my life,
> to gaze on the beauty of the Lord
> and to seek him in his temple.
> **5**
> For in the day of trouble
> he will keep me safe in his dwelling;
> he will hide me in the shelter of his sacred tent
> and set me high upon a rock.
> **6**
> Then my head will be exalted
> above the enemies who surround me;
> at his sacred tent I will sacrifice with shouts of joy;
> I will sing and make music to the Lord.
> **7**
> Hear my voice when I call, Lord;
> be merciful to me and answer me.
> **8**
> My heart says of you, "Seek his face!"
> Your face, Lord, I will seek.

April 10
Fear
Trust in God
Numbers 13:25–14:9

> I will trust in God when fear comes over me.
> I will keep my faith and live my life in victory
> When I am overwhelmed by things that will appear as giants,
> Leaving me with feeling like an ant,
> Feeling the only thing I can do is pant,
> I will trust in God, and He will rescue me.

He will save me, and I will be free.
No problem is a giant when God is with you.
God is great, ever-present, and all-powerful too.
With faith in God, when those giants appear, you will know what to do.

Fear is no longer a giant when you see it through the eyes of God.

Numbers 13:25–14:9

25 At the end of forty days they returned from exploring the land.
Report on the Exploration
26 They came back to Moses and Aaron and the whole Israelite community at Kadesh in the Desert of Paran. There they reported to them and to the whole assembly and showed them the fruit of the land. 27 They gave Moses this account: "We went into the land to which you sent us, and it does flow with milk and honey! Here is its fruit. 28 But the people who live there are powerful, and the cities are fortified and very large. We even saw descendants of Anak there. 29 The Amalekites live in the Negev; the Hittites, Jebusites and Amorites live in the hill country; and the Canaanites live near the sea and along the Jordan."
30 Then Caleb silenced the people before Moses and said, "We should go up and take possession of the land, for we can certainly do it."
31 But the men who had gone up with him said, "We can't attack those people; they are stronger than we are." 32 And they spread among the Israelites a bad report about the land they had explored. They said, "The land we explored devours those living in it. All the people we saw there are of great size. 33 We saw the Nephilim there (the descendants of Anak come from the Nephilim). We seemed like grasshoppers in our own eyes, and we looked the same to them."
The People Rebel
14 That night all the members of the community raised their voices and wept aloud. 2 All the Israelites grumbled against Moses and Aaron, and the whole assembly said to them, "If only we had died in Egypt! Or in this wilderness! 3 Why is the Lord bringing us to this land only to let us fall by the sword? Our wives and children will be taken as

plunder. Wouldn't it be better for us to go back to Egypt?" 4 And they said to each other, "We should choose a leader and go back to Egypt." 5 Then Moses and Aaron fell facedown in front of the whole Israelite assembly gathered there. 6 Joshua son of Nun and Caleb son of Jephunneh, who were among those who had explored the land, tore their clothes 7 and said to the entire Israelite assembly, "The land we passed through and explored is exceedingly good. 8 If the Lord is pleased with us, he will lead us into that land, a land flowing with milk and honey, and will give it to us. 9 Only do not rebel against the Lord. And do not be afraid of the people of the land, because we will devour them. Their protection is gone, but the Lord is with us. Do not be afraid of them."

April 11
Fear
Trust in God
Numbers 13:25–14:9

Fear came knocking on my door today.
I asked faith to answer, because he knew what to say.
Fear said he brought friends and they want to play.
Unbelief was one who wanted to come.
He explained not believing in what God wanted will be fun.
Temptation was the other friend.
He said being tempted is not a sin.
All they wanted were to be welcomed in.
Then there were wicked habits and drugs who wanted to come too.
Faith, please help me to know what I need to do.
Then panic spoke, saying how much he wished to come.
All they could talk about was having fun.
Faith told them to leave.
With their presence here, God would not be pleased.
When fear came knocking on my door today,
Faith let them know they were not welcome and they could not stay.

Giants in our lives need to be confronted by faith.

Numbers 13:25–14:9

25 At the end of forty days they returned from exploring the land.

Report on the Exploration

26 They came back to Moses and Aaron and the whole Israelite community at Kadesh in the Desert of Paran. There they reported to them and to the whole assembly and showed them the fruit of the land. 27 They gave Moses this account: "We went into the land to which you sent us, and it does flow with milk and honey! Here is its fruit. 28 But the people who live there are powerful, and the cities are fortified and very large. We even saw descendants of Anak there. 29 The Amalekites live in the Negev; the Hittites, Jebusites and Amorites live in the hill country; and the Canaanites live near the sea and along the Jordan."

30 Then Caleb silenced the people before Moses and said, "We should go up and take possession of the land, for we can certainly do it."

31 But the men who had gone up with him said, "We can't attack those people; they are stronger than we are." 32 And they spread among the Israelites a bad report about the land they had explored. They said, "The land we explored devours those living in it. All the people we saw there are of great size. 33 We saw the Nephilim there (the descendants of Anak come from the Nephilim). We seemed like grasshoppers in our own eyes, and we looked the same to them."

The People Rebel

14 That night all the members of the community raised their voices and wept aloud. 2 All the Israelites grumbled against Moses and Aaron, and the whole assembly said to them, "If only we had died in Egypt! Or in this wilderness! 3 Why is the Lord bringing us to this land only to let us fall by the sword? Our wives and children will be taken as plunder. Wouldn't it be better for us to go back to Egypt?" 4 And they said to each other, "We should choose a leader and go back to Egypt."

5 Then Moses and Aaron fell facedown in front of the whole Israelite assembly gathered there. 6 Joshua son of Nun and Caleb son of Jephunneh, who were among those who had explored the land, tore their clothes 7 and said to the entire Israelite assembly, "The land we passed through and explored is exceedingly good. 8 If the Lord is pleased with us, he will lead us into that land, a land flowing with milk and honey,

and will give it to us. 9 Only do not rebel against the Lord. And do not be afraid of the people of the land, because we will devour them. Their protection is gone, but the Lord is with us. Do not be afraid of them."

April 12
Fear
Worry
Psalm 34:1–10

Worry and fear came to visit me today.
They were sure I wanted to be with them, so they stayed.
I told them that I wanted peace to be with me.
Fear wanted to argue and let me know that cannot be.
They wanted me to focus on being in misery.
Panic should be the condition of my heart.
They did not want to depart.
They did not go. They did not want to leave.
They informed me they had more torment for me up their sleeves.
"Enough!" I said. "I will seek the Lord, and I will not be in fear."
When I called out to the LORD, He heard my cry, because He was near.
I will be at peace when I remember who God is and how He loves me so.
Fear and worry, you will have to leave.
One went left, and the other went right.
They both were completely out of sight.
So, the LORD was with me all day.
Panic was not in my heart, because fear and worry could not stay.

When you are focusing on who God is, there will be
no room to concentrate on worry and fear.

Psalm 34:1–10

Of David. When he pretended to be insane before
Abimelek, who drove him away, and he left.

1
I will extol the Lord at all times;
his praise will always be on my lips.
2
I will glory in the Lord;
let the afflicted hear and rejoice.
3
Glorify the Lord with me;
let us exalt his name together.
4
I sought the Lord, and he answered me;
he delivered me from all my fears.
5
Those who look to him are radiant;
their faces are never covered with shame.
6
This poor man called, and the Lord heard him;
he saved him out of all his troubles.
7
The angel of the Lord encamps around those who fear him,
and he delivers them.
8
Taste and see that the Lord is good;
blessed is the one who takes refuge in him.
9
Fear the Lord, you his holy people,
for those who fear him lack nothing.
10
The lions may grow weak and hungry,
but those who seek the Lord lack no good thing.

Fellowship with God
April 13
Hebrews 2:1–4

To keep my fellowship with God, what must I do?
I need to spend time with Him to learn what is true.
Learning what is true is confirmed by reading His Word, with prayer too.
I must confess my wrongs.
This will surely keep our relationship and fellowship very strong.
Interacting with other believers of Jesus Christ will help
me stay anchored to Him and not drift away.
This is exactly what I must do to have fellowship
with Him each and every day.

Jesus is the Rock that I need to be anchored to
so as not to drift away from God.

Hebrews 2:1–4

Warning to Pay Attention
2 We must pay the most careful attention, therefore, to what we have heard, so that we do not drift away. 2 For since the message spoken through angels was binding, and every violation and disobedience received its just punishment, 3 how shall we escape if we ignore so great a salvation? This salvation, which was first announced by the Lord, was confirmed to us by those who heard him. 4 God also testified to it by signs, wonders and various miracles, and by gifts of the Holy Spirit distributed according to his will.

Forgiveness
April 14
Sin
2 Samuel 22:26–37

God is my help; this I know, because the Bible tells me so.
Flawless is His Word and perfect is His way.
He shields me when I take refuge in Him every day.
He gives me strength, and He keeps me secure.
God's love for me is pure.
There are numerous difficulties in my life
causing me not to live right.
Because of sin, chaos I struggle with each day.
However, I ask God for forgiveness and to show me the way.
The way to have the power of a new and fresh start each new day.

When your life is in chaos, allow God to bring you order.

2 Samuel 22:26–37

"To the faithful you show yourself faithful,
to the blameless you show yourself blameless,
27
to the pure you show yourself pure,
but to the devious you show yourself shrewd.
28
You save the humble,
but your eyes are on the haughty to bring them low.
29
You, Lord, are my lamp;
the Lord turns my darkness into light.
30
With your help I can advance against a troop;
with my God I can scale a wall.
31

> "As for God, his way is perfect:
> The Lord's word is flawless;
> he shields all who take refuge in him.
> 32
> For who is God besides the Lord?
> And who is the Rock except our God?
> 33
> It is God who arms me with strength
> and keeps my way secure.
> 34
> He makes my feet like the feet of a deer;
> he causes me to stand on the heights.
> 35
> He trains my hands for battle;
> my arms can bend a bow of bronze.
> 36
> You make your saving help my shield;
> your help has made me great.
> 37
> You provide a broad path for my feet,
> so that my ankles do not give way.

April 15
Forgiveness
Psalm 86:5–15

Today is a new day.
An opportunity to start new.
I want to do everything, Jesus, that You tell me to do.
Lord, what do I do when I have sinned?
Will I be able to start again?
Please forgive me for the things I should have done and did not do.
As well as the things I should not have done, but did
do, which means I did not do as you told me to.

When sin leaves me feeling distressed,
I know in You I will find rest.
I need Your compassion, mercy, forgiveness, love, faithfulness, and grace.
These will help me to start afresh, and each one I will embrace.

God gives us new mercies each day.

Psalm 86:5–15

5
You, Lord, are forgiving and good,
abounding in love to all who call to you.
6
Hear my prayer, Lord;
listen to my cry for mercy.
7
When I am in distress, I call to you,
because you answer me.
8
Among the gods there is none like you, Lord;
no deeds can compare with yours.
9
All the nations you have made
will come and worship before you, Lord;
they will bring glory to your name.
10
For you are great and do marvelous deeds;
you alone are God.
11
Teach me your way, Lord,
that I may rely on your faithfulness;
give me an undivided heart,
that I may fear your name.
12
I will praise you, Lord my God, with all my heart;
I will glorify your name forever.

13
For great is your love toward me;
you have delivered me from the depths,
from the realm of the dead.
14
Arrogant foes are attacking me, O God;
ruthless people are trying to kill me—
they have no regard for you.
15
But you, Lord, are a compassionate and gracious God,
slow to anger, abounding in love and faithfulness.

Forgiveness
April 16
Ephesians 4:25–32

You did me wrong.
Please do not do it again.
I will forgive you because I'd like for us to remain friends.
The day has ended; your wrongs I will not keep.
I have asked the Lord Jesus to bless you while you sleep.
I asked Him to give me words of grace that will
edify, uplift, and encourage you.
When I talk to others about how I feel about you,
they will be encouraged and uplifted too.
When I do something wrong that has hurt you.
I know you will be willing to forgive me too.

Forgiveness is giving yourself and others another chance.

Ephesians 4:25–32

25 Therefore each of you must put off falsehood and speak truthfully to your neighbor, for we are all members of one body. 26 "In your anger do not sin": Do not let the sun go down while you are still angry, 27 and

do not give the devil a foothold. 28 Anyone who has been stealing must steal no longer, but must work, doing something useful with their own hands, that they may have something to share with those in need. 29 Do not let any unwholesome talk come out of your mouths, but only what is helpful for building others up according to their needs, that it may benefit those who listen. 30 And do not grieve the Holy Spirit of God, with whom you were sealed for the day of redemption. 31 Get rid of all bitterness, rage and anger, brawling and slander, along with every form of malice. 32 Be kind and compassionate to one another, forgiving each other, just as in Christ God forgave you.

Friendship
April 17
Compassion
Job 11:7–20

Lord, my friend came to me today for answers to
questions that I may not fully understand.
She wants my advice, and she trust my command.
What must I do? What must I say?
I do not even know all the answers to her questions anyway.
What must I do? What must I say?
Maybe this is now time for us to go to God and pray.
I hope she is aware that I do care.
As her friend, I will be there.
I hope that she will realize I may not have the answers;
however, I am listening with concern.
This is an opportunity for me to learn.
Learn that I am limited to what I know and what I can do.
This is the reason why we both need to seek You.
You are the One who has all the answers. You know what to do.
I will encourage my friend to trust in You.

It is good when people will come to you for advice; however,
let them be aware it is God who has all the answers.

Job 11:7–20

⁷
"Can you fathom the mysteries of God?
Can you probe the limits of the Almighty?
⁸
They are higher than the heavens above—what can you do?
They are deeper than the depths below—what can you know?
⁹
Their measure is longer than the earth
and wider than the sea.
¹⁰
"If he comes along and confines you in prison
and convenes a court, who can oppose him?
¹¹
Surely he recognizes deceivers;
and when he sees evil, does he not take note?
¹²
But the witless can no more become wise
than a wild donkey's colt can be born human.
¹³
"Yet if you devote your heart to him
and stretch out your hands to him,
¹⁴
if you put away the sin that is in your hand
and allow no evil to dwell in your tent,
¹⁵
then, free of fault, you will lift up your face;
you will stand firm and without fear.
¹⁶
You will surely forget your trouble,
recalling it only as waters gone by.
¹⁷
Life will be brighter than noonday,
and darkness will become like morning.

18
You will be secure, because there is hope;
you will look about you and take your rest in safety.
19
You will lie down, with no one to make you afraid,
and many will court your favor.
20
But the eyes of the wicked will fail,
and escape will elude them;
their hope will become a dying gasp."

Giving
April 18
Serving Others
Acts 20:22–35

Keep on giving.
You will experience and gain a better understanding of living.
Giving is the willingness to serve and meet others' needs.
Giving will surely refresh and bring joy to your heart indeed.
Because you will be sowing generosity seeds.
An open hand is like a cup that is filled and overflowing.
The more that is poured into it, the more it will pour out without slowing.
Be encouraged to keep on giving.
It is life that is experiencing living.

"It is more blessed to give than to receive."
Acts 20:35

Acts 20:22–35

22 "And now, compelled by the Spirit, I am going to Jerusalem, not knowing what will happen to me there. 23 I only know that in every city the Holy Spirit warns me that prison and hardships are facing me. 24 However, I consider my life worth nothing to me; my only

aim is to finish the race and complete the task the Lord Jesus has given me—the task of testifying to the good news of God's grace.
25 "Now I know that none of you among whom I have gone about preaching the kingdom will ever see me again. 26 Therefore, I declare to you today that I am innocent of the blood of any of you. 27 For I have not hesitated to proclaim to you the whole will of God. 28 Keep watch over yourselves and all the flock of which the Holy Spirit has made you overseers. Be shepherds of the church of God, which he bought with his own blood. 29 I know that after I leave, savage wolves will come in among you and will not spare the flock. 30 Even from your own number men will arise and distort the truth in order to draw away disciples after them. 31 So be on your guard! Remember that for three years I never stopped warning each of you night and day with tears.
32 "Now I commit you to God and to the word of his grace, which can build you up and give you an inheritance among all those who are sanctified. 33 I have not coveted anyone's silver or gold or clothing. 34 You yourselves know that these hands of mine have supplied my own needs and the needs of my companions.
35 In everything I did, I showed you that by this kind of hard work we must help the weak, remembering the words the Lord Jesus himself said: 'It is more blessed to give than to receive.'"

God
April 19
Genesis 12:1–4; 17:1–2

God is El Shaddai, God Almighty.
You are great and have the ability to be mighty in power in all Your ways.
How may I honor and praise You today?
Abraham was a man of profound faith.
For twenty-four years, he had to wait
to receive God's promise of a son.
His life of faith had begun.
El Shaddai, God Almighty, His promises, He will keep.
No matter how impossible it may be.

Like Abraham, I have a destiny God wants me to fulfill.
To do this, I must have faith and obey God's will.
I must walk upright in faith.
No matter how long I will have to wait.
I am ready and willing to risk the uncertainty of life.
El Shaddai, God Almighty, You are worth the sacrifice.

No matter the risk in life, God is worth it.

Genesis 12:1–4

The Call of Abram
12 The Lord had said to Abram, "Go from your country, your people and your father's household to the land I will show you.

2
"I will make you into a great nation,
and I will bless you;
I will make your name great,
and you will be a blessing.
3
I will bless those who bless you,
and whoever curses you I will curse;
and all peoples on earth
will be blessed through you."
4 So Abram went, as the Lord had told him; and Lot went with him. Abram was seventy-five years old when he set out from Harran.

Genesis 17:1–2

The Covenant of Circumcision
17 When Abram was ninety-nine years old, the Lord appeared to him and said, "I am God Almighty; walk before me faithfully and be blameless. 2 Then I will make my covenant between me and you and will greatly increase your numbers."

April 20
God
Psalm 100

To enter into God's presence, what must you do?
Enter His presence with joy that is shouting, pouring out of you.
Worship Him with a heart that is full of gladness.
To be in God's presence, there will not be any reason for any sadness.
You will be so full of joy that it will make you want to sing.
You will be singing songs telling God all about everything.
Everything He has done for you; you will be singing
songs that will be filled with the truth.
You will be so thankful and praising Him that you are one of His sheep.
This joy is filled with singing, and it will keep you dancing on your feet.
The LORD is good, loving, and faithful, and His love endures to no end.
When you are filled with God's joy, that is when
there is no need to think about sin.

Knowing the joy of the LORD will make you
worship Him with praise and thanksgiving.

Psalm 100

A psalm. For giving grateful praise.
1
Shout for joy to the Lord, all the earth.
2
Worship the Lord with gladness;
come before him with joyful songs.
3
Know that the Lord is God.
It is he who made us, and we are his;
we are his people, the sheep of his pasture.
4
Enter his gates with thanksgiving

and his courts with praise;
give thanks to him and praise his name.

5

For the Lord is good and his love endures forever;
his faithfulness continues through all generations.

April 21
Doctrine of God
2 Chronicles 20:1–13

Life has a way of delivering surprise attacks,
Rendering you feeling helpless and not knowing how to act.
These uncertainties are an opportunity to call
out to God during times of distress.
Now He will be there, and there is no reason to become depressed.
Rely on God, for He wants you to be at rest.
He uses methods that are unconventional, to say the least.
They would not bring confusion, fear, and
unbelief, but strength and peace.
Do not panic when you do not know what to do.
Depend on God, for He is reliable, trustworthy,
and faithful—and this is amazingly true.
God is dependable because He is so devoted to you.

Life has its challenges, and God knows how to handle each of them.

2 Chronicles 20:1–13

Jehoshaphat Defeats Moab and Ammon
20 After this, the Moabites and Ammonites with some of
the Meunites came to wage war against Jehoshaphat.
2 Some people came and told Jehoshaphat, "A vast army is coming
against you from Edom, from the other side of the Dead Sea. It is
already in Hazezon Tamar" (that is, En Gedi). 3 Alarmed, Jehoshaphat
resolved to inquire of the Lord, and he proclaimed a fast for all

Judah. 4 The people of Judah came together to seek help from the Lord; indeed, they came from every town in Judah to seek him. 5 Then Jehoshaphat stood up in the assembly of Judah and Jerusalem at the temple of the Lord in the front of the new courtyard 6 and said: "Lord, the God of our ancestors, are you not the God who is in heaven? You rule over all the kingdoms of the nations. Power and might are in your hand, and no one can withstand you. 7 Our God, did you not drive out the inhabitants of this land before your people Israel and give it forever to the descendants of Abraham your friend? 8 They have lived in it and have built in it a sanctuary for your Name, saying, 9 'If calamity comes upon us, whether the sword of judgment, or plague or famine, we will stand in your presence before this temple that bears your Name and will cry out to you in our distress, and you will hear us and save us.'
10 "But now here are men from Ammon, Moab and Mount Seir, whose territory you would not allow Israel to invade when they came from Egypt; so they turned away from them and did not destroy them. 11 See how they are repaying us by coming to drive us out of the possession you gave us as an inheritance. 12 Our God, will you not judge them? For we have no power to face this vast army that is attacking us. We do not know what to do, but our eyes are on you."
13 All the men of Judah, with their wives and children and little ones, stood there before the Lord.

April 22
Doctrine of God
Bible/Prayer
Judges 2:7–19

How often do we resist the temptation to go
our own way and do our own thing?
When we do, it will only lead us away from God,
and sorrow it will surely bring.
To stay close to God, we need a reminder of
His presence to be with us each day.
It is through studying His Word and the need to pray.

As a child of God, His Holy Spirit will lead you.
You must be willing to obey, and you will find that this is true;

If you live life obeying God, sin will be far away from you.
When you do not follow God's instructions, only
you will fill your life with problems.

Judges 2:7–19

7 The people served the Lord throughout the lifetime of Joshua and of the elders who outlived him and who had seen all the great things the Lord had done for Israel. 8 Joshua son of Nun, the servant of the Lord, died at the age of a hundred and ten. 9 And they buried him in the land of his inheritance, at Timnath Heres in the hill country of Ephraim, north of Mount Gaash. 10 After that whole generation had been gathered to their ancestors, another generation grew up who knew neither the Lord nor what he had done for Israel. 11 Then the Israelites did evil in the eyes of the Lord and served the Baals. 12 They forsook the Lord, the God of their ancestors, who had brought them out of Egypt. They followed and worshiped various gods of the peoples around them. They aroused the Lord's anger 13 because they forsook him and served Baal and the Ashtoreths. 14 In his anger against Israel the Lord gave them into the hands of raiders who plundered them. He sold them into the hands of their enemies all around, whom they were no longer able to resist. 15 Whenever Israel went out to fight, the hand of the Lord was against them to defeat them, just as he had sworn to them. They were in great distress. 16 Then the Lord raised up judges, who saved them out of the hands of these raiders. 17 Yet they would not listen to their judges but prostituted themselves to other gods and worshiped them. They quickly turned from the ways of their ancestors, who had been obedient to the Lord's commands. 18 Whenever the Lord raised up a judge for them, he was with the judge and saved them out of the hands of their enemies as long as the judge lived; for the Lord relented because of their groaning under those who oppressed and afflicted them. 19 But when the judge died, the people returned to ways even more corrupt than those of

their ancestors, following other gods and serving and worshiping them. They refused to give up their evil practices and stubborn ways.

April 23
Doctrine of God
Doing the Right Thing
2 Chronicles 16:7–14

Life is not simple, effortless, or child's play.
There is work of obedience that has to be done each and every day.
The history lessons to be learned of the past;
Those who were completely committed to doing God's
work are the only ones who through history will last.
We can learn from their choices and from their mistakes.
Disobedience will cause you to live in error.
This will be a life of disobedience lived in God's terror.
If you started a life living for Christ, so let it end.
Asa's life was one that ended in sin.
Depend on Jesus in all you do.
Then your life will be pleasing to God, and an example too.

How you end your life is the example that will make history.

2 Chronicles 16:7–14

7 At that time Hanani the seer came to Asa king of Judah and said to him: "Because you relied on the king of Aram and not on the Lord your God, the army of the king of Aram has escaped from your hand. 8 Were not the Cushites and Libyans a mighty army with great numbers of chariots and horsemen? Yet when you relied on the Lord, he delivered them into your hand. 9 For the eyes of the Lord range throughout the earth to strengthen those whose hearts are fully committed to him. You have done a foolish thing, and from now on you will be at war."

10 Asa was angry with the seer because of this; he was so enraged that he put him in prison. At the same time Asa brutally oppressed some of the people.
11 The events of Asa's reign, from beginning to end, are written in the book of the kings of Judah and Israel. 12 In the thirty-ninth year of his reign Asa was afflicted with a disease in his feet. Though his disease was severe, even in his illness he did not seek help from the Lord, but only from the physicians. 13 Then in the forty-first year of his reign Asa died and rested with his ancestors. 14 They buried him in the tomb that he had cut out for himself in the City of David. They laid him on a bier covered with spices and various blended perfumes, and they made a huge fire in his honor.

April 24
Doctrine of God
Protection
Joshua 20:1–9

God is the true shelter for those who need protection and peace.
He is where those who need shelter will find He
is a place of refuge, a place of release.
Release from matters and circumstances that cause
great concern that relates to your life.
You will be secure in His hands. He will make everything good and right.
He is a solid rock to which you can flee.
Always tell yourself, "God will always be with me."
In the darkest of night, God is your strong tower.
He is omnipotent. He is filled with mighty power.
He will be your hiding place.

A place that will be filled with His love and His amazing grace.
The world may put security in locks, financial funds, and guns; however, those who put their security in God will never be disappointed, because He is true security.

Joshua 20:1–9

Cities of Refuge

20 Then the Lord said to Joshua: 2 "Tell the Israelites to designate the cities of refuge, as I instructed you through Moses, 3 so that anyone who kills a person accidentally and unintentionally may flee there and find protection from the avenger of blood. 4 When they flee to one of these cities, they are to stand in the entrance of the city gate and state their case before the elders of that city. Then the elders are to admit the fugitive into their city and provide a place to live among them. 5 If the avenger of blood comes in pursuit, the elders must not surrender the fugitive, because the fugitive killed their neighbor unintentionally and without malice aforethought. 6 They are to stay in that city until they have stood trial before the assembly and until the death of the high priest who is serving at that time. Then they may go back to their own home in the town from which they fled." 7 So they set apart Kedesh in Galilee in the hill country of Naphtali, Shechem in the hill country of Ephraim, and Kiriath Arba (that is, Hebron) in the hill country of Judah. 8 East of the Jordan (on the other side from Jericho) they designated Bezer in the wilderness on the plateau in the tribe of Reuben, Ramoth in Gilead in the tribe of Gad, and Golan in Bashan in the tribe of Manasseh. 9 Any of the Israelites or any foreigner residing among them who killed someone accidentally could flee to these designated cities and not be killed by the avenger of blood prior to standing trial before the assembly.

April 25
Doctrine of God
Grace
Matthew 5:43–48

What is God's grace that I should know?
I know when I see it; it will help me grow.
Grow in maturity that God's grace is for all of humanity.

He allows His rain to fall on those who do good
and to those who do evil is the reality.
As we stand before God, we are all the same.
Sinners are filled with sin and shame.
A transformed life is what grace will do.
It will change your thinking, your attitude, and your behavior too.
I need God's grace; what about you?

God's grace is what gets us through each day.

Matthew 5:43–48

Love for Enemies
43 "You have heard that it was said, 'Love your neighbor and hate your enemy.' 44 But I tell you, love your enemies and pray for those who persecute you, 45 that you may be children of your Father in heaven. He causes his sun to rise on the evil and the good, and sends rain on the righteous and the unrighteous. 46 If you love those who love you, what reward will you get? Are not even the tax collectors doing that? 47 And if you greet only your own people, what are you doing more than others? Do not even pagans do that? 48 Be perfect, therefore, as your heavenly Father is perfect.

April 26
Doctrine of God
Strength/Suffering
Isaiah 40:27–31

Physical, emotional, and spiritual weariness affect us all.
Weariness will lead us to stumble and fall.
Fatigue will cause you to forget the goodness, strength
and the power of God and all He promises to do.
You need to know what to do when this happens to you.
Remember you need to focus on hope.

This will give you the strength to cope;
As God renews your strength for each new day.
When you experience being weary stop and pray.
Then you can soar like eagles with a pep in your stride.
So, do not allow weariness take you on its dreary ride.

When life's struggles want to make you feel weary,
allow Jesus to give you His strength.

Isaiah 40:27–31

27
Why do you complain, Jacob?
Why do you say, Israel,
"My way is hidden from the Lord;
my cause is disregarded by my God"?
28
Do you not know?
Have you not heard?
The Lord is the everlasting God,
the Creator of the ends of the earth.
He will not grow tired or weary,
and his understanding no one can fathom.
29
He gives strength to the weary
and increases the power of the weak.
30
Even youths grow tired and weary,
and young men stumble and fall;
31
but those who hope in the Lord
will renew their strength.
They will soar on wings like eagles;
they will run and not grow weary,
they will walk and not be faint.

April 27
God
Suffering/Trust
Habakkuk 3:16–19

Trials are coming today.
Trials of tragedy are on the way.
Tragedy can come in many forms.
It can last and become the norm.
Do not let fear immobilize you
when you may not understand what you are going through.
Trust God to be faithful, to be there with you.
Suffering can turn your world upside down,
Turning your smile into a frown.
Trials are a part of life.
Do not face your trials without Jesus Christ.

How do you confront tragedy and trials in your life?

Habakkuk 3:16–19

16
I heard and my heart pounded,
my lips quivered at the sound;
decay crept into my bones,
and my legs trembled.
Yet I will wait patiently for the day of calamity
to come on the nation invading us.
17
Though the fig tree does not bud
and there are no grapes on the vines,
though the olive crop fails
and the fields produce no food,
though there are no sheep in the pen
and no cattle in the stalls,

18
yet I will rejoice in the Lord,
I will be joyful in God my Savior.
19
The Sovereign Lord is my strength;
he makes my feet like the feet of a deer,
he enables me to tread on the heights.
For the director of music. On my stringed instruments.

April 28
God
Waiting on God
Numbers 14:39–45

Do not make a decision without seeking to
know what God wants you to do.
Because your ambitious nature will lead you astray
to what is not good, right, and true.
Then your ill-advised choices will take away the joy to
rejoice in the victory God had in store for you.
This can also lead you to be overly cautious and remain in fear.
Because you must know that, without seeking God, He will not be near.
Before making a decision, pray, pray, pray until you know what God has to say.
Act in obedience, doing what God wants you to do.
Then you will have the peace and victory God has planned for you.

It is challenging to be patient when you need to make decisions.

Numbers 14:39–45

39 When Moses reported this to all the Israelites, they mourned bitterly. 40 Early the next morning they set out for the highest point in the hill country, saying, "Now we are ready to go up to the land the Lord promised. Surely we have sinned!"

41 But Moses said, "Why are you disobeying the Lord's command? This will not succeed! 42 Do not go up, because the Lord is not with you. You will be defeated by your enemies, 43 for the Amalekites and the Canaanites will face you there. Because you have turned away from the Lord, he will not be with you and you will fall by the sword."

44 Nevertheless, in their presumption they went up toward the highest point in the hill country, though neither Moses nor the ark of the Lord's covenant moved from the camp. 45 Then the Amalekites and the Canaanites who lived in that hill country came down and attacked them and beat them down all the way to Hormah.

April 29
Waiting on God
Psalm 25:1–15

As I wait on God, what must I do?
God, I will wait as I trust in You.
As I wait on You, God, please show me Your ways.
God, while I wait on You, I will learn to pray.
As I wait on God, "Teach me your paths as You
guide me in Your truth" (Psalm 25:5).
God, I am waiting on You; what else should I do?
As I wait on You, God, please "Teach me, for you are my
Savior, and my hope is in you all day long" (Psalm 25:5).
God, my hope in You will make my faith and trust
help me to persevere and be strong.
God, as I wait on You, I will know exactly what I need to do.

Do you know how to wait on God?

Psalm 25:1–15

Of David.
1
In you, Lord my God,

I put my trust.

2
I trust in you;
do not let me be put to shame,
nor let my enemies triumph over me.

3
No one who hopes in you
will ever be put to shame,
but shame will come on those
who are treacherous without cause.

4
Show me your ways, Lord,
teach me your paths.

5
Guide me in your truth and teach me,
for you are God my Savior,
and my hope is in you all day long.

6
Remember, Lord, your great mercy and love,
for they are from of old.

7
Do not remember the sins of my youth
and my rebellious ways;
according to your love remember me,
for you, Lord, are good.

8
Good and upright is the Lord;
therefore he instructs sinners in his ways.

9
He guides the humble in what is right
and teaches them his way.

10
All the ways of the Lord are loving and faithful
toward those who keep the demands of his covenant.

11
For the sake of your name, Lord,

forgive my iniquity, though it is great.
12
Who, then, are those who fear the Lord?
He will instruct them in the ways they should choose.
13
They will spend their days in prosperity,
and their descendants will inherit the land.
14
The Lord confides in those who fear him;
he makes his covenant known to them.
15
My eyes are ever on the Lord,
for only he will release my feet from the snare.

April 30
God
Worship
Psalm 68:7–10, 19–20

Today's trials and challenges I will not have to face alone.
My Sovereign God will carry me as He sits on His throne.
I will have no cause for worry or for fear, I
know my Sovereign God is here.
I will praise You; daily my burdens You bear.
I know You love me and You surely care.
I worship You, God, I worship you.
I worship You with love and truth.
Praise and worship God today.

Psalm 68:7–10

7
When you, God, went out before your people,
when you marched through the wilderness,

8
the earth shook, the heavens poured down rain,
before God, the One of Sinai,
before God, the God of Israel.
9
You gave abundant showers, O God;
you refreshed your weary inheritance.
10
Your people settled in it,
and from your bounty, God, you provided for the poor.

Psalm 68:19–20

19
Praise be to the Lord, to God our Savior,
who daily bears our burdens.
20
Our God is a God who saves;
from the Sovereign Lord comes escape from death.

May 1
God's Care
Psalm 37:21–31

Your day may be filled with burdens that weigh you down,
Turning your beautiful joyous smiles into a hopeless frown.
That can change in seconds; just wait and see.
When you give your burdens to Jesus, your frown will cease to be.
Yes, that frown will be gone, and those burdens too;
Giving them to Jesus is all you have to do.
Learn to do good; do not let evil have its way.
Do not let evil have control of your day.
Speak words of wisdom, speak words of truth;
This will let you know God is living in you.

Let the law of God be in your heart, and you will not go astray.
This will keep a smile on your face throughout the day.

Humble yourselves therefore under the mighty hand of God, that he may exalt you in due time: Casting all your care upon him; for he cares for you.
1 Peter 5:6–7

Psalm 37:21–31

21
The wicked borrow and do not repay,
but the righteous give generously;
22
those the Lord blesses will inherit the land,
but those he curses will be destroyed.
23
The Lord makes firm the steps
of the one who delights in him;
24
though he may stumble, he will not fall,
for the Lord upholds him with his hand.
25
I was young and now I am old,
yet I have never seen the righteous forsaken
or their children begging bread.
26
They are always generous and lend freely;
their children will be a blessing.
27
Turn from evil and do good;
then you will dwell in the land forever.
28
For the Lord loves the just
and will not forsake his faithful ones.
Wrongdoers will be completely destroyed;
the offspring of the wicked will perish.

29
The righteous will inherit the land
and dwell in it forever.
30
The mouths of the righteous utter wisdom,
and their tongues speak what is just.
31
The law of their God is in their hearts;
their feet do not slip.

May 2
God's Care
Relationship
Acts 20:17–20, 35–38

Saying goodbye is not easy to do.
The fact is my heart is so full of love for you.
Living on earth departure is a part of life.
When you want to continue to be with someone,
departing does not feel right.
Have hope this will not always be.
Departing from those who we love will one day
come to an end when we enter into eternity.
It may feel like you are being abandoned by
those who you love and care about
God will never leave you, and this is something you never have to doubt.

You are never far from those who love you in Christ.

Acts 20:17–20

17 From Miletus, Paul sent to Ephesus for the elders of the church. 18 When they arrived, he said to them: "You know how I lived the whole time I was with you, from the first day I came into the province of Asia. 19 I served the Lord with great humility and with tears and

in the midst of severe testing by the plots of my Jewish opponents. 20 You know that I have not hesitated to preach anything that would be helpful to you but have taught you publicly and from house to house.

Acts 20:35–38

35 In everything I did, I showed you that by this kind of hard work we must help the weak, remembering the words the Lord Jesus himself said: 'It is more blessed to give than to receive.'"
36 When Paul had finished speaking, he knelt down with all of them and prayed. 37 They all wept as they embraced him and kissed him. 38 What grieved them most was his statement that they would never see his face again. Then they accompanied him to the ship.

May 3
God's Care
Psalm 116:5–9

During life challenges and trauma, how are you able to make it through?
It is not just making it through where you will find the rest.
However, it is knowing the faithfulness of God
being there to help you do your best.
It is during those times of mental flight of history that you are able to see
how God has always been there for you and for me.
He was there with His grace, righteousness, and
compassion when we could not endure.
He was there, protecting us for sure.
Experiencing God in our daily life, in circumstances beyond
our control, gives us the wisdom to know what to do.
Remind yourself of God's faithfulness, love, and
peace, which will help you make it through.
Your soul knows it needs God; how well are you listening?

Psalm 116:5–9

5
The Lord is gracious and righteous;
our God is full of compassion.
6
The Lord protects the unwary;
when I was brought low, he saved me.
7
Return to your rest, my soul,
for the Lord has been good to you.
8
For you, Lord, have delivered me from death,
my eyes from tears,
my feet from stumbling,
9
that I may walk before the Lord
in the land of the living.

May 4
God's Care
Psalm 121

How can I describe the goodness of God?
How can I make it quite clear?
I will describe His goodness as being very loving and dear.
His goodness is like taking shade underneath
an umbrella from the very hot sun.
It is like having a tissue right in hand when your nose is about to run.
In His goodness and care, He is watching over you.
Keeping you from all harm is exactly what He will do.
If the thought enters your mind, Will God always be there?
This is how I know that He truly cares:
Because He never sleeps and will not slumber.
God does not have a clock with a lot of numbers.

Describing God's goodness is not hard to do.
Think about all the wonderful things He has done and is doing for you.
How would you describe the goodness of God?

Psalm 121

A song of ascents.
1
I lift up my eyes to the mountains—
where does my help come from?
2
My help comes from the Lord,
the Maker of heaven and earth.
3
He will not let your foot slip—
he who watches over you will not slumber;
4
indeed, he who watches over Israel
will neither slumber nor sleep.
5
The Lord watches over you—
the Lord is your shade at your right hand;
6
the sun will not harm you by day,
nor the moon by night.
7
The Lord will keep you from all harm—
he will watch over your life;
8
the Lord will watch over your coming and going
both now and forevermore.

**May 5
God's Care
Psalm 139:1–18**

God has searched me, and He knows me well.
When I try to hide something, He can always tell.
My thoughts He can perceive.
He knows me so well; this I truly believe.
My ways may be peculiar; however, with them He is familiar.
Before I can think of what I need to say,
God knows it anyway.
He will guide.
He is constantly at my side.
I am always on God's mind.
His thoughts of me are immense and kind.
I could not count them on my hand,
Because they will outnumber the grains of sand.

Who could know me better than God? No one.

Psalm 139

For the director of music. Of David. A psalm.
1
You have searched me, Lord,
and you know me.
2
You know when I sit and when I rise;
you perceive my thoughts from afar.
3
You discern my going out and my lying down;
you are familiar with all my ways.
4
Before a word is on my tongue
you, Lord, know it completely.

5
You hem me in behind and before,
and you lay your hand upon me.
6
Such knowledge is too wonderful for me,
too lofty for me to attain.
7
Where can I go from your Spirit?
Where can I flee from your presence?
8
If I go up to the heavens, you are there;
if I make my bed in the depths, you are there.
9
If I rise on the wings of the dawn,
if I settle on the far side of the sea,
10
even there your hand will guide me,
your right hand will hold me fast.
11
If I say, "Surely the darkness will hide me
and the light become night around me,"
12
even the darkness will not be dark to you;
the night will shine like the day,
for darkness is as light to you.
13
For you created my inmost being;
you knit me together in my mother's womb.
14
I praise you because I am fearfully and wonderfully made;
your works are wonderful,
I know that full well.
15
My frame was not hidden from you
when I was made in the secret place,
when I was woven together in the depths of the earth.

16
Your eyes saw my unformed body;
all the days ordained for me were written in your book
before one of them came to be.
17
How precious to me are your thoughts, God!
How vast is the sum of them!
18
Were I to count them,
they would outnumber the grains of sand—
when I awake, I am still with you.

May 6
God's Care
You Matter
Ecclesiastes 1:1–11

If everything is futile, what is the point of life?
You go to work every day, but there is no joy,
because it feels more like a sacrifice.
Generations are born, and soon they will die.
Very few of them know the victory cry.
Many do not know the reason why.
The earth will remain, and this will always be.
The course of life is for eternity.
If there is nothing new under the sun, what
is the conclusion of your reality?
How is it that your existence is meant to be?
You do matter, and do not allow self-pity to control your state of being.
God has a purpose for your life, and Jesus gave His
life for you. So, put that in your reasoning.
Everything may be meaningless, but you are not.
Knowing who you are mean thinking with self-pity will have to stop.

If Jesus died for you on the cross, how valuable are you?

Ecclesiastes 1:1–11

Everything Is Meaningless
1 The words of the Teacher, son of David, king in Jerusalem:
2
"Meaningless! Meaningless!"
says the Teacher.
"Utterly meaningless!
Everything is meaningless."
3
What do people gain from all their labors
at which they toil under the sun?
4
Generations come and generations go,
but the earth remains forever.
5
The sun rises and the sun sets,
and hurries back to where it rises.
6
The wind blows to the south
and turns to the north;
round and round it goes,
ever returning on its course.
7
All streams flow into the sea,
yet the sea is never full.
To the place the streams come from,
there they return again.
8
All things are wearisome,
more than one can say.
The eye never has enough of seeing,
nor the ear its fill of hearing.
9
What has been will be again,

what has been done will be done again;
there is nothing new under the sun.
10
Is there anything of which one can say,
"Look! This is something new"?
It was here already, long ago;
it was here before our time.
11
No one remembers the former generations,
and even those yet to come
will not be remembered
by those who follow them.

May 7
God's Care
Isaiah 50:4–10

Words for the weary my soul will say today.
Whatever struggles of life you are in, to Christ, I will pray.
Words of encouragement I will speak.
To lift your spirit for the Lord to keep.
Let these words be of hope.
That will allow you to hear from Jesus to help you know how to cope.
Words of life and encouragement are what I have to give.
I pray that these words will give you the power in Christ to live.

God's Word will surely bring life to a heavy heart.

Isaiah 50:4–10

4
The Sovereign Lord has given me a well-instructed tongue,
to know the word that sustains the weary.
He wakens me morning by morning,
wakens my ear to listen like one being instructed.

5
The Sovereign Lord has opened my ears;
I have not been rebellious,
I have not turned away.
6
I offered my back to those who beat me,
my cheeks to those who pulled out my beard;
I did not hide my face
from mocking and spitting.
7
Because the Sovereign Lord helps me,
I will not be disgraced.
Therefore have I set my face like flint,
and I know I will not be put to shame.
8
He who vindicates me is near.
Who then will bring charges against me?
Let us face each other!
Who is my accuser?
Let him confront me!
9
It is the Sovereign Lord who helps me.
Who will condemn me?
They will all wear out like a garment;
the moths will eat them up.
10
Who among you fears the Lord
and obeys the word of his servant?
Let the one who walks in the dark,
who has no light,
trust in the name of the Lord
and rely on their God.

May 8
God's Cares
Christ the Savior
Psalm 34:15–22

Today has been challenging, and I do not know what else to do.
Jesus, Jesus, Jesus, I am in need of You.
Evil is all around me.
Jesus, I know You are watching and You see.
I trust You to get rid of evil and its existence for eternity.
Lord, I know when I cry out, You will hear.
You will deliver me from all my troubles and fears.
Lord, my heart is broken, and my spirit is crushed.
I cry out to You in my brokenness; my spirit will not be hushed.
Jesus, Jesus, Jesus, I am in need of You.
I do not know what else to do.
However, I will cry out to you. I know You will hear.
You will deliver me from all my troubles and fears.
The LORD will rescue his servants; no one who
takes refuge in him will be condemned.
Psalm 34:22

Psalm 34:15–22

15
The eyes of the Lord are on the righteous,
and his ears are attentive to their cry;
16
but the face of the Lord is against those who do evil,
to blot out their name from the earth.
17
The righteous cry out, and the Lord hears them;
he delivers them from all their troubles.

18
The Lord is close to the brokenhearted
and saves those who are crushed in spirit.
19
The righteous person may have many troubles,
but the Lord delivers him from them all;
20
he protects all his bones,
not one of them will be broken.
21
Evil will slay the wicked;
the foes of the righteous will be condemned.
22
The Lord will rescue his servants;
no one who takes refuge in him will be condemned.

May 9
God's Care
Grief
Psalm 34:15–22

My heart is broken. What will I do?
I need to be comforted from feeling down and blue.
Who can understand my pain? Who will
understand what I am going through?
There is no one; nonetheless, Jesus, it is only You.
You understand my pain. You understand because
of the agony on the cross that You endured.
I know You comprehend my pain; I know this for sure.
So, I will find peace in Your presence because You are always near.
No matter how much I cry, I know You will
always be there to wipe away every tear.
Thank You for grieving with me. Thank You for giving me serenity.

When you are grieving, allow Jesus to comfort you

Psalm 34:15–22

15
The eyes of the Lord are on the righteous,
and his ears are attentive to their cry;
16
but the face of the Lord is against those who do evil,
to blot out their name from the earth.
17
The righteous cry out, and the Lord hears them;
he delivers them from all their troubles.
18
The Lord is close to the brokenhearted
and saves those who are crushed in spirit.
19
The righteous person may have many troubles,
but the Lord delivers him from them all;
20
he protects all his bones,
not one of them will be broken.
21
Evil will slay the wicked;
the foes of the righteous will be condemned.
22
The Lord will rescue his servants;
no one who takes refuge in him will be condemned.

May 10
God's Care
Life Struggles
Lamentations 5:8–22

Life struggles I face every day.
Whether it is of my own doing or someone's else, I cannot say.
I am devastated, and the feeling of hopelessness will not go away.

What shall I do? Who shall I look to?
My heavenly Father, I know You understand.
I will trust You and put my life into Your mighty hands.
I know You will be gentle and patient as You
rebuild and repurpose my life.
That which has gone wrong I know You will make right.
Life is brief, but it is worth living for my Savior, Jesus Christ.

Sin destroyed life, but Jesus has restored it.

Lamentations 5:8–22

8
Slaves rule over us,
and there is no one to free us from their hands.
9
We get our bread at the risk of our lives
because of the sword in the desert.
10
Our skin is hot as an oven,
feverish from hunger.
11
Women have been violated in Zion,
and virgins in the towns of Judah.
12
Princes have been hung up by their hands;
elders are shown no respect.
13
Young men toil at the millstones;
boys stagger under loads of wood.
14
The elders are gone from the city gate;
the young men have stopped their music.
15
Joy is gone from our hearts;
our dancing has turned to mourning.

16
The crown has fallen from our head.
Woe to us, for we have sinned!
17
Because of this our hearts are faint,
because of these things our eyes grow dim
18
for Mount Zion, which lies desolate,
with jackals prowling over it.
19
You, Lord, reign forever;
your throne endures from generation to generation.
20
Why do you always forget us?
Why do you forsake us so long?
21
Restore us to yourself, Lord, that we may return;
renew our days as of old
22
unless you have utterly rejected us
and are angry with us beyond measure.

May 11
God's Care
Miracles/Trust in God
Mark 8:1–13

Lord Jesus, I have many needs today.
I will bow down on my knees and pray.
I need a miracle, so please do not delay.
I will trust in You, God, since I know You care for me.
I thank You for how You have answered my prayers so compassionately.
You did for me what I could not do.
Lord Jesus, I will always put my trust in You.

Do not be afraid to put your trust in God, as He will create miracles to care for you and meet your needs.

Mark 8:1–13

Jesus Feeds the Four Thousand

8 During those days another large crowd gathered. Since they had nothing to eat, Jesus called his disciples to him and said, 2 "I have compassion for these people; they have already been with me three days and have nothing to eat. 3 If I send them home hungry, they will collapse on the way, because some of them have come a long distance."
4 His disciples answered, "But where in this remote place can anyone get enough bread to feed them?"
5 "How many loaves do you have?" Jesus asked.
"Seven," they replied.
6 He told the crowd to sit down on the ground. When he had taken the seven loaves and given thanks, he broke them and gave them to his disciples to distribute to the people, and they did so. 7 They had a few small fish as well; he gave thanks for them also and told the disciples to distribute them. 8 The people ate and were satisfied. Afterward the disciples picked up seven basketfuls of broken pieces that were left over. 9 About four thousand were present. After he had sent them away, 10 he got into the boat with his disciples and went to the region of Dalmanutha.
11 The Pharisees came and began to question Jesus. To test him, they asked him for a sign from heaven. 12 He sighed deeply and said, "Why does this generation ask for a sign? Truly I tell you, no sign will be given to it." 13 Then he left them, got back into the boat and crossed to the other side.

May 12
God's Care
Salvation
John 10:1–11

Jesus is the Good Shepherd who knows me by my name.
He knows me so well, and I do not need to feel ashamed.
He knows my thoughts, and He knows my fears.
I know when I cry out to Him, He not only listens but also hears.
He knows my wrongs, and He is aware of what I do that is right.
My Jesus loves me, and He gives me much spiritual insight.
He knows my deepest needs.
Yes, He does indeed.
Jesus is the Good Shepherd, who became my sacrificial Lamb.
This is how He showed He loves me, because of who I am.
He died for my sins so that I will be made free.
He wants me to live with Him in eternity.
Jesus is the Good Shepherd who knows me by my name.
He knows me so well, and I do not need to feel ashamed.

Jesus knows me. Do you believe that He knows you?

John 10:1–11

The Good Shepherd and His Sheep
10 "Very truly I tell you Pharisees, anyone who does not enter the sheep pen by the gate, but climbs in by some other way, is a thief and a robber. 2 The one who enters by the gate is the shepherd of the sheep. 3 The gatekeeper opens the gate for him, and the sheep listen to his voice. He calls his own sheep by name and leads them out. 4 When he has brought out all his own, he goes on ahead of them, and his sheep follow him because they know his voice. 5 But they will never follow a stranger; in fact, they will run away from him because they do not recognize a stranger's voice." 6 Jesus used this figure of speech, but the Pharisees did not understand what he was telling them.

7 Therefore Jesus said again, "Very truly I tell you, I am the gate for the sheep. 8 All who have come before me are thieves and robbers, but the sheep have not listened to them. 9 I am the gate; whoever enters through me will be saved. They will come in and go out, and find pasture. 10 The thief comes only to steal and kill and destroy; I have come that they may have life, and have it to the full.
11 "I am the good shepherd. The good shepherd lays down his life for the sheep.

May 13
God's Care
Suffering
Psalm 55:4–23

God, I will give You the problems that I face today.
My problems are causing me to suffer in many different ways.
I acknowledge and recognize, God, that I need Your support, and I release my problems to You.
I want You to be in control in every aspect of my life,
Because You know what would be right.
You know exactly what I need to do.
I will not try to do everything in my own strength and my own effort; instead, I will find my rest in You.
Thank You for sustaining me as You see me through.

God cares about what happens to us.

Psalm 55:4–23

4
My heart is in anguish within me;
the terrors of death have fallen on me.
5
Fear and trembling have beset me;
horror has overwhelmed me.

6
I said, "Oh, that I had the wings of a dove!
I would fly away and be at rest.
7
I would flee far away
and stay in the desert;
8
I would hurry to my place of shelter,
far from the tempest and storm."
9
Lord, confuse the wicked, confound their words,
for I see violence and strife in the city.
10
Day and night they prowl about on its walls;
malice and abuse are within it.
11
Destructive forces are at work in the city;
threats and lies never leave its streets.
12
If an enemy were insulting me,
I could endure it;
if a foe were rising against me,
I could hide.
13
But it is you, a man like myself,
my companion, my close friend,
14
with whom I once enjoyed sweet fellowship
at the house of God,
as we walked about
among the worshipers.
15
Let death take my enemies by surprise;
let them go down alive to the realm of the dead,
for evil finds lodging among them.

16
As for me, I call to God,
and the Lord saves me.
17
Evening, morning and noon
I cry out in distress,
and he hears my voice.
18
He rescues me unharmed
from the battle waged against me,
even though many oppose me.
19
God, who is enthroned from of old,
who does not change—
he will hear them and humble them,
because they have no fear of God.
20
My companion attacks his friends;
he violates his covenant.
21
His talk is smooth as butter,
yet war is in his heart;
his words are more soothing than oil,
yet they are drawn swords.
22
Cast your cares on the Lord
and he will sustain you;
he will never let
the righteous be shaken.
23
But you, God, will bring down the wicked
into the pit of decay;
the bloodthirsty and deceitful
will not live out half their days.
But as for me, I trust in you.

May 14
God's Care
Trusting God
1 Chronicles 29:14–19

        Everything I have God has given to me.
I must not hold on too tightly or unwillingly to what God has bestowed.
        I must use it all as God meant for it to be used.
        Not doing what God wants will never be excused.
        Doing so will hamper the growth of my soul.
        If I do not do what God has told.
Everything I have is a gift from God; I have obtained nothing on my own.
Lord, I want to thank You for the help and love to me You have shown.
        Trusting in You is something that I must do.
        You have consistently been here to see me through.

Without God, obtaining the essentials of life would be impossible.

1 Chronicles 29:14–19

14 "But who am I, and who are my people, that we should be able to give as generously as this? Everything comes from you, and we have given you only what comes from your hand. 15 We are foreigners and strangers in your sight, as were all our ancestors. Our days on earth are like a shadow, without hope. 16 Lord our God, all this abundance that we have provided for building you a temple for your Holy Name comes from your hand, and all of it belongs to you. 17 I know, my God, that you test the heart and are pleased with integrity. All these things I have given willingly and with honest intent. And now I have seen with joy how willingly your people who are here have given to you. 18 Lord, the God of our fathers Abraham, Isaac and Israel, keep these desires and thoughts in the hearts of your people forever, and keep their hearts loyal to you. 19 And give my son Solomon the wholehearted devotion to keep your commands, statutes and decrees and to do everything to build the palatial structure for which I have provided."

May 15
God's Care
Suffering/Trust in God
Proverbs 18:4–12

Run to Me, my child
, run to Me.
The cares of this world want to do you in.
Run to Me; I am greater than any mortal friend.
Fear has a hold on you.
It always wants to control you. Telling you what to do.
It brings confusion, and this is true.
Do not run away from Me
I am right here for you; can't you see?
You alone cannot confront trouble. I will be here for you on the double.
I am right here for you.
Let it be Me telling you what you need to do.
Put your trust in Me.
Run to Me, my child, run to Me.
In Me you will find safety, and this will always be.
Run to Me, my child, run to Me.

God is our shield, our place of safety, and the
power that saves us; run to Him.

Proverbs 18:4–12

4
The words of the mouth are deep waters,
but the fountain of wisdom is a rushing stream.
5
It is not good to be partial to the wicked
and so deprive the innocent of justice.
6
The lips of fools bring them strife,
and their mouths invite a beating.

> 7
> The mouths of fools are their undoing,
> and their lips are a snare to their very lives.
> 8
> The words of a gossip are like choice morsels;
> they go down to the inmost parts.
> 9
> One who is slack in his work
> is brother to one who destroys.
> 10
> The name of the Lord is a fortified tower;
> the righteous run to it and are safe.
> 11
> The wealth of the rich is their fortified city;
> they imagine it a wall too high to scale.
> 12
> Before a downfall the heart is haughty,
> but humility comes before honor.

May 16
Goodness of God
Genesis 3:1–8

> When temptation comes, it is difficult to see
> how good God is to you and me.
> When trials come and you do not know what to do,
> Turn to God, for He is so good. He will be there for you.
> During times of grief, when comfort is what you seek,
> Remember the goodness of God, for He with you will weep.
> Our understanding is limited, and our knowledge may be too.
> The Lord is good and compassionate; He will always be there for you.
> So, when our enemy, Satan, comes along, with the temptation of
> doubt about God's goodness, wanting you to believe his lies,
> Know his lies are not true,
> Including the ones he is telling about you.
>
> God is always good.

Genesis 3:1–8

The Fall

3 Now the serpent was more crafty than any of the wild animals the Lord God had made. He said to the woman, "Did God really say, 'You must not eat from any tree in the garden'?" 2 The woman said to the serpent, "We may eat fruit from the trees in the garden, 3 but God did say, 'You must not eat fruit from the tree that is in the middle of the garden, and you must not touch it, or you will die.'" 4 "You will not certainly die," the serpent said to the woman. 5 "For God knows that when you eat from it your eyes will be opened, and you will be like God, knowing good and evil." 6 When the woman saw that the fruit of the tree was good for food and pleasing to the eye, and also desirable for gaining wisdom, she took some and ate it. She also gave some to her husband, who was with her, and he ate it. 7 Then the eyes of both of them were opened, and they realized they were naked; so they sewed fig leaves together and made coverings for themselves. 8 Then the man and his wife heard the sound of the Lord God as he was walking in the garden in the cool of the day, and they hid from the Lord God among the trees of the garden.

May 17
God's Grace
Love and Mercy
Ephesians 2:4–7

God's grace, love, and mercy, how can it be?
It is in Jesus Christ who died that I may live
together with Him for eternity.
I am saved by God's grace, unmerited favor; kindness I do not deserve.
Because I am a sinner, judgment is death; this is what my sin has reserved.
God's love is so deep. It is beyond my knowledge
and my ability to understand.

There is always plenty for every child, every woman, and every man.
God is rich in mercy, compassion, and forgiveness toward humanity.
This is the kind of love that will last for an eternity.
God asks us only to receive His grace, love, and
mercy. He does not tell us to understand.
All this is free to receive for every child, woman, and man.
He asked us to receive it through accepting His Son.
There is no other way to receive these amazing
gifts. Jesus Christ is the only One.

God is faithful in giving of Himself in grace,
love, and mercy; just receive it.

Ephesians 2:4–7

4 But because of his great love for us, God, who is rich in mercy, 5 made us alive with Christ even when we were dead in transgressions—it is by grace you have been saved. 6 And God raised us up with Christ and seated us with him in the heavenly realms in Christ Jesus, 7 in order that in the coming ages he might show the incomparable riches of his grace, expressed in his kindness to us in Christ Jesus.

God's Love
May 18
Genesis 16:1–13

The tears I shed, God will see;
They will speak for me.
God will listen to what they have to say;
He knows how to tell them to go away.
When my heart is in pain,
God's heart will feel the same.
He will understand when no one else can;
His heart knows how to take me by the hand.
My God is compassionate. He cares about me.

That is why He sent Jesus to die for me so that
I may live with Him for eternity.

God is
"The God who sees me." Genesis 16:13

Genesis 16:1–13

Hagar and Ishmael
16 Now Sarai, Abram's wife, had borne him no children.
But she had an Egyptian slave named Hagar; 2 so she said to
Abram, "The Lord has kept me from having children. Go, sleep
with my slave; perhaps I can build a family through her."
Abram agreed to what Sarai said. 3 So after Abram had
been living in Canaan ten years, Sarai his wife took her
Egyptian slave Hagar and gave her to her husband to be
his wife. 4 He slept with Hagar, and she conceived.
When she knew she was pregnant, she began to despise her mistress.
5 Then Sarai said to Abram, "You are responsible for the wrong I am
suffering. I put my slave in your arms, and now that she knows she is
pregnant, she despises me. May the Lord judge between you and me."
6 "Your slave is in your hands," Abram said. "Do with her whatever
you think best." Then Sarai mistreated Hagar; so she fled from her.
7 The angel of the Lord found Hagar near a spring in the desert; it
was the spring that is beside the road to Shur. 8 And he said, "Hagar,
slave of Sarai, where have you come from, and where are you going?"
"I'm running away from my mistress Sarai," she answered.
9 Then the angel of the Lord told her, "Go back to your mistress
and submit to her." 10 The angel added, "I will increase your
descendants so much that they will be too numerous to count."
11 The angel of the Lord also said to her:
"You are now pregnant
and you will give birth to a son.
You shall name him Ishmael,
for the Lord has heard of your misery.

> 12
> He will be a wild donkey of a man;
> his hand will be against everyone
> and everyone's hand against him,
> and he will live in hostility
> toward all his brothers."

13 She gave this name to the Lord who spoke to her: "You are the God who sees me," for she said, "I have now seen the One who sees me."

May 19
God's Love
Numbers 33:1–15, 36–37

> Step by step, Lord, please lead the way.
> Where will You lead me today?
> The way You are taking me, I do not know,
> because I have never been here before.
> I want to learn and anticipate much more!
> Each stage of life's challenges I will face.
> Each stage of life, Lord, I will take step by step with Your amazing grace.
> I will trust You to direct my way.
> Step by step, I know You will show me the way as I pray.

You need to take each stage of life step by step, with Christ at your side.

Numbers 33:1–15

Stages in Israel's Journey

33 Here are the stages in the journey of the Israelites when they came out of Egypt by divisions under the leadership of Moses and Aaron. 2 At the Lord's command Moses recorded the stages in their journey. This is their journey by stages: 3 The Israelites set out from Rameses on the fifteenth day of the first month, the day after the Passover. They marched out defiantly in full view of all the Egyptians, 4 who were burying

all their firstborn, whom the Lord had struck down among
them; for the Lord had brought judgment on their gods.
5 The Israelites left Rameses and camped at Sukkoth.
6 They left Sukkoth and camped at Etham, on the edge of the desert.
7 They left Etham, turned back to Pi Hahiroth, to the
east of Baal Zephon, and camped near Migdol.
8 They left Pi Hahiroth and passed through the sea into
the desert, and when they had traveled for three days
in the Desert of Etham, they camped at Marah.
9 They left Marah and went to Elim, where there were twelve
springs and seventy palm trees, and they camped there.
10 They left Elim and camped by the Red Sea.
11 They left the Red Sea and camped in the Desert of Sin.
12 They left the Desert of Sin and camped at Dophkah.
13 They left Dophkah and camped at Alush.
14 They left Alush and camped at Rephidim, where
there was no water for the people to drink.
15 They left Rephidim and camped in the Desert of Sinai.

Numbers 33:36-37

36 They left Ezion Geber and camped at Kadesh, in the Desert of Zin.
37 They left Kadesh and camped at Mount Hor, on the border of Edom.

May 20
God's Love
Psalm 36:5–12

Life will deplete your strength to have hope, to love, and to have faith,
Leaving you to start each day with no optimism,
no will to love, only the desire to hate.
Where can you go to be refreshed? Who will replenish you with rest?
Who will enable you to give your very best?
Whatever your needs might be, God will meet all of them indeed.
He will nurture your soul with His loving-kindness as you trust in Him.
He will fill you up as a cup that is filled to the brim.

Of love, Jesus will never run out.
His love will always pour like a gushing spout.
Come if you will, and receive.
You only need to believe.
God is abundant in love; this is the truth.
Come, come, receive from His loving hands all He will do for you.

When the world has left you empty, God will fill you up.

Psalm 36:5–12

5
Your love, Lord, reaches to the heavens,
your faithfulness to the skies.
6
Your righteousness is like the highest mountains,
your justice like the great deep.
You, Lord, preserve both people and animals.
7
How priceless is your unfailing love, O God!
People take refuge in the shadow of your wings.
8
They feast on the abundance of your house;
you give them drink from your river of delights.
9
For with you is the fountain of life;
in your light we see light.
10
Continue your love to those who know you,
your righteousness to the upright in heart.
11
May the foot of the proud not come against me,
nor the hand of the wicked drive me away.
12
See how the evildoers lie fallen—
thrown down, not able to rise!

May 21
God's Love
Lamentations 3:21–26

In God's love, I will begin my day.
With childlike faith is exactly how I will pray.
With great expectation I will watch and wait to
see what God will do with my day.
Whatever comes my way, I know God will be
faithful and His mercies will never cease.
His unfailing love and compassion will always continue to be.
No matter how my day has begun,
I know God is loving me through Jesus Christ, His holy Son.

How are you experiencing the faithfulness of God?

Lamentations 3:21–26

21
Yet this I call to mind
and therefore I have hope:
22
Because of the Lord's great love we are not consumed,
for his compassions never fail.
23
They are new every morning;
great is your faithfulness.
24
I say to myself, "The Lord is my portion;
therefore I will wait for him."
25
The Lord is good to those whose hope is in him,
to the one who seeks him;
26
it is good to wait quietly
for the salvation of the Lord.

May 22
God's Love
Serving Others
Haggai 2:15–23

As a signet ring, God has put His stamp on you.
As you display your gifts, passions, and wisdom,
you prove that God's love is true.
You show that He is reaching others by touching their lives through you.
As you respond to your call, with the privilege as God's signet ring,
As an ambassador and heir, you are bringing others
to know and worship the eternal King.

"I will make you like my signet ring, for I have
chosen you," declares the LORD.
Haggai 2:23

Haggai 2:15-23

15 "'Now give careful thought to this from this day on—consider how things were before one stone was laid on another in the Lord's temple. 16 When anyone came to a heap of twenty measures, there were only ten. When anyone went to a wine vat to draw fifty measures, there were only twenty. 17 I struck all the work of your hands with blight, mildew and hail, yet you did not return to me,' declares the Lord. 18 'From this day on, from this twenty-fourth day of the ninth month, give careful thought to the day when the foundation of the Lord's temple was laid. Give careful thought: 19 Is there yet any seed left in the barn? Until now, the vine and the fig tree, the pomegranate and the olive tree have not borne fruit.
"'From this day on I will bless you.'"
Zerubbabel the Lord's Signet Ring
20 The word of the Lord came to Haggai a second time on the twenty-fourth day of the month: 21 "Tell Zerubbabel governor of Judah that I am going to shake the heavens and the earth. 22 I will overturn royal thrones and shatter the power of the foreign

kingdoms. I will overthrow chariots and their drivers; horses and their riders will fall, each by the sword of his brother.
23 "'On that day,' declares the Lord Almighty, 'I will take you, my servant Zerubbabel son of Shealtiel,' declares the Lord, 'and I will make you like my signet ring, for I have chosen you,' declares the Lord Almighty."

May 23
God's Love
Matthew 6:25–34

Do you wonder about how valuable you are?
Who truly loves you from afar?
Who will love you for you?
When they are loving you, what all will they do?
God loves you for you.
There is so much He wishes to do.
He will never leave you alone, and He is always thinking about you.
He does not want you to worry because it is not good for you to do.
He wants you to seek Him first whenever you have a need.
Trusting in God is all you need to do indeed.

You are very valuable to God.

Matthew 6:25–34

Do Not Worry
25 "Therefore I tell you, do not worry about your life, what you will eat or drink; or about your body, what you will wear. Is not life more than food, and the body more than clothes? 26 Look at the birds of the air; they do not sow or reap or store away in barns, and yet your heavenly Father feeds them. Are you not much more valuable than they?
27 Can any one of you by worrying add a single hour to your life?
28 "And why do you worry about clothes? See how the flowers of the field grow. They do not labor or spin. 29 Yet I tell you that not even Solomon in all his splendor was dressed like one of these. 30 If that is

how God clothes the grass of the field, which is here today and tomorrow is thrown into the fire, will he not much more clothe you—you of little faith? 31 So do not worry, saying, 'What shall we eat?' or 'What shall we drink?' or 'What shall we wear?' 32 For the pagans run after all these things, and your heavenly Father knows that you need them. 33 But seek first his kingdom and his righteousness, and all these things will be given to you as well. 34 Therefore do not worry about tomorrow, for tomorrow will worry about itself. Each day has enough trouble of its own.

May 24
Love of God
Acts 9:1–19

God's grace I know I do not deserve.
It is a gift that has been given to me.
A gift for salvation from sin that has set me free.
It is a gift of forgiveness and love I am so grateful to receive.
It was given to me simply because I believe.
God's grace is so amazing to me as a sinner, who
has done nothing but with evil intent.
Knowing Jesus is my Savior because He was God sent.
There is nothing I can do to earn grace.
It is a gift that was given to the whole human race.

Grace cannot be earned because it is a gift.

Acts 9:1–19

Saul's Conversion
9 Meanwhile, Saul was still breathing out murderous threats against the Lord's disciples. He went to the high priest 2 and asked him for letters to the synagogues in Damascus, so that if he found any there who belonged to the Way, whether men or women, he might take them as prisoners to Jerusalem. 3 As he neared Damascus on his journey,

suddenly a light from heaven flashed around him. 4 He fell to the ground and heard a voice say to him, "Saul, Saul, why do you persecute me?"
5 "Who are you, Lord?" Saul asked.
"I am Jesus, whom you are persecuting," he replied. 6 "Now get up and go into the city, and you will be told what you must do."
7 The men traveling with Saul stood there speechless; they heard the sound but did not see anyone. 8 Saul got up from the ground, but when he opened his eyes he could see nothing. So they led him by the hand into Damascus. 9 For three days he was blind, and did not eat or drink anything.
10 In Damascus there was a disciple named Ananias. The Lord called to him in a vision, "Ananias!"
"Yes, Lord," he answered.
11 The Lord told him, "Go to the house of Judas on Straight Street and ask for a man from Tarsus named Saul, for he is praying. 12 In a vision he has seen a man named Ananias come and place his hands on him to restore his sight."
13 "Lord," Ananias answered, "I have heard many reports about this man and all the harm he has done to your holy people in Jerusalem. 14 And he has come here with authority from the chief priests to arrest all who call on your name."
15 But the Lord said to Ananias, "Go! This man is my chosen instrument to proclaim my name to the Gentiles and their kings and to the people of Israel. 16 I will show him how much he must suffer for my name."
17 Then Ananias went to the house and entered it. Placing his hands on Saul, he said, "Brother Saul, the Lord—Jesus, who appeared to you on the road as you were coming here—has sent me so that you may see again and be filled with the Holy Spirit." 18 Immediately, something like scales fell from Saul's eyes, and he could see again. He got up and was baptized, 19 and after taking some food, he regained his strength.

Saul in Damascus and Jerusalem
Saul spent several days with the disciples in Damascus.

May 25
God's Love
Romans 5:6–11

What is your value, if someone should ask?
Would it be the achievements you have made?
Would it be your mind, your body, or your intellect?
These are some things that might be considered of value,
and there are more than you may think to select.
Is there more to you than others would suspect?
Would it be your personality or the clothes you wear?
Would this make someone value you with care?
Do you have the value that someone would love you for you?
It would not matter who you are, what you have done, or what you will do.
Who would love you with love that would be authentically true?
This is how God loves you.
He sent to you Jesus Christ, His Son.
He died for you as if you were the only one.
The only one who needed salvation to save you from sin.
Jesus died on the cross for you as an amazing, loving, faithful Friend.
His death on the cross is how love for you should be measured.
Because, to God, this is how you are deeply treasured.

God loves you.

Romans 5:6–11

6 You see, at just the right time, when we were still powerless,
Christ died for the ungodly. 7 Very rarely will anyone die for
a righteous person, though for a good person someone might
possibly dare to die. 8 But God demonstrates his own love for
us in this: While we were still sinners, Christ died for us.
9 Since we have now been justified by his blood, how much more shall
we be saved from God's wrath through him! 10 For if, while we were
God's enemies, we were reconciled to him through the death of his Son,

how much more, having been reconciled, shall we be saved through his life! 11 Not only is this so, but we also boast in God through our Lord Jesus Christ, through whom we have now received reconciliation.

May 26
God' Love
Romans 8:12–17

Abba, Abba, Abba; Father, to You I belong.
Father God, for You my heart longs.
You watch over me, and You know me so well.
You know my thoughts and how I feel. You can always tell.
You know exactly what I will say.
You know and meet my needs before I even pray.
Intimately I want to know You.
Everything I have learned about You is true.
Your love for me will last for eternity.
I am so grateful You enjoy being with me.

A father of the fatherless and a judge for the
widows, is God in His holy habitation.
Psalm 68:5

Romans 8:12–17

12 Therefore, brothers and sisters, we have an obligation—but it is not to the flesh, to live according to it. 13 For if you live according to the flesh, you will die; but if by the Spirit you put to death the misdeeds of the body, you will live. 14 For those who are led by the Spirit of God are the children of God. 15 The Spirit you received does not make you slaves, so that you live in fear again; rather, the Spirit you received brought about your adoption to sonship. And by him we cry, "Abba, Father." 16 The Spirit himself testifies with our spirit that we are God's children. 17 Now if we are children,

then we are heirs—heirs of God and co-heirs with Christ, if indeed we share in his sufferings in order that we may also share in his glory.

May 27
God's Love
Romans 8:31–38

The way people understand love causes love not to last.
The love that people have today may not be the love that was in the past.
This kind of love can be fickle.
Making it worth less than a dime, a quarter, or even a nickel.
When love is treated this way, it will not be consistent or lasting.
The love of God is unchanging, dependable. A love that is not passing.
His love is eternal, through Jesus Christ, to all who in Him would believe.
Love that is enduring, secure, and neverending
to those who would receive.
This love is real, and it is not intended to deceive.

The love of God is eternal, and it will not change.

Romans 8:31–38

More Than Conquerors
31 What, then, shall we say in response to these things? If God is for us, who can be against us? 32 He who did not spare his own Son, but gave him up for us all—how will he not also, along with him, graciously give us all things? 33 Who will bring any charge against those whom God has chosen? It is God who justifies. 34 Who then is the one who condemns? No one. Christ Jesus who died—more than that, who was raised to life—is at the right hand of God and is also interceding for us. 35 Who shall separate us from the love of Christ? Shall trouble or hardship or persecution or famine or nakedness or danger or sword? 36 As it is written:
"For your sake we face death all day long;
we are considered as sheep to be slaughtered."

37 No, in all these things we are more than conquerors through him who loved us. 38 For I am convinced that neither death nor life, neither angels nor demons, neither the present nor the future, nor any powers,

May 28
God's Love
1 John 4:7–19

Where can I find the love of God?
It can only be found in Jesus Christ,
Because of why and what Jesus did with His life.
He sacrificed His life for the sin of man.
To comprehend this is beyond what man can understand.
You only need to believe in the love of God in order to receive.
What can separate me from God's love?
Because His love is so strong, powerful, rich, and pure,
Nothing in all creation can separate us from
God and His love. Know this for sure.
God's love will stand the test of time.
Please keep this always in your mind.

God is love. Whoever lives in love lives in God, and God in them.
1 John 4:16

1 John 4:7–19

God's Love and Ours

7 Dear friends, let us love one another, for love comes from God. Everyone who loves has been born of God and knows God. 8 Whoever does not love does not know God, because God is love. 9 This is how God showed his love among us: He sent his one and only Son into the world that we might live through him. 10 This is love: not that we loved God, but that he loved us and sent his Son as an atoning sacrifice for our sins. 11 Dear friends, since God so loved us, we also

ought to love one another. 12 No one has ever seen God; but if we love one another, God lives in us and his love is made complete in us. 13 This is how we know that we live in him and he in us: He has given us of his Spirit. 14 And we have seen and testify that the Father has sent his Son to be the Savior of the world. 15 If anyone acknowledges that Jesus is the Son of God, God lives in them and they in God. 16 And so we know and rely on the love God has for us. God is love. Whoever lives in love lives in God, and God in them. 17 This is how love is made complete among us so that we will have confidence on the day of judgment: In this world we are like Jesus. 18 There is no fear in love. But perfect love drives out fear, because fear has to do with punishment. The one who fears is not made perfect in love.
19 We love because he first loved us.

Hopelessness
May 29
Psalm 146:1–10

Look up to God, for He is worthy of praise.
Look up to God with hands raised.
Why should you praise God? What has He done for you?
What has He done that you know to be true?
He is the Maker of everything in heaven, earth, and the sea.
He made these things for you and for me.
He will forever be faithful to the very end;
Even during times when you and I have sinned.
He defends the cause of the oppressed, and the hungry He will feed.
God is faithful and true to meet all of our needs.
When the weight of this life is too heavy to bear,
God will lift us up because He truly cares.
As prisoners of sin, we want to be free;
God wants to free us to be with Him for eternity.
Because sin has blinded us to what is wrong and what is right,
God will provide us with the wisdom of spiritual insight.
God loves the righteous. For this is true.

This should give you joy and not make you feel blue.
Praise God for all He has done.
Praise Him for your salvation through Jesus Christ, His holy Son.

Have a heart of praise for who God is.

Psalm 146

1
Praise the Lord.
Praise the Lord, my soul.
2
I will praise the Lord all my life;
I will sing praise to my God as long as I live.
3
Do not put your trust in princes,
in human beings, who cannot save.
4
When their spirit departs, they return to the ground;
on that very day their plans come to nothing.
5
Blessed are those whose help is the God of Jacob,
whose hope is in the Lord their God.
6
He is the Maker of heaven and earth,
the sea, and everything in them—
he remains faithful forever.
7
He upholds the cause of the oppressed
and gives food to the hungry.
The Lord sets prisoners free,
8
the Lord gives sight to the blind,
the Lord lifts up those who are bowed down,
the Lord loves the righteous.
9

> The Lord watches over the foreigner
> and sustains the fatherless and the widow,
> but he frustrates the ways of the wicked.
> 10
> The Lord reigns forever,
> your God, O Zion, for all generations.
> Praise the Lord.

May 30
God's Presence
Hebrews 13:1–6

> How do you know God's presence is near?
> You will love others without fear.
> How do you know that God's presence is a reality?
> When you are reminded to welcome strangers with hospitality.
> How do you know that God's presence is with those who are in
> prisons or those who are being mistreated? What do you do?
> You will give them mercy and help, and with kindness too.
> They will know it is God working through you.
> What assurance do you have of God's presence in
> honoring marriage, in keeping it pure?
> God will judge when it is not; know this for sure.
> How do you know that God's presence will keep covetousness away?
> When you are content, there is very little you will have to say.
> God will never leave or forsake you;
> With confidence, you can say too,
> If God's presence is there, to me, what can man do?
>
> There is only peace in the presence of God.

Hebrews 13:1–6

Concluding Exhortations

13 Keep on loving one another as brothers and sisters. 2 Do not forget to show hospitality to strangers, for by so doing some people have shown hospitality to angels without knowing it. 3 Continue to remember those in prison as if you were together with them in prison, and those who are mistreated as if you yourselves were suffering.
4 Marriage should be honored by all, and the marriage bed kept pure, for God will judge the adulterer and all the sexually immoral. 5 Keep your lives free from the love of money and be content with what you have, because God has said,
"Never will I leave you;
never will I forsake you."
6 So we say with confidence,
"The Lord is my helper; I will not be afraid.
What can mere mortals do to me?"

May 31
Suffering
God's Love
Psalm 110

Come, come, all of you who are weak, weary, helpless, and filled with fear.
Come, come to the Lord, for He is near.
If you have doubt, because your faith is gone,
You do not have to stand alone.
What shall you do?
Come to the heavenly Father, for He waits for you.
He will renew your strength with His drink from His brook.
Come, come and see. Come and take a look.
God knows all about your situation and the trouble that you face.
Come and be comforted with spiritual strength;
Come and receive from His amazing grace.
When your situation has lowered your head and is making you feel down,
You cannot lift your head because of the weight of your frown.
Come to the Father to get the strength to carry you through.
Come; the drink from His brook is waiting for you.

Come to Father God; He is waiting to refresh you.

Have you experienced the comfort of God's love?

Psalm 110

Of David. A psalm.
1
The Lord says to my lord:
"Sit at my right hand
until I make your enemies
a footstool for your feet."
2
The Lord will extend your mighty scepter from Zion, saying,
"Rule in the midst of your enemies!"
3
Your troops will be willing
on your day of battle.
Arrayed in holy splendor,
your young men will come to you
like dew from the morning's womb.
4
The Lord has sworn
and will not change his mind:
"You are a priest forever,
in the order of Melchizedek."
5
The Lord is at your right hand;
he will crush kings on the day of his wrath.
6
He will judge the nations, heaping up the dead
and crushing the rulers of the whole earth.
7
He will drink from a brook along the way,
and so he will lift his head high.

June 1
Suffering
Job 23:1–12

Why?
What is the reason for my suffering?
Why is this happening to me?
What do I need to do from this suffering to be set free?
What have I done to cause this to be?
Lord, please help me.
I do not understand. I do not know why.
All I know is I cannot fix this, no matter how hard I try.
Are there answers to my questions so that I will know why?
All I know is I cannot fix this, no matter how hard I try.
God has the answer. He knows the reason why.
I must trust God to give me strength and
peace to weather the storms of life.
Is suffering about making a sacrifice?
He knows the purpose for this suffering of distress.
When I put my hope in God's love and promises,
my mind will have peace and rest.
I will not understand all that God has for me.
But when I am suffering, I know it will not be for an eternity.
Why?

Job 23:1–12

23 Then Job replied:
2
"Even today my complaint is bitter;
his hand is heavy in spite of my groaning.
3
If only I knew where to find him;
if only I could go to his dwelling!

4
I would state my case before him
and fill my mouth with arguments.
5
I would find out what he would answer me,
and consider what he would say to me.
6
Would he vigorously oppose me?
No, he would not press charges against me.
7
There the upright can establish their innocence before him,
and there I would be delivered forever from my judge.
8
"But if I go to the east, he is not there;
if I go to the west, I do not find him.
9
When he is at work in the north, I do not see him;
when he turns to the south, I catch no glimpse of him.
10
But he knows the way that I take;
when he has tested me, I will come forth as gold.
11
My feet have closely followed his steps;
I have kept to his way without turning aside.
12
I have not departed from the commands of his lips;
I have treasured the words of his mouth more than my daily bread.

June 2
Gratitude
Psalm 119:9–16

You can choose this day what your attitude will be.
Remember, it is a choice that others will see.
Wanting to obey God's Word is an expression of an attitude.

An attitude to see how marvelous God's Word
is will be conveyed with gratitude.
His Word will nourish your soul.
Keeping your spirit healthy for you to treasure like gold.
As you grow in Christ each day,
You will have an attitude of gratitude when you go before God to pray.
How do you see your attitude of gratitude as a child of God?

Psalm 119:9–16

ב Beth

9
How can a young person stay on the path of purity?
By living according to your word.

10
I seek you with all my heart;
do not let me stray from your commands.

11
I have hidden your word in my heart
that I might not sin against you.

12
Praise be to you, Lord;
teach me your decrees.

13
With my lips I recount
all the laws that come from your mouth.

14
I rejoice in following your statutes
as one rejoices in great riches.

15
I meditate on your precepts
and consider your ways.

16
I delight in your decrees;
I will not neglect your word.

Gratitude
June 3
Colossians 3:12–17

There are a lot of things to complain about; however,
there are numerous things to be thankful for.
Nonetheless, it is a choice whether to have an attitude
to be thankful or an attitude to grumble.
Only one of these attitudes will allow the heart to be humble.
God's Word encourages us to be compassionate, patient, gentle, and kind.
These are virtues of believers in Christ, which
they should display all the time.
Included in that list should be love, with
forgiveness and also with humility.
Whatever is done, let it all be done for Christ;
for the believer, this is a reality.
Even though there are many things to lodge complaints about,
Being thankful should be done with an attitude
of gratitude and a joyful shout.

What blessings are you complaining to God about?

Colossians 3:12–17

12 Therefore, as God's chosen people, holy and dearly loved, clothe yourselves with compassion, kindness, humility, gentleness and patience. 13 Bear with each other and forgive one another if any of you has a grievance against someone. Forgive as the Lord forgave you. 14 And over all these virtues put on love, which binds them all together in perfect unity. 15 Let the peace of Christ rule in your hearts, since as members of one body you were called to peace. And be thankful. 16 Let the message of Christ dwell among you richly as you teach and admonish one another with all wisdom through psalms, hymns, and songs from the Spirit, singing to God with gratitude in your hearts. 17 And

whatever you do, whether in word or deed, do it all in the name of the Lord Jesus, giving thanks to God the Father through him.

Grief
June 4
John 16:28–33

What hope will I have today,
That will help me navigate through life;
How will I find my way?
There are struggles, sadness, trouble of all kinds.
I want peace and joy to stay on my mind.
Where will I find this peace, this joy?
Will it be wrapped as a brand-new toy?
There is joy, but not as a brand-new toy.
The joy and peace you will find are only in Jesus Christ.
In Him alone is there peace, joy, and hope.
No matter what you are going through, He will show you how to cope.
There will be trouble in this world; there is no doubt about that.
Staying focused on Jesus is where the joy, peace, and hope are at.
Not to know Jesus is to know grief.

John 16:28–33

28 I came from the Father and entered the world; now I am leaving the world and going back to the Father."
29 Then Jesus' disciples said, "Now you are speaking clearly and without figures of speech. 30 Now we can see that you know all things and that you do not even need to have anyone ask you questions. This makes us believe that you came from God."
31 "Do you now believe?" Jesus replied. 32 "A time is coming and in fact has come when you will be scattered, each to your own home. You will leave me all alone. Yet I am not alone, for my Father is with me.

33 "I have told you these things, so that in me you may have peace. In this world you will have trouble. But take heart! I have overcome the world."

June 5
Grief
Heaven
John 11:1–4, 38–44

>Jesus will be with you during your times of grief.
>What comfort to know that Jesus will bring relief.
>Keep this truth in mind with your belief.
>Allow Him to dry your tears and take away your fears.
>Death is a part of life.
>However, Jesus's sacrifice took away death's rights.
>He conquered death and sin.
>His tomb is empty, and sin did not win.
>His death on the cross has set believers free.
>Free from hell for eternity.

>We all will die, but, for the believers, death is the beginning of life to live with Christ in eternity.

John 11:1–4

The Death of Lazarus

11 Now a man named Lazarus was sick. He was from Bethany, the village of Mary and her sister Martha. 2 (This Mary, whose brother Lazarus now lay sick, was the same one who poured perfume on the Lord and wiped his feet with her hair.) 3 So the sisters sent word to Jesus, "Lord, the one you love is sick." 4 When he heard this, Jesus said, "This sickness will not end in death. No, it is for God's glory so that God's Son may be glorified through it."

John 11:38–44

Jesus Raises Lazarus From the Dead
38 Jesus, once more deeply moved, came to the tomb. It was a cave with a stone laid across the entrance. 39 "Take away the stone," he said. "But, Lord," said Martha, the sister of the dead man, "by this time there is a bad odor, for he has been there four days." 40 Then Jesus said, "Did I not tell you that if you believe, you will see the glory of God?" 41 So they took away the stone. Then Jesus looked up and said, "Father, I thank you that you have heard me. 42 I knew that you always hear me, but I said this for the benefit of the people standing here, that they may believe that you sent me." 43 When he had said this, Jesus called in a loud voice, "Lazarus, come out!" 44 The dead man came out, his hands and feet wrapped with strips of linen, and a cloth around his face. Jesus said to them, "Take off the grave clothes and let him go."

Heaven
June 6
Colossians 3:1–11

How often do you think about heaven and the life that it will give?
It will be a life for eternity with peace. Joy filled
with love is how it will be lived.
Heaven is planned for the future for all those
who have accepted Jesus Christ.
Who believed in the salvation that was given through His sacrifice.
Life in heaven will be good, wonderful, filled with worshipping
and praising eternally to our Lord and King.
Hearts lifted up in songs to God the Father and
Jesus Christ we will joyously sing.

Is heaven expecting your arrival?

Colossians 3:1–11

Living as Those Made Alive in Christ
3 Since, then, you have been raised with Christ, set your hearts on things above, where Christ is, seated at the right hand of God. 2 Set your minds on things above, not on earthly things. 3 For you died, and your life is now hidden with Christ in God. 4 When Christ, who is your life, appears, then you also will appear with him in glory. 5 Put to death, therefore, whatever belongs to your earthly nature: sexual immorality, impurity, lust, evil desires and greed, which is idolatry. 6 Because of these, the wrath of God is coming. 7 You used to walk in these ways, in the life you once lived. 8 But now you must also rid yourselves of all such things as these: anger, rage, malice, slander, and filthy language from your lips. 9 Do not lie to each other, since you have taken off your old self with its practices 10 and have put on the new self, which is being renewed in knowledge in the image of its Creator. 11 Here there is no Gentile or Jew, circumcised or uncircumcised, barbarian, Scythian, slave or free, but Christ is all, and is in all.

June 7
Heaven
Hebrews 11:8–16

My citizenship is in heaven; in this world, I am just passing through.
When my journey on this earth is finished, it is
because there is nothing else for me to do.
I am so looking forward to seeing Jesus and
telling Him about my journey here.
In the time I have stayed, what He did on the cross has become very clear.
God's promise I will receive soon, because Jesus's return is very near.
I am longing for my home. That is where I wish to be.
The architect and builder of heaven is God, and
that is where He has made a place for me.
There is no place like home, to live for eternity.

Where is your home for eternity?

Hebrews 11:8–16

8 By faith Abraham, when called to go to a place he would later receive as his inheritance, obeyed and went, even though he did not know where he was going. 9 By faith he made his home in the promised land like a stranger in a foreign country; he lived in tents, as did Isaac and Jacob, who were heirs with him of the same promise. 10 For he was looking forward to the city with foundations, whose architect and builder is God. 11 And by faith even Sarah, who was past childbearing age, was enabled to bear children because she considered him faithful who had made the promise. 12 And so from this one man, and he as good as dead, came descendants as numerous as the stars in the sky and as countless as the sand on the seashore. 13 All these people were still living by faith when they died. They did not receive the things promised; they only saw them and welcomed them from a distance, admitting that they were foreigners and strangers on earth. 14 People who say such things show that they are looking for a country of their own. 15 If they had been thinking of the country they had left, they would have had opportunity to return. 16 Instead, they were longing for a better country—a heavenly one. Therefore God is not ashamed to be called their God, for he has prepared a city for them.

June 8
Fall/Sin
Revelation 22:1–5

When I think about the future, what will my future be?
When I think about the future, where will I live and what will I see?
My future will be with Jesus and our heavenly Father for eternity.
True life I will experience, and love will be there.
Eternal life with Jesus; there will be no care.
"No longer will there be any curse" (Revelation 22:3) to invade my life.
I will be there with Jesus, because of His love and His sacrifice.
"There will be no more night" (Revelation 22:5). What a joy that will be!
Living with Jesus in heaven, from sin I have been set free.

Because of the fall, sin controlled life and how it was lived.
Sin took life and the love it had to give.
Sin caused the fall.
Jesus gave His all.
Living in heaven is how life is meant to be.
It is living with Father God and Jesus for eternity.

What will the future hold for you?

Revelation 22:1–5

Eden Restored

22 Then the angel showed me the river of the water of life, as clear as crystal, flowing from the throne of God and of the Lamb 2 down the middle of the great street of the city. On each side of the river stood the tree of life, bearing twelve crops of fruit, yielding its fruit every month. And the leaves of the tree are for the healing of the nations. 3 No longer will there be any curse. The throne of God and of the Lamb will be in the city, and his servants will serve him. 4 They will see his face, and his name will be on their foreheads. 5 There will be no more night. They will not need the light of a lamp or the light of the sun, for the Lord God will give them light. And they will reign for ever and ever.

June 9
Heaven
Salvation
John 14:1–6

"Jesus is the way and the truth and the life" (John 14:6).
Because of sin, His life was the ultimate sacrifice.
Jesus is the only way to be set free from sin.
There is no other way that heaven will allow you to come in.
Jesus is the truth that will set you free.
To live in heaven eternally.
Jesus is the life that is to be lived.

He is the only one who knew God's love and was willing of it to give.
To go to heaven, you need to make preparations today.
You must remember: Jesus Christ will be the only way.

Use your time wisely as you prepare for eternity.

John 14:1–6

Jesus Comforts His Disciples
14 "Do not let your hearts be troubled. You believe in God; believe also in me. 2 My Father's house has many rooms; if that were not so, would I have told you that I am going there to prepare a place for you? 3 And if I go and prepare a place for you, I will come back and take you to be with me that you also may be where I am. 4 You know the way to the place where I am going."
Jesus the Way to the Father
5 Thomas said to him, "Lord, we don't know where you are going, so how can we know the way?"
6 Jesus answered, "I am the way and the truth and the life. No one comes to the Father except through me.

Holy Spirit
June 10
Exodus 4:1–12

Inadequate is exactly what I feel when I am faced with doing God's will.
This has been too much for me.
Especially when I want to do my best successfully.
The experience of fear of being in control of my
mouth has prevented me to speak.
Being lost for words in moments of feeling weak.
When I call for help, the Holy Spirit gently speaks.
Empowering me to fulfill what He has given me to do.
The Lord will always be with me, enabling me
to do what He has asked me to.

Your success in doing God's will is only through the Holy Spirit.

Exodus 4:1–12

Signs for Moses

4 Moses answered, "What if they do not believe me or listen to me and say, 'The Lord did not appear to you'?" 2 Then the Lord said to him, "What is that in your hand?"

"A staff," he replied.

3 The Lord said, "Throw it on the ground." Moses threw it on the ground and it became a snake, and he ran from it. 4 Then the Lord said to him, "Reach out your hand and take it by the tail." So Moses reached out and took hold of the snake and it turned back into a staff in his hand. 5 "This," said the Lord, "is so that they may believe that the Lord, the God of their fathers—the God of Abraham, the God of Isaac and the God of Jacob—has appeared to you."

6 Then the Lord said, "Put your hand inside your cloak." So Moses put his hand into his cloak, and when he took it out, the skin was leprous—it had become as white as snow.

7 "Now put it back into your cloak," he said. So Moses put his hand back into his cloak, and when he took it out, it was restored, like the rest of his flesh.

8 Then the Lord said, "If they do not believe you or pay attention to the first sign, they may believe the second. 9 But if they do not believe these two signs or listen to you, take some water from the Nile and pour it on the dry ground. The water you take from the river will become blood on the ground."

10 Moses said to the Lord, "Pardon your servant, Lord. I have never been eloquent, neither in the past nor since you have spoken to your servant. I am slow of speech and tongue."

11 The Lord said to him, "Who gave human beings their mouths? Who makes them deaf or mute? Who gives them sight or makes them blind? Is it not I, the Lord? 12 Now go; I will help you speak and will teach you what to say."

June 11
Holy Spirit
2 Kings 2:1–12

The work I do for Jesus will go on in spite of me.
The spirit in which I do the work will last for eternity.
It is the Holy Spirit within us who enables us to serve Christ for humanity.
Without Him, this work cannot be done, no matter how hard we may try.
What tears of joy to know He will be there, no
matter how many tears you may cry!
Make every attempt or effort to allow the
Holy Spirit to lead and guide you.

He will tell you what it is you need to do.
The Father sent the Holy Spirit to enable us
to continue the work of Christ.

2 Kings 2:1–12

Elijah Taken Up to Heaven
2 When the Lord was about to take Elijah up to heaven in a whirlwind, Elijah and Elisha were on their way from Gilgal. 2 Elijah said to Elisha, "Stay here; the Lord has sent me to Bethel."
But Elisha said, "As surely as the Lord lives and as you live, I will not leave you." So they went down to Bethel.
3 The company of the prophets at Bethel came out to Elisha and asked, "Do you know that the Lord is going to take your master from you today?"
"Yes, I know," Elisha replied, "so be quiet."
4 Then Elijah said to him, "Stay here, Elisha; the Lord has sent me to Jericho."
And he replied, "As surely as the Lord lives and as you live, I will not leave you." So they went to Jericho.
5 The company of the prophets at Jericho went up to Elisha and asked him, "Do you know that the Lord is going to take your master from you today?"

"Yes, I know," he replied, "so be quiet."
6 Then Elijah said to him, "Stay here; the Lord has sent me to the Jordan."
And he replied, "As surely as the Lord lives and as you live,
I will not leave you." So the two of them walked on.
7 Fifty men from the company of the prophets went and stood
at a distance, facing the place where Elijah and Elisha had
stopped at the Jordan. 8 Elijah took his cloak, rolled it up and
struck the water with it. The water divided to the right and to
the left, and the two of them crossed over on dry ground.
9 When they had crossed, Elijah said to Elisha, "Tell me,
what can I do for you before I am taken from you?"
"Let me inherit a double portion of your spirit," Elisha replied.
10 "You have asked a difficult thing," Elijah said, "yet if you see me
when I am taken from you, it will be yours—otherwise, it will not."
11 As they were walking along and talking together, suddenly a chariot
of fire and horses of fire appeared and separated the two of them, and
Elijah went up to heaven in a whirlwind. 12 Elisha saw this and cried out,
"My father! My father! The chariots and horsemen of Israel!" And Elisha
saw him no more. Then he took hold of his garment and tore it in two.

June 12
Holy Spirit
Acts 2:1–12

True communication will take time.
You must always bear this in mind.
In the world, numerous languages are spoken.
It can be challenging to praise God or say
thank you with an unknown token.
When the Holy Spirit comes upon you, it is
amazing what you will be able to do.
You will be in a position to connect to people in
so many different and amazing ways.
Being able to speak a new language, or languages;
saying things you never thought you could say.

The Holy Spirit will use you as God's hands and feet.
Because you are Jesus's little sheep.
When you open your mouth to speak,
The Holy Spirit will bring people through you to sit at Jesus's feet.
In bewilderment people will know and be amazed.
It is God speaking to them, and they will be
encouraged to give Him worship and praise.
What language of love has the Holy Spirit given to you to speak?

Acts 2:1–12

The Holy Spirit Comes at Pentecost

2 When the day of Pentecost came, they were all together in one place. 2 Suddenly a sound like the blowing of a violent wind came from heaven and filled the whole house where they were sitting. 3 They saw what seemed to be tongues of fire that separated and came to rest on each of them. 4 All of them were filled with the Holy Spirit and began to speak in other tongues as the Spirit enabled them.
5 Now there were staying in Jerusalem God-fearing Jews from every nation under heaven. 6 When they heard this sound, a crowd came together in bewilderment, because each one heard their own language being spoken. 7 Utterly amazed, they asked: "Aren't all these who are speaking Galileans? 8 Then how is it that each of us hears them in our native language? 9 Parthians, Medes and Elamites; residents of Mesopotamia, Judea and Cappadocia, Pontus and Asia, 10 Phrygia and Pamphylia, Egypt and the parts of Libya near Cyrene; visitors from Rome 11 (both Jews and converts to Judaism); Cretans and Arabs—we hear them declaring the wonders of God in our own tongues!" 12 Amazed and perplexed, they asked one another, "What does this mean?"

June 13
Holy Spirit
Life Struggles
John 14:16–27

Life may be filled with various struggles and
hardship. Many will agree that this is true.
Who will be there to help see you through?
As a child of God, the Holy Spirit is living within you.
He will give you the strength and wisdom to know what to do.
You will have God's peace, and you will be a witness too.
No matter the struggle, He will be there to care for you.

Allow your life struggles to be a testimony of Christ in your life.

John 14:16–27

16 And I will ask the Father, and he will give you another advocate to help you and be with you forever— 17 the Spirit of truth. The world cannot accept him, because it neither sees him nor knows him. But you know him, for he lives with you and will be in you. 18 I will not leave you as orphans; I will come to you. 19 Before long, the world will not see me anymore, but you will see me. Because I live, you also will live. 20 On that day you will realize that I am in my Father, and you are in me, and I am in you. 21 Whoever has my commands and keeps them is the one who loves me. The one who loves me will be loved by my Father, and I too will love them and show myself to them."
22 Then Judas (not Judas Iscariot) said, "But, Lord, why do you intend to show yourself to us and not to the world?"
23 Jesus replied, "Anyone who loves me will obey my teaching. My Father will love them, and we will come to them and make our home with them. 24 Anyone who does not love me will not obey my teaching. These words you hear are not my own; they belong to the Father who sent me. 25 "All this I have spoken while still with you. 26 But the Advocate, the Holy Spirit, whom the Father will send in my name, will teach you all things and will remind you of everything I have said to you.

27 Peace I leave with you; my peace I give you. I do not give to you as the world gives. Do not let your hearts be troubled and do not be afraid.

Humility
June 14
Philippians 2:1–11

Jesus humbled himself in obedience to death for me.
He gave the ultimate sacrifice for humanity.
He set the example of thinking of others and
what is best at meeting their needs.
To be like Jesus you have to follow His example in
putting others' needs first in planting seeds.
Seeds that will encourage others to do the same.
Thinking about others first and not being ashamed.
Do not be ashamed to promote unity to glorify
Christ for what He has done for humanity.

When you put others' needs first before your own,
others will put your needs first before theirs.

Philippians 2:1–11

Imitating Christ's Humility
2 Therefore if you have any encouragement from being united with Christ, if any comfort from his love, if any common sharing in the Spirit, if any tenderness and compassion, 2 then make my joy complete by being like-minded, having the same love, being one in spirit and of one mind. 3 Do nothing out of selfish ambition or vain conceit. Rather, in humility value others above yourselves, 4 not looking to your own interests but each of you to the interests of the others.
5 In your relationships with one another, have
the same mindset as Christ Jesus:
6
Who, being in very nature God,

did not consider equality with God something
to be used to his own advantage;
7
rather, he made himself nothing
by taking the very nature of a servant,
being made in human likeness.
8
And being found in appearance as a man,
he humbled himself
by becoming obedient to death—
even death on a cross!
9
Therefore God exalted him to the highest place
and gave him the name that is above every name,
10
that at the name of Jesus every knee should bow,
in heaven and on earth and under the earth,
11
and every tongue acknowledge that Jesus Christ is Lord,
to the glory of God the Father.

June 15
Injustice
Love for Others
Mark 10:13–16

Can I love me without loving you?
When injustice happens to me, can it happen to you too?
What should we do?
The kingdom of God is a choice to receive.
There is no need for injustice when you believe.
This is a place where all who believe in Jesus Christ will go.
Choosing to support one another this love will show.
It is impossible to love Christ without loving me.
It is inconceivable for me to love me without loving you for eternity.
At just the right time, when we were still
powerless, Christ died for the ungodly.

At just the right time, when we were still
powerless, Christ died for the ungodly.

Romans 5:6

Mark 10:13–16

The Little Children and Jesus
13 People were bringing little children to Jesus for him to place his hands on them, but the disciples rebuked them. 14 When Jesus saw this, he was indignant. He said to them, "Let the little children come to me, and do not hinder them, for the kingdom of God belongs to such as these. 15 Truly I tell you, anyone who will not receive the kingdom of God like a little child will never enter it." 16 And he took the children in his arms, placed his hands on them and blessed them.

June 16
Joy
Fulfilled Joy
John 16:17–24

When I call out to Jesus, will He hear?
I am learning that at the mention of His name, He is always near.
Solace is consolation in time of distress.
When I call out to Jesus, He will give me His peace and rest.
Reassuring that there will be nothing to fear.
The power in His name has made that very clear.
Jesus has made a promise to never leave or forsake me.
He wants me to know this and for the world to see.
When I am in need of Jesus and call out to Him, I know
He will be there and distress will no longer be.

Just mention His name, and Jesus will be there for you.

John 16:17–24

17 At this, some of his disciples said to one another, "What does he mean by saying, 'In a little while you will see me no more, and then after a little while you will see me,' and 'Because I am going to the Father'?" 18 They kept asking, "What does he mean by 'a little while'? We don't understand what he is saying."
19 Jesus saw that they wanted to ask him about this, so he said to them, "Are you asking one another what I meant when I said, 'In a little while you will see me no more, and then after a little while you will see me'? 20 Very truly I tell you, you will weep and mourn while the world rejoices. You will grieve, but your grief will turn to joy.
21 A woman giving birth to a child has pain because her time has come; but when her baby is born she forgets the anguish because of her joy that a child is born into the world. 22 So with you: Now is your time of grief, but I will see you again and you will rejoice, and no one will take away your joy. 23 In that day you will no longer ask me anything. Very truly I tell you, my Father will give you whatever you ask in my name. 24 Until now you have not asked for anything in my name. Ask and you will receive, and your joy will be complete.

Judging Others
June 17
John 3:9–21

Who am I to judge others in how they live for Christ?
This is not my role for their salvation, because
for them I was not made as a sacrifice.
Condemning people for their wrongs is not for me to do.
Showing them Christ's love lets the knowledge
of salvation to come through.
I want to be like Jesus and live a life that is true.
A life filled with God's love, joy, mercy, and grace

Not a life of judging and condemning, but a life
of showing love to the human race.

You have to be taught to learn how to love.

John 3:9–21

9 "How can this be?" Nicodemus asked.
10 "You are Israel's teacher," said Jesus, "and do you not understand these things? 11 Very truly I tell you, we speak of what we know, and we testify to what we have seen, but still you people do not accept our testimony. 12 I have spoken to you of earthly things and you do not believe; how then will you believe if I speak of heavenly things? 13 No one has ever gone into heaven except the one who came from heaven—the Son of Man. 14 Just as Moses lifted up the snake in the wilderness, so the Son of Man must be lifted up, 15 that everyone who believes may have eternal life in him."
16 For God so loved the world that he gave his one and only Son, that whoever believes in him shall not perish but have eternal life. 17 For God did not send his Son into the world to condemn the world, but to save the world through him. 18 Whoever believes in him is not condemned, but whoever does not believe stands condemned already because they have not believed in the name of God's one and only Son. 19 This is the verdict: Light has come into the world, but people loved darkness instead of light because their deeds were evil. 20 Everyone who does evil hates the light, and will not come into the light for fear that their deeds will be exposed. 21 But whoever lives by the truth comes into the light, so that it may be seen plainly that what they have done has been done in the sight of God.

June 18
Judging
God's Love
John 7:53–8:11

Remember, while judging others, someone is also judging you.
What occurs when you are judging others? What does it do?
It will cause you to concentrate on others who sin,
while forgetting you are a sinner too.
While condemning and judging others, mercy will not be
demonstrated or given, and forgiveness will be withheld as well.
Would Christ's love be in you? Who will be able to tell?
Now, when you sin, do you want others and Jesus to be merciless to you?
Instead, be ready and willing to forgive with
eagerness and encouragement too.
Now, this is how Jesus wants to love you.

No one wants to be judged without mercy.

John 7:53–8:11

[The earliest manuscripts and many other ancient witnesses do not have John 7:53—8:11. A few manuscripts include these verses, wholly or in part, after John 7:36, John 21:25, Luke 21:38 or Luke 24:53.]
53 Then they all went home,

8

1 but Jesus went to the Mount of Olives. 2 At dawn he appeared again in the temple courts, where all the people gathered around him, and he sat down to teach them. 3 The teachers of the law and the Pharisees brought in a woman caught in adultery. They made her stand before the group 4 and said to Jesus, "Teacher, this woman was caught in the act of adultery. 5 In the Law Moses commanded us to stone such women. Now what do you say?" 6 They were using this question as a trap, in order to have a basis for accusing him.

But Jesus bent down and started to write on the ground with his finger.
7 When they kept on questioning him, he straightened up and said
to them, "Let any one of you who is without sin be the first to throw
a stone at her." 8 Again he stooped down and wrote on the ground.
9 At this, those who heard began to go away one at a time,
the older ones first, until only Jesus was left, with the woman
still standing there. 10 Jesus straightened up and asked her,
"Woman, where are they? Has no one condemned you?"
11 "No one, sir," she said.
"Then neither do I condemn you," Jesus declared.
"Go now and leave your life of sin."

Legacy
June 19
2 Chronicles 21:4–20

What will you do with your life?
What purpose will it fulfill?
What wisdom will it give?
Your legacy will lead others to follow;
Some it will lead into their tomorrow.
A legacy lived to fulfill only selfish desires,
Will lead some to do the same, because they have been inspired.
Let your legacy be a road map that will flow;
Showing others which way they need to go.
To live a life that is meaningful with the truth.
This is a legacy that will give proof,
Of the power of Jesus Christ to provide a full meaning to life.
Life is meaningful and purposeful too.
What will your life legacy say about you?

Legacy is an inheritance that will be handed down to others as a gift.

2 Chronicles 21:4–20

Jehoram King of Judah

4 When Jehoram established himself firmly over his father's kingdom, he put all his brothers to the sword along with some of the officials of Israel. 5 Jehoram was thirty-two years old when he became king, and he reigned in Jerusalem eight years. 6 He followed the ways of the kings of Israel, as the house of Ahab had done, for he married a daughter of Ahab. He did evil in the eyes of the Lord. 7 Nevertheless, because of the covenant the Lord had made with David, the Lord was not willing to destroy the house of David. He had promised to maintain a lamp for him and his descendants forever.

8 In the time of Jehoram, Edom rebelled against Judah and set up its own king. 9 So Jehoram went there with his officers and all his chariots. The Edomites surrounded him and his chariot commanders, but he rose up and broke through by night.

10 To this day Edom has been in rebellion against Judah. Libnah revolted at the same time, because Jehoram had forsaken the Lord, the God of his ancestors. 11 He had also built high places on the hills of Judah and had caused the people of Jerusalem to prostitute themselves and had led Judah astray.

12 Jehoram received a letter from Elijah the prophet, which said: "This is what the Lord, the God of your father David, says: 'You have not followed the ways of your father Jehoshaphat or of Asa king of Judah. 13 But you have followed the ways of the kings of Israel, and you have led Judah and the people of Jerusalem to prostitute themselves, just as the house of Ahab did. You have also murdered your own brothers, members of your own family, men who were better than you. 14 So now the Lord is about to strike your people, your sons, your wives and everything that is yours, with a heavy blow. 15 You yourself will be very ill with a lingering disease of the bowels, until the disease causes your bowels to come out.'"

16 The Lord aroused against Jehoram the hostility of the Philistines and of the Arabs who lived near the Cushites. 17 They attacked Judah, invaded it and carried off all the goods found in the king's palace, together with his sons and wives. Not a son was left to him except Ahaziah, the youngest.

18 After all this, the Lord afflicted Jehoram with an incurable disease of the bowels. 19 In the course of time, at the end of the second year, his bowels came out because of the disease, and he died in great pain. His people made no funeral fire in his honor, as they had for his predecessors. 20 Jehoram was thirty-two years old when he became king, and he reigned in Jerusalem eight years. He passed away, to no one's regret, and was buried in the City of David, but not in the tombs of the kings.

June 20
Legacy
Living for Christ
Proverbs 22:1–12

Living life and living a life with a legacy are not one and the same.
How are you living your life that a legacy will be maintained?
How will this life give you a good and godly name?
What is in a name? Many may want to say.
It is how you live that will lead others to Jesus or to go astray.
Living life to leave a legacy is not easy to do.
It is living a life that is rooted in and enriched by the truth.
It is pursuing a life to live for Jesus in obedience in doing all He tells you to.
What will your name say about you?

Proverbs 22:1–12

22

A good name is more desirable than great riches;
to be esteemed is better than silver or gold.

2

Rich and poor have this in common:
The Lord is the Maker of them all.

3

The prudent see danger and take refuge,
but the simple keep going and pay the penalty.

4
Humility is the fear of the Lord;
its wages are riches and honor and life.

5
In the paths of the wicked are snares and pitfalls,
but those who would preserve their life stay far from them.

6
Start children off on the way they should go,
and even when they are old they will not turn from it.

7
The rich rule over the poor,
and the borrower is slave to the lender.

8
Whoever sows injustice reaps calamity,
and the rod they wield in fury will be broken.

9
The generous will themselves be blessed,
for they share their food with the poor.

10
Drive out the mocker, and out goes strife;
quarrels and insults are ended.

11
One who loves a pure heart and who speaks with grace
will have the king for a friend.

12
The eyes of the Lord keep watch over knowledge,
but he frustrates the words of the unfaithful.

June 21
Legacy
Stories of Faith
Psalm 145:1–13

Family history is very important in having a major impact;
From generation to generation, family history tells each generation how to act.

When the family history tells of a faith journey with Christ,
What a powerful witness of faith, of a desire to live right.
Stories of celebration of God as the Sovereign King, During
trials that put joy in the heart of songs to sing.
When the stories tell of His majesty and generosity, His
mighty acts, awesome works, and great deeds.
The stories may sound incredible, but they are planting faith seeds.
These stories must be preserved by the legacy
of faith that has been passed on.
The purpose is that the soul of many for Christ will be won.
God is good, gracious, compassionate, slow to anger and rich in love,
trustworthy in all He promises, and righteous in all His ways.
This knowledge is too precious, and it should be taught every day.
A family history of faith in Christ is strong, filled with powerful stories
of how many accepted the challenges of their generation to live right.
When that legacy has been passed down to you, how
will you use it, and with it, what will you do?
The legacy of faith is a priceless gift to give each generation.

Psalm 145:1-13

A psalm of praise. Of David.
1
I will exalt you, my God the King;
I will praise your name for ever and ever.
2
Every day I will praise you
and extol your name for ever and ever.
3
Great is the Lord and most worthy of praise;
his greatness no one can fathom.
4
One generation commends your works to another;
they tell of your mighty acts.

5
They speak of the glorious splendor of your majesty—
and I will meditate on your wonderful works.
6
They tell of the power of your awesome works—
and I will proclaim your great deeds.
7
They celebrate your abundant goodness
and joyfully sing of your righteousness.
8
The Lord is gracious and compassionate,
slow to anger and rich in love.
9
The Lord is good to all;
he has compassion on all he has made.
10
All your works praise you, Lord;
your faithful people extol you.
11
They tell of the glory of your kingdom
and speak of your might,
12
so that all people may know of your mighty acts
and the glorious splendor of your kingdom.
13
Your kingdom is an everlasting kingdom,
and your dominion endures through all generations.
The Lord is trustworthy in all he promises
and faithful in all he does.

Life Struggles
June 22
Trust in God
Isaiah 40:21–31

Life struggles have me down.
There appears to be no solution to these issues of life to be found.
This can be depressing, and it has turned my joy into a frown.
After looking at creation, I knew I did not need to wonder any longer.
There is a solution for my struggles; I only needed to ponder.
Creation gave me my answer of what I needed to know.
In all of its splendor, it clearly and will always show:
It is God who has all the answers to life.
He knows how to make life right.
When we trust and put our hope in Him, He will
give us the strength to make it through.
No matter how often we may stumble and fall, He
will give us the strength to be renewed.
God is totally awesome and never forgets who
He is and what He can and will do.
Remember, He will always be there for me,
and He will always be there for you.
It is not about how well we know life's struggles but how well
we know God, who knows what to do with those struggles.

Isaiah 40:21–31

21
Do you not know?
Have you not heard?
Has it not been told you from the beginning?
Have you not understood since the earth was founded?
22
He sits enthroned above the circle of the earth,
and its people are like grasshoppers.

He stretches out the heavens like a canopy,
and spreads them out like a tent to live in.
23
He brings princes to naught
and reduces the rulers of this world to nothing.
24
No sooner are they planted,
no sooner are they sown,
no sooner do they take root in the ground,
than he blows on them and they wither,
and a whirlwind sweeps them away like chaff.
25
"To whom will you compare me?
Or who is my equal?" says the Holy One.
26
Lift up your eyes and look to the heavens:
Who created all these?
He who brings out the starry host one by one
and calls forth each of them by name.
Because of his great power and mighty strength,
not one of them is missing.
27
Why do you complain, Jacob?
Why do you say, Israel,
"My way is hidden from the Lord;
my cause is disregarded by my God"?
28
Do you not know?
Have you not heard?
The Lord is the everlasting God,
the Creator of the ends of the earth.
He will not grow tired or weary,
and his understanding no one can fathom.
29
He gives strength to the weary
and increases the power of the weak.

> 30
> Even youths grow tired and weary,
> and young men stumble and fall;
> 31
> but those who hope in the Lord
> will renew their strength.
> They will soar on wings like eagles;
> they will run and not grow weary,
> they will walk and not be faint.

June 23
Trust in God
2 Timothy 3:10–15

> Never give up, no matter what the challenge may be.
> You must persevere with hope in letting this be your reality.
> As a child of God, persecution, and affliction
> are the suffering we each will face.
> As we persevere, we will receive and witness God's amazing grace.
> Faith in God and what His Word has to say.
> Looking to Him to be encouraged when facing discouragement
> and how to endure it each and every day.
> As we persevere, we will receive and witness God's amazing grace.
> We will be rewarded when we faithfully confront the
> challenges of suffering while finishing the race.
>
> Life is a struggle when it is lived without God.

2 Timothy 3:10–15

A Final Charge to Timothy

10 You, however, know all about my teaching, my way of life, my purpose, faith, patience, love, endurance, 11 persecutions, sufferings—what kinds of things happened to me in Antioch, Iconium and Lystra, the persecutions I endured. Yet the Lord rescued me from all of them. 12 In fact, everyone who wants to live a godly life in Christ

Jesus will be persecuted, 13 while evildoers and impostors will go from bad to worse, deceiving and being deceived. 14 But as for you, continue in what you have learned and have become convinced of, because you know those from whom you learned it, 15 and how from infancy you have known the Holy Scriptures, which are able to make you wise for salvation through faith in Christ Jesus.

Living for Christ
June 24
Matthew 5:13–16

I am salt of the earth.
Salt that Jesus says is of great worth.
Jesus says that in this world, I am His light.
Light that is the reflection of His love to a dark and
dying world that needs spiritual insight.
The opportunity to let my light shine is a real joy of mine.
Shine, shine, shine this light of mine.
Shine, shine, shine for my Jesus all the time.

Let your light shine through because the world needs to see Jesus.

Matthew 5:13–16

Salt and Light

13 "You are the salt of the earth. But if the salt loses its saltiness, how can it be made salty again? It is no longer good for anything, except to be thrown out and trampled underfoot.
14 "You are the light of the world. A town built on a hill cannot be hidden. 15 Neither do people light a lamp and put it under a bowl. Instead they put it on its stand, and it gives light to everyone in the house. 16 In the same way, let your light shine before others, that they may see your good deeds and glorify your Father in heaven.

June 25
Living for Christ
1 Peter 3:9–12

As I start this day, I need to be careful in what I do and what I say.
I must not allow evil to have any control over me in any way.
My tongue and heart must be protected from
doing and speaking evil and deceit.
I must do that which is good, while pursuing peace to
experience victory and not experience defeat.
I love my life because it is a gift from Christ.
A gift of His life, which was given as a sacrifice.
However, when I have done wrong in hurting someone with my tongue,
Forgiveness is what I must seek.
Apologizing, while being humble and meek.
I must guard my tongue and heart today.
Not allowing evil to have any victory in my
life in what I do and in what I say.

Having victory in living for Christ is knowing how to defeat evil.

1 Peter 3:9–12

9 Do not repay evil with evil or insult with insult. On the contrary, repay evil with blessing, because to this you were called so that you may inherit a blessing. 10 For,
"Whoever would love life
and see good days
must keep their tongue from evil
and their lips from deceitful speech.
11
They must turn from evil and do good;
they must seek peace and pursue it.
12
For the eyes of the Lord are on the righteous

and his ears are attentive to their prayer,
but the face of the Lord is against those who do evil."

June 26
Obedience
2 Kings 12:1–15

When living for Christ, distractions cannot get in the way;
They can come in the form of comfort, materialism, selfpromotion,
and what others might think and say.
When living for Christ, obedience in doing right is required;
It is precisely what needed for perseverance to be inspired.
Spiritual growth will be present as a legacy takes place;
It will be good to know that you did what was
right when you meet Jesus face-to-face.
God always blesses honesty.

2 Kings 12:1–15

Joash Repairs the Temple

12 In the seventh year of Jehu, Joash became king, and he reigned in Jerusalem forty years. His mother's name was Zibiah; she was from Beersheba. 2 Joash did what was right in the eyes of the Lord all the years Jehoiada the priest instructed him. 3 The high places, however, were not removed; the people continued to offer sacrifices and burn incense there. 4 Joash said to the priests, "Collect all the money that is brought as sacred offerings to the temple of the Lord—the money collected in the census, the money received from personal vows and the money brought voluntarily to the temple. 5 Let every priest receive the money from one of the treasurers, then use it to repair whatever damage is found in the temple."
6 But by the twenty-third year of King Joash the priests still had not repaired the temple. 7 Therefore King Joash summoned Jehoiada the priest and the other priests and asked them, "Why aren't you

repairing the damage done to the temple? Take no more money from your treasurers, but hand it over for repairing the temple." 8 The priests agreed that they would not collect any more money from the people and that they would not repair the temple themselves.

9 Jehoiada the priest took a chest and bored a hole in its lid. He placed it beside the altar, on the right side as one enters the temple of the Lord. The priests who guarded the entrance put into the chest all the money that was brought to the temple of the Lord. 10 Whenever they saw that there was a large amount of money in the chest, the royal secretary and the high priest came, counted the money that had been brought into the temple of the Lord and put it into bags. 11 When the amount had been determined, they gave the money to the men appointed to supervise the work on the temple. With it they paid those who worked on the temple of the Lord—the carpenters and builders, 12 the masons and stonecutters. They purchased timber and blocks of dressed stone for the repair of the temple of the Lord, and met all the other expenses of restoring the temple.

13 The money brought into the temple was not spent for making silver basins, wick trimmers, sprinkling bowls, trumpets or any other articles of gold or silver for the temple of the Lord; 14 it was paid to the workers, who used it to repair the temple. 15 They did not require an accounting from those to whom they gave the money to pay the workers, because they acted with complete honesty.

June 27
Serving Others
Ephesians 6:5–9

Lord Jesus, help me to keep this thought in mind as I start my day:
To serve You in everything, I do and everything I say.
Let it be from my heart that I pray.
I pray my heart will be filled with truthfulness,
trustworthiness, and sincerity.
I want to do and say things with integrity
People are not my focus to please in my service or to obey.
Christ is my focus to please as I live this day.

What a privilege it is to serve my Lord, and it is a joy too.
Lord Jesus, I live only to please You.

Whom do you serve, and why?

Ephesians 6:5–9

5 Slaves, obey your earthly masters with respect and fear, and with sincerity of heart, just as you would obey Christ. 6 Obey them not only to win their favor when their eye is on you, but as slaves of Christ, doing the will of God from your heart. 7 Serve wholeheartedly, as if you were serving the Lord, not people, 8 because you know that the Lord will reward each one for whatever good they do, whether they are slave or free. 9 And masters, treat your slaves in the same way. Do not threaten them, since you know that he who is both their Master and yours is in heaven, and there is no favoritism with him.

June 28
Living for Christ
Serving Others
Colossians 2:20–3:4

Rules and regulations will keep your heart from
loving and serving Christ and man.
Rules and regulations only help you to live for legalism's demands.
They will not allow you to draw closer to Christ.
They will not make your life holy and right, filled with spiritual insight.
Do not allow legalism to be in control of you.
It is counterintuitive to the Bible, and this is true.
Set your heart on God above;
This will fill you with His love.

Rules and regulations do not teach you how to love.

Colossians 2:20–3:4

20 Since you died with Christ to the elemental spiritual forces of this world, why, as though you still belonged to the world, do you submit to its rules: 21 "Do not handle! Do not taste! Do not touch!"? 22 These rules, which have to do with things that are all destined to perish with use, are based on merely human commands and teachings. 23 Such regulations indeed have an appearance of wisdom, with their selfimposed worship, their false humility and their harsh treatment of the body, but they lack any value in restraining sensual indulgence.
Living as Those Made Alive in Christ
3 Since, then, you have been raised with Christ, set your hearts on things above, where Christ is, seated at the right hand of God. 2 Set your minds on things above, not on earthly things. 3 For you died, and your life is now hidden with Christ in God. 4 When Christ, who is your life, appears, then you also will appear with him in glory.

Living Like Christ
June 29
Psalm 141:1–4

Evil is waiting to have its way with me today.
Lord Jesus, please guard my mouth in what I will say.
Keep the door of my lips so evil words will stay away.
Please keep my heart from being drawn toward that
which is evil, so wicked deeds I will not do.
Lord Jesus, I am in need of You.
I need You to soften my heart so that kind words my mouth will speak.
Today, do not allow evil to find me in being weak.
I want my prayer to be an incense to You; this is what my heart seeks.

How do you want God to use you today?

Psalm 141:1-4

A psalm of David.
1
I call to you, Lord, come quickly to me;
hear me when I call to you.
2
May my prayer be set before you like incense;
may the lifting up of my hands be like the evening sacrifice.
3
Set a guard over my mouth, Lord;
keep watch over the door of my lips.
4
Do not let my heart be drawn to what is evil
so that I take part in wicked deeds
along with those who are evildoers;
do not let me eat their delicacies.

June 30
Living Like Christ
2 Peter 1:12–21

Be firmly established in the truth.
The message of the gospel is simple, so the words
that are needed to explain it are few.
Testimony is the only thing needed.
As a witness, testify to how, through belief,
life was changed and superseded.
Simple words are not naive or dense.
When the heart wants to know the truth, they will make sense.
Simple words are direct and unpretentious.
Letting others know that their faith is genuine.

"Go and make disciples of all nations."
Matthew 28:19

2 Peter 1:12–21

Prophecy of Scripture

12 So I will always remind you of these things, even though you know them and are firmly established in the truth you now have. 13 I think it is right to refresh your memory as long as I live in the tent of this body, 14 because I know that I will soon put it aside, as our Lord Jesus Christ has made clear to me. 15 And I will make every effort to see that after my departure you will always be able to remember these things. 16 For we did not follow cleverly devised stories when we told you about the coming of our Lord Jesus Christ in power, but we were eyewitnesses of his majesty. 17 He received honor and glory from God the Father when the voice came to him from the Majestic Glory, saying, "This is my Son, whom I love; with him I am well pleased." 18 We ourselves heard this voice that came from heaven when we were with him on the sacred mountain. 19 We also have the prophetic message as something completely reliable, and you will do well to pay attention to it, as to a light shining in a dark place, until the day dawns and the morning star rises in your hearts. 20 Above all, you must understand that no prophecy of Scripture came about by the prophet's own interpretation of things. 21 For prophecy never had its origin in the human will, but prophets, though human, spoke from God as they were carried along by the Holy Spirit.

July 1
Personal Behavior/The Tongue
Psalm 141

Oh, the things this mouth of mine will say.
Lord, I need You to set a guard over it today.
Sovereign Lord, words are powerful, and this You know;
Creation clearly shows.
You spoke, and creation came to be.
It is obvious that the blind can see.
Keeping watch over my lips, so evil things out of it will not slip.

I want my words to be beautiful, gentle, meaningful, and kind.
These are the kind of words I want to think all the time.
I want to be in control over the things I will say.
Lord, please put a guard over my mouth today.

What would you do if the things you have said
to others were repeated to you?

Psalm 141

A psalm of David.
1
I call to you, Lord, come quickly to me;
hear me when I call to you.
2
May my prayer be set before you like incense;
may the lifting up of my hands be like the evening sacrifice.
3
Set a guard over my mouth, Lord;
keep watch over the door of my lips.
4
Do not let my heart be drawn to what is evil
so that I take part in wicked deeds
along with those who are evildoers;
do not let me eat their delicacies.
5
Let a righteous man strike me—that is a kindness;
let him rebuke me—that is oil on my head.
My head will not refuse it,
for my prayer will still be against the deeds of evildoers.
6
Their rulers will be thrown down from the cliffs,
and the wicked will learn that my words were well spoken.
7
They will say, "As one plows and breaks up the earth,
so our bones have been scattered at the mouth of the grave."

8
But my eyes are fixed on you, Sovereign Lord;
in you I take refuge—do not give me over to death.
9
Keep me safe from the traps set by evildoers,
from the snares they have laid for me.
10
Let the wicked fall into their own nets,
while I pass by in safety.

July 2
Living Like Christ
Ephesians 5:1–16

Living for Christ can be challenging as you
grow in the knowledge of Him.
The challenge is to grow, which is not impossible for you to do.
To live as children of the light is what Christ asks of you.
Thriving in the presence of God, let your light produce fruit from godly seeds.
Let these seeds grow into works of godly deeds.
Living in the light will not be easily done.
The challenges you will face will not be fun.
But what joy it will bring knowing you have faced
each challenge with Jesus Christ, your King.
Living in the light, darkness you cannot hide.
Living for Jesus, He will always be faithfully at your side.

Living for Christ means living a life filled with His light.

Ephesians 5:1–16

5
1 Follow God's example, therefore, as dearly loved children
2 and walk in the way of love, just as Christ loved us and gave
himself up for us as a fragrant offering and sacrifice to God.

3 But among you there must not be even a hint of sexual immorality, or of any kind of impurity, or of greed, because these are improper for God's holy people. 4 Nor should there be obscenity, foolish talk or coarse joking, which are out of place, but rather thanksgiving.
5 For of this you can be sure: No immoral, impure or greedy person—such a person is an idolater—has any inheritance in the kingdom of Christ and of God. 6 Let no one deceive you with empty words, for because of such things God's wrath comes on those who are disobedient. 7 Therefore do not be partners with them.
8 For you were once darkness, but now you are light in the Lord. Live as children of light 9 (for the fruit of the light consists in all goodness, righteousness and truth) 10 and find out what pleases the Lord. 11 Have nothing to do with the fruitless deeds of darkness, but rather expose them. 12 It is shameful even to mention what the disobedient do in secret. 13 But everything exposed by the light becomes visible—and everything that is illuminated becomes a light. 14 This is why it is said:
"Wake up, sleeper,
rise from the dead,
and Christ will shine on you."
15 Be very careful, then, how you live—not as unwise but as wise, 16 making the most of every opportunity, because the days are evil.

July 3
Living Like Christ
Philippians 4:4–9

Let me see, what choices will I make today?
Will I work, or will I play?
What will I allow in my mind today?
How will I think, and on what will I dwell?
How will my behavior tell?
I have determined that I will not be anxious about anything today.
I have decided I will get on my knees and pray.
I will thank God for guarding my heart today.
I will lift up my voice and rejoice.

I will focus on excellent and praiseworthy things.
Then I will be able to lift up my voice to rejoice and sing.
Be careful how you think today.

Philippians 4:4–9

Final Exhortations

4 Rejoice in the Lord always. I will say it again: Rejoice! 5 Let your gentleness be evident to all. The Lord is near. 6 Do not be anxious about anything, but in every situation, by prayer and petition, with thanksgiving, present your requests to God. 7 And the peace of God, which transcends all understanding, will guard your hearts and your minds in Christ Jesus. 8 Finally, brothers and sisters, whatever is true, whatever is noble, whatever is right, whatever is pure, whatever is lovely, whatever is admirable—if anything is excellent or praiseworthy—think about such things. 9 Whatever you have learned or received or heard from me, or seen in me—put it into practice. And the God of peace will be with you.

July 4
Living Like Christ
Philippians 4:4–9

The day is new, so what will I do?
I have choices to choose.
From these choices, how will my heart rule?
How shall I think to know what to do?
Lord, please tell me. I want to hear from You.
Thank You for Your peace and for guarding my heart today.
I am happy about my choice not to worry but, instead, to pray.
Now my mind is quite clear.
Because I am listening to Jesus, who will be near.
Now my mind is clear, and so is how I am to think.
I will think about the things of Jesus without a blink.
Be cautious of what you will allow into your thoughts today.

Philippians 4:4–9

Final Exhortations

4 Rejoice in the Lord always. I will say it again: Rejoice! 5 Let your gentleness be evident to all. The Lord is near. 6 Do not be anxious about anything, but in every situation, by prayer and petition, with thanksgiving, present your requests to God. 7 And the peace of God, which transcends all understanding, will guard your hearts and your minds in Christ Jesus. 8 Finally, brothers and sisters, whatever is true, whatever is noble, whatever is right, whatever is pure, whatever is lovely, whatever is admirable—if anything is excellent or praiseworthy—think about such things. 9 Whatever you have learned or received or heard from me, or seen in me— put it into practice. And the God of peace will be with you.

July 5
Living Like Christ
Colossians 3:12–17

How is the world being influenced by you?
Let your faith in Christ reflect what you will say and what you will do.
Wear the character of Jesus as your daily attire.
It will surely be an influence and greatly admired.
Dress fully in patience, kindness, gentleness,
compassion, and humility too.
You will be so well dressed, and the fit will be perfect for you.
Living like Christ for others to see,
Will surely be an influence that will be admired and believed.

Clothe yourselves with compassion, kindness,
humility, gentleness and patience.
Colossians 3:12

Colossians 3:12–17

12 Therefore, as God's chosen people, holy and dearly loved, clothe yourselves with compassion, kindness, humility, gentleness and patience. 13 Bear with each other and forgive one another if any of you has a grievance against someone. Forgive as the Lord forgave you. 14 And over all these virtues put on love, which binds them all together in perfect unity. 15 Let the peace of Christ rule in your hearts, since as members of one body you were called to peace. And be thankful. 16 Let the message of Christ dwell among you richly as you teach and admonish one another with all wisdom through psalms, hymns, and songs from the Spirit, singing to God with gratitude in your hearts. 17 And whatever you do, whether in word or deed, do it all in the name of the Lord Jesus, giving thanks to God the Father through him.

July 6
Living Like Christ
James 1:22–27

When you are listening to the Word of God, what do you hear?
Do you listen to learn, or do you only listen to hear with your ears?
When you listen to the Word of God, are you inspired?
Are you inspired to do and obey because it has become your heart desire?
Be blessed today in what you do.
Doing it with a heart's desire because you want to.
Remember to watch and be in control of what you say.
This is a practice you need to do every day.

Do you listen to hear, or do you hear to listen?

James 1:22–27

22 Do not merely listen to the word, and so deceive yourselves. Do what it says. 23 Anyone who listens to the word but does not do what it says is like someone who looks at his face in a mirror 24 and, after looking at himself, goes away and immediately forgets what he looks like. 25 But whoever looks intently into the perfect law that gives freedom, and continues in it—not forgetting what they have heard, but doing it—they will be blessed in what they do. 26 Those who consider themselves religious and yet do not keep a tight rein on their tongues deceive themselves, and their religion is worthless. 27 Religion that God our Father accepts as pure and faultless is this: to look after orphans and widows in their distress and to keep oneself from being polluted by the world.

July 7
Living Like Christ
Spiritual Transformation
James 3:1–12

Lord Jesus, I call upon You to take control
of what my mouth will say today.
This tongue of mine will say the words out of
anger. Please help me, Lord, I pray.
Lord, I ask You to help me put a guard over what I will say today.
My tongue will clearly speak my thoughts that are
careless, thoughtless, and loveless too.
Lord, I must have self-control in what I will say and as well what I will do.
I wish to thank You, Lord, because I am depending on You.
I want my words to be a blessing to others so they can see,
These words of mine are pointing them to Jesus,
who from sin will set them free.

Teach yourself to speak like Jesus.

James 3:1–12

Taming the Tongue

3 Not many of you should become teachers, my fellow believers, because you know that we who teach will be judged more strictly. 2 We all stumble in many ways. Anyone who is never at fault in what they say is perfect, able to keep their whole body in check. 3 When we put bits into the mouths of horses to make them obey us, we can turn the whole animal. 4 Or take ships as an example. Although they are so large and are driven by strong winds, they are steered by a very small rudder wherever the pilot wants to go. 5 Likewise, the tongue is a small part of the body, but it makes great boasts. Consider what a great forest is set on fire by a small spark. 6 The tongue also is a fire, a world of evil among the parts of the body. It corrupts the whole body, sets the whole course of one's life on fire, and is itself set on fire by hell. 7 All kinds of animals, birds, reptiles and sea creatures are being tamed and have been tamed by mankind, 8 but no human being can tame the tongue. It is a restless evil, full of deadly poison. 9 With the tongue we praise our Lord and Father, and with it we curse human beings, who have been made in God's likeness. 10 Out of the same mouth come praise and cursing. My brothers and sisters, this should not be. 11 Can both fresh water and salt water flow from the same spring? 12 My brothers and sisters, can a fig tree bear olives, or a grapevine bear figs? Neither can a salt spring produce fresh water.

July 8
Living Like Christ
Spiritual Transformation
James 3:1–12

Learning to control my speech is hard to do.
Especially when I want to say the things that are not always the truth.
I need to control my speech when I want to speak
of careless and thoughtless things.
Anger, lack of love is what these words will bring.

Oh, yes, my words can be heartless with a perfect aim.
That will bring nothing but heartache and much pain.
Lord, please help me.
This is not the way I wish to be.
Please bless my mouth to speak words that are loving and true.
I want my words to help people to know You.

How are your words revealing Christ in you?

James 3:1–12

Taming the Tongue

3 Not many of you should become teachers, my fellow believers, because you know that we who teach will be judged more strictly. 2 We all stumble in many ways. Anyone who is never at fault in what they say is perfect, able to keep their whole body in check. 3 When we put bits into the mouths of horses to make them obey us, we can turn the whole animal. 4 Or take ships as an example. Although they are so large and are driven by strong winds, they are steered by a very small rudder wherever the pilot wants to go. 5 Likewise, the tongue is a small part of the body, but it makes great boasts. Consider what a great forest is set on fire by a small spark. 6 The tongue also is a fire, a world of evil among the parts of the body. It corrupts the whole body, sets the whole course of one's life on fire, and is itself set on fire by hell.
7 All kinds of animals, birds, reptiles and sea creatures are being tamed and have been tamed by mankind, 8 but no human being can tame the tongue. It is a restless evil, full of deadly poison.
9 With the tongue we praise our Lord and Father, and with it we curse human beings, who have been made in God's likeness. 10 Out of the same mouth come praise and cursing. My brothers and sisters, this should not be. 11 Can both fresh water and salt water flow from the same spring? 12 My brothers and sisters, can a fig tree bear olives, or a grapevine bear figs? Neither can a salt spring produce fresh water.

Loneliness
July 9
2 Timothy 4:9–18

The walls are closing in;
Who can I call on as a friend?
I feel the coldness of life.
This is a place I do not wish to be.
How do I get out? I wish from this loneliness to be free.
I must press on to do what I have been called to do.
Lord, please help me; I am feeling painfully blue.
Who will come to my aid? Who will care? Who will be there?
God will be right there for me. I know I can trust Him to rescue me.
Loneliness will cease when I go to be with Christ, my Savior for eternity.

A touch means so much to each living person.

2 Timothy 4:9–18

Personal Remarks

9 Do your best to come to me quickly, 10 for Demas, because he loved this world, has deserted me and has gone to Thessalonica. Crescens has gone to Galatia, and Titus to Dalmatia. 11 Only Luke is with me. Get Mark and bring him with you, because he is helpful to me in my ministry. 12 I sent Tychicus to Ephesus. 13 When you come, bring the cloak that I left with Carpus at Troas, and my scrolls, especially the parchments. 14 Alexander the metalworker did me a great deal of harm. The Lord will repay him for what he has done. 15 You too should be on your guard against him, because he strongly opposed our message.
16 At my first defense, no one came to my support, but everyone deserted me. May it not be held against them. 17 But the Lord stood at my side and gave me strength, so that through me the message might be fully proclaimed and all the Gentiles might hear it. And I was delivered from the lion's mouth. 18 The Lord will rescue me from every evil attack and will bring me safely to his heavenly kingdom. To him be glory for ever and ever. Amen.

Lord's Supper
July 10
Mark 8:11–21

Be wary of those who demand signs for the proof of Jesus Christ.
Demanding God of heaven must provide a sign,
with the thought, it is their right.
Who He is and what He can do.
Expressing that they want proof that the facts about Jesus are the truth.
Watch out for the poison their influence will
have in getting you to do the same.
Not believing in Jesus Christ and the power of His name.
Let this be a reminder to you: demanding signs from
heaven is something you do not want to do.
Have faith in Jesus Christ and believe He will always be there for you.

Are you persuaded to have faith in Jesus Christ?

Mark 8:11–21

11 The Pharisees came and began to question Jesus. To test him, they asked him for a sign from heaven. 12 He sighed deeply and said, "Why does this generation ask for a sign? Truly I tell you, no sign will be given to it." 13 Then he left them, got back into the boat and crossed to the other side.
The Yeast of the Pharisees and Herod
14 The disciples had forgotten to bring bread, except for one loaf they had with them in the boat. 15 "Be careful," Jesus warned them. "Watch out for the yeast of the Pharisees and that of Herod."
16 They discussed this with one another and
said, "It is because we have no bread."
17 Aware of their discussion, Jesus asked them: "Why are you talking about having no bread? Do you still not see or understand? Are your hearts hardened? 18 Do you have eyes but fail to see, and ears but fail to hear? And don't you remember? 19 When I broke the five loaves for the five thousand, how many basketfuls of pieces did you pick up?"

"Twelve," they replied.
20 "And when I broke the seven loaves for the four thousand, how many basketfuls of pieces did you pick up?"
They answered, "Seven."
21 He said to them, "Do you still not understand?"

Love for God
July 11
Psalm 86:1–13

This life of mine I will give;
To Almighty God, with it I will live.
I will live to worship Him with praise.
With lifted hands, I will raise.
I will praise Him for all He has done for me.
I am so grateful, I will praise Him throughout eternity.
There is not anyone like my God and my King.
To You, I will eternally sing.
Sing songs about all You have done.
How You sent me a Savior, Jesus Christ, Your holy Son.

To live only for Jesus is a life that is worth living.

Psalm 86:1–13

A prayer of David.
1
Hear me, Lord, and answer me,
for I am poor and needy.
2
Guard my life, for I am faithful to you;
save your servant who trusts in you.
You are my God; 3 have mercy on me, Lord,
for I call to you all day long.

4
Bring joy to your servant, Lord,
for I put my trust in you.
5
You, Lord, are forgiving and good,
abounding in love to all who call to you.
6
Hear my prayer, Lord;
listen to my cry for mercy.
7
When I am in distress, I call to you,
because you answer me.
8
Among the gods there is none like you, Lord;
no deeds can compare with yours.
9
All the nations you have made
will come and worship before you, Lord;
they will bring glory to your name.
10
For you are great and do marvelous deeds;
you alone are God.
11
Teach me your way, Lord,
that I may rely on your faithfulness;
give me an undivided heart,
that I may fear your name.
12
I will praise you, Lord my God, with all my heart;
I will glorify your name forever.
13
For great is your love toward me;
you have delivered me from the depths,
from the realm of the dead.

July 12
Love for God
Isaiah 49:13–21

Father God loves me as I am.
I am written in the palms of His hands.
His love for me is beyond what I am able to understand.
To experience God's love is something I will always hold dear.
His love causes me never to fear.
His love is one thing I cannot keep to myself.
I am compelled to share it with everyone else.

Have you experienced God's love for you?

Isaiah 49:13–21

13
Shout for joy, you heavens;
rejoice, you earth;
burst into song, you mountains!
For the Lord comforts his people
and will have compassion on his afflicted ones.
14
But Zion said, "The Lord has forsaken me,
the Lord has forgotten me."
15
"Can a mother forget the baby at her breast
and have no compassion on the child she has borne?
Though she may forget,
I will not forget you!
16
See, I have engraved you on the palms of my hands;
your walls are ever before me.
17
Your children hasten back,
and those who laid you waste depart from you.

18
Lift up your eyes and look around;
all your children gather and come to you.
As surely as I live," declares the Lord,
"you will wear them all as ornaments;
you will put them on, like a bride.
19
"Though you were ruined and made desolate
and your land laid waste,
now you will be too small for your people,
and those who devoured you will be far away.
20
The children born during your bereavement
will yet say in your hearing,
'This place is too small for us;
give us more space to live in.'
21
Then you will say in your heart,
'Who bore me these?
I was bereaved and barren;
I was exiled and rejected.
Who brought these up?
I was left all alone,
but these—where have they come from?'"

July 13
Love for God
1 Peter 1:1–9

I have not seen Jesus, yet I believed,
He died for my salvation, which I humbly received.
Jesus, Your Word fills me with hope;
Any situation that I may find myself in, I will know how to cope.
For those who believe as I do, I always want to love,
comfort, and encourage them as well;

With Jesus, we will eternally dwell.
Though I have not seen You, I love You so.
I willingly tell others so they, too, will have the
opportunity of Your love to know.
We are one in the Father. We are one in the Son.
We are one as believers because of what Jesus has done.

How genuine is your love for Jesus?

1 Peter 1:1–9

1 Peter, an apostle of Jesus Christ,
To God's elect, exiles scattered throughout the provinces of Pontus, Galatia, Cappadocia, Asia and Bithynia, 2 who have been chosen according to the foreknowledge of God the Father, through the sanctifying work of the Spirit, to be obedient to Jesus Christ and sprinkled with his blood:
Grace and peace be yours in abundance.
Praise to God for a Living Hope
3 Praise be to the God and Father of our Lord Jesus Christ! In his great mercy he has given us new birth into a living hope through the resurrection of Jesus Christ from the dead, 4 and into an inheritance that can never perish, spoil or fade. This inheritance is kept in heaven for you, 5 who through faith are shielded by God's power until the coming of the salvation that is ready to be revealed in the last time. 6 In all this you greatly rejoice, though now for a little while you may have had to suffer grief in all kinds of trials. 7 These have come so that the proven genuineness of your faith—of greater worth than gold, which perishes even though refined by fire—may result in praise, glory and honor when Jesus Christ is revealed. 8 Though you have not seen him, you love him; and even though you do not see him now, you believe in him and are filled with an inexpressible and glorious joy, 9 for you are receiving the end result of your faith, the salvation of your souls.

Love for Others
July 14
Deuteronomy 10:12–22

Lord, thank You for blessing me to be a blessing to someone today.
How may I show them Your love in any small way?
Please let them experience Your love through me;
A love that will last for eternity.
Whatever their need might be,
Lord Jesus, let them find it by using me.
Thank You very much for an opportunity to share Your love.
Love comes only from God above.

Everyone needs Jesus's love.

Deuteronomy 10:12–22

Fear the Lord

12 And now, Israel, what does the Lord your God ask of you but to fear the Lord your God, to walk in obedience to him, to love him, to serve the Lord your God with all your heart and with all your soul, 13 and to observe the Lord's commands and decrees that I am giving you today for your own good? 14 To the Lord your God belong the heavens, even the highest heavens, the earth and everything in it. 15 Yet the Lord set his affection on your ancestors and loved them, and he chose you, their descendants, above all the nations—as it is today. 16 Circumcise your hearts, therefore, and do not be stiff-necked any longer. 17 For the Lord your God is God of gods and Lord of lords, the great God, mighty and awesome, who shows no partiality and accepts no bribes. 18 He defends the cause of the fatherless and the widow, and loves the foreigner residing among you, giving them food and clothing. 19 And you are to love those who are foreigners, for you yourselves were foreigners in Egypt. 20 Fear the Lord your God and serve him. Hold fast to him and take your oaths in his name. 21 He is the one you praise; he is your God, who performed for you those great and awesome wonders you saw with your own eyes.

22 Your ancestors who went down into Egypt were seventy in all, and now the Lord your God has made you as numerous as the stars in the sky.

July 15
Love
Luke 7:36–50

How do I love people I do not even know?
How do I let the love for them show?
How do I love someone who is different from me?
Will I have to do this for eternity?
Jesus loved with the greatest of ease;
I am sure it made the heavenly Father very pleased.
He looked beyond appearance, to the heart and the soul.
The love that Jesus gave was more precious than gold.
To see the beauty of the hearts and souls of people we encounter;
This will allow us to see them not for what they can do,
But for who they are, and this will be a blessing to you.

Loving is not always the easiest thing to do; however, when it is done right, there is nothing like the joy it brings.

Luke 7:36–50

Jesus Anointed by a Sinful Woman

36 When one of the Pharisees invited Jesus to have dinner with him, he went to the Pharisee's house and reclined at the table. 37 A woman in that town who lived a sinful life learned that Jesus was eating at the Pharisee's house, so she came there with an alabaster jar of perfume. 38 As she stood behind him at his feet weeping, she began to wet his feet with her tears. Then she wiped them with her hair, kissed them and poured perfume on them.

39 When the Pharisee who had invited him saw this, he said to himself, "If this man were a prophet, he would know who is touching him and what kind of woman she is—that she is a sinner."

40 Jesus answered him, "Simon, I have something to tell you."
"Tell me, teacher," he said.
41 "Two people owed money to a certain moneylender. One owed him five hundred denarii, and the other fifty. 42 Neither of them had the money to pay him back, so he forgave the debts of both. Now which of them will love him more?"
43 Simon replied, "I suppose the one who had the bigger debt forgiven."
"You have judged correctly," Jesus said.
44 Then he turned toward the woman and said to Simon, "Do you see this woman? I came into your house. You did not give me any water for my feet, but she wet my feet with her tears and wiped them with her hair. 45 You did not give me a kiss, but this woman, from the time I entered, has not stopped kissing my feet. 46 You did not put oil on my head, but she has poured perfume on my feet. 47 Therefore, I tell you, her many sins have been forgiven—as her great love has shown. But whoever has been forgiven little loves little."
48 Then Jesus said to her, "Your sins are forgiven."
49 The other guests began to say among themselves, "Who is this who even forgives sins?"
50 Jesus said to the woman, "Your faith has saved you; go in peace."

July 16
Love for Others
Romans 13:8–11

How do I love others?
How do I love them like Jesus, as God's holy Son?
How would I know when the love has begun?
What do I do to know that this is love and it is real?
How would I know that this is love that is healthy
and would not make someone ill?
Spiritual enablement is where love will begin.
This love will empower you to encourage others as a loving friend.
You will be able to love with the comfort and with care.

You will enable God to love through you,
because love is intended to be shared.

Everyone needs God's love.

Romans 13:8–11

Love Fulfills the Law
8 Let no debt remain outstanding, except the continuing debt to love one another, for whoever loves others has fulfilled the law.
9 The commandments, "You shall not commit adultery," "You shall not murder," "You shall not steal," "You shall not covet," and whatever other command there may be, are summed up in this one command: "Love your neighbor as yourself." 10 Love does no harm to a neighbor. Therefore love is the fulfillment of the law.
The Day Is Near
11 And do this, understanding the present time: The hour has already come for you to wake up from your slumber, because our salvation is nearer now than when we first believed.

July 17
Love of God
Christian Living/Love for Others
1 Corinthians 13

Love is not an emotion of how you feel; it is how you are to think.
To consider to be patient and kind, you may need to
remind yourself by writing it down in ink.
Now there will be times when considerable effort is
needed in order to do the things you must do.
This is the same kind of effort you will want others to show you.
To think to be respectful as you think about the interest of others too.
Remember others need to think the same way about you.
It is showing love to others when envy is not allowed to have its way.
Because boasting and being proud will want to have a field day.

Love will help you to think before you become angry
and record all the wrongs that have been done.
When others remind you of your wrongs, it is no fun.
Remember what Jesus did on the cross for you as God's beloved Son.
Love will help you remember that evil is wrong.
It will remind you that delighting in the truth will make you strong.
When you have faith and hope, love will surely be there.
Because love is from God, and that is how you know He cares.

Love comes from God. Everyone who loves has
been born of God and knows God.
1 John 4:7

1 Corinthians 13

13 If I speak in the tongues of men or of angels, but do not have love, I am only a resounding gong or a clanging cymbal. 2 If I have the gift of prophecy and can fathom all mysteries and all knowledge, and if I have a faith that can move mountains, but do not have love, I am nothing. 3 If I give all I possess to the poor and give over my body to hardship that I may boast, but do not have love, I gain nothing. 4 Love is patient, love is kind. It does not envy, it does not boast, it is not proud. 5 It does not dishonor others, it is not self-seeking, it is not easily angered, it keeps no record of wrongs. 6 Love does not delight in evil but rejoices with the truth. 7 It always protects, always trusts, always hopes, always perseveres. 8 Love never fails. But where there are prophecies, they will cease; where there are tongues, they will be stilled; where there is knowledge, it will pass away. 9 For we know in part and we prophesy in part, 10 but when completeness comes, what is in part disappears. 11 When I was a child, I talked like a child, I thought like a child, I reasoned like a child. When I became a man, I put the ways of childhood behind me. 12 For now we see only a reflection as in a mirror; then we shall see face to face. Now I know in part; then I shall know fully, even as I am fully known. 13 And now these three remain: faith, hope and love. But the greatest of these is love.

July 18
Love for Others
2 Corinthians 1:3–7

I will not focus on myself today.
I will focus on those who will need my comfort, and for them I will pray.
Lord, help me to see what needs they may have in
their trials and the troubles that they face.
I pray for words of comfort to share that will not make them feel disgrace.
I pray I can give them a hug, while extending them the gift of mercy
in Jesus's name, letting them know in Him there is no shame.
I want to serve in humility.
By sharing the love of Christ is a reality.
I want to share what was given to me,
Bringing comfort to those while on their journey to eternity.

What a comfort it is when people know you understand their pain.

2 Corinthians 1:3–7

Praise to the God of All Comfort

3 Praise be to the God and Father of our Lord Jesus Christ, the Father of compassion and the God of all comfort, 4 who comforts us in all our troubles, so that we can comfort those in any trouble with the comfort we ourselves receive from God. 5 For just as we share abundantly in the sufferings of Christ, so also our comfort abounds through Christ. 6 If we are distressed, it is for your comfort and salvation; if we are comforted, it is for your comfort, which produces in you patient endurance of the same sufferings we suffer. 7 And our hope for you is firm, because we know that just as you share in our sufferings, so also you share in our comfort.

July 19
Love for Others
Philippians 2:1–11

When I look at you, what do I see?
Is it someone who can benefit me?
From this perspective, it would not be of Christ.
Because I would have devalued your life.
Selfish ambition would have been the aim.
Vain conceit would have been how I would have played the mind game.
Valuing others above yourself is humility.
Love for others is the goal of eternity.
I need to see and treat people as Jesus would do;
That they are valued with love, and this is true.
Jesus, out of love, sacrificed His life for me,
and He sacrificed His life for you.
What a joy it is to learn how to love.
Love is only from God above.

How do you love others?

Philippians 2:1–11

Imitating Christ's Humility
2 Therefore if you have any encouragement from being united with Christ, if any comfort from his love, if any common sharing in the Spirit, if any tenderness and compassion, 2 then make my joy complete by being like-minded, having the same love, being one in spirit and of one mind. 3 Do nothing out of selfish ambition or vain conceit. Rather, in humility value others above yourselves, 4 not looking to your own interests but each of you to the interests of the others.
5 In your relationships with one another, have
the same mindset as Christ Jesus:
6
Who, being in very nature God,

did not consider equality with God something
to be used to his own advantage;

7

rather, he made himself nothing
by taking the very nature of a servant,
being made in human likeness.

8

And being found in appearance as a man,
he humbled himself
by becoming obedient to death—
even death on a cross!

9

Therefore God exalted him to the highest place
and gave him the name that is above every name,

10

that at the name of Jesus every knee should bow,
in heaven and on earth and under the earth,

11

and every tongue acknowledge that Jesus Christ is Lord,
to the glory of God the Father.

July 20
Loving Others
Living Like Christ
1 John 2:3–11

Darkness has a way of making the blind not see.
Not seeing it has a way of not making loving others as easy as it should be.
Being in darkness is continually hating, which is
disorienting, not knowing which way to go.
However, when you choose to love, because God is telling you so,
Love will not allow the darkness of unforgiveness,
frustration, and unfaithfulness to permit to be.
Choosing love instead of hate is God living inside you and me.

God's grace and mercy will make it possible for
you to know how to live in the light.
Loving others will become a delight.

It takes more effort to hate than it takes to love.
When you think of loving someone, how do
you see that as happening to you?

1 John 2:3–11

Love and Hatred for Fellow Believers

3 We know that we have come to know him if we keep his commands. 4 Whoever says, "I know him," but does not do what he commands is a liar, and the truth is not in that person. 5 But if anyone obeys his word, love for God is truly made complete in them. This is how we know we are in him: 6 Whoever claims to live in him must live as Jesus did.
7 Dear friends, I am not writing you a new command but an old one, which you have had since the beginning. This old command is the message you have heard. 8 Yet I am writing you a new command; its truth is seen in him and in you, because the darkness is passing and the true light is already shining.
9 Anyone who claims to be in the light but hates a brother or sister is still in the darkness. 10 Anyone who loves their brother and sister lives in the light, and there is nothing in them to make them stumble. 11 But anyone who hates a brother or sister is in the darkness and walks around in the darkness. They do not know where they are going, because the darkness has blinded them.

July 21
Love for Others
1 John 3:16–17

Love is a marvelous and magnificent thing that every person needs.
Love makes things grow and heals broken
hearts and lives with amazing speed.

Love comes from God, which every Christian would agree.
Being a true Christian is how love is given, so all will see.
It is given to others of sacrificial action and selfless generosity.
Love is very powerful when it is freely given to humanity.
This is the love Jesus gave to all who would believe
in Him and from sin would be set free.

Are you experiencing Christ's love in action because
you are allowing it to happen through you?

1 John 3:16–17

16 This is how we know what love is: Jesus Christ laid down his life for us. And we ought to lay down our lives for our brothers and sisters. 17 If anyone has material possessions and sees a brother or sister in need but has no pity on them, how can the love of God be in that person?

July 22
Love for Others
Confrontation
Proverbs 27:5–10

Love will feel like wounds when it comes from a friend.
Wounds from a friend can and will feel like sin.
When they tell us things that we need to hear.
They are doing this because their love for us is very dear.
They will also tell us the things that we like to hear.
When a friendship is based on honesty,
It is making love a reality.
The pain is benefiting you with the truth;
This is how God is to have a relationship with you.
Love without truth, what will it do?
Truth without love—is this what you need during
times of trouble, to make it through?
Remember the wounds from a friend;

These are not wounds that are caused from sin.

Wounds from a friend are needed in life to experience truth in love.

Proverbs 27:5–10

5
Better is open rebuke
than hidden love.
6
Wounds from a friend can be trusted,
but an enemy multiplies kisses.
7
One who is full loathes honey from the comb,
but to the hungry even what is bitter tastes sweet.
8
Like a bird that flees its nest
is anyone who flees from home.
9
Perfume and incense bring joy to the heart,
and the pleasantness of a friend
springs from their heartfelt advice.
10
Do not forsake your friend or a friend of your family,
and do not go to your relative's house when disaster strikes you—
better a neighbor nearby than a relative far away.

July 23
Love and Serving Others
James 1:22–27

To God's Word we must listen and do what it may say;
Loving and serving others is to obey.
To God, this is religion in helping those who are distressed;
The orphans and widows will receive help and rest and be refreshed.

To know how to serve others, from the pollution
of the world you must stay away;
These toxins will contaminate your faith in
Christ and cause you from him to stray.
Stay focused on him, and every day from God's Word obey.

How are you living for Christ?

James 1:22–27

22 Do not merely listen to the word, and so deceive yourselves. Do what it says. 23 Anyone who listens to the word but does not do what it says is like someone who looks at his face in a mirror 24 and, after looking at himself, goes away and immediately forgets what he looks like. 25 But whoever looks intently into the perfect law that gives freedom, and continues in it—not forgetting what they have heard, but doing it—they will be blessed in what they do. 26 Those who consider themselves religious and yet do not keep a tight rein on their tongues deceive themselves, and their religion is worthless. 27 Religion that God our Father accepts as pure and faultless is this: to look after orphans and widows in their distress and to keep oneself from being polluted by the world.

July 24
Racism
2 Corinthians 5:16–21

Divisiveness will keep hostility between those who do not understand;
The reason for unity in taking a stand;
To keep opposition of resistance from being in control;
To rule humanity without God's love will make the world feel cold.
Love for others is being in agreement to work together for peace.
Hatred will not have a place to grow, so it will cease.
Our differences are a gift from God that will meet each other's needs.
Opposition to love is hatred, and this behavior needs to stop indeed.

Every person wants to be loved.

2 Corinthians 5:16–21

16 So from now on we regard no one from a worldly point of view. Though we once regarded Christ in this way, we do so no longer. 17 Therefore, if anyone is in Christ, the new creation has come: The old has gone, the new is here! 18 All this is from God, who reconciled us to himself through Christ and gave us the ministry of reconciliation: 19 that God was reconciling the world to himself in Christ, not counting people's sins against them. And he has committed to us the message of reconciliation. 20 We are therefore Christ's ambassadors, as though God were making his appeal through us. We implore you on Christ's behalf: Be reconciled to God. 21 God made him who had no sin to be sin for us, so that in him we might become the righteousness of God.

Marriage
July 25
Prayer
1 Peter 3:7–12

Lord, as we start our day, let us get down on our knees and pray.
As the husband, let me be considerate of my wife, with respect.
At the end of this day, I will have no regrets.
I want to surrender all to You, so my prayers
to You today will not be hindered.
We pray that we will be like-minded in Christ.
This will help us in our decision in making them right.
Let us be sympathetic in expressing how one another feels.
Learning how to be empathetic will make it be very real.
Help us to be loving to each other, to be
compassionate, and to show humility.
Lord, I pray, please let this be true in me.
Please help us not repay evil for evil, or insults
with insults that will bring shame.

This is an evil game that will not bring praise to Your holy name.
Show me how to be a blessing, speaking words of life and not of deceit.
I want to speak in words that bring belief.
I want my actions not to be evil but good.
I pray I will do as a godly husband should.
I know Your eyes are watching and Your ears are listening too.
My wife and I are praying to be blessed to live godly today by You.

Talk to God; He is listening.

1 Peter 3:7–12

7 Husbands, in the same way be considerate as you live with your wives, and treat them with respect as the weaker partner and as heirs with you of the gracious gift of life, so that nothing will hinder your prayers.
Suffering for Doing Good
8 Finally, all of you, be like-minded, be sympathetic, love one another, be compassionate and humble. 9 Do not repay evil with evil or insult with insult. On the contrary, repay evil with blessing, because to this you were called so that you may inherit a blessing. 10 For,
"Whoever would love life
and see good days
must keep their tongue from evil
and their lips from deceitful speech.
11
They must turn from evil and do good;
they must seek peace and pursue it.
12
For the eyes of the Lord are on the righteous
and his ears are attentive to their prayer,
but the face of the Lord is against those who do evil."

Materialism
July 26
Idolatry
Matthew 6:24–34

Money, money, money; how much will I need of it today?
Not having enough money will make me worry, is what I have to say.
Worry, worry, worry because there is not enough
money is what I will do all day.
Then a little bird came and whispered in my ear,
"Do not worry about not having sufficient money, my dear."
Your heavenly Father will take good care of you.
You are very precious and of great worth to Him; know that this is true.
Whatever your needs may be.
God will provide for you, because He has always provided for me.

Money is not always worth the paper that it is written on;
however, God's provisions will always be enough.

Matthew 6:24–34

24 "No one can serve two masters. Either you will hate the one and love the other, or you will be devoted to the one and despise the other. You cannot serve both God and money.
Do Not Worry
25 "Therefore I tell you, do not worry about your life, what you will eat or drink; or about your body, what you will wear. Is not life more than food, and the body more than clothes? 26 Look at the birds of the air; they do not sow or reap or store away in barns, and yet your heavenly Father feeds them. Are you not much more valuable than they? 27 Can any one of you by worrying add a single hour to your life? 28 "And why do you worry about clothes? See how the flowers of the field grow. They do not labor or spin. 29 Yet I tell you that not even Solomon in all his splendor was dressed like one of these. 30 If that is how God clothes the grass of the field, which is here today and tomorrow is thrown into the fire, will he not much more clothe you—you of little

faith? 31 So do not worry, saying, 'What shall we eat?' or 'What shall we drink?' or 'What shall we wear?' 32 For the pagans run after all these things, and your heavenly Father knows that you need them. 33 But seek first his kingdom and his righteousness, and all these things will be given to you as well. 34 Therefore do not worry about tomorrow, for tomorrow will worry about itself. Each day has enough trouble of its own.

July 27
Priorities
Luke 12:22–34

Things, things, things; how they make my heart sing!
So many things, what do they bring?
Is this how success is supposed to be measured?
Is this how life should be treasured?
When they are all broken and have lost their use,
With them, what shall I do?
Into eternity these things I cannot take.
Having a lot of things, could it be a mistake?
Lord, please take this away from me.
Of the wanting of things of this life, I want to be free.
This is not what I want my life to be.
Things I do not need;
I would rather have a relationship with You, if You please.

Your relationship with Jesus Christ and with other believers is all you will be able to take into eternity.

Luke 12:22–34

Do Not Worry
22 Then Jesus said to his disciples: "Therefore I tell you, do not worry about your life, what you will eat; or about your body, what you will wear. 23 For life is more than food, and the body more than clothes. 24 Consider the ravens: They do not sow or

reap, they have no storeroom or barn; yet God feeds them. And how much more valuable you are than birds! 25 Who of you by worrying can add a single hour to your life? 26 Since you cannot do this very little thing, why do you worry about the rest?
27 "Consider how the wild flowers grow. They do not labor or spin. Yet I tell you, not even Solomon in all his splendor was dressed like one of these. 28 If that is how God clothes the grass of the field, which is here today, and tomorrow is thrown into the fire, how much more will he clothe you—you of little faith! 29 And do not set your heart on what you will eat or drink; do not worry about it. 30 For the pagan world runs after all such things, and your Father knows that you need them. 31 But seek his kingdom, and these things will be given to you as well.
32 "Do not be afraid, little flock, for your Father has been pleased to give you the kingdom. 33 Sell your possessions and give to the poor. Provide purses for yourselves that will not wear out, a treasure in heaven that will never fail, where no thief comes near and no moth destroys. 34 For where your treasure is, there your heart will be also.

Motives
July 28
Serving Others
Matthew 6:1–6

What are your motives when you are focused on praise?
Is it for Jesus, or for you, when your hands are raised?
Can your motives be perfect? Can they be true?
What are they when they are concentrated on you?
Think about why you give.
Is this why and how you live?
How, when, and why should you pray?
Is it to the Father the things you say?
Why do you fast?
If your motives for doing it will not last?
When you serve, is it done publicly for all to see?
Or do you serve anonymously?

We all have motives; this is for sure.
When your motives are tantamount to pleasing God, they will be pure.

Motives can have a way of wearing the mask of a facade.

Matthew 6:1–6

Giving to the Needy
6 "Be careful not to practice your righteousness in
front of others to be seen by them. If you do, you will
have no reward from your Father in heaven.
2 "So when you give to the needy, do not announce it with trumpets,
as the hypocrites do in the synagogues and on the streets, to be
honored by others. Truly I tell you, they have received their reward in
full. 3 But when you give to the needy, do not let your left hand know
what your right hand is doing, 4 so that your giving may be in secret.
Then your Father, who sees what is done in secret, will reward you.
Prayer
5 "And when you pray, do not be like the hypocrites, for they
love to pray standing in the synagogues and on the street corners
to be seen by others. Truly I tell you, they have received their
reward in full. 6 But when you pray, go into your room, close
the door and pray to your Father, who is unseen. Then your
Father, who sees what is done in secret, will reward you.

Obedience
July 29
Deuteronomy 5:28–33

Lord, I have failed to do whatever You have told me to.
That is sin that is against you.
How many times have I been led astray,
Because I did not do what Your Word says?
I will surrender my heart to You.
The Holy Spirit will help me in everything I will do.

He will work in me to enable me to do God's will and act accordingly,
Making it possible for me to fulfill God's purpose faithfully.
Obedience is the key to having a relationship
and living for God successfully.

Obedience is not hard when you are more focused on having
a relationship with God than doing what you want.

Deuteronomy 5:28–33

28 The Lord heard you when you spoke to me, and the Lord said to me, "I have heard what this people said to you. Everything they said was good. 29 Oh, that their hearts would be inclined to fear me and keep all my commands always, so that it might go well with them and their children forever! 30 "Go, tell them to return to their tents. 31 But you stay here with me so that I may give you all the commands, decrees and laws you are to teach them to follow in the land I am giving them to possess." 32 So be careful to do what the Lord your God has commanded you; do not turn aside to the right or to the left. 33 Walk in obedience to all that the Lord your God has commanded you, so that you may live and prosper and prolong your days in the land that you will possess.

July 30
Obedience
Deuteronomy 6:1–12

Be reminded daily how God is caring for you.
Be careful to obey what His Word has taught you to do.
Remember them as you go about your day.
Think of them when you go before God and pray.
Let God's Word be a part of you,
In all you say and all you do.
Be reminded daily of God's faithfulness to you.

In being reminded of God's faithfulness, it should
remind you of your faithfulness in obeying Him.

Deuteronomy 6:1–12

Love the Lord Your God

6 These are the commands, decrees and laws the Lord your God directed me to teach you to observe in the land that you are crossing the Jordan to possess, 2 so that you, your children and their children after them may fear the Lord your God as long as you live by keeping all his decrees and commands that I give you, and so that you may enjoy long life. 3 Hear, Israel, and be careful to obey so that it may go well with you and that you may increase greatly in a land flowing with milk and honey, just as the Lord, the God of your ancestors, promised you.
4 Hear, O Israel: The Lord our God, the Lord is one. 5 Love the Lord your God with all your heart and with all your soul and with all your strength. 6 These commandments that I give you today are to be on your hearts. 7 Impress them on your children. Talk about them when you sit at home and when you walk along the road, when you lie down and when you get up. 8 Tie them as symbols on your hands and bind them on your foreheads. 9 Write them on the doorframes of your houses and on your gates.
10 When the Lord your God brings you into the land he swore to your fathers, to Abraham, Isaac and Jacob, to give you—a land with large, flourishing cities you did not build, 11 houses filled with all kinds of good things you did not provide, wells you did not dig, and vineyards and olive groves you did not plant—then when you eat and are satisfied, 12 be careful that you do not forget the Lord, who brought you out of Egypt, out of the land of slavery.

July 31
Deuteronomy 30:11–20

The voice of God's heart wants us to obey.
So, the blessings He has for us will stay.

Choose to walk in obedience to God's Word, and you will know;
How to live and which way to go.
Obedience is the way to live life.
It is not about living in sacrifice.
When we choose not to obey, a life of death
and destruction will have its way.
It is a choice that only you can choose.
Living for God, there is no way you can lose.
God has made His demands clear.
Do not live because of the consequences that you fear.
Live to love God. That will always keep Him near.

It is always your choice what kind of life you will have: a life of obedience or a life of disobedience to God's blessings and love for you.

Deuteronomy 30:11–20

The Offer of Life or Death

11 Now what I am commanding you today is not too difficult for you or beyond your reach. 12 It is not up in heaven, so that you have to ask, "Who will ascend into heaven to get it and proclaim it to us so we may obey it?" 13 Nor is it beyond the sea, so that you have to ask, "Who will cross the sea to get it and proclaim it to us so we may obey it?" 14 No, the word is very near you; it is in your mouth and in your heart so you may obey it.
15 See, I set before you today life and prosperity, death and destruction. 16 For I command you today to love the Lord your God, to walk in obedience to him, and to keep his commands, decrees and laws; then you will live and increase, and the Lord your God will bless you in the land you are entering to possess. 17 But if your heart turns away and you are not obedient, and if you are drawn away to bow down to other gods and worship them, 18 I declare to you this day that you will certainly be destroyed. You will not live long in the land you are crossing the Jordan to enter and possess.
19 This day I call the heavens and the earth as witnesses against you that I have set before you life and death, blessings and curses.

Now choose life, so that you and your children may live 20 and that you may love the Lord your God, listen to his voice, and hold fast to him. For the Lord is your life, and he will give you many years in the land he swore to give to your fathers, Abraham, Isaac and Jacob.

August 1
Obedience
Sin
Jeremiah 7:1–11

Do you believe you sin?
Do any of your actions and ways need to be reformed and come to an end?
Do you trust in deceptive words and share with your friends?
To disobey God is something you do not want to do.
He is watching and will discipline you.
Like an intensely pungent herb that heals a
disease, God's Word is curative
for the human soul, body, and mind.
We need to feed on His Word by meditating on it all the time.
Walking in obedience will not be difficult, as you will find
God is watching what you will do.
He is watching because He loves you.
Obeying God's Word is not fighting against God's love.

Jeremiah 7:1–11

False Religion Worthless

7 This is the word that came to Jeremiah from the Lord: 2 "Stand at the gate of the Lord's house and there proclaim this message: "'Hear the word of the Lord, all you people of Judah who come through these gates to worship the Lord. 3 This is what the Lord Almighty, the God of Israel, says: Reform your ways and your actions, and I will let you live in this place. 4 Do not trust in deceptive words and say, "This is the temple of the Lord, the temple of the Lord, the temple of the Lord!" 5 If you really change

your ways and your actions and deal with each other justly, 6 if you do not
oppress the foreigner, the fatherless or the widow and do not shed innocent
blood in this place, and if you do not follow other gods to your own harm,
7 then I will let you live in this place, in the land I gave your ancestors for ever
and ever. 8 But look, you are trusting in deceptive words that are worthless.
9 "'Will you steal and murder, commit adultery and perjury,
burn incense to Baal and follow other gods you have not known,
10 and then come and stand before me in this house, which bears
my Name, and say, "We are safe"—safe to do all these detestable
things? 11 Has this house, which bears my Name, become a den
of robbers to you? But I have been watching! declares the Lord.

August 2
Spiritual Transformation
John 8:39–47

To have the facts to know the truth is one thing.
But to have the truth and not take action on
what the truth has revealed is another.
Learning the truth about Jesus and allowing that truth
to transform your life is spiritual growth.
What a world this will be when people who are looking
for the truth to know about their eternity,
Living a life of faith in Christ;
While thanking Him for His sacrifice;
You will experience being obedient in allowing Jesus to transform you.
You will have a life that will be filled with knowing the truth.

Knowing the truth can change your life.

John 8:39–47

39 "Abraham is our father," they answered.
"If you were Abraham's children," said Jesus, "then you would do what
Abraham did. 40 As it is, you are looking for a way to kill me, a man

who has told you the truth that I heard from God. Abraham did not do such things. 41 You are doing the works of your own father."

"We are not illegitimate children," they protested.

"The only Father we have is God himself."

42 Jesus said to them, "If God were your Father, you would love me, for I have come here from God. I have not come on my own; God sent me. 43 Why is my language not clear to you? Because you are unable to hear what I say. 44 You belong to your father, the devil, and you want to carry out your father's desires. He was a murderer from the beginning, not holding to the truth, for there is no truth in him. When he lies, he speaks his native language, for he is a liar and the father of lies. 45 Yet because I tell the truth, you do not believe me! 46 Can any of you prove me guilty of sin? If I am telling the truth, why don't you believe me? 47 Whoever belongs to God hears what God says. The reason you do not hear is that you do not belong to God."

August 3
Obedience
Trust in God
Jeremiah 1:4–9

God has a plan for your life.
He has something He wants you to do.
You must trust in Him to help you see it through.
This calling on your life you do not need to figure out to know what to do.
God will show you the way, but that depends on you.
Do not depend on your emotions; do not allow them to be your guide.
Remember, God will show you the way; He will always be at your side.
Be successful in obeying what God tells you to do;
This will not be easy, but always give God your very best.
Trust in God and allow Him to do the rest.

You were born with a purpose.

Jeremiah 1:4–9

The Call of Jeremiah
4 The word of the Lord came to me, saying,
5
"Before I formed you in the womb I knew you,
before you were born I set you apart;
I appointed you as a prophet to the nations."
6 "Alas, Sovereign Lord," I said, "I do not know
how to speak; I am too young."
7 But the Lord said to me, "Do not say, 'I am too young.' You must go to everyone I send you to and say whatever I command you. 8 Do not be afraid of them, for I am with you and will rescue you," declares the Lord.
9 Then the Lord reached out his hand and touched my mouth
and said to me, "I have put my words in your mouth.

August 4
Obedience
Jonah 4

A task has been laid before me to do today.
God, I do not want to do this, because I'd rather go out and play.
God has insisted that I must obey.
But, God, do I have a say?
This task is not for me. It will not be easy, and
I do not want to do it. Don't you see?
Contentment I will not find.
This task I must do is continually on my mind.
God, I ask for forgiveness for being disobedient and wasting my time.
To be obedient is all You have asked of me.
My attitude has been wrong. Now I can clearly see.
Tactical distractions were in control of me.
I will repent and obey completely.

It is better to obey God than to suffer the consequences of not doing so.

Jonah 4

Jonah's Anger at the Lord's Compassion

4 But to Jonah this seemed very wrong, and he became angry. 2 He prayed to the Lord, "Isn't this what I said, Lord, when I was still at home? That is what I tried to forestall by fleeing to Tarshish. I knew that you are a gracious and compassionate God, slow to anger and abounding in love, a God who relents from sending calamity. 3 Now, Lord, take away my life, for it is better for me to die than to live."

4 But the Lord replied, "Is it right for you to be angry?"

5 Jonah had gone out and sat down at a place east of the city. There he made himself a shelter, sat in its shade and waited to see what would happen to the city. 6 Then the Lord God provided a leafy plant and made it grow up over Jonah to give shade for his head to ease his discomfort, and Jonah was very happy about the plant. 7 But at dawn the next day God provided a worm, which chewed the plant so that it withered. 8 When the sun rose, God provided a scorching east wind, and the sun blazed on Jonah's head so that he grew faint.

He wantedto die, and said, "It would be better for me to die than to live." 9 But God said to Jonah, "Is it right for you to be angry about the plant?"

"It is," he said. "And I'm so angry I wish I were dead."

10 But the Lord said, "You have been concerned about this plant, though you did not tend it or make it grow. It sprang up overnight and died overnight. 11 And should I not have concern for the great city of Nineveh, in which there are more than a hundred and twenty thousand people who cannot tell their right hand from their left—and also many animals?"

Parenting

August 5
Stories of Faith
Psalm 78:1–8

You, my child, the stories of faith I will pass along to you.
The stories of how faith in God has brought each generation through.
Through the difficult and challenging times of life.

How that faith kept a relationship with God loving and spiritually right.
How obedience and faith in God brought us out
of darkness, into His wonderful light.
I want to teach you how to put your faith and
trust in God's Son, Jesus Christ.
Let Him become your Savior and Lord as you live your life.
It is a joy for me to teach you about having a life with God in eternity.
A life that was given to you from the hill of Calvary.

Pass the baton of faith to the next generation.

Psalm 78:1–8

A maskil of Asaph.
1
My people, hear my teaching;
listen to the words of my mouth.
2
I will open my mouth with a parable;
I will utter hidden things, things from of old—
3
things we have heard and known,
things our ancestors have told us.
4
We will not hide them from their descendants;
we will tell the next generation
the praiseworthy deeds of the Lord,
his power, and the wonders he has done.
5
He decreed statutes for Jacob
and established the law in Israel,
which he commanded our ancestors
to teach their children,
6
so the next generation would know them,
even the children yet to be born,

and they in turn would tell their children.

7

Then they would put their trust in God
and would not forget his deeds
but would keep his commands.

8

They would not be like their ancestors—
a stubborn and rebellious generation,
whose hearts were not loyal to God,
whose spirits were not faithful to him.

August 6
The Love of God
Luke 15:11–24

My child, My child, how I love you.
Please come home today.
Please come home to stay.
There is no gift that I possessed that is so precious and dear to Me.
There is no treasure that I may keep for a life of eternity.
You are that treasure that I hold so dear.
You are that treasure; I want to make that very clear.

To love you forever will bring pure joy to Me.
Come home, My child, come home to Me.
Because I want to love you and have a life with you for an eternity.
The past is over, and there is nothing that has to be done.
All that was done wrong has been left to God's holy Son.
He alone can make right what was wrong; He will make it right.
Trust in Him, because He is love and He is the Light.
Come home, My child; come home, My child; come home with Me today.
There is nothing else that I need to say.
Come home; I just want to love you, I pray.

Love was meant to last for eternity.

Luke 15:11–24

The Parable of the Lost Son

11 Jesus continued: "There was a man who had two sons. 12 The younger one said to his father, 'Father, give me my share of the estate.' So he divided his property between them.

13 "Not long after that, the younger son got together all he had, set off for a distant country and there squandered his wealth in wild living. 14 After he had spent everything, there was a severe famine in that whole country, and he began to be in need. 15 So he went and hired himself out to a citizen of that country, who sent him to his fields to feed pigs. 16 He longed to fill his stomach with the pods that the pigs were eating, but no one gave him anything.

17 "When he came to his senses, he said, 'How many of my father's hired servants have food to spare, and here I am starving to death! 18 I will set out and go back to my father and say to him: Father, I have sinned against heaven and against you. 19 I am no longer worthy to be called your son; make me like one of your hired servants.' 20 So he got up and went to his father.

"But while he was still a long way off, his father saw him and was filled with compassion for him; he ran to his son, threw his arms around him and kissed him.

21 "The son said to him, 'Father, I have sinned against heaven and against you. I am no longer worthy to be called your son.' 22 "But the father said to his servants, 'Quick! Bring the best robe and put it on him. Put a ring on his finger and sandals on his feet. 23 Bring the fattened calf and kill it. Let's have a feast and celebrate. 24 For this son of mine was dead and is alive again; he was lost and is found.' So they began to celebrate.

Patience
August 7
Galatians 5:13–26

I plan to get various things done today.
What do I do when people get in my way?
Jesus, will You help me not to be annoyed?
This is what I want to avoid.
Help me to avoid strife.
This will not help me to do what is right.
Please help me not to yield to rage.
Irritation will encourage me to become engaged.
Help me to be wise and remain calm to the day's end.
Then I will say that I have not given in to sin.

Self-control and patience are fruit of the Spirit that everyone enjoys, whether you the recipient or the giver.

Galatians 5:13–26

Life by the Spirit
13 You, my brothers and sisters, were called to be free. But do not use your freedom to indulge the flesh; rather, serve one another humbly in love. 14 For the entire law is fulfilled in keeping this one command: "Love your neighbor as yourself." 15 If you bite and devour each other, watch out or you will be destroyed by each other. 16 So I say, walk by the Spirit, and you will not gratify the desires of the flesh. 17 For the flesh desires what is contrary to the Spirit, and the Spirit what is contrary to the flesh. They are in conflict with each other, so that you are not to do whatever you want. 18 But if you are led by the Spirit, you are not under the law. 19 The acts of the flesh are obvious: sexual immorality, impurity and debauchery; 20 idolatry and witchcraft; hatred, discord, jealousy, fits of rage, selfish ambition, dissensions, factions 21 and envy; drunkenness, orgies, and the like. I warn you, as I did before, that those who live like this will not inherit the kingdom of God.

22 But the fruit of the Spirit is love, joy, peace, forbearance, kindness, goodness, faithfulness, 23 gentleness and self-control. Against such things there is no law. 24 Those who belong to Christ Jesus have crucified the flesh with its passions and desires. 25 Since we live by the Spirit, let us keep in step with the Spirit. 26 Let us not become conceited, provoking and envying each other.

Personal Behavior
August 8
Living Like Christ
Psalm 34:11–18

If I spoke like Jesus, what would I say?
If I spoke like Jesus, God, I would always pray and be willing to obey.
If I behaved like Jesus, I would love life and desire to see many good days.
Then my behavior should continue to always be this way.
If I thought like Jesus, evil would have no part of me.
I would do good in seeking peace. I would pursue it until eternity.
God, to speak and behave like Jesus, on my mouth I need a muzzle.
This will prevent me from saying those things that
will confuse and leave people feeling puzzled.
God hears when I cry.
He listens to what my tears are saying.
He will answer me without delaying.

If you spoke your own words to yourself, what would you hear?

Psalm 34:11–18

11
Come, my children, listen to me;
I will teach you the fear of the Lord.
12
Whoever of you loves life
and desires to see many good days,

¹³
keep your tongue from evil
and your lips from telling lies.
¹⁴
Turn from evil and do good;
seek peace and pursue it.
¹⁵
The eyes of the Lord are on the righteous,
and his ears are attentive to their cry;
¹⁶
but the face of the Lord is against those who do evil,
to blot out their name from the earth.
¹⁷
The righteous cry out, and the Lord hears them;
he delivers them from all their troubles.
¹⁸
The Lord is close to the brokenhearted
and saves those who are crushed in spirit.

Persecution
August 9
Acts 6:8–15; 7:59–60

To walk in Jesus's steps of persecution and suffering takes sacrificial faith.
This is the type of faith that will show love and not hate.
You will be filled with God's power and grace.
The Spirit will give you wisdom that the opposition does not want to face.
Those who have been martyred for their faith were met with brutality.
This is a way of life that living in your faith can become a reality.
Lord God, gives us the strength to confront and
endure the pain that persecution brings;
Because we want to worship Jesus Christ, our eternal King.
Let our groans of pain from suffering become songs of joy to sing.

In following Jesus, it is a journey that leads to a path of suffering.

Acts 6:8–15

Stephen Seized

8 Now Stephen, a man full of God's grace and power, performed great wonders and signs among the people. 9 Opposition arose, however, from members of the Synagogue of the Freedmen (as it was called)—Jews of Cyrene and Alexandria as well as the provinces of Cilicia and Asia—who began to argue with Stephen. 10 But they could not stand up against the wisdom the Spirit gave him as he spoke.
11 Then they secretly persuaded some men to say, "We have heard Stephen speak blasphemous words against Moses and against God."
12 So they stirred up the people and the elders and the teachers of the law. They seized Stephen and brought him before the Sanhedrin.
13 They produced false witnesses, who testified, "This fellow never stops speaking against this holy place and against the law. 14 For we have heard him say that this Jesus of Nazareth will destroy this place and change the customs Moses handed down to us."
15 All who were sitting in the Sanhedrin looked intently at Stephen, and they saw that his face was like the face of an angel.

Acts 7:59–60

59 While they were stoning him, Stephen prayed, "Lord Jesus, receive my spirit." 60 Then he fell on his knees and cried out, "Lord, do not hold this sin against them." When he had said this, he fell asleep.

August 10
Evangelism/God's Care
Jeremiah 1:1–10

Whatever the struggles, you are facing in living for Christ today,
God knows that there will be times in the midst of your struggles when there may seem to be no way.
No way to do what He has sent you to do.
Hold on to your faith as God takes you through.
Through challenges and struggles He will always be with you.

Nothing you will do for God will be in vain.
When you experience God's presence, you will never be the same.
For the committed Christian, persecution is a way of life.
Remember the cross of your Lord Jesus Christ.
No matter the challenges and struggles you are going through,
Know that God will always be with you.

"Blessed are those who are persecuted because of
righteousness, for theirs is the kingdom of heaven."
Matthew 5:10

Jeremiah 1:1–10

1 The words of Jeremiah son of Hilkiah, one of the priests at Anathoth in the territory of Benjamin. 2 The word of the Lord came to him in the thirteenth year of the reign of Josiah son of Amon king of Judah, 3 and through the reign of Jehoiakim son of Josiah king of Judah, down to the fifth month of the eleventh year of Zedekiah son of Josiah king of Judah, when the people of Jerusalem went into exile.
The Call of Jeremiah
4 The word of the Lord came to me, saying,
5
"Before I formed you in the womb I knew you,
before you were born I set you apart;
I appointed you as a prophet to the nations."
6 "Alas, Sovereign Lord," I said, "I do not know
how to speak; I am too young."
7 But the Lord said to me, "Do not say, 'I am too young.' You must go to everyone I send you to and say whatever I command you. 8 Do not be afraid of them, for I am with you and will rescue you," declares the Lord. 9 Then the Lord reached out his hand and touched my mouth and said to me, "I have put my words in your mouth. 10 See, today I appoint you over nations and kingdoms to uproot and tear down, to destroy and overthrow, to build and to plant."

Prayer
August 11
Psalm 46

Today's list is completed.
I know I will be as busy as a honeybee.
I know I need to slow down and take a rest.
This is the only way to give God my very best.
I need to be still, stop striving, and be at rest.
I need to listen to God. This can be challenging at best.
God, please help me to know how to get off my feet.
I need to be quiet, calm, and serene;
To listen to God, so He will not have to scream.
Now I am focusing, putting everything to the side.
God, I am listening, because I wish to abide

To know God, you need to be still.

Psalm 46

For the director of music. Of the Sons of Korah.
According to alamoth. A song.
1
God is our refuge and strength,
an ever-present help in trouble.
2
Therefore we will not fear, though the earth give way
and the mountains fall into the heart of the sea,
3
though its waters roar and foam
and the mountains quake with their surging.
4
There is a river whose streams make glad the city of God,
the holy place where the Most High dwells.

5
God is within her, she will not fall;
God will help her at break of day.
6
Nations are in uproar, kingdoms fall;
he lifts his voice, the earth melts.
7
The Lord Almighty is with us;
the God of Jacob is our fortress.
8
Come and see what the Lord has done,
the desolations he has brought on the earth.
9
He makes wars cease
to the ends of the earth.
He breaks the bow and shatters the spear;
he burns the shields with fire.
10
He says, "Be still, and know that I am God;
I will be exalted among the nations,
I will be exalted in the earth."
11
The Lord Almighty is with us;
the God of Jacob is our fortress.

August 12
Praying
Psalm 71:1–12

God, to You I will pray.
I am facing the encountering of terrible threats on my life this very day.
I do not know what it is that I need to do.
Lord God, I am in need of You.
The enemy is closing in.
They are convinced that they will overtake me and win.

I cannot do this alone. Please be near.
God, I am filled with much fear.
I know I may not be delivered from every situation that I will face.
I am so grateful for Your saving grace.
I know that You hear my prayers every time that I pray.
I know that You will come alongside me today.

It is comforting to know that you can call on God, and He will answer.

Psalm 71:1–12

1
In you, Lord, I have taken refuge;
let me never be put to shame.
2
In your righteousness, rescue me and deliver me;
turn your ear to me and save me.
3
Be my rock of refuge,
to which I can always go;
give the command to save me,
for you are my rock and my fortress.
4
Deliver me, my God, from the hand of the wicked,
from the grasp of those who are evil and cruel.
5
For you have been my hope, Sovereign Lord,
my confidence since my youth.
6
From birth I have relied on you;
you brought me forth from my mother's womb.
I will ever praise you.
7
I have become a sign to many;
you are my strong refuge.

8
My mouth is filled with your praise,
declaring your splendor all day long.
9
Do not cast me away when I am old;
do not forsake me when my strength is gone.
10
For my enemies speak against me;
those who wait to kill me conspire together.
11
They say, "God has forsaken him;
pursue him and seize him,
for no one will rescue him."
12
Do not be far from me, my God;
come quickly, God, to help me.

August 13
Pray
Psalm 91

Before I start my day, I must get on my knees and pray.
I do not know what the day may bring,
I find out I must pray and bring everything before the King of Kings.
It does not matter how often I may need to pray;
I know I must go to God, for this is the only way
to tend to my problems, whatever they may be.
I know God is always waiting to hear and answer me.

Every day bring everything to God in prayer;
for He always has your attention.

Psalm 91

1
Whoever dwells in the shelter of the Most High
will rest in the shadow of the Almighty.
2
I will say of the Lord, "He is my refuge and my fortress,
my God, in whom I trust."
3
Surely he will save you
from the fowler's snare
and from the deadly pestilence.
4
He will cover you with his feathers,
and under his wings you will find refuge;
his faithfulness will be your shield and rampart.
5
You will not fear the terror of night,
nor the arrow that flies by day,
6
nor the pestilence that stalks in the darkness,
nor the plague that destroys at midday.
7
A thousand may fall at your side,
ten thousand at your right hand,
but it will not come near you.
8
You will only observe with your eyes
and see the punishment of the wicked.
9
If you say, "The Lord is my refuge,"
and you make the Most High your dwelling,
10
no harm will overtake you,
no disaster will come near your tent.

11
For he will command his angels concerning you
to guard you in all your ways;
12
they will lift you up in their hands,
so that you will not strike your foot against a stone.
13
You will tread on the lion and the cobra;
you will trample the great lion and the serpent.
14
"Because he loves me," says the Lord, "I will rescue him;
I will protect him, for he acknowledges my name.
15
He will call on me, and I will answer him;
I will be with him in trouble,
I will deliver him and honor him.
16
With long life I will satisfy him
and show him my salvation."

August 14
Prayer
Psalm 122:6–9

Lord, I want and need to pray for my nation.
I pray for those who are in authority and those who make regulations.
I pray for Your peace and for Your patience.
As I pray for Your intervention, we need repentance.
Lord, You have been good to us in meeting all our needs.
Yes, You have been good to us indeed.
Please help us to be good stewards with our assets.
You are faithful, loving, and merciful, and You know what is best.
God, we need You, I must confess.

Pray for our nation to worship the Son of God, Jesus Christ.

Psalm 122:6–9

6
Pray for the peace of Jerusalem:
"May those who love you be secure.
7
May there be peace within your walls
and security within your citadels."
8
For the sake of my family and friends,
I will say, "Peace be within you."
9
For the sake of the house of the Lord our God,
I will seek your prosperity.

August 15
Prayer
1 Kings 18:41–45

Great expectations, a humble, persistent prayer will do.
Be determined to pray, regardless of your limitations too.
The earnest prayer of a righteous person has
great power, because God will hear.
Seeing what it will produce with wonderful results will
let you know that God answers, and it is very clear.
Faithfully make it an aim
to fill your life with persistent and persevering prayer, and never change.
God is faithful in answering prayers; however,
how faithful are you in praying.
Have you talked to God today?

An earnest prayer will get God's attention.

1 Kings 18:41–45

41 And Elijah said to Ahab, "Go, eat and drink, for there is the sound of a heavy rain." 42 So Ahab went off to eat and drink, but Elijah climbed to the top of Carmel, bent down to the ground and put his face between his knees.
43 "Go and look toward the sea," he told his servant. And he went up and looked.
"There is nothing there," he said.
Seven times Elijah said, "Go back."
44 The seventh time the servant reported, "A cloud as small as a man's hand is rising from the sea."
So Elijah said, "Go and tell Ahab, 'Hitch up your chariot and go down before the rain stops you.'"
45 Meanwhile, the sky grew black with clouds, the wind rose, a heavy rain started falling and Ahab rode off to Jezreel.

August 16
Prayer
2 Chronicles 6:12–21

I will pray.
I will pray about God today.
I will not concentrate on my needs.
I will concentrate on praising God while on bended knees.
I will humble myself before Almighty God and say,
"You are holy, and there is none like You. I always want to worship You with praise all day.
You are perfect and awesome in all You do.
Lord God, I desire to bring true worship to You.
I know You love and care dearly for me.
I want to thank You; from sin, You have set me free.
There is something my heart desires to ask of You.
Please keep me meek and humble in all I say and do."

Pray while focusing more on who God is instead of what He can do.

2 Chronicles 6:12–21

Solomon's Prayer of Dedication

12 Then Solomon stood before the altar of the Lord in front of the whole assembly of Israel and spread out his hands. 13 Now he had made a bronze platform, five cubits long, five cubits wide and three cubits high, and had placed it in the center of the outer court. He stood on the platform and then knelt down before the whole assembly of Israel and spread out his hands toward heaven. 14 He said: "Lord, the God of Israel, there is no God like you in heaven or on earth—you who keep your covenant of love with your servants who continue wholeheartedly in your way. 15 You have kept your promise to your servant David my father; with your mouth you have promised and with your hand you have fulfilled it—as it is today.

16 "Now, Lord, the God of Israel, keep for your servant David my father the promises you made to him when you said, 'You shall never fail to have a successor to sit before me on the throne of Israel, if only your descendants are careful in all they do to walk before me according to my law, as you have done.' 17 And now, Lord, the God of Israel, let your word that you promised your servant David come true.

18 "But will God really dwell on earth with humans? The heavens, even the highest heavens, cannot contain you. How much less this temple I have built! 19 Yet, Lord my God, give attention to your servant's prayer and his plea for mercy. Hear the cry and the prayer that your servant is praying in your presence. 20 May your eyes be open toward this temple day and night, this place of which you said you would put your Name there. May you hear the prayer your servant prays toward this place. 21 Hear the supplications of your servant and of your people Israel when they pray toward this place. Hear from heaven, your dwelling place; and when you hear, forgive.

August 17
Prayer
2 Chronicles 13:10–18

Now is the time to pray, because challenges have come my way.
Relying on God is what I must do.
Only He can bring me through.
The battle is on, and I do not know how I am to fight.
Lord Jesus, I pray to You for spiritual insight.
Jesus, I trust Your presence will be here.
My faith in You, I will always treasure, because it is very dear.
I want to thank You in advance for my victory.
Lord Jesus, You are all I will ever need. I am
glad Your presence is here with me.

How has Jesus proved Himself faithful to you?

2 Chronicles 13:10–18

10 "As for us, the Lord is our God, and we have not forsaken him. The priests who serve the Lord are sons of Aaron, and the Levites assist them. 11 Every morning and evening they present burnt offerings and fragrant incense to the Lord. They set out the bread on the ceremonially clean table and light the lamps on the gold lampstand every evening. We are observing the requirements of the Lord our God. But you have forsaken him. 12 God is with us; he is our leader. His priests with their trumpets will sound the battle cry against you. People of Israel, do not fight against the Lord, the God of your ancestors, for you will not succeed." 13 Now Jeroboam had sent troops around to the rear, so that while he was in front of Judah the ambush was behind them. 14 Judah turned and saw that they were being attacked at both front and rear. Then they cried out to the Lord. The priests blew their trumpets 15 and the men of Judah raised the battle cry. At the sound of their battle cry, God routed Jeroboam and all Israel before Abijah and Judah. 16 The Israelites fled before Judah, and God delivered them into their hands. 17 Abijah and his troops inflicted heavy losses on them, so that there

were five hundred thousand casualties among Israel's able men. 18 The Israelites were subdued on that occasion, and the people of Judah were victorious because they relied on the Lord, the God of their ancestors.

August 18
Prayer
Matthew 6:5–10

I will pray to God today.
However, I am not sure what I will say.
God, no matter what I will say, I will tell You my all anyway.
I know You will patiently listen to everything I will bring You.
I will do everything You will tell me to.
My soul will be released to speak in freedom as I please.
I will share everything with You while here on my bended knees.
When I am done, before the Father, I came
to Him through Jesus, His Son.
My secrets are safe; my mind has been set free.
Prayer has given my heavenly Father and me a
relationship that will last throughout eternity.

It feels good when I have taken everything to God in prayer.

Matthew 6:5–10

Prayer

5 "And when you pray, do not be like the hypocrites, for they love to pray standing in the synagogues and on the street corners to be seen by others. Truly I tell you, they have received their reward in full. 6 But when you pray, go into your room, close the door and pray to your Father, who is unseen. Then your Father, who sees what is done in secret, will reward you. 7 And when you pray, do not keep on babbling like pagans, for they think they will be heard because of their many words. 8 Do not be like them, for your Father knows what you need before you ask him. 9 "This, then, is how you should pray:

"'Our Father in heaven,
hallowed be your name,
10
your kingdom come,
your will be done,
on earth as it is in heaven.

August 19
Prayer
Matthew 16:1–4

Most would agree: Prayer is important when you are in need,
Especially if it is for guidance in knowing which way you should go.
But how do you pray when you do not know?
Do you ask for signs so you will know the way?
Or do you seek feelings as you pray?
Staying focused on God's nature is the way.
The more you learn about who God is and His
attributes, the more you will know how to pray.
By developing a relationship with the Father,
signs or feeling you will not need.
The more you learn about the attributes of God,
how you pray will change indeed.

Remember, God knows who you are, but how well do you know Him?

Matthew 16:1–4

The Demand for a Sign
16 The Pharisees and Sadducees came to Jesus and tested
him by asking him to show them a sign from heaven.
2 He replied, "When evening comes, you say, 'It will be fair weather,
for the sky is red,' 3 and in the morning, 'Today it will be stormy, for
the sky is red and overcast.' You know how to interpret the appearance
of the sky, but you cannot interpret the signs of the times. 4 A wicked

and adulterous generation looks for a sign, but none will be given it except the sign of Jonah." Jesus then left them and went away.

August 20
Prayer
Doctrine of God
Ephesians 3:14–21

I want to pray God's blessings over your life today.
I pray that you will be strengthened through God's Spirit as you obey.
I request you will grasp and experience the
depth of Christ's love as a treasure.
His love for you cannot be measured.
I pray you will embrace that which has been given to you:
Forgiveness, hope, and encouragement too.
I pray that God will give you the power to live
a new life filled with the truth.
Your expectations are limited if they are measured.
God's power cannot be measured; embrace
this as a blessing to be treasured.

Remember, God is bigger than your imagination.

Ephesians 3:14–21

A Prayer for the Ephesians
14 For this reason I kneel before the Father, 15 from whom every family in heaven and on earth derives its name. 16 I pray that out of his glorious riches he may strengthen you with power through his Spirit in your inner being, 17 so that Christ may dwell in your hearts through faith. And I pray that you, being rooted and established in love, 18 may have power, together with all the Lord's holy people, to grasp how wide and long and high and deep is the love of Christ, 19 and to know this love that surpasses knowledge— that you may be filled to the measure of all the fullness of God.

20 Now to him who is able to do immeasurably more than all we ask or imagine, according to his power that is at work within us, 21 to him be glory in the church and in Christ Jesus throughout all generations, for ever and ever! Amen.

August 21
Prayer
1 Thessalonians 5:12–28

Intimacy with God is what prayer will do for you.
It will be time well spent as you tell Him what you are going through.
Unload your heart of all its hurt and pain.
As your intimacy grows, you will never be the same.
Tell Him of your troubles, weaknesses, needs, and temptations.
In the time of intimacy with God, He will give you new revelations.
Intimacy with God is what prayer will do for you.
It is experiencing God and His Word, the Living Truth.
Jesus often withdrew to lonely places and prayed.
Luke 5:16

1 Thessalonians 5:12–28

Final Instructions
12 Now we ask you, brothers and sisters, to acknowledge those who work hard among you, who care for you in the Lord and who admonish you. 13 Hold them in the highest regard in love because of their work. Live in peace with each other. 14 And we urge you, brothers and sisters, warn those who are idle and disruptive, encourage the disheartened, help the weak, be patient with everyone. 15 Make sure that nobody pays back wrong for wrong, but always strive to do what is good for each other and for everyone else. 16 Rejoice always, 17 pray continually, 18 give thanks in all circumstances; for this is God's will for you in Christ Jesus.

19 Do not quench the Spirit. 20 Do not treat prophecies with contempt 21 but test them all; hold on to what is good, 22 reject every kind of evil. 23 May God himself, the God of peace, sanctify you through and through. May your whole spirit, soul and body be kept blameless at the coming of our Lord Jesus Christ. 24 The one who calls you is faithful, and he will do it. 25 Brothers and sisters, pray for us. 26 Greet all God's people with a holy kiss. 27 I charge you before the Lord to have this letter read to all the brothers and sisters. 28 The grace of our Lord Jesus Christ be with you.

August 22
Prayer
Fellowship with God
Matthew 14:13–23

In a relationship with God, don't become haggard and hurried;
Instead, come to rest in Him and leave behind your worries.
In Him, you will find your rest.
No matter the circumstances, He will enable you to do your very best.
In fellowshipping with God, each day, you need to nurture a bond.
A bond that will cultivate growing closer to Him
is through a relationship with His Son.
Taking time to be alone with Him each day to
experience His strength and fulfillment.
As you draw near to God, your mind will be refreshed and renewed.
It will bring much needed rest to you.

Time alone with God is a time that is never wasted.

Matthew 14:13–23

Jesus Feeds the Five Thousand
13 When Jesus heard what had happened, he withdrew by boat privately to a solitary place. Hearing of this, the crowds followed

him on foot from the towns. 14 When Jesus landed and saw a large crowd, he had compassion on them and healed their sick. 15 As evening approached, the disciples came to him and said, "This is a remote place, and it's already getting late. Send the crowds away, so they can go to the villages and buy themselves some food." 16 Jesus replied, "They do not need to go away. You give them something to eat." 17 "We have here only five loaves of bread and two fish," they answered. 18 "Bring them here to me," he said. 19 And he directed the people to sit down on the grass. Taking the five loaves and the two fish and looking up to heaven, he gave thanks and broke the loaves. Then he gave them to the disciples, and the disciples gave them to the people. 20 They all ate and were satisfied, and the disciples picked up twelve basketfuls of broken pieces that were left over. 21 The number of those who ate was about five thousand men, besides women and children.

Jesus Walks on the Water

22 Immediately Jesus made the disciples get into the boat and go on ahead of him to the other side, while he dismissed the crowd. 23 After he had dismissed them, he went up on a mountainside by himself to pray. Later that night, he was there alone,

August 23
Prayer
God's Care
Matthew 6:25–34

All my needs have been met today.
I will thank the Lord as I pray.
There will be no worries for me.
God has met all of my needs faithfully.
Night and day, He is always there.
I trust Him; He will never abandon me, because He cares.
He knows me intimately and knows when I am in
need. Yes, God faithfully cares for me indeed.

What a privilege to know God will take care of those who belong to Him.

Matthew 6:25–34

Do Not Worry

25 "Therefore I tell you, do not worry about your life, what you will eat or drink; or about your body, what you will wear. Is not life more than food, and the body more than clothes? 26 Look at the birds of the air; they do not sow or reap or store away in barns, and yet your heavenly Father feeds them. Are you not much more valuable than they? 27 Can any one of you by worrying add a single hour to your life? 28 "And why do you worry about clothes? See how the flowers of the field grow. They do not labor or spin. 29 Yet I tell you that not even Solomon in all his splendor was dressed like one of these. 30 If that is how God clothes the grass of the field, which is here today and tomorrow is thrown into the fire, will he not much more clothe you—you of little faith? 31 So do not worry, saying, 'What shall we eat?' or 'What shall we drink?' or 'What shall we wear?' 32 For the pagans run after all these things, and your heavenly Father knows that you need them. 33 But seek first his kingdom and his righteousness, and all these things will be given to you as well. 34 Therefore do not worry about tomorrow, for tomorrow will worry about itself. Each day has enough trouble of its own.

August 24
Prayer
Matthew 26:39–42; 27:45–46

When you tell God what is on your heart and mind,
Know that when you receive an answer, it is always in His time.
We must relinquish our rights to let God do what is best.
Know that by trusting Him, you will be put to the test.
Knowing what you do not know and what you cannot see;
You just have to trust God and let it be.
Know as you trust in God, He is listening and will do what is best for you.
This is what prayer is meant to do.
Once you understand what prayer is and how to pray,

You will be talking to God each and every day.

When you are in a position to pray, God is in a position to listen.

Matthew 26:39–42

39 Going a little farther, he fell with his face to the ground and prayed, "My Father, if it is possible, may this cup be taken from me. Yet not as I will, but as you will." 40 Then he returned to his disciples and found them sleeping. "Couldn't you men keep watch with me for one hour?" he asked Peter. 41 "Watch and pray so that you will not fall into temptation. The spirit is willing, but the flesh is weak." 42 He went away a second time and prayed, "My Father, if it is not possible for this cup to be taken away unless I drink it, may your will be done."

Matthew 27:45–46

The Death of Jesus
45 From noon until three in the afternoon darkness came over all the land. 46 About three in the afternoon Jesus cried out in a loud voice, "Eli, Eli, lema sabachthani?" (which means "My God, my God, why have you forsaken me?").

August 25
Holy Spirit Intercession
Romans 8:22–34

Spiritual warfare is so thick,
It is paralyzing and is making me sick.
I cannot face and fight this alone.
I do not possess the strength; it is all gone.
Jesus, Jesus, hear me, please,
As I pray to You while on bended knees.
Thank You and the Holy Spirit for interceding before the Father for me;

> I will be thanking You for eternity.
> Knowing You are always praying for me is so
> amazing, astonishing, and extraordinary too.
> Jesus, I am so in need of You.
> Thank You, for loving me so;
> This is something that I want to always know.

When you are not praying, Jesus and the Holy Spirit are.

Romans 8:22–34

22 We know that the whole creation has been groaning as in the pains of childbirth right up to the present time. 23 Not only so, but we ourselves, who have the firstfruits of the Spirit, groan inwardly as we wait eagerly for our adoption to sonship, the redemption of our bodies. 24 For in this hope we were saved. But hope that is seen is no hope at all. Who hopes for what they already have? 25 But if we hope for what we do not yet have, we wait for it patiently.
26 In the same way, the Spirit helps us in our weakness. We do not know what we ought to pray for, but the Spirit himself intercedes for us through wordless groans. 27 And he who searches our hearts knows the mind of the Spirit, because the Spirit intercedes for God's people in accordance with the will of God.
28 And we know that in all things God works for the good of those who love him, who have been called according to his purpose. 29 For those God foreknew he also predestined to be conformed to the image of his Son, that he might be the firstborn among many brothers and sisters. 30 And those he predestined, he also called; those he called, he also justified; those he justified, he also glorified.

More Than Conquerors

31 What, then, shall we say in response to these things? If God is for us, who can be against us? 32 He who did not spare his own Son, but gave him up for us all—how will he not also, along with him, graciously give us all things? 33 Who will bring any charge against those whom God has chosen? It is God who justifies. 34 Who then is the one who

condemns? No one. Christ Jesus who died—more than that, who was raised to life—is at the right hand of God and is also interceding for us.

August 26
Prayer
Rest/Serving Others
Luke 9:1–2, 10–17

There comes a time for work, and there is a time to rest.
Taking time to rest will enable you to give your very best.
Having time alone with the Savior is the most effective way for solitude.
This will enable you, in your service to others,
to always have the right attitude.
Jesus has shown us the way, how we should live each day,
Quieting ourselves to be alone with God to
be able to hear what he has to say,
Knowing in this moment of solitude, it will
bring us rest and help us to pray.
Life can be noisy with distractions of various kinds.
Taking a moment to be alone with your Lord, you will
experience peace and rest in your soul, body, and mind.

Turn the volume of life down to hear God better.

Luke 9:1–2

Jesus Sends Out the Twelve
9 When Jesus had called the Twelve together, he gave them power and authority to drive out all demons and to cure diseases, 2 and he sent them out to proclaim the kingdom of God and to heal the sick.

Luke 9:10–17

Jesus Feeds the Five Thousand

10 When the apostles returned, they reported to Jesus what they had done. Then he took them with him and they withdrew by themselves to a town called Bethsaida, 11 but the crowds learned about it and followed him. He welcomed them and spoke to them about the kingdom of God, and healed those who needed healing.

12 Late in the afternoon the Twelve came to him and said, "Send the crowd away so they can go to the surrounding villages and countryside and find food and lodging, because we are in a remote place here."

13 He replied, "You give them something to eat."

They answered, "We have only five loaves of bread and two fish—unless we go and buy food for all this crowd."

14 (About five thousand men were there.)

But he said to his disciples, "Have them sit down in groups of about fifty each." 15 The disciples did so, and everyone sat down. 16 Taking the five loaves and the two fish and looking up to heaven, he gave thanks and broke them. Then he gave them to the disciples to distribute to the people. 17 They all ate and were satisfied, and the disciples picked up twelve basketfuls of broken pieces that were left over.

August 27
Prayer
Spiritual Discipline
Matthew 14:22–36

A quiet and peaceful place I need to find.
I need to be alone with Jesus, with no distractions;
That is what I will need to bear in mind.
I need to hear what He has to say,
About how He wants me to live for Him today.
There is much I need to understand.
How to pray for the needs of the people in this land.

A daily time of solitude will surely change my attitude.
I will pour out my heart before God in prayer;
He always will listen with care.
How will I know what the Father wants me to do?
Jesus, I will not know until I come in prayer before You.

God is very good about listening to us; how
effective are we in listening to Him?

Matthew 14:22–36

Jesus Walks on the Water
22 Immediately Jesus made the disciples get into the boat and go on ahead of him to the other side, while he dismissed the crowd. 23 After he had dismissed them, he went up on a mountainside by himself to pray. Later that night, he was there alone, 24 and the boat was already a considerable distance from land, buffeted by the waves because the wind was against it.
25 Shortly before dawn Jesus went out to them, walking on the lake. 26 When the disciples saw him walking on the lake, they were terrified. "It's a ghost," they said, and cried out in fear.
27 But Jesus immediately said to them: "Take courage! It is I. Don't be afraid."
28 "Lord, if it's you," Peter replied, "tell me to come to you on the water."
29 "Come," he said.
Then Peter got down out of the boat, walked on the water and came toward Jesus. 30 But when he saw the wind, he was afraid and, beginning to sink, cried out, "Lord, save me!"
31 Immediately Jesus reached out his hand and caught him. "You of little faith," he said, "why did you doubt?"
32 And when they climbed into the boat, the wind died down. 33 Then those who were in the boat worshiped him, saying, "Truly you are the Son of God."
34 When they had crossed over, they landed at Gennesaret. 35 And when the men of that place recognized Jesus, they sent word to all the surrounding country. People brought all their sick to him 36 and begged him to let the sick just touch the edge of his cloak, and all who touched it were healed.

August 28
Prayer
Suffering
2 Kings 19:9–20

The enemy has come with his taunts to defeat.
I feel afraid, and I want to retreat.
What do I do to defend my honor?
I do not want everyone to know that I have been cornered.
I will fall down on my knees and to my Savior, Jesus Christ, I will pray.
I know He will listen and will show me the way;
Which way I am to go and what it is I need to do.
My Lord is faithful to see me through.
When facing the enemy, suffering will be at hand,
But it must leave at God's command.
Look for the victory, and praise God with worship when it transpires;
Keeping a heart filled with gratitude is the kind of worship God desires.

You may look hopeless and defenseless to the enemy, but
when you pray for God's help, you will not be.

2 Kings 19:9–20

9 Now Sennacherib received a report that Tirhakah, the king of Cush, was marching out to fight against him. So he again sent messengers to Hezekiah with this word: 10 "Say to Hezekiah king of Judah: Do not let the god you depend on deceive you when he says, 'Jerusalem will not be given into the hands of the king of Assyria.' 11 Surely you have heard what the kings of Assyria have done to all the countries, destroying them completely. And will you be delivered? 12 Did the gods of the nations that were destroyed by my predecessors deliver them—the gods of Gozan, Harran, Rezeph and the people of Eden who were in Tel Assar? 13 Where is the king of Hamath or the king of Arpad? Where are the kings of Lair, Sepharvaim, Hena and Ivvah?" Hezekiah's Prayer 14 Hezekiah received the

letter from the messengers and read it.
Then he went up to the temple of the Lord and spread it out before the Lord. 15 And Hezekiah prayed to the Lord: "Lord, the God of Israel, enthroned between the cherubim, you alone are God over all the kingdoms of the earth. You have made heaven and earth. 16 Give ear, Lord, and hear; open your eyes, Lord, and see; listen to the words Sennacherib has sent to ridicule the living God.
17 "It is true, Lord, that the Assyrian kings have laid waste these nations and their lands. 18 They have thrown their gods into the fire and destroyed them, for they were not gods but only wood and stone, fashioned by human hands. 19 Now, Lord our God, deliver us from his hand, so that all the kingdoms of the earth may know that you alone, Lord, are God."
Isaiah Prophesies Sennacherib's Fall
20 Then Isaiah son of Amoz sent a message to Hezekiah: "This is what the Lord, the God of Israel, says: I have heard your prayer concerning Sennacherib king of Assyria.

August 29
Prayer
Isaiah 37:9–22, 33

Trouble came and demanded that I obey,
Threatening me with words, but I did not know what to say.
I was scared, and fear was in control of me.
What was I to do? The only thing that came to mind was to flee.
I cried out to God for help, to know what I should do:
"Heavenly Father, I truly am in need of You."
I told Him about the problem, and I told Him of my fear.
He told me not to worry but to be still and know that He was near.
As I prayed about my worries, God gave me peace.
From trouble and its demands I was released.
God commanded trouble that it was to cease.

Turn worrying into praying.

Isaiah 37:9–22

9 Now Sennacherib received a report that Tirhakah, the king of Cush, was marching out to fight against him. When he heard it, he sent messengers to Hezekiah with this word: 10 "Say to Hezekiah king of Judah: Do not let the god you depend on deceive you when he says, 'Jerusalem will not be given into the hands of the king of Assyria.' 11 Surely you have heard what the kings of Assyria have done to all the countries, destroying them completely. And will you be delivered? 12 Did the gods of the nations that were destroyed by my predecessors deliver them—the gods of Gozan, Harran, Rezeph and the people of Eden who were in Tel Assar? 13 Where is the king of Hamath or the king of Arpad? Where are the kings of Lair, Sepharvaim, Hena and Ivvah?"

Hezekiah's Prayer

14 Hezekiah received the letter from the messengers and read it. Then he went up to the temple of the Lord and spread it out before the Lord. 15 And Hezekiah prayed to the Lord: 16 "Lord Almighty, the God of Israel, enthroned between the cherubim, you alone are God over all the kingdoms of the earth. You have made heaven and earth. 17 Give ear, Lord, and hear; open your eyes, Lord, and see; listen to all the words Sennacherib has sent to ridicule the living God. 18 "It is true, Lord, that the Assyrian kings have laid waste all these peoples and their lands. 19 They have thrown their gods into the fire and destroyed them, for they were not gods but only wood and stone, fashioned by human hands. 20 Now, Lord our God, deliver us from his hand, so that all the kingdoms of the earth may know that you, Lord, are the only God."

Sennacherib's Fall

21 Then Isaiah son of Amoz sent a message to Hezekiah: "This is what the Lord, the God of Israel, says: Because you have prayed to me concerning Sennacherib king of Assyria, 22 this is the word the Lord has spoken against him:

"Virgin Daughter Zion
despises and mocks you.
Daughter Jerusalem
tosses her head as you flee.

Isaiah 37:33

33 "Therefore this is what the Lord says concerning the king of Assyria:
"He will not enter this city
or shoot an arrow here.
He will not come before it with shield
or build a siege ramp against it.

August 30
Prayer
Luke 18:1–8

Lord, I am having difficulties today;
Please show me the way.
I need You to guard my heart and the words I will say;
Lord, I need You today.
Demands are being made on me;
I need You, Lord, as I fall to my knees.
I need You, Lord, as You can see.
Decisions need to be made, and people are counting on me;
They are expecting me to know how things are supposed to be.
I know prayer will change everything;
This is what I know my faith will bring.
As I fall on my face, Lord, I ask for Your mercy and saving grace.
Please show me the way,
As I get down on my knees to pray.

Pray, pray, pray; there is no other way.

Luke 18:1–8

The Parable of the Persistent Widow
18 Then Jesus told his disciples a parable to show them that they should always pray and not give up. 2 He said: "In a certain town there was a judge who neither feared God nor cared what people

thought. 3 And there was a widow in that town who kept coming to him with the plea, 'Grant me justice against my adversary.' 4 "For some time he refused. But finally he said to himself, 'Even though I don't fear God or care what people think, 5 yet because this widow keeps bothering me, I will see that she gets justice, so that she won't eventually come and attack me!'" 6 And the Lord said, "Listen to what the unjust judge says. 7 And will not God bring about justice for his chosen ones, who cry out to him day and night? Will he keep putting them off? 8 I tell you, he will see that they get justice, and quickly. However, when the Son of Man comes, will he find faith on the earth?"

August 31
Prayer
Suffering
John 17:6–19

It is during times of difficulties that I need to pray.
I will pray for others and myself every day.
It is during these times that prayer is all I am able to do.
It is during these times, Lord Jesus, that I am truly in need of you.
I know that with Your help, You will see me through.
I am encouraged not to focus on the difficulties
and the suffering they will bring.
I will keep my eyes on you, Jesus, and the song my heart can sing.

There are times when looking and thinking about others and their difficulties will give you a different perspective on yours.

John 17:6–19

Jesus Prays for His Disciples
6 "I have revealed you to those whom you gave me out of the world. They were yours; you gave them to me and they have obeyed your word. 7 Now they know that everything you have given me comes from you. 8 For I gave them the words you gave me and they accepted them. They knew with

certainty that I came from you, and they believed that you sent me. 9 I pray for them. I am not praying for the world, but for those you have given me, for they are yours. 10 All I have is yours, and all you have is mine. And glory has come to me through them. 11 I will remain in the world no longer, but they are still in the world, and I am coming to you. Holy Father, protect them by the power of your name, the name you gave me, so that they may be one as we are one. 12 While I was with them, I protected them and kept them safe by that name you gave me. None has been lost except the one doomed to destruction so that Scripture would be fulfilled. 13 "I am coming to you now, but I say these things while I am still in the world, so that they may have the full measure of my joy within them. 14 I have given them your word and the world has hated them, for they are not of the world any more than I am of the world. 15 My prayer is not that you take them out of the world but that you protect them from the evil one. 16 They are not of the world, even as I am not of it. 17 Sanctify them by the truth; your word is truth. 18 As you sent me into the world, I have sent them into the world. 19 For them I sanctify myself, that they too may be truly sanctified.

September 1
Prayer
1 Thessalonians 5:16–28

Prayer is critical. Most people will agree.
It is what is needed from worry to keep the mind free.
But to maintain a consistent prayer life is the challenge a believer will face.
It is difficult, and we are in need of God's mercy and grace.
A life of prayer is like a long-lasting marathon, a difficult task to maintain.
You must go before God, pouring out your heart
to Him like a downpour of rain.
Don't give up, because your life will never be the same.
Be devoted to prayer, remaining faithful to pray.
You will need to do this each day.
God wants to have an intimate relationship with you.
It will also deepen your communication with Him too.

It may be a struggle to pray, but the power will
allow God to do the impossible.

1 Thessalonians 5:16–28

16 Rejoice always, 17 pray continually, 18 give thanks in all circumstances; for this is God's will for you in Christ Jesus. 19 Do not quench the Spirit. 20 Do not treat prophecies with contempt 21 but test them all; hold on to what is good, 22 reject every kind of evil. 23 May God himself, the God of peace, sanctify you through and through. May your whole spirit, soul and body be kept blameless at the coming of our Lord Jesus Christ. 24 The one who calls you is faithful, and he will do it.
25 Brothers and sisters, pray for us. 26 Greet all God's people with a holy kiss. 27 I charge you before the Lord to have this letter read to all the brothers and sisters.
28 The grace of our Lord Jesus Christ be with you.

September 2
Prayer
Hebrews 4:14–16

No one can understand the reason to pray.
Jesus does, because He prayed to the Father each day.
He trusted the Father to hear His plea.
He knew the Father would answer His every need.
He trusted the outcome of God's decision.
He knew God's answer would be a with complete provision.
God, I want to come before Your throne of grace.
With confidence, I come to seek You face-to-face.
I need Your mercy and Your grace during my time of need.
I thank You for Your help with a humble heart indeed.

Jesus knows why we need to pray.

Hebrews 4:14–16

Jesus the Great High Priest
14 Therefore, since we have a great high priest who has ascended into heaven, Jesus the Son of God, let us hold firmly to the faith we profess. 15 For we do not have a high priest who is unable to empathize with our weaknesses, but we have one who has been tempted in every way, just as we are—yet he did not sin. 16 Let us then approach God's throne of grace with confidence, so that we may receive mercy and find grace to help us in our time of need.

Purpose
September 3
Spiritual Gifts/Serving Others
1 Peter 4:7–11

You have a purpose. Yes, this is true.
Knowing this is what you must do.
Know God has a purpose especially for you.
Be sober in using sensible and responsible judgment,
keeping alert and vigilant at all times.
Being watchful and observant needs to stay on your mind.
While keeping God's plan in mind, be hospitable; serving
without grumbling, just be loving and kind.
Serving in God's strength as He provides.
"You have been fearfully and wonderfully made" (Psalm 139:16), because God had a plan with an intent in mind.
Whatever challenges you may face today, do not allow them to make you feel useless or meaningless in any way.
You have purpose. Yes, this is true.
Knowing this is what you must do.
Then know, God has a purpose especially for you.

You are a person with a purpose.

1 Peter 4:7–11

7 The end of all things is near. Therefore be alert and of sober mind so that you may pray. 8 Above all, love each other deeply, because love covers over a multitude of sins. 9 Offer hospitality to one another without grumbling. 10 Each of you should use whatever gift you have received to serve others, as faithful stewards of God's grace in its various forms. 11 If anyone speaks, they should do so as one who speaks the very words of God. If anyone serves, they should do so with the strength God provides, so that in all things God may be praised through Jesus Christ. To him be the glory and the power for ever and ever. Amen.

Relationships
September 4
Enemies/Listening
1 Samuel 25:14–33

An offense will cause you to want to strike back,
Having a behavior to be on the attack.
Nevertheless, be on guard, being gracious, so as to avoid having regret,
After having made a decision that, later, you will wish to forget.
Have the desire to please God and not look
for an opportunity to retaliate;
Having the goal to please God in the situation will
show discipline in love and not giving in to hate.
He will make your enemies be at peace with you.
Perhaps you are right in reasoning that an attack is the right thing to do;
However, learn to listen as to how to act when
wrong has been done to you.
This is learning how to be at peace with your enemy,
and it is the goal of what God wants you to do.

Learn how to show love when you have been wronged.

1 Samuel 25:14–33

14 One of the servants told Abigail, Nabal's wife, "David sent messengers from the wilderness to give our master his greetings, but he hurled insults at them. 15 Yet these men were very good to us. They did not mistreat us, and the whole time we were out in the fields near them nothing was missing. 16 Night and day they were a wall around us the whole time we were herding our sheep near them. 17 Now think it over and see what you can do, because disaster is hanging over our master and his whole household. He is such a wicked man that no one can talk to him."

18 Abigail acted quickly. She took two hundred loaves of bread, two skins of wine, five dressed sheep, five seahs of roasted grain, a hundred cakes of raisins and two hundred cakes of pressed figs, and loaded them on donkeys. 19 Then she told her servants, "Go on ahead; I'll follow you." But she did not tell her husband Nabal.

20 As she came riding her donkey into a mountain ravine, there were David and his men descending toward her, and she met them. 21 David had just said, "It's been useless—all my watching over this fellow's property in the wilderness so that nothing of his was missing. He has paid me back evil for good. 22 May God deal with David, be it ever so severely, if by morning I leave alive one male of all who belong to him!"

23 When Abigail saw David, she quickly got off her donkey and bowed down before David with her face to the ground. 24 She fell at his feet and said: "Pardon your servant, my lord, and let me speak to you; hear what your servant has to say. 25 Please pay no attention, my lord, to that wicked man Nabal. He is just like his name—his name means Fool, and folly goes with him. And as for me, your servant, I did not see the men my lord sent. 26 And now, my lord, as surely as the Lord your God lives and as you live, since the Lord has kept you from bloodshed and from avenging yourself with your own hands, may your enemies and all who are intent on harming my lord be like Nabal. 27 And let this gift, which your servant has brought to my lord, be given to the men who follow you.

28 "Please forgive your servant's presumption. The Lord your God will certainly make a lasting dynasty for my lord, because you fight the Lord's battles, and no wrongdoing will be found in you as long as you live. 29 Even though someone is pursuing you to take your life, the life

of my lord will be bound securely in the bundle of the living by the Lord your God, but the lives of your enemies he will hurl away as from the pocket of a sling. 30 When the Lord has fulfilled for my lord every good thing he promised concerning him and has appointed him ruler over Israel, 31 my lord will not have on his conscience the staggering burden of needless bloodshed or of having avenged himself. And when the Lord your God has brought my lord success, remember your servant."
32 David said to Abigail, "Praise be to the Lord, the God of Israel, who has sent you today to meet me. 33 May you be blessed for your good judgment and for keeping me from bloodshed this day and from avenging myself with my own hands.

September 5
Relationships
Evangelism
Luke 19:1–9

Life is short, and this is true.
Come, I want to spend some time with you.
How are you, and what is new?
It is so good to see and visit with you.
I know life is challenging, and I would like to encourage you with God's grace.
I know it will put a smile on your face.
I am so grateful to share this moment of life with you.
It is the best gift to give in investing in a relationship that I want to be loving and true.

Spending time with people is the best gift to be given.

Luke 19:1–9

Zacchaeus the Tax Collector
19 Jesus entered Jericho and was passing through. 2 A man was there by the name of Zacchaeus; he was a chief tax collector and

was wealthy. 3 He wanted to see who Jesus was, but because he was short he could not see over the crowd. 4 So he ran ahead and climbed a sycamore-fig tree to see him, since Jesus was coming that way.
5 When Jesus reached the spot, he looked up and said to him, "Zacchaeus, come down immediately. I must stay at your house today." 6 So he came down at once and welcomed him gladly.
7 All the people saw this and began to mutter,
"He has gone to be the guest of a sinner."
8 But Zacchaeus stood up and said to the Lord, "Look, Lord! Here and now I give half of my possessions to the poor, and if I have cheated anybody out of anything, I will pay back four times the amount."
9 Jesus said to him, "Today salvation has come to this house, because this man, too, is a son of Abraham.

September 6
Relationships
Forgiving Others
Luke 6:27–36

When a relationship has gone wrong,
God, we ask You, How are we to be strong?
How are we to respond so this will not continue on for too long?
Forgiveness is the key that will permit healing to come in.
Remember, we are all sinners who need each other as friends.
Pray for God's grace.
It is amazing during those difficult times that we need to face.
It takes courage to face someone in a conflict that needs to be resolved.
Involving Jesus is the only way it will be solved.

Permit your heart to be change when there needs to be forgiveness.

Luke 6:27–36

Love for Enemies

27 "But to you who are listening I say: Love your enemies, do good to those who hate you, 28 bless those who curse you, pray for those who mistreat you. 29 If someone slaps you on one cheek, turn to them the other also. If someone takes your coat, do not withhold your shirt from them. 30 Give to everyone who asks you, and if anyone takes what belongs to you, do not demand it back. 31 Do to others as you would have them do to you.
32 "If you love those who love you, what credit is that to you? Even sinners love those who love them. 33 And if you do good to those who are good to you, what credit is that to you? Even sinners do that. 34 And if you lend to those from whom you expect repayment, what credit is that to you? Even sinners lend to sinners, expecting to be repaid in full. 35 But love your enemies, do good to them, and lend to them without expecting to get anything back. Then your reward will be great, and you will be children of the Most High, because he is kind to the ungrateful and wicked. 36 Be merciful, just as your Father is merciful.

September 7
Relationships
Leadership/Love
Philemon 8–18

When thinking about relationships, think how long they will last.
Will they be ones that will last into eternity?
There are many kinds of relationships in life to obtain;
All will be different, but one thing should remain the same.
Love should be involved in each relationship,
because of those it will affect;
All who are involved will experience the effect.
Love's involvement in all your relationships is
something that should be a matter of concern;

As you grow in each relationship, there will be much you will learn.
Whether you are a leader, parent, or friend,
By learning to love in your relationships, peace will always be welcome in.

Love, and being loved, is how life is supposed to be lived.

Philemon 8–18

Paul's Plea for Onesimus
8 Therefore, although in Christ I could be bold and order you to do what you ought to do, 9 yet I prefer to appeal to you on the basis of love. It is as none other than Paul—an old man and now also a prisoner of Christ Jesus— 10 that I appeal to you for my son Onesimus, who became my son while I was in chains. 11 Formerly he was useless to you, but now he has become useful both to you and to me.
12 I am sending him—who is my very heart—back to you. 13 I would have liked to keep him with me so that he could take your place in helping me while I am in chains for the gospel. 14 But I did not want to do anything without your consent, so that any favor you do would not seem forced but would be voluntary. 15 Perhaps the reason he was separated from you for a little while was that you might have him back forever— 16 no longer as a slave, but better than a slave, as a dear brother. He is very dear to me but even dearer to you, both as a fellow man and as a brother in the Lord.
17 So if you consider me a partner, welcome him as you would welcome me. 18 If he has done you any wrong or owes you anything, charge it to me.

September 8
Relationships
Spiritual Transformation
Proverbs 27:5–17

As a friend, you would want to be sharpened as iron in
your relationship to lead your friends into eternity;

This will allow love in your friendship to be free.
This will take fondness, gentleness, patience, and care,
Letting your friends know that for them you will continue to be there.
They should do the same thing for you;
This is how iron sharpens iron, because this is what friends do.
It is during these times that words will sound
rough, harsh but spoken in truth;
This is what a friendship with love will do for you.
Keep in mind you will do the same thing;
This is how we are bringing worship with praise to glorify Jesus, our King.

How is iron sharpening iron happening in your relationships?

Proverbs 27:5–17

5
Better is open rebuke
than hidden love.
6
Wounds from a friend can be trusted,
but an enemy multiplies kisses.
7
One who is full loathes honey from the comb,
but to the hungry even what is bitter tastes sweet.
8
Like a bird that flees its nest
is anyone who flees from home.
9
Perfume and incense bring joy to the heart,
and the pleasantness of a friend
springs from their heartfelt advice.
10
Do not forsake your friend or a friend of your family,
and do not go to your relative's house when disaster strikes you—
better a neighbor nearby than a relative far away.

11
Be wise, my son, and bring joy to my heart;
then I can answer anyone who treats me with contempt.
12
The prudent see danger and take refuge,
but the simple keep going and pay the penalty.
13
Take the garment of one who puts up security for a stranger;
hold it in pledge if it is done for an outsider.
14
If anyone loudly blesses their neighbor early in the morning,
it will be taken as a curse.
15
A quarrelsome wife is like the dripping
of a leaky roof in a rainstorm;
16
restraining her is like restraining the wind
or grasping oil with the hand.
17
As iron sharpens iron,
so one person sharpens another.

September 9
Relationships
Spiritual Transformation
Proverbs 27:5–17

Good friendships are notoriously difficult to find;
Please bear this in mind.
Are you willing to do what a good friendship needs?
When it calls for iron to sharpen iron, could you agree?
Could you in all faithfulness and patience heed?
Could you speak the truth, no matter what it will take?
Could you do this without thinking that it would be a mistake?
Could you receive it when it is something that you need to hear?

Could you respond with "Thank you, my dear,
That was something that I needed to hear"?
Good friendships are difficult to find;
We all need to bear this thought in mind.
Wounds from a friend can be trusted,
but an enemy multiplies kisses. Proverbs 27:6

Proverbs 27:5–17

5
Better is open rebuke
than hidden love.
6
Wounds from a friend can be trusted,
but an enemy multiplies kisses.
7
One who is full loathes honey from the comb,
but to the hungry even what is bitter tastes sweet.
8
Like a bird that flees its nest
is anyone who flees from home.
9
Perfume and incense bring joy to the heart,
and the pleasantness of a friend
springs from their heartfelt advice.
10
Do not forsake your friend or a friend of your family,
and do not go to your relative's house when disaster strikes you—
better a neighbor nearby than a relative far away.
11
Be wise, my son, and bring joy to my heart;
then I can answer anyone who treats me with contempt.
12
The prudent see danger and take refuge,
but the simple keep going and pay the penalty.

13
Take the garment of one who puts up security for a stranger;
hold it in pledge if it is done for an outsider.
14
If anyone loudly blesses their neighbor early in the morning,
it will be taken as a curse.
15
A quarrelsome wife is like the dripping
of a leaky roof in a rainstorm;
16
restraining her is like restraining the wind
or grasping oil with the hand.
17
As iron sharpens iron,
so one person sharpens another.

Repentance
September 10
Christ/Messiah
Isaiah 40:1–11

Tender mercy I will speak,
To bring comfort to your heart when it is weak.
Weak from the burden of fear that is laced with sin;
These words of tender mercy, please welcome them in.
Jesus the Messiah has paid for your sins;
He is the Sovereign Lord who wants to become your Eternal Friend.
When pride in your heart rises up as high as a mountaintop,
You need to quickly stop.
Repent. When your emotions travel to the low land of despair,
These words of tender mercy will remind you that Jesus is there.
Words of tender mercy I will speak to you.
Jesus loves you and knows that this is true.

Have you prepared your heart for Jesus?

Isaiah 40:1–11

Comfort for God's People

40 Comfort, comfort my people,
  says your God.
2
Speak tenderly to Jerusalem,
  and proclaim to her
that her hard service has been completed,
  that her sin has been paid for,
that she has received from the Lord's hand
  double for all her sins.
3
A voice of one calling:
"In the wilderness prepare
  the way for the Lord;
make straight in the desert
  a highway for our God.
4
Every valley shall be raised up,
  every mountain and hill made low;
the rough ground shall become level,
  the rugged places a plain.
5
And the glory of the Lord will be revealed,
  and all people will see it together.
For the mouth of the Lord has spoken."
6
A voice says, "Cry out."
  And I said, "What shall I cry?"
"All people are like grass,
and all their faithfulness is like the flowers of the field.
7
The grass withers and the flowers fall,

because the breath of the Lord blows on them.
Surely the people are grass.

8

The grass withers and the flowers fall,
but the word of our God endures forever."

9

You who bring good news to Zion,
go up on a high mountain.
You who bring good news to Jerusalem,
lift up your voice with a shout,
lift it up, do not be afraid;
say to the towns of Judah,
"Here is your God!"

10

See, the Sovereign Lord comes with power,
and he rules with a mighty arm.
See, his reward is with him,
and his recompense accompanies him.

11

He tends his flock like a shepherd:
He gathers the lambs in his arms
and carries them close to his heart;
he gently leads those that have young.

September 11
Repentance
Salvation
Mark 10:17–27

It takes courage and faith to follow Jesus every day.
Do not put your trust in things and in people,
believing everything that they may say.
Seeking Jesus is something you must do every day.
Do what Jesus says we must do.
It will help you to walk your salvation through.

Every day there will be challenges you will face.
Jesus will give you the strength, mercy, and grace.
Do not allow the things of this world to be a
distraction or a hindrance to you.
Living for Jesus will not be easy to do.
Repentance is wanting change that will give you true life.
Living for Jesus will be a sacrifice.

Is it worth it to live for Jesus?

Mark 10:17–27

The Rich and the Kingdom of God
17 As Jesus started on his way, a man ran up to him
and fell on his knees before him. "Good teacher," he
asked, "what must I do to inherit eternal life?"
18 "Why do you call me good?" Jesus answered. "No one is good—except
God alone. 19 You know the commandments: 'You shall not murder,
you shall not commit adultery, you shall not steal, you shall not give
false testimony, you shall not defraud, honor your father and mother.'"
20 "Teacher," he declared, "all these I have kept since I was a boy."
21 Jesus looked at him and loved him. "One thing you lack,"
he said. "Go, sell everything you have and give to the poor, and
you will have treasure in heaven. Then come, follow me."
22 At this the man's face fell. He went away
sad, because he had great wealth.
23 Jesus looked around and said to his disciples, "How
hard it is for the rich to enter the kingdom of God!"
24 The disciples were amazed at his words. But Jesus said
again, "Children, how hard it is to enter the kingdom of God!
25 It is easier for a camel to go through the eye of a needle than
for someone who is rich to enter the kingdom of God."
26 The disciples were even more amazed, and said
to each other, "Who then can be saved?"
27 Jesus looked at them and said, "With man this is impossible,
but not with God; all things are possible with God."

September 12
Sin
Psalm 51:7–17

God, I am broken over my sins.
There are many things I have done against
You, my family, and my friends.
Every one of them I need to confess.
To have the right relationship with You, I know that would be best.
My sins I will confess so I will by You be blessed.
Wash me so I will be clean.
To me, this is what it will mean.
A heart that will be pure with a renewed steadfast spirit too.
There is more I need You to do.
My joy will be restored with a willing spirit to obey that will sustain me.
Father, I want my soul to be free.
Free to sing songs of praise to You for an eternity.
Deliver me from my guilt and shame.
I am the only one to blame.
I only have a broken spirit and a broken heart to give You.
What else can I do?
Sin is a heavy weight to bear.

Psalm 51:7–17

7
Cleanse me with hyssop, and I will be clean;
wash me, and I will be whiter than snow.
8
Let me hear joy and gladness;
let the bones you have crushed rejoice.
9
Hide your face from my sins
and blot out all my iniquity.

10
Create in me a pure heart, O God,
and renew a steadfast spirit within me.
11
Do not cast me from your presence
or take your Holy Spirit from me.
12
Restore to me the joy of your salvation
and grant me a willing spirit, to sustain me.
13
Then I will teach transgressors your ways,
so that sinners will turn back to you.
14
Deliver me from the guilt of bloodshed, O God,
you who are God my Savior,
and my tongue will sing of your righteousness.
15
Open my lips, Lord,
and my mouth will declare your praise.
16
You do not delight in sacrifice, or I would bring it;
you do not take pleasure in burnt offerings.
17
My sacrifice, O God, is a broken spirit;
a broken and contrite heart
you, God, will not despise.

September 13
Repentance
Sin
1 Samuel 25:1–12

Oh, when sin has a hold of me;
I will do foolish things that are irrational,
illogical, unreasonable completely.

Stubbornness and recklessness would describe my way of life.
For others it made their life difficult, because I did not treat them right.
I was concerned with no one but me.
This is not how life is supposed to be.
Lord, I want You to change my ways.
I do not want to live like this another day.
I want to repent; this I pray.
I do not want sin to have a hold of me.
I want of sin to be set free.
Show me how to make my wrongs right.
My desire is to be guided by Your spiritual insight.

Self-centeredness is a world that has a population of one.

1 Samuel 25:1–12

David, Nabal and Abigail
25 Now Samuel died, and all Israel assembled and mourned for him; and they buried him at his home in Ramah.
Then David moved down into the Desert of Paran.
2 A certain man in Maon, who had property there at Carmel, was very wealthy. He had a thousand goats and three thousand sheep, which he was shearing in Carmel. 3 His name was Nabal and his wife's name was Abigail. She was an intelligent and beautiful woman, but her husband was surly and mean in his dealings—he was a Calebite.
4 While David was in the wilderness, he heard that Nabal was shearing sheep. 5 So he sent ten young men and said to them, "Go up to Nabal at Carmel and greet him in my name. 6 Say to him: 'Long life to you! Good health to you and your household! And good health to all that is yours!
7 "'Now I hear that it is sheep-shearing time. When your shepherds were with us, we did not mistreat them, and the whole time they were at Carmel nothing of theirs was missing. 8 Ask your own servants and they will tell you. Therefore be favorable toward my men, since we come at a festive time. Please give your servants and your son David whatever you can find for them.'"

9 When David's men arrived, they gave Nabal this message in David's name. Then they waited.
10 Nabal answered David's servants, "Who is this David? Who is this son of Jesse? Many servants are breaking away from their masters these days. 11 Why should I take my bread and water, and the meat I have slaughtered for my shearers, and give it to men coming from who knows where?"
12 David's men turned around and went back. When they arrived, they reported every word.

September 14
Repentance
Forgiveness of Sin
Joel 2:12–17

Lord, my heart wants to speak to You today.
It is from my heart that I need to pray.
It is of sin that I need to confess;
Because of sin, my life is in a complete mess.
Lord, I ask You to please forgive me of my sin.
I am filled with regret, and it is from deep within;
Of my heart, soul, and mind.
Please forgive me, Lord. This sin is depressing me all the time.
Please change me, cleanse me, and make me new;
I want to serve only You.
You are gracious, compassionate, slow to anger, and abounding in love.
This could not come from anyone else but only from Almighty God above.

When the heart speaks, God will always listen.

Joel 2:12–17

Rend Your Heart
12
"Even now," declares the Lord

"return to me with all your heart,
with fasting and weeping and mourning."
13
Rend your heart
and not your garments.
Return to the Lord your God,
for he is gracious and compassionate,
slow to anger and abounding in love,
and he relents from sending calamity.
14
Who knows? He may turn and relent
and leave behind a blessing—
grain offerings and drink offerings
for the Lord your God.
15
Blow the trumpet in Zion,
declare a holy fast,
call a sacred assembly.
16
Gather the people,
consecrate the assembly;
bring together the elders,
gather the children,
those nursing at the breast.
Let the bridegroom leave his room
and the bride her chamber.
17
Let the priests, who minister before the Lord,
weep between the portico and the altar.
Let them say, "Spare your people, Lord.
Do not make your inheritance an object of scorn,
a byword among the nations.
Why should they say among the peoples,
'Where is their God?'"

Respect
September 15
Ezra 5:6–17

There will be occasions when you will need to plead your case;
Remember, you need to be in God's grace.
Seek to have God's wisdom to respond respectfully and with admiration;
This should be your attitude in any situation.
Trust God to be in control, and the outcome will be as He desires;
Your attitude and gratitude will leave others to be inspired ...
Knowing you will confront without confrontation will
cause many to think you worthy to be admired.

Your goal should be to please God with worship and praise.

Ezra 5:6–17

6 This is a copy of the letter that Tattenai, governor of Trans-Euphrates, and Shethar-Bozenai and their associates, the officials of Trans-Euphrates, sent to King Darius. 7 The report they sent him read as follows:
To King Darius:
Cordial greetings.
8 The king should know that we went to the district of Judah, to the temple of the great God. The people are building it with large stones and placing the timbers in the walls. The work is being carried on with diligence and is making rapid progress under their direction.
9 We questioned the elders and asked them, "Who authorized you to rebuild this temple and to finish it?"
10 We also asked them their names, so that we could write down the names of their leaders for your information.
11 This is the answer they gave us:
"We are the servants of the God of heaven and earth, and we are rebuilding the temple that was built many years ago, one that a great king of Israel built and finished. 12 But because

our ancestors angered the God of heaven, he gave them into the
hands of Nebuchadnezzar the Chaldean, king of Babylon, who
destroyed this temple and deported the people to Babylon.
13 "However, in the first year of Cyrus king of Babylon, King Cyrus
issued a decree to rebuild this house of God. 14 He even removed
from the temple of Babylon the gold and silver articles of the house of
God, which Nebuchadnezzar had taken from the temple in Jerusalem
and brought to the temple in Babylon. Then King Cyrus gave them
to a man named Sheshbazzar, whom he had appointed governor,
15 and he told him, 'Take these articles and go and deposit them in
the temple in Jerusalem. And rebuild the house of God on its site.'
16 "So this Sheshbazzar came and laid the foundations of
the house of God in Jerusalem. From that day to the present
it has been under construction but is not yet finished."
17 Now if it pleases the king, let a search be made in the
royal archives of Babylon to see if King Cyrus did in fact
issue a decree to rebuild this house of God in Jerusalem.
Then let the king send us his decision in this matter.

Rest
September 16
Exodus 18:14–24

The load is heavy, and the weight of it is weighing me down;
The burden of it all is turning my smile into a frown.
Lord, please refresh my spirit and soul today;
Rest will help me, and time to enjoy some play.
I want to live a balanced life that is effective
and successful—that is my desire;
Getting the proper rest during times of stress is strongly required.
When I have been refreshed, I will be stimulated and inspired.

When you are refreshed, you feel like a new person.

Exodus 18:14–24

14 When his father-in-law saw all that Moses was doing for the people, he said, "What is this you are doing for the people? Why do you alone sit as judge, while all these people stand around you from morning till evening?" 15 Moses answered him, "Because the people come to me to seek God's will. 16 Whenever they have a dispute, it is brought to me, and I decide between the parties and inform them of God's decrees and instructions." 17 Moses' father-in-law replied, "What you are doing is not good. 18 You and these people who come to you will only wear yourselves out. The work is too heavy for you; you cannot handle it alone. 19 Listen now to me and I will give you some advice, and may God be with you. You must be the people's representative before God and bring their disputes to him. 20 Teach them his decrees and instructions, and show them the way they are to live and how they are to behave. 21 But select capable men from all the people—men who fear God, trustworthy men who hate dishonest gain—and appoint them as officials over thousands, hundreds, fifties and tens. 22 Have them serve as judges for the people at all times, but have them bring every difficult case to you; the simple cases they can decide themselves. That will make your load lighter, because they will share it with you. 23 If you do this and God so commands, you will be able to stand the strain, and all these people will go home satisfied."
24 Moses listened to his father-in-law and did everything he said.

September 17
Rest
Mark 6:7–13, 30–32

I have a long busy day ahead of me.
Many things to do. Appointments to keep and people to see.
Will there be time to rest for me?
It is challenging to find time to rest when there
are so many things on my mind.
How can I make the time?

Jesus, I need You to come with me.
Help me to find that place of rest that will be quiet and peachy.
There I will be able to relax, sitting aside the agenda for today.
This will be the time to relax even from play.
In God's presence I will tune out the distractions,
the tension, and all the noises too.
In Your presence, God, I want to think about Your
wonders and faithfulness; I want to hear only You.
I want to enter into Your rest, because You know what is best.

Another way to look at the human race is that we are
people who are in a race to get some rest.

Mark 6:7–13

7 Calling the Twelve to him, he began to send them out two
by two and gave them authority over impure spirits.
8 These were his instructions: "Take nothing for the journey except a staff—no bread, no bag, no money in your belts. 9 Wear sandals but not an extra shirt. 10 Whenever you enter a house, stay there until you leave that town. 11 And if any place will not welcome you or listen to you, leave that place and shake the dust off your feet as a testimony against them."
12 They went out and preached that people should
repent. 13 They drove out many demons and anointed
many sick people with oil and healed them.

Mark 6:30–32

Jesus Feeds the Five Thousand
30 The apostles gathered around Jesus and reported to him all they had done and taught. 31 Then, because so many people were coming and going that they did not even have a chance to eat, he said to them, "Come with me by yourselves to a quiet place and get some rest."
32 So they went away by themselves in a boat to a solitary place.

September 18
Rest
God's Care
Matthew 11:25–30

Be still, my soul, be still.
The presence of God is what I need to feel.
I am weary and burdened with the cares of this life.
From them, my soul cries out for rest and spiritual insight.
Who but Jesus can calm my weary soul?
Bringing warmth of love to a soul that is burdensome, restless, and cold.
I will keep my mind on Jesus for the rest He has for me.
This rest will bring me the peace I will have for eternity.
"Be still, and know that I am God."
Psalm 46:10

Matthew 11:25–30)

The Father Revealed in the Son
25 At that time Jesus said, "I praise you, Father, Lord of heaven and earth, because you have hidden these things from the wise and learned, and revealed them to little children.
26 Yes, Father, for this is what you were pleased to do.
27 "All things have been committed to me by my Father. No one knows the Son except the Father, and no one knows the Father except the Son and those to whom the Son chooses to reveal him.
28 "Come to me, all you who are weary and burdened, and I will give you rest. 29 Take my yoke upon you and learn from me, for I am gentle and humble in heart, and you will find rest for your souls. 30 For my yoke is easy and my burden is light."

September 19
Resting
Waiting/Witnessing
John 4:4–14

A time of resting is a good time to reflect.
God wants us to use that time, so He can interject.
The perfect time to know to witness to the lost.
The time for rest while waiting is a good time for
anticipating, not focusing on the cost,
But those who are lost.
Sharing the gospel of Jesus Christ and what He has done;
It will bring joy to you, and it can be fun.
Watching others whose lives are being made anew,
Because you have shared the gospel as Jesus wants you to.
When you thirst for Jesus, a spring of living
water will become alive in you,
A spring of water that will make you brand-new.
This living water, come taste and see;
It is water you will want to have for an eternity.

How many lost souls do you notice around you?

John 4:4–14

4 Now he had to go through Samaria. 5 So he came to a town in Samaria called Sychar, near the plot of ground Jacob had given to his son Joseph. 6 Jacob's well was there, and Jesus, tired as he was from the journey, sat down by the well. It was about noon.
7 When a Samaritan woman came to draw water, Jesus said to her, "Will you give me a drink?" 8 (His disciples had gone into the town to buy food.)
9 The Samaritan woman said to him, "You are a Jew and I am a Samaritan woman. How can you ask me for a drink?" (For Jews do not associate with Samaritans.)

10 Jesus answered her, "If you knew the gift of God and who it is that asks you for a drink, you would have asked him and he would have given you living water."
11 "Sir," the woman said, "you have nothing to draw with and the well is deep. Where can you get this living water? 12 Are you greater than our father Jacob, who gave us the well and drank from it himself, as did also his sons and his livestock?"
13 Jesus answered, "Everyone who drinks this water will be thirsty again, 14 but whoever drinks the water I give them will never thirst. Indeed, the water I give them will become in them a spring of water welling up to eternal life."

Salvation
September 20
Isaiah 12

Jesus is my peace.
This is the way life should be.
What will I find by drawing deep into God's will?
I will be refreshed and strengthened with joy that will never fail.
Repentance and confession will lead me to the
waters of joy that are cool and deep,
That are everlasting and sweet to keep.
God's well of salvation will never run dry;
I will not feel depleted and spiritually die.
God's grace, His strength, and joy, will always be there for me.
This causes my heart to praise with gratitude for all the world to see;
Gratitude that will last for all eternity.

God's love will never die.

Isaiah 12

Songs of Praise
12 In that day you will say:

"I will praise you, Lord.
Although you were angry with me,
your anger has turned away
and you have comforted me.
2
Surely God is my salvation;
I will trust and not be afraid.
The Lord, the Lord himself, is my strength and my defense;
he has become my salvation."
3
With joy you will draw water
from the wells of salvation.
4 In that day you will say:
"Give praise to the Lord, proclaim his name;
make known among the nations what he has done,
and proclaim that his name is exalted.
5
Sing to the Lord, for he has done glorious things;
let this be known to all the world.
6
Shout aloud and sing for joy, people of Zion,
for great is the Holy One of Israel among you."

September 21
Salvation
Psalm 146

Why should I praise the LORD?
What has He done for me?
As a prisoner of sin, He has set me free.
Why should I praise the LORD?
Why should I put my trust in Him?
Humans cannot save, so I will not put my trust in them.
Why should I praise the LORD?
In life's stresses, He gives me hope.

Now I understand how I am to cope.
It is He who made heaven and earth;
For that alone, of praise, He is worthy.
He is there for the oppressed.
He understands their stress.
He gives sight to the blind, and He loves the righteous too.
He watches over foreigners, and He is watching over you.
He will put the ways of the wicked to an end.
I know why I will praise the LORD, because He died for man's sin.

Do not be a prisoner of sin. Let Jesus set you free.

Psalm 146

1
Praise the Lord.
Praise the Lord, my soul.
2
I will praise the Lord all my life;
I will sing praise to my God as long as I live.
3
Do not put your trust in princes,
in human beings, who cannot save.
4
When their spirit departs, they return to the ground;
on that very day their plans come to nothing.
5
Blessed are those whose help is the God of Jacob,
whose hope is in the Lord their God.
6
He is the Maker of heaven and earth,
the sea, and everything in them—
he remains faithful forever.
7
He upholds the cause of the oppressed
and gives food to the hungry.

The Lord sets prisoners free,
8
the Lord gives sight to the blind,
the Lord lifts up those who are bowed down,
the Lord loves the righteous.
9
The Lord watches over the foreigner
and sustains the fatherless and the widow,
but he frustrates the ways of the wicked.
10
The Lord reigns forever,
your God, O Zion, for all generations.
Praise the Lord.

September 22
Salvation
Mark 2:13–17

Jesus's arms are open wide to welcome in His heart
all sinners who are lost to come inside.
Come, come if you are a sinner like me.
Come and follow Him and receive a new life and see;
This new life will give you joy and peace for eternity.
You will want to change, you will not want to remain the same.
His love for you is real.
Especially when it is love, you do not feel.
Come, come and see;
This love and new life is a gift for you for all eternity.

Jesus's love for you is amazing.

Mark 2:13–17

Jesus Calls Levi and Eats With Sinners

13 Once again Jesus went out beside the lake. A large crowd came to him, and he began to teach them. 14 As he walked along, he saw Levi son of Alphaeus sitting at the tax collector's booth. "Follow me," Jesus told him, and Levi got up and followed him. 15 While Jesus was having dinner at Levi's house, many tax collectors and sinners were eating with him and his disciples, for there were many who followed him. 16 When the teachers of the law who were Pharisees saw him eating with the sinners and tax collectors, they asked his disciples: "Why does he eat with tax collectors and sinners?" 17 On hearing this, Jesus said to them, "It is not the healthy who need a doctor, but the sick. I have not come to call the righteous, but sinners."

September 23
Salvation
Luke 1:67–79

A gift has been given to me and to you:
The gift of salvation with forgiveness, and love came with it too.
The gift is free.
It is meant to be kept for eternity.
However, the cost to the giver was costly, to say the least.
It cost Him His life, which He gave as a sacrifice.
He gave it out of love, which came from the heavenly Father above.
Salvation is a gift to all who wish to receive.
It is given from the heart of Jesus to those who will believe.

Have you received your gift of salvation?

Luke 1:67–79

Zechariah's Song

67 His father Zechariah was filled with the Holy Spirit and prophesied:

68
"Praise be to the Lord, the God of Israel,
because he has come to his people and redeemed them.

69
He has raised up a horn of salvation for us
in the house of his servant David

70
(as he said through his holy prophets of long ago),

71
salvation from our enemies
and from the hand of all who hate us—

72
to show mercy to our ancestors
and to remember his holy covenant,

73
the oath he swore to our father Abraham:

74
to rescue us from the hand of our enemies,
and to enable us to serve him without fear

75
in holiness and righteousness before him all our days.

76
And you, my child, will be called a prophet of the Most High;
for you will go on before the Lord to prepare the way for him,

77
to give his people the knowledge of salvation
through the forgiveness of their sins,

78
because of the tender mercy of our God,
by which the rising sun will come to us from heaven

79
to shine on those living in darkness

and in the shadow of death,
to guide our feet into the path of peace."

September 24
Salvation
Luke 4:14–21

Sin has left me broken and oppressed.
Every day, I am feeling down, depressed with distress.
I have been dehumanized by sin.
Whom can I trust as my friend?
I am suffering from brokenness and sorrow.
Which gives me no hope for tomorrow.
Then someone shared Jesus with me.
I was told how Jesus died from sin so I can be free.
I believed those words to be true.
My heart was no longer feeling blue.
Jesus, thank You for Your mercy. Thank You for Your grace.
I no longer feel dehumanized as part of the human race.
Salvation has been granted to me.
From the bondage of sin, I have been set free.

Sin wants to keep you in bondage, while salvation wants to set you free.

Luke 4:14–21

Jesus Rejected at Nazareth
14 Jesus returned to Galilee in the power of the Spirit, and news about him spread through the whole countryside. 15 He was teaching in their synagogues, and everyone praised him.
16 He went to Nazareth, where he had been brought up, and on the Sabbath day he went into the synagogue, as was his custom. He stood up to read, 17 and the scroll of the prophet Isaiah was handed to him. Unrolling it, he found the place where it is written:

18
"The Spirit of the Lord is on me,
because he has anointed me
to proclaim good news to the poor.
He has sent me to proclaim freedom for the prisoners
and recovery of sight for the blind,
to set the oppressed free,
19
to proclaim the year of the Lord's favor."
20 Then he rolled up the scroll, gave it back to the attendant
and sat down. The eyes of everyone in the synagogue
were fastened on him. 21 He began by saying to them,
"Today this scripture is fulfilled in your hearing."

September 25
Salvation
Christ, Savior and Messiah
Romans 3:21–26

A costly price has been paid for salvation.
Jesus was the only One who could bring restoration,
Which enabled God and man to have reconciliation.
We all needed redemption from sin.
Jesus was the only One who could pay the
price. He paid it as a loyal Friend.
It is through faith in Jesus Christ that you must believe,
To have salvation that brings restoration to have
reconciliation; it is there for you to receive.

To enter heaven is free.

Romans 3:21–26

Righteousness Through Faith

21 But now apart from the law the righteousness of God has been made known, to which the Law and the Prophets testify. 22 This righteousness is given through faith in Jesus Christ to all who believe. There is no difference between Jew and Gentile, 23 for all have sinned and fall short of the glory of God, 24 and all are justified freely by his grace through the redemption that came by Christ Jesus. 25 God presented Christ as a sacrifice of atonement, through the shedding of his blood—to be received by faith. He did this to demonstrate his righteousness, because in his forbearance he had left the sins committed beforehand unpunished— 26 he did it to demonstrate his righteousness at the present time, so as to be just and the one who justifies those who have faith in Jesus.

September 26
Salvation
John 1:1–14

Take a good look at the world as it is today.
What do you have to say?
What do you see?
Is the world the way it ought to be?
How are you doing your part for humanity?
What are you doing to bring peace and tranquillity to make it a reality?
Man does not have the ability to bring peace into the world or replace the world of darkness with a world of love and light.
However, God did send one man who brought salvation for man's sin.
To all who received and accepted Him, He became their Friend.
Jesus Christ is that man.
What He did on the cross very few truly understand.
As the Word, the Light of the World, as Life and the True Light, are you willing to take Him by the hand and live by His command?

Do you have hope in Jesus?

John 1:1–14

The Word Became Flesh

1 In the beginning was the Word, and the Word was with God, and the Word was God. 2 He was with God in the beginning. 3 Through him all things were made; without him nothing was made that has been made. 4 In him was life, and that life was the light of all mankind. 5 The light shines in the darkness, and the darkness has not overcome it.

6 There was a man sent from God whose name was John.
7 He came as a witness to testify concerning that light, so that through him all might believe. 8 He himself was not the light; he came only as a witness to the light.
9 The true light that gives light to everyone was coming into the world. 10 He was in the world, and though the world was made through him, the world did not recognize him. 11 He came to that which was his own, but his own did not receive him. 12 Yet to all who did receive him, to those who believed in his name, he gave the right to become children of God— 13 children born not of natural descent, nor of human decision or a husband's will, but born of God.
14 The Word became flesh and made his dwelling among us. We have seen his glory, the glory of the one and only Son, who came from the Father, full of grace and truth.

September 27
Salvation
John 6:53–69

Are you a follower of Jesus Christ?
Willing to live for Him with all of your life?
Do you understand His teaching, and are you willing to obey?
Do you seize the opportunity to witness to someone today?
When facing challenges, do you look to Him first and pray?
Are you a follower of Jesus today?
Do you believe He is the Son of God and nothing less?

Do you give to Him your very best?
Are you a follower of Jesus; will others say that about you?
Are you a follower of Jesus? Will this be true?

Are you a follower of Jesus? If so, why?

John 6:53–69

53 Jesus said to them, "Very truly I tell you, unless you eat the flesh of the Son of Man and drink his blood, you have no life in you. 54 Whoever eats my flesh and drinks my blood has eternal life, and I will raise them up at the last day. 55 For my flesh is real food and my blood is real drink. 56 Whoever eats my flesh and drinks my blood remains in me, and I in them. 57 Just as the living Father sent me and I live because of the Father, so the one who feeds on me will live because of me. 58 This is the bread that came down from heaven. Your ancestors ate manna and died, but whoever feeds on this bread will live forever."
59 He said this while teaching in the synagogue in Capernaum.

Many Disciples Desert Jesus

60 On hearing it, many of his disciples said, "This is a hard teaching. Who can accept it?"
61 Aware that his disciples were grumbling about this, Jesus said to them, "Does this offend you? 62 Then what if you see the Son of Man ascend to where he was before! 63 The Spirit gives life; the flesh counts for nothing. The words I have spoken to you—they are full of the Spirit and life. 64 Yet there are some of you who do not believe." For Jesus had known from the beginning which of them did not believe and who would betray him. 65 He went on to say, "This is why I told you that no one can come to me unless the Father has enabled them."
66 From this time many of his disciples turned back and no longer followed him.
67 "You do not want to leave too, do you?" Jesus asked the Twelve. 68 Simon Peter answered him, "Lord, to whom shall we go? You have the words of eternal life. 69 We have come to believe and to know that you are the Holy One of God."

September 28
Salvation
John 8:31–37

What is salvation, and how did it come to be?
It was a battle that was fought for the souls of
men to live with God for eternity.
Jesus fought the battle against sin.
He fought the battle for humanity, a battle that we could not win.
The battle freed us from the slavery of brokenness and sin.
Jesus became our Savior, our Lord, and a faithful, loyal Friend.
Jesus paid the price for sin so we could be free.
To live with Him and have a life that will be filled
with love, peace, and joy for eternity.

Salvation. Do you have it?

John 8:31–37

Dispute Over Whose Children Jesus' Opponents Are
31 To the Jews who had believed him, Jesus said, "If you hold to my teaching, you are really my disciples. 32 Then you will know the truth, and the truth will set you free." 33 They answered him, "We are Abraham's descendants and have never been slaves of anyone. How can you say that we shall be set free?" 34 Jesus replied, "Very truly I tell you, everyone who sins is a slave to sin. 35 Now a slave has no permanent place in the family, but a son belongs to it forever. 36 So if the Son sets you free, you will be free indeed. 37 I know that you are Abraham's descendants. Yet you are looking for a way to kill me, because you have no room for my word.

September 29
Salvation
Hebrews 10:19–25

As you grow in God, share your faith to help
strengthen other believers in Christ.
Come together to encourage each other as you
face the many spiritual struggles in life.
The day is approaching for Christ's return.
There is much to do and much to learn.
The right to access into God's presence has
been given to enter at any time.
This will give you hope to persevere; please keep this in mind.
There is no barrier between God and man.
Christ has removed that barrier, so in God's
presence, you can humbly stand.

God welcomes all who want to spend time with Him.

Hebrews 10:19–25

A Call to Persevere in Faith
19 Therefore, brothers and sisters, since we have confidence to enter the Most Holy Place by the blood of Jesus, 20 by a new and living way opened for us through the curtain, that is, his body, 21 and since we have a great priest over the house of God, 22 let us draw near to God with a sincere heart and with the full assurance that faith brings, having our hearts sprinkled to cleanse us from a guilty conscience and having our bodies washed with pure water. 23 Let us hold unswervingly to the hope we profess, for he who promised is faithful. 24 And let us consider how we may spur one another on toward love and good deeds, 25 not giving up meeting together, as some are in the habit of doing, but encouraging one another—and all the more as you see the Day approaching.

September 30
Salvation
1 Peter 1:3–9

A new birth and a living hope are what salvation will give you.
It is the resurrection of Jesus Christ that it is through.
It cannot perish or spoil, and it will never fade away.
It can be become your inheritance today.
You may have suffered in all kinds of trials that have caused you grief.
Your inheritance is being kept in heaven under
God's protection because of your belief.
You will have great joy when Jesus Christ is
revealed it will bring you such relief.
You have not seen him, but you love and believe in Him just the same.
The joy you are filled with will bring praise to His holy name.
You will receive the end result of your faith,
which is the salvation of your soul.
This is worth more than pure gold.

The promise of heaven can be yours.

1 Peter 1:3–9

Praise to God for a Living Hope

3 Praise be to the God and Father of our Lord Jesus Christ! In his great mercy he has given us new birth into a living hope through the resurrection of Jesus Christ from the dead, 4 and into an inheritance that can never perish, spoil or fade. This inheritance is kept in heaven for you, 5 who through faith are shielded by God's power until the coming of the salvation that is ready to be revealed in the last time. 6 In all this you greatly rejoice, though now for a little while you may have had to suffer grief in all kinds of trials. 7 These have come so that the proven genuineness of your faith—of greater worth than gold, which perishes even though refined by fire—may result in praise, glory and honor when Jesus Christ is revealed. 8 Though you have not seen him, you love him; and even though you do not see him now, you believe

in him and are filled with an inexpressible and glorious joy, 9 for you are receiving the end result of your faith, the salvation of your souls.

October 1
Salvation
1 Peter 1:17–23

Do you know what you are worth?
Are you more valuable than everything on this earth?
Gold and silver are considered to be of great worth that is treasured.
Would you use this as a means for your worth to be measured?
Whether you are a slave or free,
Jesus died for you and me.
He paid the costly price to rescue us from sin.
No human could do that, not even a very close friend.
God's love for you is priceless, and this is true.
That is why He sent Jesus to die for you.

The next time you feel worthless, remember how much
God loves you—as someone worth dying for.

1 Peter 1:17–23

17 Since you call on a Father who judges each person's work impartially, live out your time as foreigners here in reverent fear. 18 For you know that it was not with perishable things such as silver or gold that you were redeemed from the empty way of life handed down to you from your ancestors, 19 but with the precious blood of Christ, a lamb without blemish or defect. 20 He was chosen before the creation of the world, but was revealed in these last times for your sake. 21 Through him you believe in God, who raised him from the dead and glorified him, and so your faith and hope are in God. 22 Now that you have purified yourselves by obeying the truth so that you have sincere love for each other, love one another deeply, from

the heart. 23 For you have been born again, not of perishable seed, but of imperishable, through the living and enduring word of God.

October 2
Salvation
1 Peter 2:4–10

Each believer is a precious stone that builds the house of God.
Each one is of His chosen people, a royal priesthood, a holy nation.
Because Christ was the propitiation.
Each one has been forgiven of sin and has been granted salvation.
Each one has been called out of darkness that
concealed what was truly sin.
Each one has been welcomed into the light that
with true love each believer has entered in.
God's holy priesthood is to offer themselves daily as a spiritual sacrifice.
Daily laying aside their desire for life, instead, to live
for Christ in the way that is spiritually right.
Having the desire to follow and to trust Him in all they say and do,
Jesus has become their cornerstone, and now
their lives are filled with what is true.

Darkness conceals what is true about spiritual death;
however, the light will reveal what is truly there.

1 Peter 2:4–10

The Living Stone and a Chosen People
4 As you come to him, the living Stone—rejected by humans but chosen by God and precious to him— 5 you also, like living stones, are being built into a spiritual house to be a holy priesthood, offering spiritual sacrifices acceptable to God through Jesus Christ. 6 For in Scripture it says:
"See, I lay a stone in Zion,
a chosen and precious cornerstone,

and the one who trusts in him
will never be put to shame."
7 Now to you who believe, this stone is precious.
But to those who do not believe,
"The stone the builders rejected
has become the cornerstone,"
8 and,
"A stone that causes people to stumble
and a rock that makes them fall."
They stumble because they disobey the message—
which is also what they were destined for.
9 But you are a chosen people, a royal priesthood, a holy nation, God's special possession, that you may declare the praises of him who called you out of darkness into his wonderful light. 10 Once you were not a people, but now you are the people of God; once you had not received mercy, but now you have received mercy.

October 3
Salvation
Spiritual Growth
Philippians 3:1–8

Okay, I may know that I am a sinner, but what does that mean?
I have abilities that have enabled me to achieve so many wonderful things.
What should I do with all my accomplishments
and the rewards they will bring?
I do not feel fulfilled, nor does my heart have a song to sing.
I am feeling emotionally empty with a life that is hollow, idle, and vain.
If this is what life is, then I am in considerable pain.
Christ wants to transform my life for eternity.
With restoration to live life as it should be.
Turning over my life to Christ, He will make it into
something beautiful that will be good and new.
I will be a new person who will be useful to
others and filled with the truth.

Living for Christ, I will have nothing to lose,
But the emptiness of having rubbish that I no longer choose.

Do not put trust in people, but in Jesus Christ,
who will restore the true meaning of life.

Philippians 3:1–8

No Confidence in the Flesh

3 Further, my brothers and sisters, rejoice in the Lord! It is no trouble for me to write the same things to you again, and it is a safeguard for you. 2 Watch out for those dogs, those evildoers, those mutilators of the flesh. 3 For it is we who are the circumcision, we who serve God by his Spirit, who boast in Christ Jesus, and who put no confidence in the flesh— 4 though I myself have reasons for such confidence. If someone else thinks they have reasons to put confidence in the flesh, I have more: 5 circumcised on the eighth day, of the people of Israel, of the tribe of Benjamin, a Hebrew of Hebrews; in regard to the law, a Pharisee; 6 as for zeal, persecuting the church; as for righteousness based on the law, faultless.
7 But whatever were gains to me I now consider loss for the sake of Christ. 8 What is more, I consider everything a loss because of the surpassing worth of knowing Christ Jesus my Lord, for whose sake I have lost all things. I consider them garbage, that I may gain Christ

Satan
October 4
Temptation
Genesis 3:1–7

Pay attention; to be watchful and alert, and you must be awake.
Temptation is constantly on the prowl, wanting you to make mistakes.
He is your enemy who prowls.
You must use your spiritual eyes like an owl.

Temptation is from Satan, who prowls like a roaring
lion looking for someone to be his prey.
Do not be his victim; you must stay on your knees and pray.
For any hint of self-will,
Satan will surely use it for real.
He will use it to make you a victim for the kill.
To escape from temptation, to God you must run.
Causing you to stand firm in your faith in Jesus Christ, God's holy Son.

The best way to escape temptation is to know that is what it is.

Genesis 3:1–7

The Fall
3 Now the serpent was more crafty than any of the wild animals
the Lord God had made. He said to the woman, "Did God
really say, 'You must not eat from any tree in the garden'?"
2 The woman said to the serpent, "We may eat fruit from the trees in the
garden, 3 but God did say, 'You must not eat fruit from the tree that is
in the middle of the garden, and you must not touch it, or you will die.'"
4 "You will not certainly die," the serpent said to the woman.
5 "For God knows that when you eat from it your eyes will be
opened, and you will be like God, knowing good and evil."
6 When the woman saw that the fruit of the tree was good
for food and pleasing to the eye, and also desirable for gaining
wisdom, she took some and ate it. She also gave some to her
husband, who was with her, and he ate it. 7 Then the eyes of both
of them were opened, and they realized they were naked; so they
sewed fig leaves together and made coverings for themselves.

October 5
Temptation
Genesis 3:1–7

Satan is the deceiver that we all need to know.
He wants to deceive you; so, to hell with him he wants you to go.
He wants you to have knowledge of things that are not true.
Like a roaring lion, Satan wants to devour you.
From the time he was in the Garden of Eden, lies he still tells.
He wants all of God's children to go to hell.
Giving his truth of what is pleasing to the eyes he wants you to see.
How great it would be to be with him in eternity.
From the lust of the flesh, pleasures he wants you to enjoy.
Now he is playing with you as if you are a toy.
From pride of life, he wants you to think no one can be greater than you.
He wants you to be so full of yourself that what you
think about yourself, you think others will too.
Satan is the deceiver that we all need to know.
He will deceive you; so, to hell with him is where he wants you to go.

Be on your guard; stand firm in the faith.
1 Corinthians 16:13

Genesis 3:1–7

3 Now the serpent was more crafty than any of the wild animals the Lord God had made. He said to the woman, "Did God really say, 'You must not eat from any tree in the garden'?" 2 The woman said to the serpent, "We may eat fruit from the trees in the garden, 3 but God did say, 'You must not eat fruit from the tree that is in the middle of the garden, and you must not touch it, or you will die.'"
4 "You will not certainly die," the serpent said to the woman.
5 "For God knows that when you eat from it your eyes will be opened, and you will be like God, knowing good and evil."

6 When the woman saw that the fruit of the tree was good for food and pleasing to the eye, and also desirable for gaining wisdom, she took some and ate it. She also gave some to her husband, who was with her, and he ate it. 7 Then the eyes of both of them were opened, and they realized they were naked; so they sewed fig leaves together and made coverings for themselves.

October 6
Temptation
Mark 14:32–42

Temptation comes when we least expect it and
when we are vulnerable and weak.
Our enemy, Satan, is ready to strike. This is not the time to sleep.
Be on guard and pray.
Satan is looking for someone to attack today.
We must be on the alert and know what we need to do.
We must remain watchful, praying for self and
for others, and with Bible study too.
The Holy Spirit will empower you in resistance.
Staying on guard and being alert, you must be consistent with persistence.
If Satan is planning an attack, you will know how to act.

"Watch and pray so that you will not fall into temptation."
Mark 14:38

Mark 14:32–42

Gethsemane
32 They went to a place called Gethsemane, and Jesus said to his disciples, "Sit here while I pray." 33 He took Peter, James and John along with him, and he began to be deeply distressed and troubled. 34 "My soul is overwhelmed with sorrow to the point of death," he said to them. "Stay here and keep watch."

35 Going a little farther, he fell to the ground and prayed that if possible the hour might pass from him. 36 "Abba, Father," he said, "everything is possible for you. Take this cup from me. Yet not what I will, but what you will."
37 Then he returned to his disciples and found them sleeping. "Simon," he said to Peter, "are you asleep? Couldn't you keep watch for one hour? 38 Watch and pray so that you will not fall into temptation. The spirit is willing, but the flesh is weak."
39 Once more he went away and prayed the same thing. 40 When he came back, he again found them sleeping, because their eyes were heavy. They did not know what to say to him.
41 Returning the third time, he said to them, "Are you still sleeping and resting? Enough! The hour has come. Look, the Son of Man is delivered into the hands of sinners. 42 Rise! Let us go! Here comes my betrayer!"

Serving Others
October 7
Serving
Exodus 31:1–11

Work, work; what does it mean to me?
Is this how life is to be lived? Is this how it is supposed to be?
Will I have to work when I go to heaven for eternity?
My attitude toward work will be how I will perform the task.
I am to give and do my very best; that is all God has asked.
All work is not hard, and some work will be fun.
I should do all my work as unto Jesus, God's holy Son.
Work is intended to serve with an attitude of gratitude,
So others will receive.
It is all about serving Jesus and what He did for
you that made you in Him believe.

How much work are you willing to do for Jesus?

Exodus 31:1–11

Bezalel and Oholiab

31 Then the Lord said to Moses, 2 "See, I have chosen Bezalel son of Uri, the son of Hur, of the tribe of Judah, 3 and I have filled him with the Spirit of God, with wisdom, with understanding, with knowledge and with all kinds of skills— 4 to make artistic designs for work in gold, silver and bronze, 5 to cut and set stones, to work in wood, and to engage in all kinds of crafts. 6 Moreover, I have appointed Oholiab son of Ahisamak, of the tribe of Dan, to help him. Also I have given ability to all the skilled workers to make everything I have commanded you: 7 the tent of meeting, the ark of the covenant law with the atonement cover on it, and all the other furnishings of the tent— 8 the table and its articles, the pure gold lampstand and all its accessories, the altar of incense, 9 the altar of burnt offering and all its utensils, the basin with its stand— 10 and also the woven garments, both the sacred garments for Aaron the priest and the garments for his sons when they serve as priests, 11 and the anointing oil and fragrant incense for the Holy Place. They are to make them just as I commanded you."

October 8
Serving
1 Kings 12:1–15

What is a leader, and what does a leader do?
Can anyone be a leader? Can this be true?
A leader who knows how to lead will be a servant to all.
He will understand and learn how to lead when he accepts the call.
This kind of leader will have a humble servant's
heart of passion and empathy.
Be willing to give of himself with sympathy.
Leading with compassion and humility is a leader who wants to be;
Leading people to unite in unity and will have love for all humanity.

Jesus taught that a good leader is a servant.

1 Kings 12:1–15

Israel Rebels Against Rehoboam

12 Rehoboam went to Shechem, for all Israel had gone there to make him king. 2 When Jeroboam son of Nebat heard this (he was still in Egypt, where he had fled from King Solomon), he returned from Egypt. 3 So they sent for Jeroboam, and he and the whole assembly of Israel went to Rehoboam and said to him: 4 "Your father put a heavy yoke on us, but now lighten the harsh labor and the heavy yoke he put on us, and we will serve you."

5 Rehoboam answered, "Go away for three days and then come back to me." So the people went away.

6 Then King Rehoboam consulted the elders who had served his father Solomon during his lifetime. "How would you advise me to answer these people?" he asked.

7 They replied, "If today you will be a servant to these people and serve them and give them a favorable answer, they will always be your servants."

8 But Rehoboam rejected the advice the elders gave him and consulted the young men who had grown up with him and were serving him.

9 He asked them, "What is your advice? How should we answer these people who say to me, 'Lighten the yoke your father put on us'?"

10 The young men who had grown up with him replied, "These people have said to you, 'Your father put a heavy yoke on us, but make our yoke lighter.' Now tell them, 'My little finger is thicker than my father's waist. 11 My father laid on you a heavy yoke; I will make it even heavier. My father scourged you with whips; I will scourge you with scorpions.'"

12 Three days later Jeroboam and all the people returned to Rehoboam, as the king had said, "Come back to me in three days."

13 The king answered the people harshly. Rejecting the advice given him by the elders, 14 he followed the advice of the young men and said, "My father made your yoke heavy; I will make it even heavier. My father scourged you with whips; I will scourge you with scorpions." 15 So the king did not listen to the people, for this turn of events was from the Lord, to fulfill the word the Lord had spoken to Jeroboam son of Nebat through Ahijah the Shilonite.

October 9
Serving Others
Galatians 6:2–10

>Carrying one another's burdens in living for Christ,
>Will help to reduce the pain while living life.
>Sharing our joy as well as sharing our pain,
>Experiencing burden bearing, life will never be the same.
>Being aware of those around us who are in need.
>When you become aware, stay on bended knees.
>Praying to Jesus to answer your prayer with a plea.
>You may be the one Jesus uses in order to meet their need.
>Always do everything you can to meet those who
>are in need in the family of Christ.
>They are your family for eternal life.
>Carrying another person's burden is loving Christ.

Galatians 6:2–10

2 Carry each other's burdens, and in this way you will fulfill the law of Christ. 3 If anyone thinks they are something when they are not, they deceive themselves. 4 Each one should test their own actions. Then they can take pride in themselves alone, without comparing themselves to someone else, 5 for each one should carry their own load. 6 Nevertheless, the one who receives instruction in the word should share all good things with their instructor. 7 Do not be deceived: God cannot be mocked. A man reaps what he sows. 8 Whoever sows to please their flesh, from the flesh will reap destruction; whoever sows to please the Spirit, from the Spirit will reap eternal life. 9 Let us not become weary in doing good, for at the proper time we will reap a harvest if we do not give up. 10 Therefore, as we have opportunity, let us do good to all people, especially to those who belong to the family of believers.

October 10
Serving Others
Love
Philippians 1:27–2:4

In serving others in the name of love, there four
things God's Word tells us to do.
We are to stand firm in one spirit, striving together as
one to be unyielding, to not desert the truth.
Because of our faith in the gospel, there will be those
who want to frighten us and who will oppose us.
So, we must stand together for Christ in all we do.
God wants us to be joyful as we think the same.
Having only one goal will be our aim.
Which is having the same mind-set: to bring glory to Jesus's holy name.
The joy of being loving, being in one spirit and of one mind.
This is how we need to be thinking all the time.
In humility is how this will be done.
Then stand firm in the hope you have in Christ Jesus, God's holy Son.
When we stand firm in our faith in Jesus Christ, let us do it in love.

Philippians 1:27–2:4

Life Worthy of the Gospel
27 Whatever happens, conduct yourselves in a manner worthy of the gospel of Christ. Then, whether I come and see you or only hear about you in my absence, I will know that you stand firm in the one Spirit, striving together as one for the faith of the gospel 28 without being frightened in any way by those who oppose you. This is a sign to them that they will be destroyed, but that you will be saved—and that by God. 29 For it has been granted to you on behalf of Christ not only to believe in him, but also to suffer for him, 30 since you are going through the same struggle you saw I had, and now hear that I still have.
Imitating Christ's Humility

2 Therefore if you have any encouragement from being united with Christ, if any comfort from his love, if any common sharing in the Spirit, if any tenderness and compassion, 2 then make my joy complete by being like-minded, having the same love, being one in spirit and of one mind. 3 Do nothing out of selfish ambition or vain conceit. Rather, in humility value others above yourselves, 4 not looking to your own interests but each of you to the interests of the others.

October 11
Serving Others
Stewardship and Giving
Matthew 25:31–40

What may I do for you?
How may I help you with what you may be going through?
I want to serve you in any way to help you get through the day;
Whatever your need may be.
I want to give what I have generously.
Whether it is of time, money, or love,
It is truly God who will be giving from above.
It is He who will provide for me to give to you in love and graciously.
I want to do it generously.
Giving is a part of experiencing God's power and
love in your life as you share it with others.

Matthew 25:31–40

The Sheep and the Goats
31 "When the Son of Man comes in his glory, and all the angels with him, he will sit on his glorious throne. 32 All the nations will be gathered before him, and he will separate the people one from another as a shepherd separates the sheep from the goats. 33 He will put the sheep on his right and the goats on his left.

34 "Then the King will say to those on his right, 'Come, you who are blessed by my Father; take your inheritance, the kingdom prepared for you since the creation of the world. 35 For I was hungry and you gave me something to eat, I was thirsty and you gave me something to drink, I was a stranger and you invited me in, 36 I needed clothes and you clothed me, I was sick and you looked after me, I was in prison and you came to visit me.'
37 "Then the righteous will answer him, 'Lord, when did we see you hungry and feed you, or thirsty and give you something to drink? 38 When did we see you a stranger and invite you in, or needing clothes and clothe you? 39 When did we see you sick or in prison and go to visit you?'
40 "The King will reply, 'Truly I tell you, whatever you did for one of the least of these brothers and sisters of mine, you did for me.'

Sin
October 12
Forgiveness
Romans 7:14–25

One day, I looked in the mirror, and what did I see?
A person filled with sin looking back at me.
Sin has a hold on me. This hold that I do not wish to be.
Why do I do the things I do not mean and want to do?
Sometimes I wonder if you experience this too.
I find myself doing the very thing, I do not want to do.
Sinning, which I know will leave me feeling sad and blue.
No matter how hard I may try not to, I will sin, and this is true.
Jesus, please help me.
I need Your forgiveness from the power of sin to be set free.

Forgiveness is a beautiful word that does the soul good.

Romans 7:14–25

14 We know that the law is spiritual; but I am unspiritual, sold as a slave to sin. 15 I do not understand what I do. For what I want to do I do not do, but what I hate I do. 16 And if I do what I do not want to do, I agree that the law is good. 17 As it is, it is no longer I myself who do it, but it is sin living in me. 18 For I know that good itself does not dwell in me, that is, in my sinful nature. For I have the desire to do what is good, but I cannot carry it out. 19 For I do not do the good I want to do, but the evil I do not want to do—this I keep on doing. 20 Now if I do what I do not want to do, it is no longer I who do it, but it is sin living in me that does it. 21 So I find this law at work: Although I want to do good, evil is right there with me. 22 For in my inner being I delight in God's law; 23 but I see another law at work in me, waging war against the law of my mind and making me a prisoner of the law of sin at work within me. 24 What a wretched man I am! Who will rescue me from this body that is subject to death? 25 Thanks be to God, who delivers me through Jesus Christ our Lord! So then, I myself in my mind am a slave to God's law, but in my sinful nature a slave to the law of sin.

October 13
Spiritual Growth
Roman 7:15–25

A prisoner of sin I do not want to be.
I find myself doing things that make me feel shame and not have integrity.
As a prisoner of sin, what can I do?
I am doing things that I do not want to do,
and I find that this is always true.
I am caught in a cycle of trying harder to be good
in obeying the rules, as I am obligated to.
No matter how hard I try, I fail, and this makes me feel blue.
Help! Help me, Lord. I very much need You.
Please let me know what I need to do.

I need Your strength, and I need Your grace. I do not
want this cycle of sin in my life to have a place.
I will focus on Jesus; this is what I will do.
I know He will always be there to help me through.
Through times of trials, when sin wants to win,
Jesus will be there for me as a true, devoted, faithful, and loyal Friend.

We all find ourselves in situations we got ourselves into and wishing we had not; however, the only way out is through Jesus. Depend on Him.

Romans 7:15–25

15 I do not understand what I do. For what I want to do I do not do, but what I hate I do. 16 And if I do what I do not want to do, I agree that the law is good. 17 As it is, it is no longer I myself who do it, but it is sin living in me. 18 For I know that good itself does not dwell in me, that is, in my sinful nature. For I have the desire to do what is good, but I cannot carry it out. 19 For I do not do the good I want to do, but the evil I do not want to do—this I keep on doing. 20 Now if I do what I do not want to do, it is no longer I who do it, but it is sin living in me that does it.
21 So I find this law at work: Although I want to do good, evil is right there with me. 22 For in my inner being I delight in God's law; 23 but I see another law at work in me, waging war against the law of my mind and making me a prisoner of the law of sin at work within me. 24 What a wretched man I am! Who will rescue me from this body that is subject to death? 25 Thanks be to God, who delivers me through Jesus Christ our Lord!
So then, I myself in my mind am a slave to God's law,
but in my sinful nature a slave to the law of sin.

October 14
Sin
Temptation
Genesis 4:1–8

There are many ways sin will entice.
These will make you feel that you have a right,
To have all your physical senses satisfied;
Convinced that living right should not be used as a guide.
Sin wants to be in complete control.
It will make you think that to sin is to be bold.
There is one way out from sin's trap.
However, to find the approach you must use God's map.
When you walk with the Spirit, your flesh will not be pleased,
Because you will not meet its demanding and selfish needs.
When facing temptation, you must do it with resistance;
God will be there to give you divine assistance.
From temptation, you must flee;
As you resist, it will let you be.

When you know you are being tempted, you have the authority to resist.

Genesis 4:1–8

Cain and Abel

4 Adam made love to his wife Eve, and she became pregnant and gave birth to Cain. She said, "With the help of the Lord I have brought forth a man." 2 Later she gave birth to his brother Abel. Now Abel kept flocks, and Cain worked the soil. 3 In the course of time Cain brought some of the fruits of the soil as an offering to the Lord. 4 And Abel also brought an offering—fat portions from some of the firstborn of his flock. The Lord looked with favor on Abel and his offering, 5 but on Cain and his offering he did not look with favor. So Cain was very angry, and his face was downcast.
6 Then the Lord said to Cain, "Why are you angry? Why is your face downcast? 7 If you do what is right, will you not be

accepted? But if you do not do what is right, sin is crouching at your door; it desires to have you, but you must rule over it."
8 Now Cain said to his brother Abel, "Let's go out to the field." While they were in the field, Cain attacked his brother Abel and killed him.

October 15
Sin
Temptation
1 Corinthians 10:1–13

How do we sin?
It is when we set our hearts on evil things;
Then we have to face the consequences that it brings.
Sin, why do you tempt me so?
Tell me, tell me; I want to know.
It is not sin when we aren't tempted, but it is a
sin when we surrender to its demands.
Temptation will come. But, sin, I would not heed to your commands.
I am putting my trust in God and in His loving hands.
Temptation, when you come, I will leave;
Because God has made an escape for me.
Temptation, you are not my friend;
Given the fact you want me to go against God and sin.

And God is faithful; he would not let you be
tempted beyond what you can bear.
1 Corinthians 10:13.

1 Corinthians 10:1–13

Warnings From Israel's History
10 For I do not want you to be ignorant of the fact, brothers and sisters, that our ancestors were all under the cloud and that they all passed through the sea. 2 They were all baptized into Moses in the cloud and in the sea. 3 They all ate the same spiritual food 4 and drank the same

spiritual drink; for they drank from the spiritual rock that accompanied them, and that rock was Christ. 5 Nevertheless, God was not pleased with most of them; their bodies were scattered in the wilderness. 6 Now these things occurred as examples to keep us from setting our hearts on evil things as they did. 7 Do not be idolaters, as some of them were; as it is written: "The people sat down to eat and drink and got up to indulge in revelry." 8 We should not commit sexual immorality, as some of them did—and in one day twentythree thousand of them died. 9 We should not test Christ, as some of them did—and were killed by snakes. 10 And do not grumble, as some of them did—and were killed by the destroying angel. 11 These things happened to them as examples and were written down as warnings for us, on whom the culmination of the ages has come. 12 So, if you think you are standing firm, be careful that you don't fall! 13 No temptation has overtaken you except what is common to mankind. And God is faithful; he will not let you be tempted beyond what you can bear. But when you are tempted, he will also provide a way out so that you can endure it.

October 16
Sin
Temptation
1 Corinthians 10:1–13

Temptation came to visit one day.
He wanted to know if he could visit or perhaps stay.
Temptation, temptation, I do not know.
Temptation replied, "Let me stay, please. I have much to show.
Life can be so boring when there is nothing to do.
Please let me spend the day with you."
Temptation, temptation, that sounds risky at best.
Is this some kind of test?
This is no test, and you will see.
It is learning how to have fun before eternity.
The last time you came to visit, God had made an escape for me.

He did not want me to sin.
Temptation, you are not my friend.
Particularly when you entice me to sin.
Go away, and never come back again.
If you think you are standing firm, be careful that you don't fall!
1 Corinthians 10:12

1 Corinthians 10:1–13

Warnings From Israel's History
10 For I do not want you to be ignorant of the fact, brothers and sisters, that our ancestors were all under the cloud and that they all passed through the sea. 2 They were all baptized into Moses in the cloud and in the sea. 3 They all ate the same spiritual food 4 and drank the same spiritual drink; for they drank from the spiritual rock that accompanied them, and that rock was Christ. 5 Nevertheless, God was not pleased with most of them; their bodies were scattered in the wilderness.
6 Now these things occurred as examples to keep us from setting our hearts on evil things as they did. 7 Do not be idolaters, as some of them were; as it is written: "The people sat down to eat and drink and got up to indulge in revelry." 8 We should not commit sexual immorality, as some of them did—and in one day twentythree thousand of them died. 9 We should not test Christ, as some of them did—and were killed by snakes. 10 And do not grumble, as some of them did—and were killed by the destroying angel.
11 These things happened to them as examples and were written down as warnings for us, on whom the culmination of the ages has come. 12 So, if you think you are standing firm, be careful that you don't fall! 13 No temptation has overtaken you except what is common to mankind. And God is faithful; he will not let you be tempted beyond what you can bear. But when you are tempted, he will also provide a way out so that you can endure it.

Spiritual Gifts
October 17
1 Corinthians 12:4–14

As believers in Christ, we are uniquely one;
We are united in the body of God's holy Son.
We each have been given gifts to faithfully serve;
So the knowledge of Jesus Christ will be reserved.
Lord, we ask that You will help us to use our gifts in serving faithfully.
There are many different kinds of work for each believer to do.
When we work in unity, we are proving God's Word is true.
We are to express Your love as You want it to be.
Leading unbelievers to know You and Your love for them for eternity.

Each believer is unique in God's eyes.

1 Corinthians 12:4–14

4 There are different kinds of gifts, but the same Spirit distributes them. 5 There are different kinds of service, but the same Lord. 6 There are different kinds of working, but in all of them and in everyone it is the same God at work. 7 Now to each one the manifestation of the Spirit is given for the common good. 8 To one there is given through the Spirit a message of wisdom, to another a message of knowledge by means of the same Spirit, 9 to another faith by the same Spirit, to another gifts of healing by that one Spirit, 10 to another miraculous powers, to another prophecy, to another distinguishing between spirits, to another speaking in different kinds of tongues, and to still another the interpretation of tongues. 11 All these are the work of one and the same Spirit, and he distributes them to each one, just as he determines.
Unity and Diversity in the Body
12 Just as a body, though one, has many parts, but all its many parts form one body, so it is with Christ. 13 For we were all baptized by one Spirit so as to form one body—whether Jews or Gentiles,

slave or free—and we were all given the one Spirit to drink.
14 Even so the body is not made up of one part but of many.

Spiritual Growth
October 18
Proverbs 2:1–5

What hidden treasure will I find
When I explore Your commands with all my mind?
I will listen to Your wisdom and apply my heart to understand,
The hidden treasure of Your commands.
I will search out this treasure as if I searching
for silver hidden deep in the earth.
This hidden wisdom, to me, is of great worth.
It is all I will need to know and understand,
The fear and knowledge of God, which give
me joy to obey His commands.

The Bible is filled with great treasure that will
enable you to live and enjoy life.

Proverbs 2:1–5

Moral Benefits of Wisdom
2
My son, if you accept my words
and store up my commands within you,
2
turning your ear to wisdom
and applying your heart to understanding—
3
indeed, if you call out for insight
and cry aloud for understanding,
4
and if you look for it as for silver

and search for it as for hidden treasure,
5
then you will understand the fear of the Lord
and find the knowledge of God.

October 19
Spiritual Growth
Luke 19:1–10

I want to see Jesus in my life today.
I will read the Bible and get down on my knees and pray.
Jesus tells me from the Bible that in my heart I have pride.
It my imagined self-sufficiency that has caused corrosion inside.
I need to see Jesus as my counselor for each day;
He showed me that to do away with pride, I must repent and pray.
Anxiety has filled my thoughts, and I have no peace.
Jesus tells me I need to see Him as the Prince of
Peace, so my anxious thoughts need to cease.
Jesus tells me that focusing on fulfilling my status of having
wealth and prestige will please no one but me.
I need to see Him as the Bread of Life.
I need to remember how and why He died for me as a sacrifice.
I want to see You, Jesus, in my life today.
Without You, Jesus, I will be lost in the world of life and not find my way.

Pursue Jesus will all you have.

Luke 19:1–10

Zacchaeus the Tax Collector
19 Jesus entered Jericho and was passing through. 2 A man was there by the name of Zacchaeus; he was a chief tax collector and was wealthy. 3 He wanted to see who Jesus was, but because he was short he could not see over the crowd. 4 So he ran ahead and climbed a sycamore-fig tree to see him, since Jesus was coming that way.

5 When Jesus reached the spot, he looked up and said to him, "Zacchaeus, come down immediately. I must stay at your house today." 6 So he came down at once and welcomed him gladly. 7 All the people saw this and began to mutter, "He has gone to be the guest of a sinner." 8 But Zacchaeus stood up and said to the Lord, "Look, Lord! Here and now I give half of my possessions to the poor, and if I have cheated anybody out of anything, I will pay back four times the amount." 9 Jesus said to him, "Today salvation has come to this house, because this man, too, is a son of Abraham. 10 For the Son of Man came to seek and to save the lost."

October 20
Spiritual Growth
Living with Other Believers
Ephesians 4:1–16

I want to grow in Christ.
I want to learn how to live healthy and right.
I will look to the church, to those who are spiritually mature,
Who will be patient, in love, with me, for sure.
Facilitating my Christian journey, how to live out my faith;
Pastors who will shepherd me as Jesus's sheep,
Providing spiritual guidance that I can keep,
Teachers who will instruct in showing me the way,
As I learn how I am to live every day.
Spiritual mentors I will need as I strive in my Christian life to mature;
Knowing that, one day, I will be there to help others to grow, for sure.

As the body of Christ grows, we are all here to help each other to grow.

Ephesians 4:1–16

Unity and Maturity in the Body of Christ

4 As a prisoner for the Lord, then, I urge you to live a life worthy of the calling you have received. 2 Be completely humble and gentle; be patient, bearing with one another in love. 3 Make every effort to keep the unity of the Spirit through the bond of peace. 4 There is one body and one Spirit, just as you were called to one hope when you were called; 5 one Lord, one faith, one baptism; 6 one God and Father of all, who is over all and through all and in all.

7 But to each one of us grace has been given as Christ apportioned it. 8 This is why it says:

"When he ascended on high,
he took many captives
and gave gifts to his people."

9 (What does "he ascended" mean except that he also descended to the lower, earthly regions? 10 He who descended is the very one who ascended higher than all the heavens, in order to fill the whole universe.) 11 So Christ himself gave the apostles, the prophets, the evangelists, the pastors and teachers, 12 to equip his people for works of service, so that the body of Christ may be built up 13 until we all reach unity in the faith and in the knowledge of the Son of God and become mature, attaining to the whole measure of the fullness of Christ.

14 Then we will no longer be infants, tossed back and forth by the waves, and blown here and there by every wind of teaching and by the cunning and craftiness of people in their deceitful scheming. 15 Instead, speaking the truth in love, we will grow to become in every respect the mature body of him who is the head, that is, Christ. 16 From him the whole body, joined and held together by every supporting ligament, grows and builds itself up in love, as each part does its work.

Spiritual Transformation
October 21
Romans 12:1–8

Allow your mind to be renewed today.
Do not get influenced by this world in what it does and what it says.
Be transformed in your mind.

You must do this all the time.
Let maturity be your goal to achieve.
This digital age will bombard you with information
that may difficult to believe.
Let God's Word shape your mind.
This is the type of influence you need to have all the time.

Spiritual transformation is being renewed in your mind.

Romans 12:1–8

A Living Sacrifice

12 Therefore, I urge you, brothers and sisters, in view of God's mercy, to offer your bodies as a living sacrifice, holy and pleasing to God—this is your true and proper worship. 2 Do not conform to the pattern of this world, but be transformed by the renewing of your mind. Then you will be able to test and approve what God's will is—his good, pleasing and perfect will.

Humble Service in the Body of Christ

3 For by the grace given me I say to every one of you: Do not think of yourself more highly than you ought, but rather think of yourself with sober judgment, in accordance with the faith God has distributed to each of you. 4 For just as each of us has one body with many members, and these members do not all have the same function, 5 so in Christ we, though many, form one body, and each member belongs to all the others. 6 We have different gifts, according to the grace given to each of us. If your gift is prophesying, then prophesy in accordance with your faith; 7 if it is serving, then serve; if it is teaching, then teach; 8 if it is to encourage, then give encouragement; if it is giving, then give generously; if it is to lead, do it diligently; if it is to show mercy, do it cheerfully.

October 22
Spiritual Transformation
1 Corinthians 9:24–27

The race is on; how well will you do?

Others in the race will make every possible effort
to do their best, and what about you?
The prize is the focus, but who will win?
However, this race is about competing against sin.
You must be in training to be transformed for change to take place.
This is an incredible challenge for the whole human race.
No longer allowing old and bad behaviors be in charge, causing you to sin.
No longer demanding your rights and that things
must go your way, refusing to give in.
This is the challenge that your faith in Christ will enable you to win.
Transformation will take time as you prepare for the race.
As you become like Christ, in heaven you will have a winner's place.

Discipline your mind to stay focused on Christ.

1 Corinthians 9:24–27

The Need for Self-Discipline
24 Do you not know that in a race all the runners run, but only one gets the prize? Run in such a way as to get the prize. 25 Everyone who competes in the games goes into strict training. They do it to get a crown that will not last, but we do it to get a crown that will last forever. 26 Therefore I do not run like someone running aimlessly; I do not fight like a boxer beating the air. 27 No, I strike a blow to my body and make it my slave so that after I have preached to others, I myself will not be disqualified for the prize.

October 23
Spiritual Transformation
2 Corinthians 5:12–21

Leave the past behind in your new life in Christ.
Your new life will be filled with joy, peace, love, and spiritual insight.
You were once dominated by sin.
When you repented, into your heart Jesus came.

You have been transformed. So, let your old life fade away.
You are a new person in Christ today.
You have been reconciled to God through Christ.
Now the Holy Spirit will empower you to live right.
Life will not be easy. Old ways and habits will have to end.
They will only lead you back into sin.
The Holy Spirit will give you inner strength to make it through.
Giving you the understanding that Jesus will never leave or forsake you.

Life feels great when you know you're forgiven.

2 Corinthians 5:12–21

12 We are not trying to commend ourselves to you again, but are giving you an opportunity to take pride in us, so that you can answer those who take pride in what is seen rather than in what is in the heart. 13 If we are "out of our mind," as some say, it is for God; if we are in our right mind, it is for you. 14 For Christ's love compels us, because we are convinced that one died for all, and therefore all died. 15 And he died for all, that those who live should no longer live for themselves but for him who died for them and was raised again. 16 So from now on we regard no one from a worldly point of view. Though we once regarded Christ in this way, we do so no longer. 17 Therefore, if anyone is in Christ, the new creation has come: The old has gone, the new is here! 18 All this is from God, who reconciled us to himself through Christ and gave us the ministry of reconciliation: 19 that God was reconciling the world to himself in Christ, not counting people's sins against them. And he has committed to us the message of reconciliation. 20 We are therefore Christ's ambassadors, as though God were making his appeal through us. We implore you on Christ's behalf: Be reconciled to God. 21 God made him who had no sin to be sin for us, so that in him we might become the righteousness of God.

October 24
Spiritual Transformation
Galatians 5:16–25

You need to change.
I need to change.
As believers in Christ, we cannot remain the same.
By means of the Holy Spirit, He will not allow us in sin to remain.
It is through the Holy Spirit that this change will take place.
We need to be consciously dependent on
Him to receive God's saving grace.
We need to be consciously dependent on Him to help
us in changing our attitude to have gratitude.
Our old sinful way of life needs to be changed to live for Jesus Christ.
It is not our effort that allows the change to take place.
It is in surrendering moment by moment in trusting
Christ that our victory will be based.

Our efforts will never bring change of spiritual
transformation in our lives.

Galatians 5:16–25

16 So I say, walk by the Spirit, and you will not gratify the desires of the flesh. 17 For the flesh desires what is contrary to the Spirit, and the Spirit what is contrary to the flesh. They are in conflict with each other, so that you are not to do whatever you want.
18 But if you are led by the Spirit, you are not under the law.
19 The acts of the flesh are obvious: sexual immorality, impurity and debauchery; 20 idolatry and witchcraft; hatred, discord, jealousy, fits of rage, selfish ambition, dissensions, factions 21 and envy; drunkenness, orgies, and the like. I warn you, as I did before, that those who live like this will not inherit the kingdom of God.
22 But the fruit of the Spirit is love, joy, peace, forbearance, kindness, goodness, faithfulness, 23 gentleness and self-control. Against such things there is no law. 24 Those who belong to

Christ Jesus have crucified the flesh with its passions and desires.
25 Since we live by the Spirit, let us keep in step with the Spirit.

October 25
Spiritual Transformation
Revelation 2:12–17

As a follower of Christ, I am a new person, and I have a new name too.
I belong to Jesus, so what about you?
My identity has been changed; I am no longer the same.
I am a new creation,
Because I have salvation.
I am filled with joy, love, and delight.
The Holy Spirit has given me great spiritual insight.
Spiritual transformation has happened to me.
I have a new name and a new identity.

When I go to heaven, I will be brand-new.

Revelation 2:12–17

To the Church in Pergamum
12 "To the angel of the church in Pergamum write:
These are the words of him who has the sharp, double-edged sword. 13 I know where you live—where Satan has his throne. Yet you remain true to my name. You did not renounce your faith in me, not even in the days of Antipas, my faithful witness, who was put to death in your city—where Satan lives.
14 Nevertheless, I have a few things against you: There are some among you who hold to the teaching of Balaam, who taught Balak to entice the Israelites to sin so that they ate food sacrificed to idols and committed sexual immorality. 15 Likewise, you also have those who hold to the teaching of the Nicolaitans. 16 Repent therefore! Otherwise, I will soon come to you and will fight against them with the sword of my mouth.
17 Whoever has ears, let them hear what the Spirit says to the churches. To the one who is victorious, I will give some of the hidden manna. I will also give that person a white stone with a new name written on it, known only to the one who receives it.

October 26
Spiritual Transformation
God's Care
2 Peter 1:1–10

God has given us everything we need to live godly and right.
Because God has unlimited power, we are not
lacking in any spiritual insight.
To live for Him, God has graciously provided us all that we need.
We are given grace and peace in abundance indeed.
Do not attempt to live in your own strength. What will it profit you?
It will cause you to be blind and shortsighted too,
Causing you to forget that you have been cleansed from past sins.
This blindness and shortsightedness will be
the reason for you to stumble again.

Once you have received Christ as your Savior and Lord, you
have everything you need in order to live a godly life.

2 Peter 1:1–10

1 Simon Peter, a servant and apostle of Jesus Christ,
To those who through the righteousness of our God and Savior
Jesus Christ have received a faith as precious as ours:
2 Grace and peace be yours in abundance through
the knowledge of God and of Jesus our Lord.
Confirming One's Calling and Election
3 His divine power has given us everything we need for a godly life through our knowledge of him who called us by his own glory and goodness. 4 Through these he has given us his very great and precious promises, so that through them you may participate in the divine nature, having escaped the corruption in the world caused by evil desires.

5 For this very reason, make every effort to add to your faith goodness; and to goodness, knowledge; 6 and to knowledge, self-control; and to self-control, perseverance; and to perseverance, godliness; 7 and to godliness, mutual affection; and to mutual affection, love. 8 For if you possess these qualities in increasing measure, they will keep you from being ineffective and unproductive in your knowledge of our Lord Jesus Christ. 9 But whoever does not have them is nearsighted and blind, forgetting that they have been cleansed from their past sins. 10 Therefore, my brothers and sisters, make every effort to confirm your calling and election. For if you do these things, you will never stumble,

October 27
Spiritual Transformation
God's Love
1 Corinthians 6:9–11; 13:4–7

What are your struggles, and what brokenness do you face?
God's love will bring about spiritual transformation to you from
your experiences, from hurt and pain, and from the human race.
Only God can heal a broken life and transform
it through His amazing grace.
He will do it with His love that will be patient and kind to you.
His love is not envy in being resentful. When you experience
His love, you will learn that this is absolutely true.
His love is not boastful or proud, it does not dishonor others, it is not
self-seeking, and it is not easily angered; it just always wants to love you.
His love will not keep a record of wrongs,
Because His love for you is very strong.
His love takes no delight in evil, but the truth is what it rejoices in.
Rejoicing in the truth will prevent you from wanting to sin.
His love will protect and make it easy to trust, to persevere with hope.
This kind of love will always be here to help you in your
struggles and brokenness and to know how to cope.

Only through God's grace can a life experience spiritual transformation.

1 Corinthians 6:9–11

9 Or do you not know that wrongdoers will not inherit the kingdom of God? Do not be deceived: Neither the sexually immoral nor idolaters nor adulterers nor men who have sex with men 10 nor thieves nor the greedy nor drunkards nor slanderers nor swindlers will inherit the kingdom of God. 11 And that is what some of you were. But you were washed, you were sanctified, you were justified in the name of the Lord Jesus Christ and by the Spirit of our God.

1 Corinthians 13:4–7

4 Love is patient, love is kind. It does not envy, it does not boast, it is not proud. 5 It does not dishonor others, it is not self-seeking, it is not easily angered, it keeps no record of wrongs. 6 Love does not delight in evil but rejoices with the truth. 7 It always protects, always trusts, always hopes, always perseveres.

October 28
Spiritual Transformation
Holy Spirit
Ezekiel 18:25–32

Seeking a new start will be choosing to change.
Knowing what sin has done to your life, you
do not wish to remain the same.
Through the power of Jesus's resurrection,
the Holy Spirit will empower you.
You will be able to have change to your heart, because this is true.
God will give you a new heart and a new attitude in
everything you will say and everything you will do.
It is a choice to choose to want change.
No longer allowing sin to be in control so
you will always remain the same.
This will be a revolution that can begin today.

Just start by asking God for forgiveness; telling Him
you want a new life in Him is all you need to say.

Be transformed by the way you think.

Ezekiel 18:25–32

25 "Yet you say, 'The way of the Lord is not just.' Hear, you Israelites: Is my way unjust? Is it not your ways that are unjust? 26 If a righteous person turns from their righteousness and commits sin, they will die for it; because of the sin they have committed they will die. 27 But if a wicked person turns away from the wickedness they have committed and does what is just and right, they will save their life. 28 Because they consider all the offenses they have committed and turn away from them, that person will surely live; they will not die. 29 Yet the Israelites say, 'The way of the Lord is not just.' Are my ways unjust, people of Israel? Is it not your ways that are unjust? 30 "Therefore, you Israelites, I will judge each of you according to your own ways, declares the Sovereign Lord. Repent! Turn away from all your offenses; then sin will not be your downfall. 31 Rid yourselves of all the offenses you have committed, and get a new heart and a new spirit. Why will you die, people of Israel? 32 For I take no pleasure in the death of anyone, declares the Sovereign Lord. Repent and live!

October 29
Spiritual Transformation
Loving Others
Ephesians 2:1–10

I was once dead to life in my transgressions and my sins.
God transformed my life, then Jesus came in.
I once followed the ways of this world;
Gratifying the craving of my flesh, wanting to be like my friends.
This is how sin in my life came in.
God, who is rich in mercy, it is by His grace that I have been made free.

Sin no longer has control over me.
I was created to do good works that I cannot boast about.
I am just so filled with joy and empowered to pursue
life that it makes me jump and shout.
I used to be dead in sin.
Now I am alive to live because into my heart Jesus came in.

Let your light shine before others, that they may see your
good deeds and glorify our Father in heaven.
Matthew 5:16

Ephesians 2:1–10

Made Alive in Christ

2 As for you, you were dead in your transgressions and sins, 2 in which you used to live when you followed the ways of this world and of the ruler of the kingdom of the air, the spirit who is now at work in those who are disobedient. 3 All of us also lived among them at one time, gratifying the cravings of our flesh and following its desires and thoughts. Like the rest, we were by nature deserving of wrath. 4 But because of his great love for us, God, who is rich in mercy, 5 made us alive with Christ even when we were dead in transgressions—it is by grace you have been saved. 6 And God raised us up with Christ and seated us with him in the heavenly realms in Christ Jesus, 7 in order that in the coming ages he might show the incomparable riches of his grace, expressed in his kindness to us in Christ Jesus. 8 For it is by grace you have been saved, through faith—and this is not from yourselves, it is the gift of God— 9 not by works, so that no one can boast. 10 For we are God's handiwork, created in Christ Jesus to do good works, which God prepared in advance for us to do.

October 30
Spiritual Transformation
Living Like Christ
Psalm 138:7–8; Ephesians 2:6–10

As a child of God, I must be transformed into the image of Christ.
The transformation will not be easy as I surrender my life.
God's saving grace through faith will accomplish this work in me.
It will continue until I enter into eternity.
The process is wonderful and painful too.
In the end, Jesus, I will be just like You.

Spiritual transformation into the image of Christ is not easy,
but it will make a difference in how you experience life.

Psalm 138:7–8

7
Though I walk in the midst of trouble,
you preserve my life.
You stretch out your hand against the anger of my foes;
with your right hand you save me.
8
The Lord will vindicate me;
your love, Lord, endures forever—
do not abandon the works of your hands.

Ephesians 2:6–10

6 And God raised us up with Christ and seated us with him in the heavenly realms in Christ Jesus, 7 in order that in the coming ages he might show the incomparable riches of his grace, expressed in his kindness to us in Christ Jesus. 8 For it is by grace you have been saved, through faith— and this is not from yourselves, it is the gift of God— 9 not by works, so that no one can boast. 10 For we are God's handiwork, created in Christ Jesus to do good works, which God prepared in advance for us to do.

Suffering
October 31
Psalm 40:1–5

During times of suffering, it is difficult to see the light.
For this reason, you are in a fight.
The fight is to wait patiently for God to answer you.
During this time, putting your trust in Him is all you must do.
During times of suffering do not be tempted to turn
to those who are wise in their own ways.
This is the perfect time to be on your knees; to Jesus you must pray.
Let Christ be your solid Rock on which to stand.
Your suffering He surely understands.
God of wonders, who can compare to You?
To tell of all Your deeds is too numerous to count to.

When you are waiting on God, is it for an answer? Or is
He waiting on you to find out more about who He is?

Psalm 40:1–5

For the director of music. Of David. A psalm.
1
I waited patiently for the Lord;
he turned to me and heard my cry.
2
He lifted me out of the slimy pit,
out of the mud and mire;
he set my feet on a rock
and gave me a firm place to stand.
3
He put a new song in my mouth,
a hymn of praise to our God.
Many will see and fear the Lord
and put their trust in him.

4
Blessed is the one
who trusts in the Lord,
who does not look to the proud,
to those who turn aside to false gods.
 5
Many, Lord my God,
are the wonders you have done,
the things you planned for us.
None can compare with you;
were I to speak and tell of your deeds,
they would be too many to declare.

November 1
God
Exodus 13:17–22

Suffering has many lessons to teach about life.
The lessons you must learn may not all seem to be good and right.
You may seek the short and easy road to travel through life,
thinking this is the right or correct choice to make.
This road may be filled with many obstacles that will
cause you to make many unnecessary mistakes.
These mistakes will not alarm you or warrant the need to hesitate.
To know that there are things and situations that need
to be avoided because a disaster could be near.
Now this obstacle has brought you much to fear.
Now the long road may be hard with much work to do.
In the long run, this will surely be very beneficial to you.
It should help you to seek God's guidance and
allow Him to show you the way.
It will encourage you to think and know how to pray.
You may not understand all the reasons for this
journey's path and how long it will last.
It is a journey that has a lesson that you will learn very fast.

When you understand you do not know how life is
supposed to be lived, you will seek God, because it was
He who created life and the way it should be lived.

Exodus 13:17–22

Crossing the Sea
17 When Pharaoh let the people go, God did not lead them on the road through the Philistine country, though that was shorter. For God said, "If they face war, they might change their minds and return to Egypt." 18 So God led the people around by the desert road toward the Red Sea. The Israelites went up out of Egypt ready for battle.
19 Moses took the bones of Joseph with him because Joseph had made the Israelites swear an oath. He had said, "God will surely come to your aid, and then you must carry my bones up with you from this place."
20 After leaving Sukkoth they camped at Etham on the edge of the desert. 21 By day the Lord went ahead of them in a pillar of cloud to guide them on their way and by night in a pillar of fire to give them light, so that they could travel by day or night. 22 Neither the pillar of cloud by day nor the pillar of fire by night left its place in front of the people.

November 2
Suffering
Isaiah 61:1–4

The world we live in is fallen, where there is brokenness, pain, and despair.
These experiences will leave you to believe that little can be
done to change things and that no one really cares.
However, this is not true.
The hopelessness of the world situation will always be.
God has sent a Savior to rescue you and me.
Our Savior, Jesus Christ, has done what no one else could do.
He sacrificed His life on the cross to save this world from sin, and this is true.
His love for us has turned our mourning to dancing.
This is good news that all need to hear.

We have a Savior who will always be here for us,
because His Word has made that very clear.

Only Jesus can give you a song to sing that will
turn your mourning to dancing.

Isaiah 61:1–4

The Year of the Lord's Favor
61
The Spirit of the Sovereign Lord is on me,
because the Lord has anointed me
to proclaim good news to the poor.
He has sent me to bind up the brokenhearted,
to proclaim freedom for the captives
and release from darkness for the prisoners,
2
to proclaim the year of the Lord's favor
and the day of vengeance of our God,
to comfort all who mourn,
3
and provide for those who grieve in Zion—
to bestow on them a crown of beauty
instead of ashes,
the oil of joy
instead of mourning,
and a garment of praise
instead of a spirit of despair.
They will be called oaks of righteousness,
a planting of the Lord
for the display of his splendor.
4
They will rebuild the ancient ruins
and restore the places long devastated;
they will renew the ruined cities
that have been devastated for generations.

November 3
Suffering
God's Care
Psalm 35:17–28

How long must I wait before this suffering ends?
How long must I anticipate in dealing with the presence of sin?
These burdens may be overwhelming, and the hardship too.
Lord God, I will put my trust in You.
You will give me the strength to endure my suffering and pain.
When it is over, I know I will not be the same.
My trust in You will have grown deeper with
the intimacy of knowing You.
Suffering has a season of testing of your faith. This is so very true.
It will encourage spiritual growth as you learn in
suffering, while waiting, what to do.

While you are experiencing suffering, seek God.

Psalm 35:17–28

17
How long, Lord, will you look on?
Rescue me from their ravages,
my precious life from these lions.
18
I will give you thanks in the great assembly;
among the throngs I will praise you.
19
Do not let those gloat over me
who are my enemies without cause;
do not let those who hate me without reason
maliciously wink the eye.
20
They do not speak peaceably,

but devise false accusations
against those who live quietly in the land.

21

They sneer at me and say, "Aha! Aha!
With our own eyes we have seen it."

22

Lord, you have seen this; do not be silent.
Do not be far from me, Lord.

23

Awake, and rise to my defense!
Contend for me, my God and Lord.

24

Vindicate me in your righteousness, Lord my God;
do not let them gloat over me.

25

Do not let them think, "Aha, just what we wanted!"
or say, "We have swallowed him up."

26

May all who gloat over my distress
be put to shame and confusion;
may all who exalt themselves over me
be clothed with shame and disgrace.

27

May those who delight in my vindication
shout for joy and gladness;
may they always say, "The Lord be exalted,
who delights in the well-being of his servant."

28

My tongue will proclaim your righteousness,
your praises all day long.

November 4
Suffering
God's Care
Psalm 55:4–23

God, I will give you the problems that I face today.
My problems are causing me to suffer in many different ways.
I acknowledge and recognize, God, that I need Your
support, and I release my problems to You.
I want You to be in control and be in every aspect of my life,
Because You know what would be right.
You will know what it is that I need to do.
I will not try to do everything in my own strength and
my own effort, but I will find my rest in You.
Thank You for sustaining me as You see me through.
God cares about what happens to us.

Psalm 55:4–23

4
My heart is in anguish within me;
the terrors of death have fallen on me.
5
Fear and trembling have beset me;
horror has overwhelmed me.
6
I said, "Oh, that I had the wings of a dove!
I would fly away and be at rest.
7
I would flee far away
and stay in the desert;
8
I would hurry to my place of shelter,
far from the tempest and storm."

9
Lord, confuse the wicked, confound their words,
for I see violence and strife in the city.
10
Day and night they prowl about on its walls;
malice and abuse are within it.
11
Destructive forces are at work in the city;
threats and lies never leave its streets.
12
If an enemy were insulting me,
I could endure it;
if a foe were rising against me,
I could hide.
13
But it is you, a man like myself,
my companion, my close friend,
14
with whom I once enjoyed sweet fellowship
at the house of God,
as we walked about
among the worshipers.
15
Let death take my enemies by surprise;
let them go down alive to the realm of the dead,
for evil finds lodging among them.
16
As for me, I call to God,
and the Lord saves me.
17
Evening, morning and noon
I cry out in distress,
and he hears my voice.
18
He rescues me unharmed
from the battle waged against me,
even though many oppose me.

19
God, who is enthroned from of old,
who does not change—
he will hear them and humble them,
because they have no fear of God.
20
My companion attacks his friends;
he violates his covenant.
21
His talk is smooth as butter,
yet war is in his heart;
his words are more soothing than oil,
yet they are drawn swords.
22
Cast your cares on the Lord
and he will sustain you;
he will never let
the righteous be shaken.
23
But you, God, will bring down the wicked
into the pit of decay;
the bloodthirsty and deceitful
will not live out half their days.
But as for me, I trust in you.

November 5
Suffering
God's Care
John 14:15–21

While on life's journey, the road ahead I cannot always see;
I have no idea what will be ahead of me.
Whatever I may encounter, I know as I trust in Jesus, He will be there;
Because He truly cares.

On the road of life's journey, there may be mountains,
valley, and rivers with challenges waiting for me.
I will call out to the Lord Jesus for directions so that I can see.
I need to see the highs and the lows, the heartache,
the solitude, and the sorrows.
I need to know the terrain, the crowded highways, and
the lonely roads that will be my tomorrow.
I not only needed to be reminded of my challenges but also
of the truth that God will always be here with me.
These challenges of life will not imprison me, because
Jesus's death on the cross has set me free.
I am free to travel through this life to be prepared for life in eternity.
Life journey is meant to be traveled with Jesus.

John 14:15–21

Jesus Promises the Holy Spirit
15 "If you love me, keep my commands. 16 And I will ask the Father, and he will give you another advocate to help you and be with you forever— 17 the Spirit of truth. The world cannot accept him, because it neither sees him nor knows him. But you know him, for he lives with you and will be in you. 18 I will not leave you as orphans; I will come to you. 19 Before long, the world will not see me anymore, but you will see me. Because I live, you also will live. 20 On that day you will realize that I am in my Father, and you are in me, and I am in you. 21 Whoever has my commands and keeps them is the one who loves me. The one who loves me will be loved by my Father, and I too will love them and show myself to them."

November 6
Heaven
Philippians 1:12–26

What is it to suffer for Christ?
What from it is there to gain in this life?
The chains of suffering give you confidence in the
Lord, to proclaim the gospel without fear.
Because Jesus gave a promise, He will never
leave you; He will always be near.
Now, there are various reasons why the gospel is preached.
Some are from envy and rivalry.
From this motive, the inspiration or incentive does
not understand the reason for Calvary.
But when it is done out of goodwill and out of love,
Then it is done in and for God in heaven above.
Whether the motives are false or true, you have
to know why Christ died for you.
Suffering for Christ to bring the kingdom of
heaven to those who are in need.
Your suffering will never be in vain indeed,
Because it is planting salvation seeds.

How would you describe your suffering for Christ?

Philippians 1:12–26

Paul's Chains Advance the Gospel
12 Now I want you to know, brothers and sisters, that what has happened to me has actually served to advance the gospel. 13 As a result, it has become clear throughout the whole palace guard and to everyone else that I am in chains for Christ. 14 And because of my chains, most of the brothers and sisters have become confident in the Lord and dare all the more to proclaim the gospel without fear.
15 It is true that some preach Christ out of envy and rivalry, but others out of goodwill. 16 The latter do so out of love, knowing that

I am put here for the defense of the gospel. 17 The former preach Christ out of selfish ambition, not sincerely, supposing that they can stir up trouble for me while I am in chains. 18 But what does it matter? The important thing is that in every way, whether from false motives or true, Christ is preached. And because of this I rejoice. Yes, and I will continue to rejoice, 19 for I know that through your prayers and God's provision of the Spirit of Jesus Christ what has happened to me will turn out for my deliverance. 20 I eagerly expect and hope that I will in no way be ashamed, but will have sufficient courage so that now as always Christ will be exalted in my body, whether by life or by death. 21 For to me, to live is Christ and to die is gain. 22 If I am to go on living in the body, this will mean fruitful labor for me. Yet what shall I choose? I do not know! 23 I am torn between the two: I desire to depart and be with Christ, which is better by far; 24 but it is more necessary for you that I remain in the body. 25 Convinced of this, I know that I will remain, and I will continue with all of you for your progress and joy in the faith, 26 so that through my being with you again your boasting in Christ Jesus will abound on account of me.

November 7
Suffering
Salvation
Psalm 119:71–75

Broken as I am, whole is what I want to be.
Jesus, my brokenness, please take it and bring healing to me.
You can make me new.
This is what I need you to do.
I have been afflicted because of sin.
Jesus, please help me and show me how to begin again.

When you are broken, it is the best time to seek Jesus.

Psalm 119:71–75

71
It was good for me to be afflicted
so that I might learn your decrees.
72
The law from your mouth is more precious to me
than thousands of pieces of silver and gold.
י Yodh
73
Your hands made me and formed me;
give me understanding to learn your commands.
74
May those who fear you rejoice when they see me,
for I have put my hope in your word.
75
I know, Lord, that your laws are righteous,
and that in faithfulness you have afflicted me.

November 8
Suffering
Trust in God
James 1:2–12

How will trials and suffering help me to grow?
Is the purpose of trials and suffering to allow spiritual maturity to show?
Spiritual growth from trials and suffering equips me
to find out how to live for Jesus correctly.
This will enable the world to see Jesus through me accurately.
My trials will attain God's purpose when I
trust them in His mighty hands.
They will shape me into the resemblance of Jesus, and
now my trials and suffering I understand.

When going through trials and suffering, it is difficult
to understand why it is happening to you.

James 1:2–12

Trials and Temptations
2 Consider it pure joy, my brothers and sisters, whenever you face trials of many kinds, 3 because you know that the testing of your faith produces perseverance. 4 Let perseverance finish its work so that you may be mature and complete, not lacking anything. 5 If any of you lacks wisdom, you should ask God, who gives generously to all without finding fault, and it will be given to you. 6 But when you ask, you must believe and not doubt, because the one who doubts is like a wave of the sea, blown and tossed by the wind.
7 That person should not expect to receive anything from the Lord.
8 Such a person is double-minded and unstable in all they do.
9 Believers in humble circumstances ought to take pride in their high position. 10 But the rich should take pride in their humiliation—since they will pass away like a wild flower. 11 For the sun rises with scorching heat and withers the plant; its blossom falls and its beauty is destroyed. In the same way, the rich will fade away even while they go about their business.
12 Blessed is the one who perseveres under trial because, having stood the test, that person will receive the crown of life that the Lord has promised to those who love him.

Temptation
November 9
Isaiah 53:1–6

Like sheep, we children of God will go astray;
We will do this to God every day.
We go our own way to do our own thing;
God's Word tells us sorrow it will surely bring.
Like sheep, we need a shepherd to guard our souls,

Every day as we grow old.
Jesus is willing to lead if we will follow;
Lead us away from the temptation of today so
we can be blessed with tomorrow.
Like sheep, we have gone astray;
Jesus, as our Good Shepherd, we need You each and every day.

Sheep without a shepherd will always be lost.

Isaiah 53:1–6

53
Who has believed our message
and to whom has the arm of the Lord been revealed?
2
He grew up before him like a tender shoot,
and like a root out of dry ground.
He had no beauty or majesty to attract us to him,
nothing in his appearance that we should desire him.
3
He was despised and rejected by mankind,
a man of suffering, and familiar with pain.
Like one from whom people hide their faces
he was despised, and we held him in low esteem.
4
Surely he took up our pain
and bore our suffering,
yet we considered him punished by God,
stricken by him, and afflicted.
5
But he was pierced for our transgressions,
he was crushed for our iniquities;
the punishment that brought us peace was on him,
and by his wounds we are healed.
6
We all, like sheep, have gone astray,

each of us has turned to our own way;
and the Lord has laid on him
the iniquity of us all.

November 10
Christ/Savior
Hebrews 2:10–18

Jesus Christ was fully human in every way;
He lived on earth like every man, facing temptation every day.
He understands our struggles, and He knows our hurts and pain.
His life's purpose on earth was to die for the
souls of man; this was His main aim.
His death on the cross was surely not in vain.
He spoke with understanding and encouragement too;
He wanted those of you who are suffering to
know that He will be there for you.
With every temptation you face, Christ will be at your side,
Giving you strength, hope, and encouragement,
and He will be your guide.
He will guide you through your struggles with temptation
as you experience His presence in your life today.
Temptation will be powerless in your life when you go to Christ and pray.

No one understands temptation better than Jesus Christ.

Hebrews 2:10–18

10 In bringing many sons and daughters to glory, it was fitting that God, for whom and through whom everything exists, should make the pioneer of their salvation perfect through what he suffered. 11 Both the one who makes people holy and those who are made holy are of the same family. So Jesus is not ashamed to call them brothers and sisters. 12 He says,
"I will declare your name to my brothers and sisters;
in the assembly I will sing your praises."

13 And again,
"I will put my trust in him."
And again he says,
"Here am I, and the children God has given me."
14 Since the children have flesh and blood, he too shared in their humanity so that by his death he might break the power of him who holds the power of death—that is, the devil— 15 and free those who all their lives were held in slavery by their fear of death. 16 For surely it is not angels he helps, but Abraham's descendants.
17 For this reason he had to be made like them, fully human in every way, in order that he might become a merciful and faithful high priest in service to God, and that he might make atonement for the sins of the people. 18 Because he himself suffered when he was tempted, he is able to help those who are being tempted.

Thankfulness
November 11
Job 40:1–14

I did not create the oceans, and I did not create the seas.
I did not create the earth and all the animals, plants, and trees.
But how do I thank God who created all these wonderful things?
How often do I thank Him with worship for all the
marvelous accommodations each of these brings?
God, please forgive me for being just so rude,
Having an attitude that is absent of gratitude is so very crude.
I want to express my appreciation for all the things
that I have that You have given to me.
I do not mean to focus any longer on what I think
I do not have and what it should bring.
I want to be appreciative with a heart of thankfulness
that to You will sing, sing, sing.
You are my wonderful, fantastic, indescribable Savior, Lord, and King.

Every day, give thanks to God for His goodness, mercy, and grace.

Job 40:1–14

40 The Lord said to Job:

2

"Will the one who contends with the Almighty correct him?
Let him who accuses God answer him!"

3 Then Job answered the Lord:

4

"I am unworthy—how can I reply to you?
I put my hand over my mouth.

5

I spoke once, but I have no answer—
twice, but I will say no more."

6 Then the Lord spoke to Job out of the storm:

7

"Brace yourself like a man;
I will question you,
and you shall answer me.

8

"Would you discredit my justice?
Would you condemn me to justify yourself?

9

Do you have an arm like God's,
and can your voice thunder like his?

10

Then adorn yourself with glory and splendor,
and clothe yourself in honor and majesty.

11

Unleash the fury of your wrath,
look at all who are proud and bring them low,

12

look at all who are proud and humble them,
crush the wicked where they stand.

13

Bury them all in the dust together;
shroud their faces in the grave.

14
Then I myself will admit to you
that your own right hand can save you.

November 12
Thankfulness
Creation
Psalm 136:1–9

When I woke up this morning, what did I see?
A world of creation filled with beauty standing before me.
Who could create such beauty that would give me so much delight?
I know it was done in love, with might and much insight.
It makes me ponder on the craftsmanship and the care with which
each thing was constructed and designed with a purpose to perform.
The more I pondered, the more I wanted to be informed.
The answer is clearly obvious, and it is not out of the norm.
Man could not have done this, and it is plain to see;
Only the mighty hands of God could create this world for me.
How grateful I am to know the truth.
Lord God, I want to know more about You.

God is loving, and He has made everything
beautiful, which includes you and me.

Psalm 136:1–9

1
Give thanks to the Lord, for he is good.
His love endures forever.
2
Give thanks to the God of gods.
His love endures forever.
3
Give thanks to the Lord of lords:

His love endures forever.

4

to him who alone does great wonders,
His love endures forever.

5

who by his understanding made the heavens,
His love endures forever.

6

who spread out the earth upon the waters,
His love endures forever.

7

who made the great lights—
His love endures forever.

8

the sun to govern the day,
His love endures forever.

9

the moon and stars to govern the night;
His love endures forever.

November 13
Thankfulness
Worship
Psalm 139:14–18

I will worship You, God, for making me.
I am so grateful You did not make me like a tree.
I am thankful because of how You created me.
I am fearfully and wonderfully made for the world to see.
As a creation of God, I am precious in His sight.
His thoughts of me will keep me counting all
through the night, till the morning light.
They are too vast in number the sum of them all.
How I love to worship Him, and His name I will always call.

Thank You, Lord God, for making me.
I am as grateful with joy as I can be.

What are you thanking God for?

Psalm 139:14–18

14
I praise you because I am fearfully and wonderfully made;
your works are wonderful,
I know that full well.
15
My frame was not hidden from you
when I was made in the secret place,
when I was woven together in the depths of the earth.
16
Your eyes saw my unformed body;
all the days ordained for me were written in your book
before one of them came to be.
17
How precious to me are your thoughts, God!
How vast is the sum of them!
18
Were I to count them,
they would outnumber the grains of sand—
when I awake, I am still with you.

The Tongue
November 14
James 3:1–12

I want to speak; what shall I say?
Will it be helpful to someone today?
If I say something to you,

Will it be true? Will I say something to help or harm you?
My tongue, my tongue, what will you say today?
A tame tongue, who can find?
Who has that kind of control that is always on their mind?

How often do you think before you speak?

James 3:1–12

Taming the Tongue
3 Not many of you should become teachers, my fellow believers, because you know that we who teach will be judged more strictly. 2 We all stumble in many ways. Anyone who is never at fault in what they say is perfect, able to keep their whole body in check. 3 When we put bits into the mouths of horses to make them obey us, we can turn the whole animal. 4 Or take ships as an example. Although they are so large and are driven by strong winds, they are steered by a very small rudder wherever the pilot wants to go. 5 Likewise, the tongue is a small part of the body, but it makes great boasts. Consider what a great forest is set on fire by a small spark. 6 The tongue also is a fire, a world of evil among the parts of the body. It corrupts the whole body, sets the whole course of one's life on fire, and is itself set on fire by hell.
7 All kinds of animals, birds, reptiles and sea creatures are being tamed and have been tamed by mankind, 8 but no human being can tame the tongue. It is a restless evil, full of deadly poison.
9 With the tongue we praise our Lord and Father, and with it we curse human beings, who have been made in God's likeness. 10 Out of the same mouth come praise and cursing. My brothers and sisters, this should not be. 11 Can both fresh water and salt water flow from the same spring? 12 My brothers and sisters, can a fig tree bear olives, or a grapevine bear figs? Neither can a salt spring produce fresh water.

The Tongue
November 15
James 3:1–12

Little tongue wants to speak; what shall you say?
Little tongue, will you be helpful to someone today?
Little tongue, if you speak, will it be true?
Little tongue, when you speak, will it make someone feel sad and blue?
Little tongue, are your words tame to speak words of life?
Little tongue, will you give good advice?
Little tongue, are you tame? A tame tongue, who can find?
Little tongue, who has that kind of control that is always on their mind?
Little tongue, small you may be, but the power you
have can give orders to make an army flee.
Little tongue, you can bring life or death, speak
what is right or what is wrong.
Little tongue, you may be little, but you are very powerful and very strong.

How do you use your tongue to speak?

James 3:1–12

Taming the Tongue
3 Not many of you should become teachers, my fellow believers, because you know that we who teach will be judged more strictly. 2 We all stumble in many ways. Anyone who is never at fault in what they say is perfect, able to keep their whole body in check. 3 When we put bits into the mouths of horses to make them obey us, we can turn the whole animal. 4 Or take ships as an example. Although they are so large and are driven by strong winds, they are steered by a very small rudder wherever the pilot wants to go. 5 Likewise, the tongue is a small part of the body, but it makes great boasts. Consider what a great forest is set on fire by a small spark. 6 The tongue also is a fire, a world of evil among the parts of the body. It corrupts the whole body, sets the whole course of one's life on fire, and is itself set on fire by hell.

7 All kinds of animals, birds, reptiles and sea creatures are being tamed and have been tamed by mankind, 8 but no human being can tame the tongue. It is a restless evil, full of deadly poison. 9 With the tongue we praise our Lord and Father, and with it we curse human beings, who have been made in God's likeness. 10 Out of the same mouth come praise and cursing. My brothers and sisters, this should not be. 11 Can both fresh water and salt water flow from the same spring? 12 My brothers and sisters, can a fig tree bear olives, or a grapevine bear figs? Neither can a salt spring produce fresh water.

Trials
November 16
Psalm 13:1–6

When trials and challenges come my way,
I feel so alone. It is difficult to know how to manage my day.
How long will this continue?
How long will my soul find no peace?
Lord, please stop this pain; please stop this grief.
Lord, how I want this all to cease.
I will trust in Your mercy, because salvation You have given to me.
Your joy causes my spirit to sing, so joyfully, of the
blessings You have given so bountifully.

Never stay focused on the trials; instead, stay
focused on what God is doing in the trials.

Psalm 13

For the director of music. A psalm of David.
1
How long, Lord? Will you forget me forever?
How long will you hide your face from me?
2
How long must I wrestle with my thoughts

and day after day have sorrow in my heart?
How long will my enemy triumph over me?
3
Look on me and answer, Lord my God.
Give light to my eyes, or I will sleep in death,
4
and my enemy will say, "I have overcome him,"
and my foes will rejoice when I fall.
5
But I trust in your unfailing love;
my heart rejoices in your salvation.
6
I will sing the Lord's praise,
for he has been good to me.

November 17
God's Will
1 Peter 1:1–9

Today, I will serve my God and my King.
It does not matter what trials the situation may bring;
God's will is what concerns me.
God, I pray that in these trials of mine, You will
be praised, honored, and glorified.
The plans I have made may not be meant to be;
Doing God's will is preparing me for eternity.
God has written His plan in permanent ink, while I have to
write my plan in pencil, because God's plan never changes.

1 Peter 1:1–9

1 Peter, an apostle of Jesus Christ,
To God's elect, exiles scattered throughout the provinces
of Pontus, Galatia, Cappadocia, Asia and Bithynia, 2 who

have been chosen according to the foreknowledge of God
the Father, through the sanctifying work of the Spirit, to be
obedient to Jesus Christ and sprinkled with his blood:
Grace and peace be yours in abundance.
Praise to God for a Living Hope
3 Praise be to the God and Father of our Lord Jesus Christ! In his
great mercy he has given us new birth into a living hope through the
resurrection of Jesus Christ from the dead, 4 and into an inheritance
that can never perish, spoil or fade. This inheritance is kept in heaven
for you, 5 who through faith are shielded by God's power until the
coming of the salvation that is ready to be revealed in the last time. 6 In
all this you greatly rejoice, though now for a little while you may have
had to suffer grief in all kinds of trials. 7 These have come so that the
proven genuineness of your faith—of greater worth than gold, which
perishes even though refined by fire—may result in praise, glory and
honor when Jesus Christ is revealed. 8 Though you have not seen him,
you love him; and even though you do not see him now, you believe in
him and are filled with an inexpressible and glorious joy, 9 for you are
receiving the end result of your faith, the salvation of your souls.'

November 18
God's Sovereignty
Psalm 121

What is life that I must know?
It is a road that is slow, winding with troubles,
problems of stress and unrest.
We each have a path to travel to get to our destination in life.
How will I travel this road of life?
What must I do, and what must I sacrifice?
Each step must be planned, being obedient to
follow the leading of God's mighty hand.
He will preserve my going out and my coming in.
This will surely keep me far away from the darkness and the death of sin.

Yes, life is a winding road filled with trials and
adventures, but which way will it lead?
To the path which will cause me to want to flee or
to the path of the providence of God's plan,
Which has been designed for me with His mighty, loving hand.

No one knows what the future holds, but God does.

Psalm 121

A song of ascents.
1
I lift up my eyes to the mountains—
where does my help come from?
2
My help comes from the Lord,
the Maker of heaven and earth.
3
He will not let your foot slip—
he who watches over you will not slumber;
4
indeed, he who watches over Israel
will neither slumber nor sleep.
5
The Lord watches over you—
the Lord is your shade at your right hand;
6
the sun will not harm you by day,
nor the moon by night.
7
The Lord will keep you from all harm—
he will watch over your life;
8
the Lord will watch over your coming and going
both now and forevermore.

November 19
God's Love
Job 7:11–21

Why, God? Why are these trials in my life? I do not understand.
Whatever the reason, Lord, my life is in your mighty loving hand.
Help me not to focus on the trials; reassure me that it is all part of Your loving plan.
Please keep me close to You while I am in the midst
of my trial; it will help me to understand.
Trials will make life seem dark, but God's love
will bring light to help you see clearly.

Job 7:11–21

11
"Therefore I will not keep silent;
I will speak out in the anguish of my spirit,
I will complain in the bitterness of my soul.
12
Am I the sea, or the monster of the deep,
that you put me under guard?
13
When I think my bed will comfort me
and my couch will ease my complaint,
14
even then you frighten me with dreams
and terrify me with visions,
15
so that I prefer strangling and death,
rather than this body of mine.
16
I despise my life; I would not live forever.
Let me alone; my days have no meaning.
17

"What is mankind that you make so much of them,
that you give them so much attention,
18
that you examine them every morning
and test them every moment?
19
Will you never look away from me,
or let me alone even for an instant?
20
If I have sinned, what have I done to you,
you who see everything we do?
Why have you made me your target?
Have I become a burden to you?
21
Why do you not pardon my offenses
and forgive my sins?
For I will soon lie down in the dust;
you will search for me, but I will be no more."

November 20
Surrender
John 16:25–33

Where and how can I escape the risk and danger of this world?
Where can I go from this broken world to tranquillity that I may find?
Where can I find assurance that will give me peace of mind?
All the world has to offer is tribulation. The revelation of this is true.
However, put your trust in Jesus because He loves you.
Having a relationship with Him will show His faithfulness too.
He has overcome this world with all its trials and pain.
Believe in His written Word, because it will never change.

Reading the newspaper lets you know what has
happened and what is happening;
however, the Bible tells you what will happen, and why.

John 16:25–33

25 "Though I have been speaking figuratively, a time is coming when I will no longer use this kind of language but will tell you plainly about my Father. 26 In that day you will ask in my name. I am not saying that I will ask the Father on your behalf. 27 No, the Father himself loves you because you have loved me and have believed that I came from God. 28 I came from the Father and entered the world; now I am leaving the world and going back to the Father."
29 Then Jesus' disciples said, "Now you are speaking clearly and without figures of speech. 30 Now we can see that you know all things and that you do not even need to have anyone ask you questions. This makes us believe that you came from God."
31 "Do you now believe?" Jesus replied. 32 "A time is coming and in fact has come when you will be scattered, each to your own home. You will leave me all alone. Yet I am not alone, for my Father is with me.
33 "I have told you these things, so that in me you may have peace. In this world you will have trouble. But take heart! I have overcome the world."

Surrender
November 21
Psalm 94:3–23

The futile thoughts of man God understands.
The insolent speech of the wicked boast about themselves,
Applauding themselves with their evil hands.
Thinking that God does not see them in their work of iniquity,
Bringing harm to the righteous of humanity.
However, they are greatly mistaken in thinking that
God has forsaken the righteous who are His own.
Our God is still sitting on His throne.
He is our solid Rock.
The wicked will be shocked to know that He is dependable and strong.
Our refuge is in Him; He provides safety from all wrong.

God is our defender, to evil we do not have to surrender,
In fearing what the wicked will do.
We trust in our God, because He is faithful and true.
So, when trials come into this life,
Just remember this is why Jesus gave His life as a sacrifice.

When you face trials, remember Jesus is a refuge.

Psalm 94:3–23

3
How long, Lord, will the wicked,
how long will the wicked be jubilant?
4
They pour out arrogant words;
all the evildoers are full of boasting.
5
They crush your people, Lord;
they oppress your inheritance.
6
They slay the widow and the foreigner;
they murder the fatherless.
7
They say, "The Lord does not see;
the God of Jacob takes no notice."
8
Take notice, you senseless ones among the people;
you fools, when will you become wise?
9
Does he who fashioned the ear not hear?
Does he who formed the eye not see?
10
Does he who disciplines nations not punish?
Does he who teaches mankind lack knowledge?
11
The Lord knows all human plans;

he knows that they are futile.
12
Blessed is the one you discipline, Lord,
the one you teach from your law;
13
you grant them relief from days of trouble,
till a pit is dug for the wicked.
14
For the Lord will not reject his people;
he will never forsake his inheritance.
15
Judgment will again be founded on righteousness,
and all the upright in heart will follow it.
16
Who will rise up for me against the wicked?
Who will take a stand for me against evildoers?
17
Unless the Lord had given me help,
I would soon have dwelt in the silence of death.
18
When I said, "My foot is slipping,"
your unfailing love, Lord, supported me.
19
When anxiety was great within me,
your consolation brought me joy.
20
Can a corrupt throne be allied with you—
a throne that brings on misery by its decrees?
21
The wicked band together against the righteous
and condemn the innocent to death.
22
But the Lord has become my fortress,
and my God the rock in whom I take refuge.
23
He will repay them for their sins

and destroy them for their wickedness;
the Lord our God will destroy them.

November 22
God's Grace
Lamentations 3:1–3, 25–33

When you face hardship, pain, and sorrow,
Do not become submerged in self-pity,
Thinking there will be no tomorrow.
From suffering you may not be spared.
This does not mean God does not care.
He can spare you from this pain.
His love for you will not change;
It will always remain the same.
Though He causes grief, yet He will show compassion.
Lamentations 3:32

Lamentations 3:1–3

3

I am the man who has seen affliction
by the rod of the Lord's wrath.

2

He has driven me away and made me walk
in darkness rather than light;

3

indeed, he has turned his hand against me
again and again, all day long.
Lamentations 3:25–33

25

The Lord is good to those whose hope is in him,

  to the one who seeks him;
26
it is good to wait quietly
for the salvation of the Lord.
27
It is good for a man to bear the yoke
while he is young.
28
Let him sit alone in silence,
for the Lord has laid it on him.
29
Let him bury his face in the dust—
there may yet be hope.
30
Let him offer his cheek to one who would strike him,
and let him be filled with disgrace.
31
For no one is cast off
by the Lord forever.
32
Though he brings grief, he will show compassion,
so great is his unfailing love.
33
For he does not willingly bring affliction
or grief to anyone.

November 23
Trust
Psalm 107:23–32

When the storms of life toss you to and fro,
You are not sure how you are to row,
Through the crashing waves of grief and pain,
Leaving your face with worry stained.
As the storms of life rage on with pain and grief,

Fill your mind with thoughts of the Lord, Jesus Christ, and
Trust in Him to bring you through with peace and relief.

Life is all about living with challenges, but victory is
about facing the challenges that life brings.

Psalm 107:23–32

23
Some went out on the sea in ships;
they were merchants on the mighty waters.
24
They saw the works of the Lord,
his wonderful deeds in the deep.
25
For he spoke and stirred up a tempest
that lifted high the waves.
26
They mounted up to the heavens and went down to the depths;
in their peril their courage melted away.
27
They reeled and staggered like drunkards;
they were at their wits' end.
28
Then they cried out to the Lord in their trouble,
and he brought them out of their distress.
29
He stilled the storm to a whisper;
the waves of the sea were hushed.
30
They were glad when it grew calm,
and he guided them to their desired haven.
31
Let them give thanks to the Lord for his unfailing love
and his wonderful deeds for mankind.
32

Let them exalt him in the assembly of the people
and praise him in the council of the elders.

November 24
Trials
Psalm 32:1–6; Matthew 11:28–30

Unconfessed sin can be a heavy burden to bear.
The weight of denial cannot be sustained;
Confession with repentance needs to be maintained.
You will find the weight of it will be all gone,
When you give it to Christ Jesus, God's holy Son.
Sin and the burden of it is weight no man can bear.

Psalm 32:1–6

Of David. A maskil.
1
Blessed is the one
whose transgressions are forgiven,
whose sins are covered.
2
Blessed is the one
whose sin the Lord does not count against them
and in whose spirit is no deceit.
3
When I kept silent,
my bones wasted away
through my groaning all day long.
4
For day and night
your hand was heavy on me;
my strength was sapped
as in the heat of summer.

5
Then I acknowledged my sin to you
and did not cover up my iniquity.
I said, "I will confess
my transgressions to the Lord."
And you forgave
the guilt of my sin.
6
Therefore let all the faithful pray to you
while you may be found;
surely the rising of the mighty waters
will not reach them.

Matthew 11:28–30

28 "Come to me, all you who are weary and burdened, and I will give you rest. 29 Take my yoke upon you and learn from me, for I am gentle and humble in heart, and you will find rest for your souls. 30 For my yoke is easy and my burden is light."

November 25
Trials
Matthew 5:38–48

The storms of life have much to bring to encourage
you to be strong in your faith.
Faith in Christ is what it will take to prepare
you to have unwavering faith.
Trials in life will let you know you will be wrong.
But your unwavering faith will keep you strong.
So, love and bless when you are put to the test.
Do good and pray as God sends you on your way today.

Trials are there to strengthen your faith in Christ.

Matthew 5:38–48

Eye for Eye

38 "You have heard that it was said, 'Eye for eye, and tooth for tooth.' 39 But I tell you, do not resist an evil person. If anyone slaps you on the right cheek, turn to them the other cheek also. 40 And if anyone wants to sue you and take your shirt, hand over your coat as well. 41 If anyone forces you to go one mile, go with them two miles. 42 Give to the one who asks you, and do not turn away from the one who wants to borrow from you.

Love for Enemies

43 "You have heard that it was said, 'Love your neighbor and hate your enemy.' 44 But I tell you, love your enemies and pray for those who persecute you, 45 that you may be children of your Father in heaven. He causes his sun to rise on the evil and the good, and sends rain on the righteous and the unrighteous. 46 If you love those who love you, what reward will you get? Are not even the tax collectors doing that? 47 And if you greet only your own people, what are you doing more than others? Do not even pagans do that? 48 Be perfect, therefore, as your heavenly Father is perfect.

November 26
God's Presence
John 16:25–33

When trouble and sorrow happen, coming in with the force of a tsunami,
God, are You there?
Your Word tells me how much You care.
When troubles and sorrows come against me and knock me off my feet,
Leaving me feeling wounded and thinking I am beat,
The Holy Spirit reminds me God's love never fails; He
will not forget me, and He is never too late.
God is to be trusted, because He will not forsake.

Don't let your troubles or sorrow be so big that you cannot see God.

John 16:25–33

25 "Though I have been speaking figuratively, a time is coming when I will no longer use this kind of language but will tell you plainly about my Father. 26 In that day you will ask in my name. I am not saying that I will ask the Father on your behalf. 27 No, the Father himself loves you because you have loved me and have believed that I came from God. 28 I came from the Father and entered the world; now I am leaving the world and going back to the Father."
29 Then Jesus' disciples said, "Now you are speaking clearly and without figures of speech. 30 Now we can see that you know all things and that you do not even need to have anyone ask you questions. This makes us believe that you came from God."
31 "Do you now believe?" Jesus replied. 32 "A time is coming and in fact has come when you will be scattered, each to your own home. You will leave me all alone. Yet I am not alone, for my Father is with me.
33 "I have told you these things, so that in me you may have peace. In this world you will have trouble. But take heart! I have overcome the world."

November 27
God's Sovereignty
James 1:1–8

Trials will test a believer's faith to produce patience for the test.
In the trials of testing, wisdom is what is needed
to have faith that will be resilient at best.
Tribulation will enable you to work through your
salvation, and wisdom will do the rest.
If wisdom is what you need, God will give it to you liberally.
This is how you are to prepare for trials; with
patience and wisdom you will succeed,
In having the faith to grow in His promised grace—
this, God will give to you indeed.

You will not know what patience is until your faith has been put to the test.

James 1:1–8

1 James, a servant of God and of the Lord Jesus Christ,
To the twelve tribes scattered among the nations:
Greetings.
Trials and Temptations
2 Consider it pure joy, my brothers and sisters, whenever you face trials of many kinds, 3 because you know that the testing of your faith produces perseverance. 4 Let perseverance finish its work so that you may be mature and complete, not lacking anything. 5 If any of you lacks wisdom, you should ask God, who gives generously to all without finding fault, and it will be given to you. 6 But when you ask, you must believe and not doubt, because the one who doubts is like a wave of the sea, blown and tossed by the wind. 7 That person should not expect to receive anything from the Lord. 8 Such a person is double-minded and unstable in all they do.

Trust in God
November 28
Exodus 16:11–31

God will provide in ways I cannot imagine, I dare say.
He can and will do this each and every day.
I am limited, though, in how I think about what God can do.
I must have faith in what I know of Him that is true.
The impossible is the norm; this is the pattern of
how God will work and what He will do.
When you seek God for help, know that He will always be there for you.
He will never abandon you; He will always see you through.
God is a loving God who will love and take care of you.

Believe in the impossible and know that God can do it.

Exodus 16:11–31

11 The Lord said to Moses, 12 "I have heard the grumbling of the Israelites. Tell them, 'At twilight you will eat meat, and in the morning you will be filled with bread. Then you will know that I am the Lord your God.'"
13 That evening quail came and covered the camp, and in the morning there was a layer of dew around the camp. 14 When the dew was gone, thin flakes like frost on the ground appeared on the desert floor. 15 When the Israelites saw it, they said to each other, "What is it?" For they did not know what it was. Moses said to them, "It is the bread the Lord has given you to eat.
16 This is what the Lord has commanded: 'Everyone is to gather as much as they need. Take an omer for each person you have in your tent.'"
17 The Israelites did as they were told; some gathered much, some little. 18 And when they measured it by the omer, the one who gathered much did not have too much, and the one who gathered little did not have too little. Everyone had gathered just as much as they needed.
19 Then Moses said to them, "No one is to keep any of it until morning."
20 However, some of them paid no attention to Moses; they kept part of it until morning, but it was full of maggots and began to smell. So Moses was angry with them.
21 Each morning everyone gathered as much as they needed, and when the sun grew hot, it melted away. 22 On the sixth day, they gathered twice as much—two omers for each person—and the leaders of the community came and reported this to Moses. 23 He said to them, "This is what the Lord commanded: 'Tomorrow is to be a day of sabbath rest, a holy sabbath to the Lord. So bake what you want to bake and boil what you want to boil. Save whatever is left and keep it until morning.'"
24 So they saved it until morning, as Moses commanded, and it did not stink or get maggots in it. 25 "Eat it today," Moses said, "because today is a sabbath to the Lord. You will not find any of it on the ground today. 26 Six days you are to gather it, but on the seventh day, the Sabbath, there will not be any."
27 Nevertheless, some of the people went out on the seventh day to gather it, but they found none. 28 Then the Lord said to Moses, "How long will

you refuse to keep my commands and my instructions? 29 Bear in mind that the Lord has given you the Sabbath; that is why on the sixth day he gives you bread for two days. Everyone is to stay where they are on the seventh day; no one is to go out." 30 So the people rested on the seventh day. 31 The people of Israel called the bread manna. It was white like coriander seed and tasted like wafers made with honey.

November 29
Trust in God
Judges 7:1–8

God has called me to do a job that I just cannot do.
The challenge is too great, and this is the truth.
The resources are not there, and what little I have is dwindling away.
God, without Your strength, I cannot do this; there is no other way.
I cried out to You for the wisdom to know what it is that I need to do.
I want the circumstances to be clear that the victory is mine;
However, the success did not come from me.
It is from the Lord, who made that which is not become what is to be.
All the credit goes to God; no one will do what He can do.
Acknowledgment and recognition are His
because this is the absolute truth.
When I am weak, God, You are strong.
To give You worship and praise would not be wrong.

Depending on God and not man is the way to get any job done.

Judges 7:1–8

Gideon Defeats the Midianites
7 Early in the morning, Jerub-Baal (that is, Gideon) and all his men camped at the spring of Harod. The camp of Midian was north of them in the valley near the hill of Moreh. 2 The Lord said to Gideon, "You have too many men. I cannot deliver Midian into their hands, or Israel would boast against me, 'My own strength has saved me.' 3 Now announce to

the army, 'Anyone who trembles with fear may turn back and leave Mount Gilead.'" So twenty-two thousand men left, while ten thousand remained. 4 But the Lord said to Gideon, "There are still too many men. Take them down to the water, and I will thin them out for you there. If I say, 'This one shall go with you,' he shall go; but if I say, 'This one shall not go with you,' he shall not go." 5 So Gideon took the men down to the water. There the Lord told him, "Separate those who lap the water with their tongues as a dog laps from those who kneel down to drink." 6 Three hundred of them drank from cupped hands, lapping like dogs. All the rest got down on their knees to drink. 7 The Lord said to Gideon, "With the three hundred men that lapped I will save you and give the Midianites into your hands. Let all the others go home." 8 So Gideon sent the rest of the Israelites home but kept the three hundred, who took over the provisions and trumpets of the others. Now the camp of Midian lay below him in the valley.

November 30
Trust in God
Psalm 18:1–6

What challenges will I face today?
To prepare myself, I will get down on my knees and pray.
The advice of man I will not find,
Because Jesus's Word is always on my mind.
I know that when I cry out to God, He will hear.
Even when I whisper in His ears.
He is my Rock.
Nothing that I will do will make Him shocked.
He is my Fortress, where my mind will be at rest.
As my Deliverer, He will always do His best.
I will not panic when facing the challenges that may come my way today.
I will just get down on my knees and to God I will pray.

The world will make me panic, but God will give me His peace.

Psalm 18:1–6

For the director of music. Of David the servant of the Lord. He sang to the Lord the words of this song when the Lord delivered him from the hand of all his enemies and from the hand of Saul. He said:

1
I love you, Lord, my strength.

2
The Lord is my rock, my fortress and my deliverer;
my God is my rock, in whom I take refuge,
my shield and the horn of my salvation, my stronghold.

3
I called to the Lord, who is worthy of praise,
and I have been saved from my enemies.

4
The cords of death entangled me;
the torrents of destruction overwhelmed me.

5
The cords of the grave coiled around me;
the snares of death confronted me.

6
In my distress I called to the Lord;
I cried to my God for help.
From his temple he heard my voice;
my cry came before him, into his ears.

December 1
Trust in God
Psalm 20

Changes, changes, changes; nothing stays the same.
This is happening all around us, but can you put your
trust in it? Asking that should be the aim.
Trust is essential; security is too.

Who and what do you put your trust in when
things look weary, hopeless, and blue?
Should you put your trust in things, possessions, people, or wealth?
Will you feel secure to trust in their help?
Will they disappoint or let you down?
Turning your joyous smile into a disappointed, hopeless frown.
Putting your trust in Jesus is the thing you need to do.
No matters what happens, you can always
depend on Him to see you through.
He is the same yesterday, today, and tomorrow; He always will be too.
Put your trust in Jesus, because He loves taking care of you.

You change, people and the world change, but God never changes.

Psalm 20

For the director of music. A psalm of David.
1
May the Lord answer you when you are in distress;
may the name of the God of Jacob protect you.
2
May he send you help from the sanctuary
and grant you support from Zion.
3
May he remember all your sacrifices
and accept your burnt offerings.
4
May he give you the desire of your heart
and make all your plans succeed.
5
May we shout for joy over your victory
and lift up our banners in the name of our God.
May the Lord grant all your requests.
6
Now this I know:
The Lord gives victory to his anointed.

He answers him from his heavenly sanctuary
with the victorious power of his right hand.
7
Some trust in chariots and some in horses,
but we trust in the name of the Lord our God.
8
They are brought to their knees and fall,
but we rise up and stand firm.
9
Lord, give victory to the king!
Answer us when we call!

December 2
Trust in God
Psalm 77:1–15

When you feel like quitting, because you have had enough,
Life has become too difficult, hard, and tough,
Look to God and pray; tell Him how you honestly feel.
He will not criticize you, because He knows
these feelings of yours are real.
Think back and remember all that God has done in the past.
Then you will remember these emotions of
depression and know that they will not last.
Now look forward, thinking about what God will do.
He will bring good out of the situation, because He
wants to be there to love and help you.
Now think again about your situation and the circumstances
you are in, and do so with genuine faith.
Reminding yourself who God is, think about
quitting, and you will not want to debate.

When you have problems, remember, God will always have the solutions.

Psalm 77:1–15

For the director of music. For Jeduthun. Of Asaph. A psalm.

1
I cried out to God for help;
I cried out to God to hear me.

2
When I was in distress, I sought the Lord;
at night I stretched out untiring hands,
and I would not be comforted.

3
I remembered you, God, and I groaned;
I meditated, and my spirit grew faint.

4
You kept my eyes from closing;
I was too troubled to speak.

5
I thought about the former days,
the years of long ago;

6
I remembered my songs in the night.
My heart meditated and my spirit asked:

7
"Will the Lord reject forever?
Will he never show his favor again?

8
Has his unfailing love vanished forever?
Has his promise failed for all time?

9
Has God forgotten to be merciful?
Has he in anger withheld his compassion?"

10
Then I thought, "To this I will appeal:
the years when the Most High stretched out his right hand.

11
I will remember the deeds of the Lord;
yes, I will remember your miracles of long ago.
12
I will consider all your works
and meditate on all your mighty deeds."
13
Your ways, God, are holy.
What god is as great as our God?
14
You are the God who performs miracles;
you display your power among the peoples.
15
With your mighty arm you redeemed your people,
the descendants of Jacob and Joseph.

December 3
Trust in God
Proverbs 3:1–18

When temptation comes, it wants to lure you in,
Getting you excited with the desire to want to sin.
When you are tempted, know it can be a powerful,
dominant focus, more powerful than you.
How should you handle temptation? What do you need to do?
Temptation is always an opportunity to put your
trust in God, because He loves you.
Temptation wants you to depend on your own understanding,
Causing you to give in to what it is demanding.
God is the One you should trust;
When facing temptation, this is an absolute must.
Do not think it is good to be wise in what and how you think;
When you do that, you will surely give in to temptation, and then you will
sink.

Turning to God is the only way to face temptation.

Proverbs 3:1–18

Wisdom Bestows Well-Being

3

My son, do not forget my teaching,
but keep my commands in your heart,

2

for they will prolong your life many years
and bring you peace and prosperity.

3

Let love and faithfulness never leave you;
bind them around your neck,
write them on the tablet of your heart.

4

Then you will win favor and a good name
in the sight of God and man.

5

Trust in the Lord with all your heart
and lean not on your own understanding;

6

in all your ways submit to him,
and he will make your paths straight.

7

Do not be wise in your own eyes;
fear the Lord and shun evil.

8

This will bring health to your body
and nourishment to your bones.

9

Honor the Lord with your wealth,
with the firstfruits of all your crops;

10

then your barns will be filled to overflowing,
and your vats will brim over with new wine.

11

My son, do not despise the Lord's discipline,

and do not resent his rebuke,
12
because the Lord disciplines those he loves,
as a father the son he delights in.
13
Blessed are those who find wisdom,
those who gain understanding,
14
for she is more profitable than silver
and yields better returns than gold.
15
She is more precious than rubies;
nothing you desire can compare with her.
16
Long life is in her right hand;
in her left hand are riches and honor.
17
Her ways are pleasant ways,
and all her paths are peace.
18
She is a tree of life to those who take hold of her;
those who hold her fast will be blessed.

December 4
Trust in God
God's Care/Suffering
Proverbs 18:4–12

Run to Me, My child, run to Me.
The cares of this world want to do you in.
Run to Me; I am greater than a friend.
Fear has a hold on you.
It always wants to control you, telling you what to do;
It brings confusion, and this is true.
Do not run away from Me!

I am right here for you; can't you see?
You alone cannot confront trouble; I will be here for you on the double.
I am right here for you;
Let it be Me telling you what you need to do.
Put your trust in Me.
Run to Me, My child, run to Me.
In Me you will find safety, and this will always be.
Run to Me, My child, run to Me.
God is our Shield, a place of safety and power that saves us; run to Him.

Proverbs 18:4-12

4
The words of the mouth are deep waters,
but the fountain of wisdom is a rushing stream.

5
It is not good to be partial to the wicked
and so deprive the innocent of justice.

6
The lips of fools bring them strife,
and their mouths invite a beating.

7
The mouths of fools are their undoing,
and their lips are a snare to their very lives.

8
The words of a gossip are like choice morsels;
they go down to the inmost parts.

9
One who is slack in his work
is brother to one who destroys.

10
The name of the Lord is a fortified tower;
the righteous run to it and are safe.

11
The wealth of the rich is their fortified city;

they imagine it a wall too high to scale.
12
Before a downfall the heart is haughty,
but humility comes before honor.

December 5
Trust in God
Isaiah 55:6–13

There are times when life does not make any sense,
Which can leave you with the feeling of being tense.
Of God, how much do you understand?
Do you comprehend His thinking, His law, and His commands?
His thoughts are not the same as yours and mine.
His ways of doing things are beyond us, which has been clearly defined.
You may not comprehend God and all His ways.
You will learn you must put your trust in Him every day.

"For my thoughts are not your thoughts, neither are
your ways my ways," declares the LORD.
Isaiah 55:8

Isaiah 55:6–13

6
Seek the Lord while he may be found;
call on him while he is near.
7
Let the wicked forsake their ways
and the unrighteous their thoughts.
Let them turn to the Lord, and he will have mercy on them,
and to our God, for he will freely pardon.
8
"For my thoughts are not your thoughts,
neither are your ways my ways,"

declares the Lord.

9

"As the heavens are higher than the earth,
so are my ways higher than your ways
and my thoughts than your thoughts.

10

As the rain and the snow
come down from heaven,
and do not return to it
without watering the earth
and making it bud and flourish,
so that it yields seed for the sower and bread for the eater,

11

so is my word that goes out from my mouth:
It will not return to me empty,
but will accomplish what I desire
and achieve the purpose for which I sent it.

12

You will go out in joy
and be led forth in peace;
the mountains and hills
will burst into song before you,
and all the trees of the field
will clap their hands.

13

Instead of the thornbush will grow the juniper,
and instead of briers the myrtle will grow.
This will be for the Lord's renown,
for an everlasting sign,
that will endure forever."

December 6
Trust in God
Isaiah 55:6–13

"Seek the LORD today" (Isaiah 55:6).
Seek Him as you pray.
"Call on him while he is near." (Isaiah 55:6)
Especially when you are in fear.
That which is evil do not do.
Do not think this way too.
Turn to God, and mercy He will show.
He will forgive you; this you need to know.
God's thoughts are not as your thoughts.
His ways are not as your ways.
You will see this each and every day.
When God speaks His Word, it will accomplish
everything He wants it to do.
This is why you need to trust in God, because
He will always be here for you.
Trust God to be there for you.

Isaiah 55:6–13

6
Seek the Lord while he may be found;
call on him while he is near.
7
Let the wicked forsake their ways
and the unrighteous their thoughts.
Let them turn to the Lord, and he will have mercy on them,
and to our God, for he will freely pardon.
8
"For my thoughts are not your thoughts,
neither are your ways my ways,"
declares the Lord.

9
"As the heavens are higher than the earth,
so are my ways higher than your ways
and my thoughts than your thoughts.
10
As the rain and the snow
come down from heaven,
and do not return to it
without watering the earth
and making it bud and flourish,
so that it yields seed for the sower and bread for the eater,
11
so is my word that goes out from my mouth:
It will not return to me empty,
but will accomplish what I desire
and achieve the purpose for which I sent it.
12
You will go out in joy
and be led forth in peace;
the mountains and hills
will burst into song before you,
and all the trees of the field
will clap their hands.
13
Instead of the thornbush will grow the juniper,
and instead of briers the myrtle will grow.
This will be for the Lord's renown,
for an everlasting sign,
that will endure forever."

December 7
Trust in God
Matthew 8:23–28

When the storms of life come your way, what do you do?
When you are confronted with the uncertainties
of life, whom do you turn to?
Do you wait to listen to see what God will do for you?
He will do amazing things,
Because He is the Kings of Kings.
As you sail through the storms of life,
Let Him navigate you through the course that is right;
He knows what to do, and the storms of life He will show how to fight.
In the uncertainties of life that you will face,
do not be afraid and do not hesitate.
God will be at your side; He will guide you through.
He will tell you what to do; He will always be here to help you.

The most important thing to remember and think about
regarding the future is that God knows what to do.

Matthew 8:23–28

Jesus Calms the Storm
23 Then he got into the boat and his disciples followed him.
24 Suddenly a furious storm came up on the lake, so that the waves
swept over the boat. But Jesus was sleeping. 25 The disciples went
and woke him, saying, "Lord, save us! We're going to drown!"
26 He replied, "You of little faith, why are you so afraid?" Then he got
up and rebuked the winds and the waves, and it was completely calm.
27 The men were amazed and asked, "What kind of man
is this? Even the winds and the waves obey him!"
Jesus Restores Two Demon-Possessed Men
28 When he arrived at the other side in the region of the
Gadarenes, two demon-possessed men coming from the tombs
met him. They were so violent that no one could pass that way.

December 8
Trust in God
Honesty
Luke 16:1–10

People of integrity will display the virtue of trust.
They will be trustworthy in both little and much.
Children of God's behavior will be the same; whatever they do,
It will bring glory to Jesus's name.
Now, to some, honesty is no big deal.
They see what they want and, in taking it,
they will call it a find not a steal.
They find themselves having to look over their
shoulders for what they have done;
Living this way cannot be fun.
Yes, honesty is the best policy, as many will say.
Is honesty how you live your life today?

A dishonest person calls honesty what they do to others,
but they do not want it to be done to them.

Luke 16:1–10

The Parable of the Shrewd Manager
16 Jesus told his disciples: "There was a rich man whose manager was accused of wasting his possessions. 2 So he called him in and asked him, 'What is this I hear about you? Give an account of your management, because you cannot be manager any longer.'
3 "The manager said to himself, 'What shall I do now? My master is taking away my job. I'm not strong enough to dig, and I'm ashamed to beg— 4 I know what I'll do so that, when I lose my job here, people will welcome me into their houses.'
5 "So he called in each one of his master's debtors. He asked the first, 'How much do you owe my master?'
6 "'Nine hundred gallons of olive oil,' he replied.

"The manager told him, 'Take your bill, sit down
quickly, and make it four hundred and fifty.'
7 "Then he asked the second, 'And how much do you owe?'
"'A thousand bushels of wheat,' he replied.
"He told him, 'Take your bill and make it eight hundred.'
8 "The master commended the dishonest manager because he had
acted shrewdly. For the people of this world are more shrewd in
dealing with their own kind than are the people of the light. 9 I
tell you, use worldly wealth to gain friends for yourselves, so that
when it is gone, you will be welcomed into eternal dwellings.
10 "Whoever can be trusted with very little can also
be trusted with much, and whoever is dishonest with
very little will also be dishonest with much.

December 9
Trust in God
Hebrews 10:32–11:6

How may I please God today?
How may I please Him in what I do and what I say?
Faith is the only way God wants to be pleased.
Having faith in Him while praying on my knees;
Keeping my faith in God should never cease.
Faith is what I believe even though I cannot see;
It is having confidence, hope, and assurance
that God will be right there for me.
I must persevere by trusting in the Lord at any cost;
Through the trials and tribulations, I may face great loss.
Faith does not work from a magic formula that
will give victory and triumph in glory.
Sometimes when there is no victory in sight, I still need
to keep the faith in God to tell my faith story.
Faith is the only way God wants to be pleased.
I will put my faith, hope, and trust in Him while praying on my knees.

> ... without faith it is impossible to please God.
> Hebrews 11:6

Hebrews 10:32–11:6

32 Remember those earlier days after you had received the light, when you endured in a great conflict full of suffering. 33 Sometimes you were publicly exposed to insult and persecution; at other times you stood side by side with those who were so treated. 34 You suffered along with those in prison and joyfully accepted the confiscation of your property, because you knew that you yourselves had better and lasting possessions. 35 So do not throw away your confidence; it will be richly rewarded. 36 You need to persevere so that when you have done the will of God, you will receive what he has promised. 37 For,

"In just a little while,
he who is coming will come
and will not delay."

38 And,

"But my righteous one will live by faith.
And I take no pleasure
in the one who shrinks back."

39 But we do not belong to those who shrink back and are destroyed, but to those who have faith and are saved.

Faith in Action

11 Now faith is confidence in what we hope for and assurance about what we do not see. 2 This is what the ancients were commended for. 3 By faith we understand that the universe was formed at God's command, so that what is seen was not made out of what was visible. 4 By faith Abel brought God a better offering than Cain did. By faith he was commended as righteous, when God spoke well of his offerings. And by faith Abel still speaks, even though he is dead. 5 By faith Enoch was taken from this life, so that he did not experience death: "He could not be found, because God had taken him away." For before he was taken, he was commended

as one who pleased God. 6 And without faith it is impossible to please God, because anyone who comes to him must believe that he exists and that he rewards those who earnestly seek him.

December 10
Trust in God
Revelation 3:7–13

Persevere in your faith when faced with great trials and opposition.
Cling to your Savior; seek His strength for resistance.
Hold on to His promises while persevering in your faith.
Your circumstances may be harsh, and when
your sorrows you can no longer take,
Hold on, hold on. Your Savior will be there for you.
He will keep His promises; believe and know that this is true.
Hold on, hold on. Your Savior will be there for you.
Hold on, hold on; persevere in your faith.
Circumstances may be harsh; hold on to your faith and do not hesitate.
Christ will keep His promise. His return is sooner than you think.

Revelation 3:7–13

To the Church in Philadelphia
7 "To the angel of the church in Philadelphia write:
These are the words of him who is holy and true, who holds the key of David. What he opens no one can shut, and what he shuts no one can open. 8 I know your deeds. See, I have placed before you an open door that no one can shut. I know that you have little strength, yet you have kept my word and have not denied my name. 9 I will make those who are of the synagogue of Satan, who claim to be Jews though they are not, but are liars—I will make them come and fall down at your feet and acknowledge that I have loved you. 10 Since you have kept my command to endure patiently, I will also keep you from the hour of trial that is going to come on the whole world to test the inhabitants of the earth.

11 I am coming soon. Hold on to what you have, so that no one will take your crown. 12 The one who is victorious I will make a pillar in the temple of my God. Never again will they leave it. I will write on them the name of my God and the name of the city of my God, the new Jerusalem, which is coming down out of heaven from my God; and I will also write on them my new name. 13 Whoever has ears, let them hear what the Spirit says to the churches.

December 11
Trust in God
Fear
Numbers 14:1–9

Be unfazed when new challenges enter your life or existence.
Do not permit your mind to think with fear; instead, use resistance.
When concentrating on the obstacles, it will bring
panic, and you will be discouraged.
However, accurately assess the situation and be encouraged.
As a follower of Christ, regardless of whether the challenges
are a real threat or a phantom, be confident in Christ.
He will help you to differentiate between
what is real and what is not right.
Living in our fears of the unknown brings in darkness, not light.
Live in your faith, and that will enable you to trust
Christ with your life and existence.
Now you can face your fears with resistance.

The worst enemy to your progress is your fear.

Numbers 14:1–9

The People Rebel
14 That night all the members of the community raised their voices and wept aloud. 2 All the Israelites grumbled against Moses and Aaron, and the whole assembly said to them, "If only we had died in Egypt!

Or in this wilderness! 3 Why is the Lord bringing us to this land only to let us fall by the sword? Our wives and children will be taken as plunder. Wouldn't it be better for us to go back to Egypt?" 4 And they said to each other, "We should choose a leader and go back to Egypt." 5 Then Moses and Aaron fell facedown in front of the whole Israelite assembly gathered there. 6 Joshua son of Nun and Caleb son of Jephunneh, who were among those who had explored the land, tore their clothes 7 and said to the entire Israelite assembly, "The land we passed through and explored is exceedingly good. 8 If the Lord is pleased with us, he will lead us into that land, a land flowing with milk and honey, and will give it to us. 9 Only do not rebel against the Lord. And do not be afraid of the people of the land, because we will devour them. Their protection is gone, but the Lord is with us. Do not be afraid of them."

December 12
Trust in God
Suffering
2 Kings 6:8–17

Whatever challenges you will face today,
trust in God to show you the way.
You may have no idea what God is doing. You may not
see how He is helping you to get through today.
Trust in God; He will make a way.
When you are suffering, feeling under pressure, you see
nothing but your problems. What do you do?
Go to Jesus. He will be there for you.
Jesus understands suffering, and He knows what to do.
He will open your eyes and show you the way.
Trust in Jesus. Trust in Him today.

It is difficult to know what to do when the
pressure of life is all you can see.

2 Kings 6:8–17

Elisha Traps Blinded Arameans

8 Now the king of Aram was at war with Israel. After conferring with his officers, he said, "I will set up my camp in such and such a place." 9 The man of God sent word to the king of Israel: "Beware of passing that place, because the Arameans are going down there." 10 So the king of Israel checked on the place indicated by the man of God. Time and again Elisha warned the king, so that he was on his guard in such places.

11 This enraged the king of Aram. He summoned his officers and demanded of them, "Tell me! Which of us is on the side of the king of Israel?"

12 "None of us, my lord the king," said one of his officers, "but Elisha, the prophet who is in Israel, tells the king of Israel the very words you speak in your bedroom."

13 "Go, find out where he is," the king ordered, "so I can send men and capture him." The report came back: "He is in Dothan." 14 Then he sent horses and chariots and a strong force there. They went by night and surrounded the city.

15 When the servant of the man of God got up and went out early the next morning, an army with horses and chariots had surrounded the city. "Oh no, my lord! What shall we do?" the servant asked.

16 "Don't be afraid," the prophet answered. "Those who are with us are more than those who are with them."

17 And Elisha prayed, "Open his eyes, Lord, so that he may see." Then the Lord opened the servant's eyes, and he looked and saw the hills full of horses and chariots of fire all around Elisha.

December 13
Trust in God
Suffering
2 Kings 6:8–17

My vision is dim, and I cannot see beyond
the problems that are before me.
I do not have a solution for what I should do.
Lord Jesus, I am in the need of You.
Jesus, opens my eyes so I will see
the solution to my problems You have prepared for me.
Life may have a way of keeping me focused
on my suffering, pain, and fears.
But, You, Jesus, no matter what, let me know that You are always near.

Life has problems, but Jesus has all the solutions.

2 Kings 6:8–17

Elisha Traps Blinded Arameans
8 Now the king of Aram was at war with Israel. After conferring with his officers, he said, "I will set up my camp in such and such a place." 9 The man of God sent word to the king of Israel: "Beware of passing that place, because the Arameans are going down there." 10 So the king of Israel checked on the place indicated by the man of God. Time and again Elisha warned the king, so that he was on his guard in such places.
11 This enraged the king of Aram. He summoned
his officers and demanded of them, "Tell me! Which
of us is on the side of the king of Israel?"
12 "None of us, my lord the king," said one of his officers,
"but Elisha, the prophet who is in Israel, tells the king of
Israel the very words you speak in your bedroom."
13 "Go, find out where he is," the king ordered, "so I can
send men and capture him." The report came back: "He is in

Dothan." 14 Then he sent horses and chariots and a strong force there. They went by night and surrounded the city.
15 When the servant of the man of God got up and went out early the next morning, an army with horses and chariots had surrounded the city. "Oh no, my lord! What shall we do?" the servant asked.
16 "Don't be afraid," the prophet answered. "Those who are with us are more than those who are with them."
17 And Elisha prayed, "Open his eyes, Lord, so that he may see." Then the Lord opened the servant's eyes, and he looked and saw the hills full of horses and chariots of fire all around Elisha.

December 14
Suffering
Philippians 4:8–13

Life at times can feel like fog is all around,
Keeping the sunlight that wants to penetrate your life bound.
Misery and gloom are in control, making life feel as if it is on hold.
How can the sunlight pierce through when you are feeling so blue?
This is when you need to set your mind on the things above;
This will be God's love.
Let your mind ponder on heavenly things.
This is exactly what it will bring:
Thoughts of things that are admirable, excellent,
praiseworthy, noble, lovely, pure, and right.
Now your life will be filled with godly penetrating sunlight.

You can have sunlight on a foggy day.

Philippians 4:8–13

8 Finally, brothers and sisters, whatever is true, whatever is noble, whatever is right, whatever is pure, whatever is lovely, whatever is admirable—if anything is excellent or praiseworthy—think about such

things. 9 Whatever you have learned or received or heard from me, or seen in me—put it into practice. And the God of peace will be with you.

Thanks for Their Gifts

10 I rejoiced greatly in the Lord that at last you renewed your concern for me. Indeed, you were concerned, but you had no opportunity to show it. 11 I am not saying this because I am in need, for I have learned to be content whatever the circumstances. 12 I know what it is to be in need, and I know what it is to have plenty. I have learned the secret of being content in any and every situation, whether well fed or hungry, whether living in plenty or in want. 13 I can do all this through him who gives me strength.

December 15
Suffering/Trust
Hebrews 12:1–11

When you are persecuted for your faith, remain
true to your conviction and do not hesitate.
Persevere in the race for your faith and do not give up,
keeping your eyes on Jesus and what he has done.
Remember who he is, as God's holy faithful Son.
He suffered and died for our sins.
He will be there to help you to endure, for He is a faithful Friend.
Don't quit! You will win.
You will finish strong,
No matter what might go wrong.
The race is keeping your eyes on Christ;
Persevere in the race to the finish of eternal life.

The race of life is to have the gift of eternal life.

Hebrews 12:1–11

12 Therefore, since we are surrounded by such a great cloud of witnesses, let us throw off everything that hinders and the sin that so easily

entangles. And let us run with perseverance the race marked out for us, 2 fixing our eyes on Jesus, the pioneer and perfecter of faith. For the joy set before him he endured the cross, scorning its shame, and sat down at the right hand of the throne of God. 3 Consider him who endured such opposition from sinners, so that you will not grow weary and lose heart.

God Disciplines His Children

4 In your struggle against sin, you have not yet resisted to the point of shedding your blood. 5 And have you completely forgotten this word of encouragement that addresses you as a father addresses his son? It says,

"My son, do not make light of the Lord's discipline,
and do not lose heart when he rebukes you,
6
because the Lord disciplines the one he loves,
and he chastens everyone he accepts as his son."

7 Endure hardship as discipline; God is treating you as his children. For what children are not disciplined by their father? 8 If you are not disciplined—and everyone undergoes discipline—then you are not legitimate, not true sons and daughters at all. 9 Moreover, we have all had human fathers who disciplined us and we respected them for it. How much more should we submit to the Father of spirits and live! 10 They disciplined us for a little while as they thought best; but God disciplines us for our good, in order that we may share in his holiness. 11 No discipline seems pleasant at the time, but painful. Later on, however, it produces a harvest of righteousness and peace for those who have been trained by it.

December 16
Suffering
James 1:2–4

During times of suffering, be at rest;
God is working, and He will do His very best.
While you face trials, He will give you His love and His grace,
Enabling you to endure the challenges that you face.

In each trial there, are blessings with lessons
to learn in trusting God with belief;
He will bring you out of each trial, and you will find relief.
God is always in control of what is happening to you;
Instant solutions and quick fixes will not do.
During times of suffering, there are things you must accept and receive.
God is good, loving, and is gracious; during times
of trials and suffering, you must believe.

Only God can bring true comfort during times of suffering.

James 1:2–4

Trials and Temptations
2 Consider it pure joy, my brothers and sisters, whenever you face trials of many kinds, 3 because you know that the testing of your faith produces perseverance. 4 Let perseverance finish its work so that you may be mature and complete, not lacking anything.

December 17
Temptation
Genesis 39:1–12

Pray for the strength and wisdom to walk away
when temptation comes today.
Temptation will come knocking at your door; it wants you to let it in.
It wants to have fun with you in getting you to agree with it to sin.
Temptation has a way of sticking around, getting
you to believe it can be a good friend.
When temptation comes and wants you to take its bait,
God is faithful to show you how to escape; take
the way out and do not hesitate.
He will provide an opportunity for a way out so
you can endure (1 Corinthians 10:13).
This is in the Bible; know this for sure.

When temptation comes knocking on your door,
Do not answer or respond to it, because it is not your friend.
It has a goal, so keep this in mind:
Temptation wants to get you to sin all the time.
Temptation can be a bully in demanding you to do things its way.
Let it know you will not give in and you will take
the moment to go to God to pray.

There is one thing good about being tempted: it is
always the right moment to go to God.

Genesis 39:1–12

Joseph and Potiphar's Wife
39 Now Joseph had been taken down to Egypt. Potiphar, an Egyptian who was one of Pharaoh's officials, the captain of the guard, bought him from the Ishmaelites who had taken him there.
2 The Lord was with Joseph so that he prospered, and he lived in the house of his Egyptian master. 3 When his master saw that the Lord was with him and that the Lord gave him success in everything he did, 4 Joseph found favor in his eyes and became his attendant. Potiphar put him in charge of his household, and he entrusted to his care everything he owned. 5 From the time he put him in charge of his household and of all that he owned, the Lord blessed the household of the Egyptian because of Joseph. The blessing of the Lord was on everything Potiphar had, both in the house and in the field. 6 So Potiphar left everything he had in Joseph's care; with Joseph in charge, he did not concern himself with anything except the food he ate. Now Joseph was well-built and handsome, 7 and after a while his master's wife took notice of Joseph and said, "Come to bed with me!"
8 But he refused. "With me in charge," he told her, "my master does not concern himself with anything in the house; everything he owns he has entrusted to my care. 9 No one is greater in this house than I am. My master has withheld nothing from me except you, because you are his wife. How then could I do such a wicked

thing and sin against God?" 10 And though she spoke to Joseph day after day, he refused to go to bed with her or even be with her. 11 One day he went into the house to attend to his duties, and none of the household servants was inside. 12 She caught him by his cloak and said, "Come to bed with me!" But he left his cloak in her hand and ran out of the house.

December 18
Waiting on God
1 Chronicles 17:1–20

Our plans for our life are not the same plans God has for us.
When our plans do not work out the way we want, we
will often fuss and throw temper tantrums.
Commit your plans to the Lord, and everything will work out for you.
You do not have to figure things out and know
what you are supposed to do.
You will find satisfaction and peace in the Lord;
know that this is the exact truth.
Achieving your hopes, dreams, and ambitions—
how significant is this to you?
If God's plans are different from yours, what are you going to do?

You are important to God, and He dearly loves you.

1 Chronicles 17:1–20

God's Promise to David

17 After David was settled in his palace, he said to Nathan the prophet, "Here I am, living in a house of cedar, while the ark of the covenant of the Lord is under a tent." 2 Nathan replied to David, "Whatever you have in mind, do it, for God is with you."
3 But that night the word of God came to Nathan, saying:
4 "Go and tell my servant David, 'This is what the Lord says: You are not the one to build me a house to dwell in. 5 I have not dwelt in

a house from the day I brought Israel up out of Egypt to this day. I have moved from one tent site to another, from one dwelling place to another. 6 Wherever I have moved with all the Israelites, did I ever say to any of their leaders whom I commanded to shepherd my people, "Why have you not built me a house of cedar?"'

7 "Now then, tell my servant David, 'This is what the Lord Almighty says: I took you from the pasture, from tending the flock, and appointed you ruler over my people Israel. 8 I have been with you wherever you have gone, and I have cut off all your enemies from before you. Now I will make your name like the names of the greatest men on earth. 9 And I will provide a place for my people Israel and will plant them so that they can have a home of their own and no longer be disturbed. Wicked people will not oppress them anymore, as they did at the beginning 10 and have done ever since the time I appointed leaders over my people Israel. I will also subdue all your enemies.

"'I declare to you that the Lord will build a house for you: 11 When your days are over and you go to be with your ancestors, I will raise up your offspring to succeed you, one of your own sons, and I will establish his kingdom. 12 He is the one who will build a house for me, and I will establish his throne forever. 13 I will be his father, and he will be my son. I will never take my love away from him, as I took it away from your predecessor. 14 I will set him over my house and my kingdom forever; his throne will be established forever.'"

15 Nathan reported to David all the words of this entire revelation.

David's Prayer

16 Then King David went in and sat before the Lord, and he said: "Who am I, Lord God, and what is my family, that you have brought me this far? 17 And as if this were not enough in your sight, my God, you have spoken about the future of the house of your servant. You, Lord God, have looked on me as though I were the most exalted of men.

18 "What more can David say to you for honoring your servant? For you know your servant, 19 Lord. For the sake of your servant and according to your will, you have done this great thing and made known all these great promises.

20 "There is no one like you, Lord, and there is no God but you, as we have heard with our own ears.

Unity
December 19
Ephesians 4:1–6

Lord Jesus, help me to grow in patience, gentleness, and in humility;
These attitudes will enable me to work with
other believers, all of us in unity.
Despite our differences, let us live in unity with one another in love;
Because we have been reconciled, through Christ's death, to God above.
Through the Holy Spirit, unity will bond us in peace;
As the body of Christ, we are members of God's
family, and this union will never cease.

God's family is one family, where unity is for eternity.

Ephesians 4:1–6

Unity and Maturity in the Body of Christ
4 As a prisoner for the Lord, then, I urge you to live a life worthy of the calling you have received. 2 Be completely humble and gentle; be patient, bearing with one another in love. 3 Make every effort to keep the unity of the Spirit through the bond of peace. 4 There is one body and one Spirit, just as you were called to one hope when you were called; 5 one Lord, one faith, one baptism; 6 one God and Father of all, who is over all and through all and in all.

Wisdom
December 20
1 Kings 4:29–34

Minds filled with wisdom will think differently from the rest.
Wise minds think with the mind of God to carry out their very best.
Which should be desirable, wisdom or intelligence?
Which is significant to want to possess?
How are they different in the manner in which they are processed?

They both demand diligence to complete the task at hand.
Discipline in direction when given a command.
Learning to develop each skill must be acquired.
This is essential in making decisions that would be inspired.
Nevertheless, wisdom understands how to apply
intelligence in being aware what to do.
Wisdom knows how to speak and act at the same time too.

Solomon would tell you that to have wisdom is one
thing, but to know how to use it is another.

1 Kings 4:29–34

Solomon's Wisdom

29 God gave Solomon wisdom and very great insight, and a breadth of understanding as measureless as the sand on the seashore. 30 Solomon's wisdom was greater than the wisdom of all the people of the East, and greater than all the wisdom of Egypt. 31 He was wiser than anyone else, including Ethan the Ezrahite—wiser than Heman, Kalkol and Darda, the sons of Mahol. And his fame spread to all the surrounding nations. 32 He spoke three thousand proverbs and his songs numbered a thousand and five. 33 He spoke about plant life, from the cedar of Lebanon to the hyssop that grows out of walls. He also spoke about animals and birds, reptiles and fish. 34 From all nations people came to listen to Solomon's wisdom, sent by all the kings of the world, who had heard of his wisdom

December 21
Discernment
Proverbs 19:15–25

Listen to hear the Word of God.
Let it counsel you, as you apply it to your life, in teaching you how to live.
Great wisdom and discernment it will surely give.
In life, mistakes we will make, learning from them will
help us to be dependent on God while we wait;

Waiting on His faithfulness will keep you from making life's mistakes.
Let the wisdom of God's Word grow in you.
Let its roots grow deep, so you will always know what to do.

The wisdom to discern will give you God's view of the world.

Proverbs 19:15–25

15
Laziness brings on deep sleep,
and the shiftless go hungry.
16
Whoever keeps commandments keeps their life,
but whoever shows contempt for their ways will die.
17
Whoever is kind to the poor lends to the Lord,
and he will reward them for what they have done.
18
Discipline your children, for in that there is hope;
do not be a willing party to their death.
19
A hot-tempered person must pay the penalty;
rescue them, and you will have to do it again.
20
Listen to advice and accept discipline,
and at the end you will be counted among the wise.
21
Many are the plans in a person's heart,
but it is the Lord's purpose that prevails.
22
What a person desires is unfailing love;
better to be poor than a liar.
23
The fear of the Lord leads to life;
then one rests content, untouched by trouble.
24

A sluggard buries his hand in the dish;
he will not even bring it back to his mouth!
25
Flog a mocker, and the simple will learn prudence;
rebuke the discerning, and they will gain knowledge.

December 22
Mentor
Ecclesiastes 12:6–14

Come, and God will teach you how to think,
With wisdom from His Holy Word that has been written in holy ink.
A mentor His Son, Jesus, will be to you,
Shepherding you to use your gifts to serve others with love and the truth,
because God loves you.
As you travel on life's journey, this will make
you be a reflection of God's heart.
Being filled with His love, truth, and wisdom, He
will not allow this from you to depart.
The importance of wisdom is using words that reflect the mind of God.

Ecclesiastes 12:6–14

6
Remember him—before the silver cord is severed,
and the golden bowl is broken;
before the pitcher is shattered at the spring,
and the wheel broken at the well,
7
and the dust returns to the ground it came from,
and the spirit returns to God who gave it.
8
"Meaningless! Meaningless!" says the Teacher.
"Everything is meaningless!"

The Conclusion of the Matter
9 Not only was the Teacher wise, but he also imparted
knowledge to the people. He pondered and searched out and set
in order many proverbs. 10 The Teacher searched to find just
the right words, and what he wrote was upright and true.
11 The words of the wise are like goads, their collected
sayings like firmly embedded nails—given by one shepherd.
12 Be warned, my son, of anything in addition to them.
Of making many books there is no end, and much study wearies the body.
13
Now all has been heard;
here is the conclusion of the matter:
Fear God and keep his commandments,
for this is the duty of all mankind.
14
For God will bring every deed into judgment,
including every hidden thing,
whether it is good or evil.

December 23
Counsel
1 Corinthians 1:18–25

How wise are you to counsel with wisdom that will
lead others from the road of destruction?
What words of enlightenment would you speak
that could cause others to seek?
To not be led from a mind of corruption?
Be wise in your thinking and know with confidence,
God's wisdom is not the same as man's providence.
Man is limited in what he knows as well as in what he understands.
Destruction and corruption are the work of his hands.
Wise counsel should be pursued; with much diligence do proceed;
From the Word of God, godly wisdom you will receive.

When you look for wise counsel, make sure the
person understands what godly wisdom is.

1 Corinthians 1:18–25

Christ Crucified Is God's Power and Wisdom
18 For the message of the cross is foolishness to those who are perishing, but to us who are being saved it is the power of God. 19 For it is written:
"I will destroy the wisdom of the wise;
the intelligence of the intelligent I will frustrate."
20 Where is the wise person? Where is the teacher of the law? Where is the philosopher of this age? Has not God made foolish the wisdom of the world? 21 For since in the wisdom of God the world through its wisdom did not know him, God was pleased through the foolishness of what was preached to save those who believe. 22 Jews demand signs and Greeks look for wisdom, 23 but we preach Christ crucified: a stumbling block to Jews and foolishness to Gentiles, 24 but to those whom God has called, both Jews and Greeks, Christ the power of God and the wisdom of God. 25 For the foolishness of God is wiser than human wisdom, and the weakness of God is stronger than human strength.

December 24
Wisdom
Faith/Grace
James 1:1–8

To live in this world today, you will need wisdom; to get
wisdom, you must get on your knees and pray.
Because wisdom is grown in the rich soil of the hardship of life,
You will need God's grace to face a life of sacrifice.
You will learn that life trials can be overwhelming each day;
You must learn how to rest in God's grace's and learn how to pray.
When you ask God for wisdom, you must believe that you will receive;
Do not doubt, because it will lead you to be deceived.
This will cause you to be like the waves of the sea;

You will be tossed to and fro,
Not knowing what to do in life as you go.
Trials in life will feel dark; however, as time goes on,
God's grace will be a reflection of the Light
through Jesus Christ, His holy Son.

God's grace and wisdom are here to help you go through the trials of life.

James 1:1–8

1 James, a servant of God and of the Lord Jesus Christ,
To the twelve tribes scattered among the nations:
Greetings.
Trials and Temptations
2 Consider it pure joy, my brothers and sisters, whenever you face trials of many kinds, 3 because you know that the testing of your faith produces perseverance. 4 Let perseverance finish its work so that you may be mature and complete, not lacking anything. 5 If any of you lacks wisdom, you should ask God, who gives generously to all without finding fault, and it will be given to you. 6 But when you ask, you must believe and not doubt, because the one who doubts is like a wave of the sea, blown and tossed by the wind. 7 That person should not expect to receive anything from the Lord. 8 Such a person is double-minded and unstable in all they do.

December 25
Wisdom
James 3:13–17

The meekness of wisdom is what I want my conduct to be.
Having bitter envy and self-seeking in my heart,
this I do not want to be a part of me.
But the wisdom that is from above is the wisdom that is from God's love.
It is pure, peaceable, gentle, willing to yield; this
wisdom will help keep life morally real.

It is without partiality, in not being biased or unfair in any way.
This is God's wisdom, and I will obey.
I have put His Word in my heart, and it is there to stay.
It is not hypocrisy, so I do not have to pretend
to be something that is not really me.
God's wisdom is transforming my life into the likeness of His Son,
Jesus Christ; so, you see, when of the time of wisdom I am in need,
I will pray to God, and I know I will receive.
Wisdom is knowing you are in need of it and
being willing to ask God for it.

James 3:13–17

Two Kinds of Wisdom

13 Who is wise and understanding among you? Let them show it by their good life, by deeds done in the humility that comes from wisdom. 14 But if you harbor bitter envy and selfish ambition in your hearts, do not boast about it or deny the truth. 15 Such "wisdom" does not come down from heaven but is earthly, unspiritual, demonic. 16 For where you have envy and selfish ambition, there you find disorder and every evil practice. 17 But the wisdom that comes from heaven is first of all pure; then peace-loving, considerate, submissive, full of mercy and good fruit, impartial and sincere.

Witnessing
December 26
Testimony
2 Corinthians 3:1–11

See my testimony written in me;
The story of salvation, of forgiveness, of compassion,
patience, love, and generosity.
The Spirit of God has given me life;
The life that Jesus lived and on the cross was sacrificed.

My soul, He has set free;
Blessing me to live with Him for all eternity.

Let your life be a testimony and witness of who Jesus Christ is.

2 Corinthians 3:1–11

3 Are we beginning to commend ourselves again? Or do we need, like some people, letters of recommendation to you or from you? 2 You yourselves are our letter, written on our hearts, known and read by everyone. 3 You show that you are a letter from Christ, the result of our ministry, written not with ink but with the Spirit of the living God, not on tablets of stone but on tablets of human hearts. 4 Such confidence we have through Christ before God. 5 Not that we are competent in ourselves to claim anything for ourselves, but our competence comes from God. 6 He has made us competent as ministers of a new covenant—not of the letter but of the Spirit; for the letter kills, but the Spirit gives life.

The Greater Glory of the New Covenant

7 Now if the ministry that brought death, which was engraved in letters on stone, came with glory, so that the Israelites could not look steadily at the face of Moses because of its glory, transitory though it was, 8 will not the ministry of the Spirit be even more glorious? 9 If the ministry that brought condemnation was glorious, how much more glorious is the ministry that brings righteousness! 10 For what was glorious has no glory now in comparison with the surpassing glory. 11 And if what was transitory came with glory, how much greater is the glory of that which lasts!

December 27
Wisdom
Acts 8:26–35

I have accepted Jesus Christ; now I am a witness
to how He has changed my life.

Living for self is no longer a desire;
Living for Jesus, the Holy Spirit has set my soul on fire.
Now I am a tool of God,
He will speak through my lips, work through my
hands, fulfilling His kingdom plan.
Yes, I am a witness.
Knowing what sin has done to my life,
I am truly thankful for forgiveness and Jesus's sacrifice.
As a witness for Christ, let the whole world know
you have something that is worth sharing.

Acts 8:26–35

Philip and the Ethiopian

26 Now an angel of the Lord said to Philip, "Go south to the road—the desert road—that goes down from Jerusalem to Gaza." 27 So he started out, and on his way he met an Ethiopian eunuch, an important official in charge of all the treasury of the Kandake (which means "queen of the Ethiopians"). This man had gone to Jerusalem to worship, 28 and on his way home was sitting in his chariot reading the Book of Isaiah the prophet. 29 The Spirit told Philip, "Go to that chariot and stay near it." 30 Then Philip ran up to the chariot and heard the man reading Isaiah the prophet. "Do you understand what you are reading?" Philip asked.

31 "How can I," he said, "unless someone explains it to me?"

So he invited Philip to come up and sit with him.

32 This is the passage of Scripture the eunuch was reading:

"He was led like a sheep to the slaughter,
and as a lamb before its shearer is silent,
so he did not open his mouth.
33
In his humiliation he was deprived of justice.
Who can speak of his descendants?
For his life was taken from the earth."

34 The eunuch asked Philip, "Tell me, please, who is the prophet talking about, himself or someone else?" 35 Then Philip began with that very passage of Scripture and told him the good news about Jesus.

December 28
The Call
1 Samuel 3:1–10

The Savior is calling; can you hear?
Listen, listen to His tender voice; do not fear.
He is pleading for you to come follow Him. Please do not delay.
The time to come to Jesus is today.
A plan for your life He has for you;
Something special He wants you to do.
The plan of salvation He wants you to work through;
Listen, listen; the Savior, Jesus, is calling you.

Our plans for our lives are short term. Jesus's plan for our lives is eternal.

1 Samuel 3:1–10

The Lord Calls Samuel

3 The boy Samuel ministered before the Lord under Eli. In those days the word of the Lord was rare; there were not many visions. 2 One night Eli, whose eyes were becoming so weak that he could barely see, was lying down in his usual place. 3 The lamp of God had not yet gone out, and Samuel was lying down in the house of the Lord, where the ark of God was. 4 Then the Lord called Samuel. Samuel answered, "Here I am." 5 And he ran to Eli and said, "Here I am; you called me."
But Eli said, "I did not call; go back and lie down." So he went and lay down.
6 Again the Lord called, "Samuel!" And Samuel got up and went to Eli and said, "Here I am; you called me."
"My son," Eli said, "I did not call; go back and lie down."

7 Now Samuel did not yet know the Lord: The word
of the Lord had not yet been revealed to him.
8 A third time the Lord called, "Samuel!" And Samuel got
up and went to Eli and said, "Here I am; you called me."
Then Eli realized that the Lord was calling the boy. 9 So Eli told
Samuel, "Go and lie down, and if he calls you, say, 'Speak, Lord, for
your servant is listening.'" So Samuel went and lay down in his place.
10 The Lord came and stood there, calling as at
the other times, "Samuel! Samuel!"
Then Samuel said, "Speak, for your servant is listening."

Worship
December 29
The Doctrine of God
Psalm 100

God is good, merciful, loving, and kind.
You are always in God's mind.
His mercy endures forever, and His faithfulness too.
There is nothing that God will not do for you.
Praise Him, praise Him for who He is.
Praise Him, praise Him, for His love for you is very real.
Bring your worship and praise to God today, and let it be strong.
Praise and worship God all day long.

Give God your praise and worship today.

Psalm 100

A psalm. For giving grateful praise.
1
Shout for joy to the Lord, all the earth.
2
Worship the Lord with gladness;
come before him with joyful songs.

> **3**
> Know that the Lord is God.
> It is he who made us, and we are his;
> we are his people, the sheep of his pasture.
> **4**
> Enter his gates with thanksgiving
> and his courts with praise;
> give thanks to him and praise his name.
> **5**
> For the Lord is good and his love endures forever;
> his faithfulness continues through all generations.

December 30
Worship
Ezra 3:7–13

What do you do when it is time to worship the
Lord, your God, with adoration?
Is your heart prepared to glorify Him with exaltation?
When you see God's wonders, how do you feel?
To bring Him worship emotions of joy and thanksgiving will become real.
In worshipping God in songs of praise, your voice
is lifted, and your hands are raised.
When those songs are a reminder to us of our sin,
Feelings of remorse and repentance slowly come in.
When worshipping God, it can bring laughter, and it will bring tears.
God is holy, and we should have reverence for Him with godly fear.

How do you feel when you are worshipping God?

Ezra 3:7–13

Rebuilding the Temple
7 Then they gave money to the masons and carpenters, and
gave food and drink and olive oil to the people of Sidon

and Tyre, so that they would bring cedar logs by sea from Lebanon to Joppa, as authorized by Cyrus king of Persia. 8 In the second month of the second year after their arrival at the house of God in Jerusalem, Zerubbabel son of Shealtiel, Joshua son of Jozadak and the rest of the people (the priests and the Levites and all who had returned from the captivity to Jerusalem) began the work. They appointed Levites twenty years old and older to supervise the building of the house of the Lord. 9 Joshua and his sons and brothers and Kadmiel and his sons (descendants of Hodaviah) and the sons of Henadad and their sons and brothers—all Levites—joined together in supervising those working on the house of God. 10 When the builders laid the foundation of the temple of the Lord, the priests in their vestments and with trumpets, and the Levites (the sons of Asaph) with cymbals, took their places to praise the Lord, as prescribed by David king of Israel. 11 With praise and thanksgiving they sang to the Lord:
"He is good;
his love toward Israel endures forever."
And all the people gave a great shout of praise to the Lord, because the foundation of the house of the Lord was laid. 12 But many of the older priests and Levites and family heads, who had seen the former temple, wept aloud when they saw the foundation of this temple being laid, while many others shouted for joy. 13 No one could distinguish the sound of the shouts of joy from the sound of weeping, because the people made so much noise. And the sound was heard far away.

December 31
Worship
Encouragement
Acts 4:32–37; 9:26–27

The gift of encouragement God always wants to give to you.
To those who are anxiously waiting to be encouraged
through a timely word of truth,

A phone call or a prayer can strengthen and support them in
their faith in Jesus Christ with what they are going through.
This means of encouragement is a gift of generousness.
It is given out of selflessness.

Worship God by giving encouragement to others
to accomplish God's works in them.

Acts 4:32–37

The Believers Share Their Possessions
32 All the believers were one in heart and mind. No one claimed that
any of their possessions was their own, but they shared everything
they had. 33 With great power the apostles continued to testify
to the resurrection of the Lord Jesus. And God's grace was so
powerfully at work in them all 34 that there were no needy persons
among them. For from time to time those who owned land or houses
sold them, brought the money from the sales 35 and put it at the
apostles' feet, and it was distributed to anyone who had need.
36 Joseph, a Levite from Cyprus, whom the apostles called
Barnabas (which means "son of encouragement"), 37 sold a field he
owned and brought the money and put it at the apostles' feet.

Acts 9:26–27

26 When he came to Jerusalem, he tried to join the disciples,
but they were all afraid of him, not believing that he really
was a disciple. 27 But Barnabas took him and brought him to
the apostles. He told them how Saul on his journey had seen
the Lord and that the Lord had spoken to him, and how in
Damascus he had preached fearlessly in the name of Jesus.

Scriptures Index

Old Testament

Genesis
3:1–7 .... OCTOBER 4, 5 .... 366, 367, 368
3:1–8 .... MAY 16 .... 185, 186
4:1–8 .... OCTOBER 14 379
12:1–4 .... APRIL 19 .... 145, 146
16:1–13 .... MAY 18 .... 187, 188
17:1–2 .... APRIL 19 146
39:1–12 .... DECEMBER 17 .... 466, 467

Exodus
1:22–2:10 .... JANUARY 1 3
4:1–12 .... JUNE 10 .... 216, 217
13:17–22 .... NOVEMBER 1 .... 400, 401
16:11–31 .... NOVEMBER 28 .... 438, 439
17:8–16 .... MARCH 11 .... 96, 97
18:14–24 .... SEPTEMBER 16 .... 344, 345
31:1–11 .... OCTOBER 7 .... 370, 371

Numbers
13:25–14:9 .... APRIL 10, 11 .... 131, 132, 133, 134
14:1–9 .... DECEMBER 11 459
14:39–45 .... APRIL 28 157
33:1–15, 36–37 .... MAY 19 189

Deuteronomy
5:28–33 .... JULY 29 .... 278, 279
6:1–12 .... JANUARY 19; JULY 30 .... 27, 279, 280
10:12–22 .... JULY 14 261
30:11–20 .... JULY 31 .... 280, 281
34:1–12 .... JANUARY 4 7

Joshua
20:1–9 .... APRIL 24 .... 152, 153

Judges
2:7–19 .... APRIL 22 .... 149, 150
7:1–8 .... NOVEMBER 29 440

1 Samuel
3:1–10 JANUARY 16; DECEMBER 28 .... 23, 480
25:1–12 .... SEPTEMBER 13 .... 339, 340
25:14–33 .... SEPTEMBER 4 .... 325, 326

2 Samuel
22:26–37 .... APRIL 14 138

1 Kings
4:29–34 .... DECEMBER 20 .... 470, 471
12:1–15 .... OCTOBER 8 .... 371, 372
18:41–45 .... AUGUST 15 .... 301, 302

2 Kings
2:1–12 .... JUNE 11 218
6:8–17 .... DECEMBER 12, 13 .... 460, 461, 462
12:1–15 .... JUNE 26 239
19:9–20 .... AUGUST 28 317

1 Chronicles
17:1–20 .... DECEMBER 18 468
29:14–19 .... MAY 14 183

2 Chronicles
6:12–21 .... AUGUST 16 .... 302, 303
13:10–18 .... AUGUST 17 304
16:7–14 .... APRIL 23 151
20:1–13 .... APRIL 21 148
21:4–20 .... JUNE 19 .... 228, 229

Ezra
3:7–13 .... DECEMBER 30 482
5:6–17 .... SEPTEMBER 15 343

Nehemiah
8:1–8 .... JANUARY 9 14
8:2–6 .... JANUARY 10 15

Job
7:11–21 .... NOVEMBER 19 426
11:7–20 .... APRIL 17 .... 142, 143
23:1–12 .... JUNE 1 206
40:1–14 .... NOVEMBER 11 .... 415, 416

Psalms
13:1–6 .... NOVEMBER 16 422
18:1–6 .... NOVEMBER 30 .... 441, 442
20 .... DECEMBER 1 .... 442, 443
22:1–10 .... FEBRUARY 8 .... 53, 54
25:1–15 .... APRIL 29 158
27:1–8 .... APRIL 9 130
32:1–6 .... NOVEMBER 24 434
34:1–10 .... APRIL 12 135
34:11–18 .... AUGUST 8 291
34:15–22 .... MAY 8, 9 .... 173, 174, 175
35:17–28 .... NOVEMBER 3 403
36:5–12 .... MAY 20 .... 190, 191
37:21–31 .... MAY 1, 2 .... 161, 162
40:1–5 .... OCTOBER 31 399
42 .... MARCH 18 104
46 .... AUGUST 11 .... 295, 347
51:7–17 .... SEPTEMBER 12 338
55:4–23 .... MAY 13; NOVEMBER 4 .... 180, 405
68:7–10, 19–20 .... APRIL 30 160
71:1–12 .... AUGUST 12 .... 296, 297
77:1–15 .... DECEMBER 2 .... 444, 445
78:1–8 .... AUGUST 5 .... 286, 287
86:1–13 .... JULY 11 256
86:5–15 .... APRIL 15 .... 139, 140
91 .... AUGUST 13 .... 298, 299
92:12–15 .... JANUARY 5 9
94:3–23 .... NOVEMBER 21 .... 428, 429
100 .... APRIL 20; DECEMBER 29 .... 147, 481
103:1–18 .... JANUARY 2; FEBRUARY 12 .... 4, 5, 58, 59
107:23–32 .... NOVEMBER 23 .... 432, 433

110 .... MAY 31 .... 204, 205
116:5–9 .... MAY 3 .... 164, 165
119:9–16 .... JUNE 2 .... 207, 208
119:17–19, 130–134 .... JANUARY 15 21
119:71–75 .... NOVEMBER 7 .... 410, 411
119:89–96 .... JANUARY 11 .... 16, 17
119:97–104 .... JANUARY 17 24
119:161–168 .... JANUARY 12 18
121 .... MAY 4; NOVEMBER 18 .... 165, 166, 424, 425
122:6–9 .... AUGUST 14 .... 300, 301
136:1–9 .... NOVEMBER 12 417
138:7–8 .... OCTOBER 30 398
139:1–18 .... MAY 5 167
139:14–18 .... NOVEMBER 13 .... 418, 419
141:1–4 .... JUNE 29 242
141 .... JULY 1 .... 242, 243, 244, 245
145:1–13 .... JUNE 21 231
146:1–10 .... MAY 29 201
146 .... SEPTEMBER 21 .... 201, 202, 350, 351

Proverbs
2:1–5 .... OCTOBER 18 384
3:1–18 .... DECEMBER 3 .... 446, 447
18:4–12 .... MAY 15; DECEMBER 4 .... 184, 448
19:15–25 .... DECEMBER 21 .... 471, 472
22:1–12 .... JUNE 20 230
22:1–16 .... MARCH 10 .... 94, 95
27:5–10 .... JULY 22 .... 270, 271
27:5–17 .... SEPTEMBER 8, 9 .... 330, 331, 332, 333

Ecclesiastes
1:1–11 .... MAY 6; MARCH 2 .... 84, 85, 169, 170
12:6–14 .... DECEMBER 22 473

Isaiah
9:1–7 .... FEBRUARY 13 61
12 .... SEPTEMBER 20 349
37:9–22, 33 .... AUGUST 29 318
40:1–11 .... SEPTEMBER 10 .... 334, 335
40:21–31 .... JUNE 22 234

40:27–31 .... APRIL 26 .... 154, 155
46:4–13 .... JANUARY 6 10
49:13–21 .... JULY 12 258
50:4–10 .... MAY 7 171
53:1–6 .... NOVEMBER 9 .... 412, 413
55:6–13 .... DECEMBER 5, 6 .... 450, 452
61:1–4 .... NOVEMBER 2 .... 401, 402

Jeremiah
1:1–10 .... AUGUST 10 .... 293, 294
1:4–9 .... AUGUST 3 .... 284, 285
7:1–11 .... AUGUST 1 282

Lamentations
3:1–3, 25–33 .... NOVEMBER 22 431
3:21–26 .... MAY 21 192
5:8–22 .... MAY 10 .... 175, 176

Ezekiel
18:25–32 .... OCTOBER 28 .... 395, 396

Joel
2:12–17 .... SEPTEMBER 14 341

Jonah
4 .... AUGUST 4 .... 285, 286

Nahum
1:7–15 .... JANUARY 20 .... 28, 29

Habakkuk
3:16–19 .... APRIL 27 156

Haggai
2:15–23 .... MAY 22 193

New Testament

Matthew
5:1–16 .... MARCH 19 .... 106, 107
5:13–16 .... JUNE 24 237
5:43–48 .... APRIL 25; NOVEMBER 25 .... 153, 154
6:1–6 .... JULY 28 .... 277, 278
6:5–10 .... AUGUST 18 305
6:24–34 .... JULY 26 275
6:25–34 .... FEBRUARY 29; MAY 23; JULY 26; AUGUST 23 .... 82, 83, 194, 310, 311
7:12–23 .... APRIL 7 .... 127, 128
8:23–28 .... DECEMBER 7 454
10:26–32 .... MARCH 28 117
10:35–42 .... FEBRUARY 2 46
11:25–30 .... SEPTEMBER 18 347
11:28–30 .... NOVEMBER 24 .... 434, 435
14:13–23 .... AUGUST 22 309
14:22–36 .... AUGUST 27 .... 315, 316
16:1–4 .... AUGUST 19 306
20:1–16 .... MARCH 5 .... 88, 89
25:1–13 .... FEBRUARY 19 69
25:31–40 .... OCTOBER 11 375
26:39–42 .... AUGUST 24 .... 311, 312
27:45–46 .... AUGUST 24 312
28:16–20 .... JANUARY 22 .... 31, 32

Mark
1:16–22 .... MARCH 26 115
2:13–17 .... SEPTEMBER 22 .... 352, 353
4:35–5:1 .... APRIL 8 129
5:1–20 .... MARCH 20 108
6:7–13, 30–32 .... SEPTEMBER 17 345
8:1–13 .... MAY 11 .... 177, 178
8:11–21 .... JULY 10 255
10:13–16 .... JUNE 15 .... 223, 224
10:17–27 .... SEPTEMBER 11 .... 336, 337
14:3–9 .... MARCH 30 119
14:32–39 .... JANUARY 23 .... 32, 33
14:32–42 .... OCTOBER 6 369

Luke
1:67–79 .... SEPTEMBER 23 .... 353, 354
2:8–14 .... FEBRUARY 14 63
2:8–20 .... JANUARY 24, 25 .... 33, 34, 35
2:21–35 .... FEBRUARY 20 .... 70, 71
2:25–38 .... FEBRUARY 4 .... 48, 49
4:14–21 .... SEPTEMBER 24 355
5:27–32 .... APRIL 1 121
6:27–36 .... SEPTEMBER 6 .... 328, 329
7:36–50 .... JULY 15 262
8:40–48 .... MARCH 31 120
9:1–2, 10–17 .... AUGUST 26 314
9:57–62 .... MARCH 8, 9 .... 92, 93, 94
10:38–11:4 .... FEBRUARY 5 50
12:22–34 .... JULY 27 276
15:11–24 .... AUGUST 6 .... 288, 289
16:1–10 .... DECEMBER 8 455
18:1–8 .... AUGUST 30 320
19:1–9 .... SEPTEMBER 5 327
19:1–10 .... OCTOBER 19 385
22:39–46 .... FEBRUARY 6 .... 51, 52
24:13–32 .... FEBRUARY 15 64
24:13–35 .... FEBRUARY 24 76

John
1:1–4 .... JANUARY 26 .... 19, 20
1:1–8 .... MARCH 25 .... 100, 114
1:1–14 .... SEPTEMBER 26 .... 36, 37, 357, 358
3:9–21 .... JUNE 17 .... 225, 226
4:4–14 .... SEPTEMBER 19 348
4:31–34 .... FEBRUARY 7 .... 52, 53
6:34–51 .... MARCH 21, 22 .... 109, 110, 111
6:53–69 .... SEPTEMBER 27 .... 358, 359
7:53–8:11 .... JUNE 18 227
8:12–20 .... JANUARY 21 .... 30, 31
8:31–37 .... SEPTEMBER 28 360
8:31–38 .... FEBRUARY 1 45
8:39–47 .... AUGUST 2 283
10:1–9 .... JANUARY 27 38
10:1–11 .... MAY 12 179
11:1–4, 38–44 .... JUNE 5 211

11:17–27 .... MARCH 6 .... 90, 91
14:1–6 .... JUNE 9 .... 215, 216
14:15–21 .... NOVEMBER 5 .... 407, 408
14:16–27 .... JUNE 13 221
15:12–17 .... JANUARY 28 .... 39, 40
16:17–24 .... JUNE 16 .... 224, 225
16:25–33 .... NOVEMBER 20, 26 .... 427, 428, 436, 437
16:28–33 .... JUNE 4 210
17:1–5 .... FEBRUARY 9 55
17:6–19 .... AUGUST 31 321
18:10–14, 36–37 .... FEBRUARY 16 65
20:24–31 .... FEBRUARY 10 56

Acts
1:1–8 .... MARCH 23 .... 112, 113
2:1–12 .... JUNE 12 .... 219, 220
2:42–47 .... MARCH 1 .... 83, 84
4:32–37 .... DECEMBER 31 .... 483, 484
6:8–15 .... AUGUST 9 .... 292, 293
7:59–60 .... AUGUST 9 293
8:4–8 .... JANUARY 10 .... 15, 16
8:26–35 .... DECEMBER 27 .... 478, 479
9:1–19 .... MAY 24 195
9:26–27 .... DECEMBER 31 484
20:17–20, 35–38 .... MAY 2 163
20:22–35 .... APRIL 18 144

Romans
3:21–26 .... FEBRUARY 17; SEPTEMBER 25 .... 67, 356, 357
4:18–25 .... APRIL 4 124
5:6–11 .... MAY 25 197
7:14–25 .... OCTOBER 12 .... 376, 377
7:15–25 .... OCTOBER 13 378
8:12–17 .... MAY 26 198
8:22–34 .... AUGUST 25 .... 312, 313
8:31–38 .... MAY 27 199
12:1–8 .... OCTOBER 21 .... 387, 388
13:8–11 .... JULY 16 .... 263, 264
15:1–7 .... FEBRUARY 26 .... 78, 79

1 Corinthians

1:18–25 .... DECEMBER 23 .... 474, 475
1:18–31 .... JANUARY 29 .... 40, 41
6:9–11 .... OCTOBER 27 .... 394, 395
9:24–27 .... OCTOBER 22 .... 388, 389
10:1–13 .... OCTOBER 15, 16 .... 380, 381, 382
12:4–14 .... OCTOBER 17 383
13:4–7 .... OCTOBER 27 395
13 .... JULY 17 .... 264, 265, 395
14:6–12, 26 .... FEBRUARY 27 80

2 Corinthians

1:3–7 .... FEBRUARY 28; JULY 18 .... 81, 82, 266
2:12–17 .... MARCH 29 118
2:14–17 .... MARCH 24 .... 113, 114
3:1–11 .... DECEMBER 26 .... 477, 478
4:1–6 .... APRIL 2, 3 .... 122, 123
5:12–21 .... OCTOBER 23 .... 389, 390
5:16–21 .... JULY 24 .... 272, 273
12:6–10 .... MARCH 4 .... 87, 88

Galatians

5:13–26 .... AUGUST 7 290
5:16–25 .... OCTOBER 24 391
6:2–10 .... OCTOBER 9 373

Ephesians

2:1–10 .... OCTOBER 29 .... 396, 397
2:4–7 .... MAY 17 .... 186, 187
2:6–10 .... OCTOBER 30 398
3:14–21 .... AUGUST 20 307
4:1–6 .... DECEMBER 19 470
4:1–16 .... OCTOBER 20 386
4:2–6 .... MARCH 16 102
4:25–32 .... JANUARY 8; MARCH 12 APRIL 16 .... 13, 97, 98, 141
5:1–16 .... JULY 2 246
6:5–9 .... JUNE 27 .... 240, 241

Philippians

1:12–26 .... NOVEMBER 6 409

1:27–2:4 .... OCTOBER 10 374
1:27–30 .... JANUARY 14 .... 20, 21
2:1–11 .... JANUARY 30; JUNE 14; JULY 19 .... 42, 222, 267
3:1–8 .... OCTOBER 3 .... 365, 366
3:17–21 .... MARCH 27 116
4:4–9 .... JULY 3, 4 .... 247, 248, 249
4:8–13 .... DECEMBER 14 463
4:10–19 .... MARCH 3 86

Colossians
2:20–3:4 .... JUNE 28 .... 241, 242
3:1–11 .... JUNE 6 .... 212, 213
3:12–17 .... JANUARY 3; JUNE 3; JULY 5 .... 6, 7, 209, 249, 250

1 Thessalonians
4:1–12 .... MARCH 13, 15 .... 98, 99, 101
4:13–18 .... FEBRUARY 21; MARCH 7 .... 72, 91, 92
5:12–28 .... AUGUST 21 308
5:16–28 .... SEPTEMBER 1 .... 322, 323

2 Thessalonians
1:3–12 .... FEBRUARY 23 .... 74, 75

1 Timothy
4:6–11 .... JANUARY 7 12

2 Timothy
3:10–15 .... JUNE 23 236
4:9–18 .... JULY 9 254

Philemon
8–18 .... SEPTEMBER 7 .... 329, 330

Hebrews
1:1–12 .... JANUARY 18 .... 25, 26
2:1–4 .... APRIL 13 137
2:10–18 .... NOVEMBER 10 414
4:14–16 .... SEPTEMBER 2 .... 323, 324
9:19–28 .... FEBRUARY 11 .... 57, 58
10:19–25 .... SEPTEMBER 29 361

10:32–11:6 . . . . DECEMBER 9 . . . . 456, 457
11:8–16 . . . . APRIL 6; JUNE 7 . . . . 126, 127, 213, 214
11:32–12:3 . . . . MARCH 17 103
12:1–11 . . . . DECEMBER 15 464
13:1–6 . . . . MAY 30 203

James

1:1–8 . . . . NOVEMBER 27; DECEMBER 24 . . . . 437, 438, 475, 476
1:2–4 . . . . DECEMBER 16 . . . . 465, 466
1:2–12 . . . . NOVEMBER 8 . . . . 411, 412
1:22–27 . . . . JULY 6, 23 . . . . 250, 251, 271, 272
2:8–26 . . . . JANUARY 31 . . . . 43, 44
3:1–12 . . . . JULY 7, 8; NOVEMBER 14, 15 . . . . 251, 252, 253, 419, 420, 421
3:13–17 . . . . DECEMBER 25 . . . . 476, 477

1 Peter

1:1–9 . . . . JULY 13; NOVEMBER 17 . . . . 259, 260, 423
1:3–9 . . . . SEPTEMBER 30 362
1:17–23 . . . . OCTOBER 1 363
2:4–10 . . . . OCTOBER 2 364
2:9–12 . . . . FEBRUARY 3 . . . . 47, 48
3:7–12 . . . . JULY 25 . . . . 273, 274
3:8–16 . . . . FEBRUARY 18 68
3:9–12 . . . . JUNE 25 238
4:7–11 . . . . SEPTEMBER 3 . . . . 324, 325

2 Peter

1:1–10 . . . . OCTOBER 26 393
1:12–21 . . . . JUNE 30 . . . . 243, 244
3:8–15 . . . . FEBRUARY 25 . . . . 77, 78

1 John

1:1–4 . . . . JANUARY 13 . . . . 19, 20
2:3–11 . . . . JULY 20 . . . . 268, 269
3:16–17 . . . . JULY 21 . . . . 269, 270
4:7–19 . . . . MAY 28 200
5:1–13 . . . . APRIL 5 125

3 John

1:1–8 . . . . MARCH 14 100

Revelation
2:12–17 .... OCTOBER 25 392
3:7–13 .... DECEMBER 10 458
22:1–5 .... JUNE 8 .... 214, 215
22:12–21 .... FEBRUARY 22 .... 73, 74

Asking for salvation

After reading this book if you want to invite Jesus into your life as your Savior and Lord.
Pray this simple prayer to invite Jesus into your life.

Steps
Trust Jesus Christ today! ...
Admit that you are a sinner and that you need God's help. ...
Be willing to change your mind and turn from your sin (repent). ...
Believe that Jesus Christ died for you, was buried, and rose from the dead. ...
Through prayer, invite Jesus into your heart to become your personal Lord and Savior. ...

Pray:
Father, I know that I have broken your laws and my sins have separated me from you. I am truly sorry, and now I want to turn away from my past sinful life toward you. Please forgive me, and help me avoid sinning again. I believe that your son, Jesus Christ died for my sins, was resurrected from the dead, is alive, and hears my prayer. I invite Jesus to become the Lord of my life, to rule and reign in my heart from this day forward. Please send your Holy Spirit to help me obey You, and to do Your will for the rest of my life. In Jesus' name, I pray, Amen."

www.ingramcontent.com/pod-product-compliance
Lightning Source LLC
Chambersburg PA
CBHW071800080526
44589CB00012B/628